THE SCREENWRITER'S HANDBOOK

Barry Turner has worked on both sides of publishing, as an editor and marketing director and as an author. He started his career as a journalist with the *Observer* before moving on to television and radio. He has written over twenty books including *A Place in the Country*, which inspired a television series, and a best-selling biography of the actor Richard Burton.

His recent work includes *Suez 1956: The Forgotten War*, *Countdown to Victory*, a book about the last months of World War II, a radio play, travel articles, serialising books for *The Times*, editing the magazine *Country* and writing a one-man show based on the life of the legendary theatre critic James Agate. Barry has also been the editor of *The Writer's Handbook* for over twenty years and editor of *The Statesman's Yearbook* for ten.

THE
SCREENWRITER'S
HANDBOOK

Edited by BARRY TURNER

MACMILLAN

First published 2007 by Macmillan
an imprint of Pan Macmillan Ltd
Pan Macmillan, 20 New Wharf Road, London N1 9RR
Basingstoke and Oxford
Associated companies throughout the world
www.panmacmillan.com

ISBN 978-0-2300-1404-6

9 8 7 6 5 4 3 2 1

A CIP catalogue record for this book is available from
the British Library.

Typeset by Macmillan India Ltd
Printed and bound in Great Britain by
Mackays of Chatham plc, Chatham, Kent

Credits

Editor Barry Turner   *Assistant Editor* Daniel Smith   *Editorial Assistant* Bruno Vincent

Consultant Pete Daly   *Research* Steven Hall, Pranushka Naidoo, Olivia Shean

Production Wayne Hayward, Gail Bailey, Mark Davies, Andrew Joseph

Contents

INTRODUCTION

Of all the literary arts, screenwriting seems to have the strongest appeal for young people. It is easy to see why. A successful book is read by thousands, a successful play on stage or small screen is seen by hundreds of thousands, but a movie, even one that is not rated five stars, can reach millions. Fame, fortune and fulfilment beckon.

The downside, at least for writers who value their independence, is that moviemaking is a collaborative effort with a pecking order that puts the director and producer in prime position. For the screenwriter, the readiness to work with tough-minded associates with ideas of their own is as important as the ability to plot a convincing and marketable story. That, and patience, since it is a safe general rule that a movie takes longer to come to fruition than, say, a novel or even a stage play.

But none of this will dissuade the writer who has caught the movie virus – as the number of requests in recent years for a companion volume to the annual *Writer's Handbook* has proved. This first edition of *The Screenwriter's Handbook* is the logical outcome. Following the pattern of the *Writer's Handbook*, the aim is for the *Screenwriter's Handbook* to become an annual publication, with an accompanying website to provide regular updates, professional support for newcomers and a forum for discussion.

International telephone codes have been omitted for brevity's sake and because the book is itself international and thus unable to keep track of regional variations for codes.

Suggestions for further developments are welcome. Please do write or email: screenwriters@macmillan.com

WRITING IN A PARTNERSHIP

Rob Sprackling & John Smith reflect on writing relationships

John Smith

Why choose to write with another person when you could be claiming sole credit for your masterpiece or taking all that filthy lucre and lifting your BAFTA single-handed?

Firstly, many all-time TV classics – especially sitcoms – and some of the finest films have been penned by two people shuffling bits of paper back and forth (or these days clicking 'send'). So when they work writing partnerships can bring big rewards.

Furthermore, you might be better suited to working in a partnership. This sounds frivolous, but writing can be a lonely business, spending hours every day at your word processor with only an agent for an ally. And who can you rely on for genuine, impartial feedback on your writing? The opinions of your nearest and dearest count for nothing. They love you so they'll want to be nice.

Your writing partner is somebody with whom you can share the highs – 'we've just sold our first script, let's get wildly drunk' – and the lows – 'they turned us down, let's get wildly drunk'. The importance of keeping each other's morale high cannot be overstated. Writing partnerships are like marriages; it's all peaks and troughs. If you've written a hit your agent will be delighted (read: it's good business), the actors ecstatic (read: work, darling) and your friends thrilled (read: jealous and possibly depressed). The only person who can truly understand how you feel is your writing partner. So, what makes a good writing partner?

It helps if you like your writing partner, although it's not essential. But you must respect each other's opinion. You will from time to time have major creative differences; you might even have full-scale rows. But compromise is the name of the game. You must learn you will never get it wholly your own way. If you want to be top dog why are you in a partnership?

Good writing partners also offer complementary strengths and weaknesses. The job of writing demands a broad set of skills. You're not going to be good at every aspect of the job. One of you might be brilliant at dreaming up hugely original and highly arresting concepts, but it might take the other to make it come alive in front of a bunch of jaded producers. You might have a good ear for clean crisp dialogue but your partner might demonstrate a better understanding of story structure. With a bit of luck your partner's yin butts up neatly against your yang.

If writing comedy it might be useful to be able to make each other laugh (though, of course, you don't have to terrify each other to write a horror or fall in love to do romance). Writing partnerships historically have gravitated towards writing comedy because comedy is what you might call an externalized creative process. It has an objective that can be mutually explored: the search for laughs. So it helps if you find the same things funny – although subtly divergent tonal qualities can help give the finished product an interesting tension.

Partnerships are better suited to writing scripts than prose or poetry. Long passages of purple prose tend to be for the solitary scribe in a lofty garret. If you guard your writing against interference because you draw your inspiration from deeply personal experience then think again about writing in a partnership. Are you going to be fair to your own talents or the talents of your partner if you revere your 'creative vision' above anything else? Working with a colleague who will demand the right to change your work might not be the right thing for you. A good writing partner will give it to you straight. You might not like them trampling over your words but you have to respect their opinions and, if they're voicing concerns over the writing, others will too.

Of course, the final and most sobering reason of all for writing in a partnership is possibly the most significant. Deep down, perhaps you are honest enough to admit – you're simply not as good writing on your own.

Rob Sprackling

The other benefit of a writing partnership is that you can leave your mate to do most of the writing while you relax. And that is clearly what has happened in this case!

I believe the key to a fruitful writing partnership is the correct division of labour. You don't have to be together all the time. In particular, don't both sit at the computer when creating your first draft, with one person typing and the other saying 'Isn't "the" better than "a"?' This is extremely unproductive and will often result in the premature end of a promising writing partnership (and some wrestling).

There are, however, various stages of the writing process which benefit from being together in the room. In particular the initial brainstorm – where you have an original idea and bounce it back and forth. A good partnership will have each of you finishing the other's sentences when ideas are flying – two people on the same wavelength can bring the best out in each other. Good ideas inspire better ideas. You get excited, you develop a joint vision, and you prevent one another from heading off down creative blind alleys. When this works, it is the best thing about the job.

Rewriting should also be done together; it deploys a different part of the brain to creating the scenes, characters and dialogue from scratch. It allows both writers to read stuff back aloud and to discuss it objectively. Also the process of editing, improving and reinventing suits a consultative approach and doesn't interfere too much with the creative flow.

So partnerships are great as long as you know when to leave each other alone. My advice is to follow this simple three point plan.

1. Generate the ideas, characters, scenes and story together.
2. Write the first draft separately, either splitting the script in half or one person doing it alone.
3. Come together again for subsequent drafts; if one partner has written the first draft, the other will be able to use their fresh perspective to take the lead on future drafts.

My final suggestion for making a partnership work is the same for any marriage. Try not to be nasty to each other, forgive quickly, give each other space, enjoy each other's company and fuck like rabbits. Actually no – scratch the last one.

Rob Sprackling & John Smith are a professional screenwriting partnership. Their credits include the successful movie Mike Bassett: England Manager. *They work regularly for production companies in the UK and US.*

PRODUCTION
COMPANIES

PRODUCTION COMPANIES

 Cinema   Computer games   Television

UNITED STATES OF AMERICA

1492 PICTURES

c/o Warner Brothers 4000 Warner Boulevard
Bldg. 3 Burbank CA 91522
T   818 954 4939

Founded in 1995 by director Chris Columbus,
producing films such as *Jingle All the Way*, the
first three instalments in the *Harry Potter* series
and *Night at the Museum*.

Submissions Policy
Does not accept unsolicited material.

20TH CENTURY FOX

10201 West Pico Boulevard Los Angeles
CA 90035
T   310 369 1000
W www.foxmovies.com

The Fox Film Corp was founded in 1914 and
merged with 20th Century Pictures in 1935 to
form 20th Century Fox, one of America's
leading film production companies. 20th
Century Fox has produced Academy Award-
winning films such as *The Sound of Music*, *The
King and I*, *Alien* and *Titannic*. Recent output
includes *Star Wars Episode III*, *Mr. & Mrs.
Smith*, *Walk the Line*, *Ice Age: The Meltdown*,
X-Men: The Last Stand, *The Devil Wears
Prada*, *Eragon* and *Night at the Museum*.

20TH CENTURY FOX TELEVISION

10201 W Pico Boulevard Bldg 88 Los Angeles
CA 90035
T   310 369 1000
W www.foxhome.com

Founded in 1949, 20th Century Fox Television
is the television production division of the 20th

Century Fox movie studio, a subsidiary of News
Corporation. It has produced successful shows
such as *The Simpsons*, *Prison Break* and *24*.

2929 ENTERTAINMENT

9100 Wilshire Boulevard Suite 500 West
Beverly Hills CA 90212
T   310 309 5200
F   310 309 5716
W www.2929entertainment.com

Founded in 2005, producing independent
feature films such as *Good Night and Good
Luck* (nominated for 6 Academy Awards
including Best Picture) and *Akeelah and the
Bee* (starring Academy Award-nominees
Laurence Fishburne and Angela Basset).

Submissions Policy
Submit a brief 2–3 paragraph synopsis of
project via website.

3 ARTS ENTERTAINMENT

9460 Wilshire Boulevard 7th Floor
Beverly Hills CA 90212
T   310 888 3200

Produced films such as *I am Legend*,
Carpoolers, *Bio-Dome* and *A Scanner Darkly*,
which won the Austin Film Critics Award and
was nominated for the Saturn award for Best
Animated Film.

ACTIVISION, INC.

Corporate Headquarters 3100 Ocean Park
Boulevard Santa Monica CA 90405
T   310 255 2000
W www.activision.com

A leading international publisher of interactive
entertainment software products. Produces

games across genres for an array of markets and platforms. Has development agreements with the likes of DreamWorks, Hasbro Properties and Harrah's Entertainment, Inc. and has created successful brands such as *True Crime* and *Call of Duty*.

AEI

c/o AEI Submissions 9601 Wilshire Boulevard Box 1202 Beverly Hills CA 90210
T 323 932 0407
E submissions@aeionline.com
W www.aeionline.com

A one-stop full-service literary management and motion picture production company. Offers development, sales, marketing, production and licensing services.

Submissions Policy
Send query letters only. Additional material will be discarded unread. No calls. Allow 8–10 weeks for a response on manuscripts, non-fiction proposals and screenplays. Send sae for reply and return of material. Full submission guidelines available on website.

AGAMEMNON FILMS INC.

650 N. Bronson Avenue Ste. B-225
Los Angeles CA 90004
T 323 960 4066
W www.agamemnon.com

Founded in 1981 by Fraser and Charlton Heston (*Ben Hur*). Produced films such as *The Bible* and the animated version of *Ben Hur*.

ALPINE PICTURES, INC.

3500 W. Magnolia Boulevard Burbank
CA 91505
T 818 333 2600
F 818 902 5015
E scottv@alpinepix.com
W www.alpinepix.com

Founded in 1995. Credits include *Dorothy of Oz*, *Dark Honeymoon* and *Love is the Drug*.

Submissions Policy
Does not accept unsolicited manuscripts. To submit an idea or synopsis, approach via email.

AMERICAN ZOETROPE

916 Kearny Street San Francisco CA 94133

Founded by Francis Ford Coppola and George Lucas in the late 1960s. Has received no less than 15 Academy Awards and 68 nominations. Output includes *Lost in Translation*, *Kinsey* and *The Godfather* trilogy.

CRAIG ANDERSON PRODUCTIONS

9696 Culver Boulevard Suite 208 Culver City
CA 90232
T 310 841 2555
E info@cappix.com
W www.cappix.com

Founded in 1990, producing films such as *The Christmas Blessing*, *American Meltdown* and *Wilder Days*.

Submissions Policy
In first instance submit a 2–5 page synopsis of the project.

ANTIDOTE INTERNATIONAL FILMS, INC.

200 Varick Street Suite 502 New York
NY 10014-4810
T 646 486 4344
F 646 486 5885
E info@antidotefilms.com
W www.antidotefilms.com

Founded in 2000 by producer Jeffrey Levy-Hinte. Has produced such titles as *The Hawk is Dying*, *Mysterious Skin* (nominated for IFP Gotham and Independent Spirit Awards), *Thirteen* (starring Holly Hunter and Evan Rachel Wood) and *Chain*.

Submissions Policy
Does not accept any unsolicited submissions.

APERTURA

535 Main Street Oxford NH 03777
T   603 353 9067
F   603 353 4646
E   karol@apertura.org
W   www.apertura.org

Contacts
John Karol *Producer/Filmmaker*

Founded in 1969, producing documentary
features and television programmes. Nominated
for an Academy Award for Best Documentary
Feature.

Submissions Policy
Welcomes unsolicited manuscripts by mail or
email.

ARDEN ENTERTAINMENT

12034 Riverside Drive Suite 200 North
Hollywood CA 91607
T   818 985 4600
F   818 985 3021
E   chris@ardenentertainment.com
W   www.ardenentertainment.com

Founded in 2000, producing for television.
Output includes the documentary series
Growing Up, the studio-based reality series
Dream Decoders and the docu-soap *K9 Karma*.

Submissions Policy
Does not accept unsolicited materials or
programme proposals.

ARENAS ENTERTAINMENT

100 North Crescent Drive Garden Level
Beverly Hills CA 90210
T   310 385 4401
F   310 385 4402
E   info@arenasgroup.com
W   www.arenasgroup.com

Founded in 1988. Produces, acquires, markets
and distributes films in all media including
theatrical, video and television that target the
US Latino market. Produced the award-winning

film *Nicotina* starring Diego Luna, and
co-produced *Imagining Argentina*, starring
Antonio Banderas and Emma Thompson.

THE ARTISTS' COLONY

256 S. Robertson Boulevard Suite 1500
Beverley Hills CA 90211
T   310 720 8300
E   theartistscolony@sbcglobal.net
W   www.theartistscolony.com

Contacts
Lloyd A. Silverman *President/CEO/Producer*

Founded in 1997, creating content for film, TV
and the web. Specializes in drama, thrillers and
documentaries. Credits include *Snow Falling on
Cedars*, *Shattered Image*, *12* and *A Girl, Three
Guys and a Gun*. Has recently launched a
corporate identity/branding and
communications firm in conjunction with other
film and TV companies, called communic8.

Submissions Policy
Only packaged projects will be considered.
Approach by email.

ASCENDANT PICTURES

9350 Civic Center Drive Suite 110
Beverly Hills CA 90210
T   310 288 4600
F   310 288 4601
E   info@ascendantpictures.com
W   www.ascendantpictures.com

Founded in 2002. Produced the film *The Big
White* and has co-produced titles including
Lord of War, *Ask the Dust* and *Lucky
Number Slevin*.

A-V-A PRODUCTIONS

4760 E. 65th Street Indianapolis IN 46220
T   317 255 6457
F   317 253 6448
E   avaprods@aol.com

Contacts
Bud Osborne *Owner and Executive Producer*

Established in 1980, an award-winning television production company specializing in documentaries. Past productions include documentary segments for The History Channel, The Discovery Channel and E! Entertainment Network.

Submissions Policy
Accepts unsolicited manuscripts by mail. Welcomes the opportunity to see new writers' work and 'will give feedback about what we like and don't like'.

AVATAR PRODUCTIONS

329 270 Sparta Avenue Ste 104 Sparta NJ 07871
T 973 486 2875
E contactavatar@avatarproductions.com

Has been providing production services for broadcast, industrial and corporate television for over 20 years. Has received several awards, including 2 Emmy awards.

AXIAL ENTERTAINMENT

20 West 21st Street 8th Floor New York NY 10010
E submissions@axialentertainment.com
W www.axialentertainment.com

Production and management company, with a model loosely based on the "hot house" studio environment of the 1940s. Brings writers and film executives together to encourage the development process before studios, networks or producers become involved. Allows for a chance to be taken on a new writer or original idea.

Submissions Policy
It is company policy not to accept unsolicited materials. If interested in submitting work, email a 1-page brief summary of material.

BARNSTORM FILMS

73 Market Street Venice CA 90291
T 310 396 5937
F 310 450 4988
E tony@barnstormfilms.com

Contacts
Tony Bill *President*

Film production company founded in 1975. Recent credits include *Flyboys*, *North Country* and *A Home of our Own*. Company president Tony Bill won a Best Picture Oscar for *The Sting*.

Submissions Policy
Welcomes new writing. Send a one-page synopsis.

BELLADONNA PRODUCTIONS

118 West 22nd Street Suite 3 New York NY 10011
T 212 807 0108
F 212 807 6263
E cordelia@belladonna.bz
W www.belladonna.bz

Contacts
Cordelia Stephens *Head of Development*

Produces a range of media content, including feature films, documentaries and TV shows. Output includes *A Guide to Recognizing Your Saints* and *Transamerica*.

Submissions Policy
Sometimes welcomes unsolicited manuscripts.

BENDERSPINK

6735 Yucca Street Hollywood CA 90028
T 323 845 1640
F 323 512 5347
W www.benderspink.com

Founded in 1998, this management/production company has sold over 20 client scripts and co-produced *American Pie* with Universal

Pictures in its first year. Also co-produced *American Pie 2, Final Destination* and *Cats & Dogs*. Produced the television series *Kyle XY*.

Submissions Policy
Always accepting query letters for screenplays and short or feature films of all genres. Submit a brief synopsis via email.

BEYOND PIX

950 Battery Street San Francisco CA 94111
T 415 4341027
F 415 434 1032
W www.beyondpix.com

Production company offering broadcasting, production, editorial and internet media services. It produces the weekly programme *For the Record* for Bloomberg Television.

BLIZZARD ENTERTAINMENT

PO Box 18979 Irvine CA 92623
W www.blizzard.com

A major developer and publisher of entertainment software. Founded in 1991 as Silicon & Synapse and relaunched in 1994 as Blizzard. Examples of games include *World of Warcraft, Diablo* and *StarCraft*. The company's research and development group includes over 250 designers, producers, programmers, artists, and sound engineers.

BLUE RIDER PICTURES

2801 Ocean Park Boulevard Suite 193
Santa Monica CA 90405
T 310 314 8405
F 310 314 8402
E info@blueriderpictures.com
W www.blueriderpictures.com

Founded in 1991. Has produced over 100 movies and TV projects. Involved in the production of *Around The World In 80 Days, The Call of the Wild* and *The Incredible Mrs.*

Ritchie, starring James Caan and Gena Rowlands, which won an Emmy Award.

Submissions Policy
For submissions, send an email in first instance.

BLUE SKY STUDIOS

44 South Broadway White Plains New York
NY 10601
T 914 259 6500
F 914 259 6499
E info@blueskystudios.com
W www.blueskystudios.com

A division of Fox Filmed Entertainment since 1997. Produces pioneering animated content for film and television. Credits include *Bunny* and *Ice Age*.

BOCA PRODUCTIONS LLC

44314 Date Avenue Lancaster CA 93534
T 661 949 2848
E bocaproductions@yahoo.com
W bocaproductions.scriptmania.com

Contacts
Gary L. Myers *Executive Producer*

Founded in 2001, producing feature films and made-for-TV features. Production credits include *BOCA, Emissary* and *Evan's Heaven*. Welcomes original screenplays 'with financing in place' or 'adaptations of successful novels where rights have been acquired'.

BRILLSTEIN-GREY ENTERTAINMENT

9150 Wilshire Boulevard Ste 350 Beverly Hills
CA 90212
T 310 275 6135
F 310 275 6180

Brillstein-Grey Entertainment is a Hollywood agency that includes Brad Pitt and Courteney Cox in its clientele. The company also produces movies such as *The Wedding Singer* and television shows such as *Just Shoot Me*.

BROOKLYN FILMS

PO Box 20412 New York NY 10021
T   212 744 2845
E   inquiry@brooklynfilms.com
W   www.brooklynfilms.com

Brooklyn Films was founded in 1988. They
have produced feature films, television series
and HDTV productions. Past titles include
Flesh-Eating Mothers and *The Suckling*.

BROOKWELL/MCNAMARA ENTERTAINMENT

1600 Rosecrans Boulevard Raleigh Studios Bldg.
6A 3rd Floor North Wing Manhattan Beach
CA 90266
T   310 727 3353
F   310 727 3354
W   www.bmetvfilm.com

Has produced films including *Cake, Beyond the
Break* and *Dance Revolution*. Other credits
include the award-winning television series
That's So Raven from 2002 to 2006.

JERRY BRUCKHEIMER FILMS

1631 10th Street Santa Monica CA 90404
W   www.jbfilms.com

Produces films and television series in the genre
of action, drama and science fiction. Most of
these big-budget productions feature trademark
elaborate special effects. Credits include *Top
Gun*, *The Rock*, *Armageddon* and *Pirates of
the Caribbean*. Also produces television shows
including *CSI: Crime Scene Investigation*,
E-ring and *The Amazing Race*.

C2 PICTURES

2308 Broadway Santa Monica CA 90404
T   310 315 6000
F   310 828 0443

Cinergi Pictures Entertainment was a small
production company formed in 1992 and
produced films such as *Tombstone*, *Nixon* and

Evita. In 2002, it merged with Carolco Pictures
to form C2 Pictures. Output includes
Terminator 3: Rise of the Machines and *Basic
Instinct 2*.

C3 ENTERTAINMENT INC.

1415 Gardena Avenue Glendale CA 91204
T   818 956 1337
W   www.c3entertainment.com

Founded in 1959 as Comedy III Productions by
the Three Stooges. Produced the television
movie *The Three Stooges* in association with
Mel Gibson, and also co-produced *The Three
Stooges Greatest Hits* with Sony Pictures
Television.

Submissions Policy
See website for information on screenplay
submissions.

CAPCOM USA, INC.

Capcom Entertainment Inc. 800 Concar Drive
Suite 300 San Mateo CA 94402-2649
T   650 350 6500
W   www.capcom.com

Founded in Japan in 1979, manufacturing and
distributing electronic game machines. In 1983
Capcom Co., Ltd was established and over 25
years has produced some of the most successful
games franchises in the world. Titles include
Resident Evil, *Street Fighter*, *Breath of Fire*
and *Mega Man*. Offices in Tokyo, Osaka,
California, England, Germany and Hong Kong.

CARSEY-WERNER, LLC.

4024 Radford Avenue Ste. 3 Studio City
CA 91604
T   818 655 5598
F   818 655 6067
W   www.cwm.com

Established by Marcy Carsey and Tom Werner
in 1981, incorporating production and
distribution arms. Particular reputation for its
hit TV comedy series. Output includes *3rd*

Rock from the Sun, A Different World, Cybill, Grace Under Fire, Roseanne, That '70s Show and *The Cosby Show.*

CASTLE ROCK ENTERTAINMENT

Warner Bros. Studios 4000 Warner Boulevard
Burbank CA 91522
T   310 285 2300
F   310 285 2345
W   www2.warnerbros.com

Founded in 1987 by Martin Shafer, director Rob Reiner, Andy Scheinman, Glenn Padnick and Alan Horn, with Columbia Pictures as a strategic partner. Has produced a number of award-winning feature films and television shows. Titles include *When Harry Met Sally, A Few Good Men, The Polar Express, Music and Lyrics,* and the television show *Seinfeld.*

CHARNJIT FILMS

1209 Liberty Avenue Union NJ 07083
T   212 302 1906
F   212 302 0500
E   charnjitfilms@aol.com

Contacts
Chani Singh

Founded in 2001, producing Bollywood films. Recent productions include *Bollywood Rocks.*

Submissions Policy
Does not welcome unsolicited manuscripts.

CHERRY ROAD FILMS

10960 Wilshire Boulevard Suite 980
Los Angeles CA 90024
E   info@cherryroadfilms.com
W   www.cherryroadfilms.com

Founded in 2002, with credits including *Spring Break in Bosnia, White Jazz* and *Illegal Superman.*

Submissions Policy
Company policy not to accept unsolicited manuscripts.

CINETEL FILMS

8255 Sunset Boulevard Los Angeles
CA 90046
T   323 654 4000
F   323 650 6400
E   info@cinetelfilms.com
W   www.cinetelfilms.com

Founded in 1980. Has produced films including *Deadly Surveillance, Solar Attack* and *The Bone Eater.*

Submissions Policy
Company policy not to accept unsolicited manuscripts.

COLUMBIA TRISTAR MOTION PICTURE GROUP/SONY PICTURES

10202 W Washington Boulevard Culver City
CA 90232
T   310 244 4000
F   310 244 2626
W   www.sonypictures.com

Columbia TriStar Motion Pictures is part of Sony Pictures Entertainment Inc. It releases about 25 films per year and has 12 Academy Award Best Picture films in its library. Recent output includes *The Da Vinci Code, Talladega Nights, Casino Royale, Rocky Balboa, The Benchwarmers, Ghost Rider* and *Spider-Man 3.*

CRANE WEXELBLATT ENTERTAINMENT LTD

6061 Galahad Drive Malibu CA 90265
T   310 457 4821
F   310 457 3888
E   twomoguls@aol.com

Contacts
Peter Crane *Producer*

Established in 1978, producing drama and comedy for film and television.

Submissions Policy
Welcomes unsolicited ideas; send a synopsis by email.

CRITERION GAMES

E   mailbag@criteriongames.com
w   www.criteriongames.com

Owned by the giant Electronic Arts, specializing in developing leading video games such as the *Burnout* series and *Black*.

THE CROSLEY COMPANY

PO Box 1545 Edmond OK 73083
T   405 348 1628

Contacts
Richard Crosley *Producer*

Over 30-years experience in commercial and educational television producing, directing and writing. Working mostly for corporate clients.

Submissions Policy
Welcomes new writing.

DAKOTA FILMS

4133 Lankershim Boulevard North Hollywood CA 91602
T   818 760 0099
F   818 760 1070
E   info@dakotafilms.com
w   www.dakotafilms.com

Dakota Films specializes in reality based programming as well as scripted series and specials. Notable productions include Billy Crystal's opening films for the Oscars, HBO's *Tenacious D* and MTV's *Viva La Bam*.

Submissions Policy
Does not accept unsolicited material.

DARK HORSE ENTERTAINMENT

421 S. Beverly Drive Beverly Hills CA 90212
T   310 789 4751
w   www.dhentertainment.com

Founded in 1992, producers of *The Mask*, *TimeCop*, *Barb Wire*, *The Mystery Men* and *Hellboy*.

DINO DE LAURENTIIS COMPANY

100 Universal City Plaza Bungalow 5195
Universal City CA 91608
T   818 777 7191
F   818 866 5566
E   ddlcoffice@ddlc.net
w   www.ddlc.net

Contacts
Dino De Laurentiis *Producer*

Film production company producing narrative feature films. Established in 1983, past credits include *Hannibal Rising*, *U-571* and *Breakdown*.

Submissions Policy
Does not accept unsolicited manuscripts.

DEEGEE ENTERTAINMENT

366 N. La Cienega Boulevard Los Angeles
CA 90048
T   310 652 0999
F   310 652 0718
w   www.coronet-theatrela.com

Founded in 1986, producing films including *Ricochet River* (starring Kate Hudson and Jason James Richter), *Hostile* (starring Rob Lowe) and *The Wedding Planner* (starring Matthew McConaughey and Jennifer Lopez). Also run a writer's lab once a week.

DIMENSION FILMS

375 Greenwich St 4th Floor New York
NY 10013
w   www.weinsteinco.com

Founded in 1995, Dimension Films is a subsidiary of the Weinstein Company. Its credits include the *Scream* horror trilogy, *Spy Kids* and the *Scary Movie* franchise.

DINGO PRODUCTION LLC

12 Havemeyer Street #3L Brooklyn NY 11211
T 718 554 3558
F 510 856 3973
E enquiries@dingoproduction.com
W www.dingoproduction.com

Contacts
Nan Sandle *Producer*

Founded in 2006, producing a range of media content including feature films, podcasts, documentaries and advertising.

Submissions Policy
Welcomes unsolicited manuscripts by email.

DISNEY INTERACTIVE STUDIOS, INC.

500 South Buena Vista Street Burbank CA 91521
T 818 553 5000
W www.disney.go.com/disneyinteractivestudios

The interactive entertainment arm of the Walt Disney Company. Self-publishes and licences a range of games for many platforms and all markets.

DISTANT HORIZON

Suite A 8282 Sunset Boulevard Los Angeles CA 90046
T 323 848 4140
F 323 848 4144
E la@distant-horizon.com
W www.distant-horizon.com

Has produced in the US, Canada, United Kingdom and Africa. Credits include *Chain of Desire*, *Dead Beat*, *Scorpion Spring* and *I Capture the Castle*. Also has an office in London.

DREAMWORKS SKG

Universal City Plaza Bungalow 5121 Universal City CA 91608
T 818 733 7000
F 818 695 7574
W www.dreamworks.com

Founded in 1994. Major American film studios. Develops, produces and distributes films, video games and television programming. Won three consecutive Best Picture Academy Awards in 1999, 2000 and 2001 for *American Beauty*, *Gladiator* and *A Beautiful Mind* (the latter two with Universal). Also produces the television series *Into the West*, *Las Vegas*, *Rescue Me* and *The Contender*. Sold to Viacom (parent company of Paramount Pictures) in 2006. Independent animation branch DreamWorks Animation SKG spun off in 2004 and now produces two CG animated family features per year. Recent credits include *Shark Tale*, *Shrek*, *Shrek 2* and *Madagascar*.

EDMONDS ENTERTAINMENT

1635 N. Cahuenga Boulevard Los Angeles CA 90028
T 323 860 1550
F 323 860 1554
W www.edmondsent.com

Founded by Grammy-winning singer/producer Kenneth "Babyface" Edmonds and his wife Tracy. It has produced films including *Light it Up*, *Hav Plenty*, *College Hill* and *Soul Food*, which spawned the award-winning television drama series of the same name.

EL DORADO PICTURES

725 Arizona Avenue Ste. 100 Santa Monica CA 90401
T 310 458 4800
F 310 458 4802
W www.alecbaldwin.com/eldorado

Founded by actor Alec Baldwin, with credits including *State and Main* (winner of the Jury

Award at the Ft. Lauderdale International Film Festival), *Second Nature* and *The Devil and Daniel Webster*.

ELECTRIC ENTERTAINMENT

5707 Melrose Avenue Hollywood CA 90038
T   323 817 1300
F   323 467 7280
W   www.electric-entertainment.com

Founded in 2001, and responsible for films such as *Flyboys*, *Eight Legged Freaks*, *Cellular* (starring Kim Basinger) and *Who Killed the Electric Car?* (nominated by the Writer's Guild of America for Best Documentary Screenplay and by the Broadcast Film Critics Association for Best Documentary Feature). Also produced the made-for-television film *The Librarian*, starring Noah Wyle.

ELECTRO-FISH MEDIA LLC

PO Box 301348 Austin TX 78703
T   512 351 7133
E   info@electro-fish.com
W   electro-fish.com

Contacts
Chris Elley *Director*

Founded in 2004, film and television production companies primarily specializing in documentaries. Recent titles include *Barbecue: A Texas Love Story* and *Ghost Town: 24 Hours in Terlihgua*.

Submissions Policy
Prefers introductory contact before submissions are sent.

ELECTRONIC ARTS (EA)

209 Redwood Shores Parkway Redwood City CA 94065
T   650 628 1500
F   650 628 1414
W   www.ea.com

Founded in 1982, one of the giants of the gaming world, employing over 7,000 people worldwide. An independent developer and publisher of interactive entertainment software for advanced entertainment systems. Works with storywriters and film directors. Among its properties are *Need for Speed*, *The Sims*, *FIFA Soccer*, *Fight Night*, *Tiger Woods PGA Tour* and *The Lord of the Rings*. Its five hub studios are in Redwood Shores (US), Los Angeles (US), Orlando (US), Vancouver (Canada) and Surrey (UK).

ELIXIR FILMS

8033 W. Sunset Boulevard West Hollywood CA 90046
T   323 848 9867
F   323 848 5945
E   info@elixirfilms.com
W   www.elixirfilms.com

Made its first film in 2001 with the screen adaptation of Eric Bogosian's *Wake Up and Smell the Coffee*. Also produced the films *Where the Red Fern Grows*, *The Good Thief*, and the documentary *Long Way Round* (starring Ewan McGregor and Charley Boorman).

ENERGY ENTERTAINMENT

999 N. Doheny Drive #711 Los Angeles CA 90069
T   310 274 3440
W   www.energyentertainment.net

Founded in 2001, its film credits include *The Number 23*, starring Jim Carrey.

EVAMERE ENTERTAINMENT LLC

575 Broadway 6th Floor New York NY 10012
T   212 475 7555
F   212 475 1717
W   www.evamere.com

Founded as Hart Sharp Entertainment, partner John Hart launched Evamere in February 2007 after the team decided to part ways. This new production company will focus on feature films and Broadway theatrical productions. Forthcoming features include *Life During Wartime* and *Alice Goes To Harlem*.

Submissions Policy
Does not accept unsolicited material.

EVERGREEN FILMS LLC

1515 Palisades Drive Suite N Pacific Palisades CA 90272
T   319 573 9978
F   310 573 1137
W   www.evergreenfilms.com

Has produced films including *The Secret Adventures of Jules Verne*, *When Dinosaurs Roamed America*, *Red Flag*, and the mini-series *Alien Planet*.

FILM POLICE!

4310 North Mozart Street Chicago IL 60618
T   773 463 4010
F   773 463 4009
E   info@filmpolice.com
W   www.filmpolice.com

Contacts
Phillip Koch *Producer*

Founded in 1980, producing feature films and documentaries. Output includes *Medua Challenger*, *Pink Nights* and *The American Flag* (a documentary for PBS).

Submissions Policy
No unsolicited manuscripts. In first instance, send an inquiry.

FIRELIGHT MEDIA

2600 Tenth Street Suite 636 Berkeley CA 94710
T   510 704 9200
F   510 704 9201
E   info@firelightmedia.org
W   www.firelightmedia.org

An independent non-profit production company dedicated to telling stories of people, places, cultures and issues that are underrepresented in the mainstream media. Most Firelight Media productions are created for national broadcast on PBS. They have produced films including *Jonestown: The Life and Death of Peoples Temple*, and the documentary *Beyond Beats and Rhymes* (which examines representations of manhood, sexism and homophobia in hip-hop culture).

FLEXITOON

46 West 73 Street #3A NY 10023
T   212 877 2757
F   212 799 1987
E   craigmarin@flexitoon.com
W   www.flexitoon.com

Contacts
Craig Marin *Co-owner*

Founded in 1979 by puppeteers Olga Felgemacher and Craig Marin, specializing in family entertainment and commercials across a wide range of media. Past children's programmes include *Hamlin*, *Loopy Sloop* and *Pinwheel*.

Submissions Policy
Does not welcome unsolicited manuscripts.

FOCUS FEATURES

65 Bleecker St 3rd Floor New York NY 10012
T   212 539 4000
W   www.focusfeatures.com

Formed in 2002, Focus Features is the art house film division of NBC Universal's Universal Studios. It also serves as a producer and distributor of low-budget action/horror films through its Rogue Pictures. Focus has produced Academy Awarding-winning films such as *Gosford Park*, *Traffic*, *The Constant Gardner*, *Pride and Prejudice* and *Brokeback Mountain*.

FORTRESS FEATURES INC.

E   info@fortressfeatures.com
w   www.fortress-ent.com

Founded in 2004, it has produced films such as
Pride, *The Road Back* and *The Midnight Man*.
Also produces television shows including the
series *Ultimate Battles*, *I.A* and *Susan Powter*.

Submissions Policy
Accepts film screenplay submissions of any
genre. Submit a logline (50 words or less) and a
brief synopsis (250 words or less) to:
scripts@fortress-ent.com.

FOX ATOMIC

10201 West Pico Boulevard Bldg. 38
Los Angeles CA 90035
T   310 369 1000
F   310 369 2000
w   www.foxatomic.com

A division of 20th Century Fox, founded in
2006 and producing films, comics and digital
content for young adults. Output includes
Turistas, *The Hills Have Eyes II* and
28 Weeks Later.

FOX SEARCHLIGHT PICTURES

10201 W Pico Boulevard Bldg 38 Los Angeles
CA 90035
w   www.foxsearchlight.com

Fox Searchlight Pictures was established in 1994
as a specialty film division of 20th Century Fox
to produce and distribute indie styled films. It
has produced Academy Award-winning movies
such as *Boys Don't Cry*, *Sideways*, *The Last
King of Scotland* and *Little Miss Sunshine*.

FRIES FILM GROUP

22817 Ventura Boulevard Ste 909 Woodland
Hills CA 91364
T   818 888 3052
F   818 888 3042

Production/distribution company founded in
1994. Output includes *Treasure Island*,
Wildflowers and *LAPD: To Protect and Serve*.

FURST FILMS

8954 West Pico Boulevard 2nd Floor
Los Angeles CA 90035
T   310 278 6468
F   310 278 7401
E   info@furstfilms.com
w   www.furstfilms.com

Founded in 1999. Films output includes *The
Matador* (starring Pierce Brosnan, Greg
Kinnear, and Hope Davis), *The Cooler*
(starring Alec Baldwin and William H. Macy)
and *Owning Mahowny* (starring Philip
Seymour Hoffman, Minnie Driver and John
Hurt). Also produced the television show
Tough Trade.

FUTURE FILMS USA, LLC

1531 14th Street Santa Monica CA 90404
T   310 393 7124
F   310 393 7251
E   info@futurefilmgroup.com
w   www.futurefilmgroup.com

Formed in 2000, providing a full range of
services from pre-financing to post-production.
Highly experienced as both a co-producer on
international productions and as executive
producer on other productions.

GHOSTHOUSE PICTURES

E   info@ghosthousepictures.com
w   www.ghosthousepictures.com

Founded in 2002 by filmmakers Sam Raimi and
Rob Tapert. Has produced horror films such as
The Grudge 2, *30 Days of Night*, *The
Messengers*, *Dibbuk Box* and *Rise*.

Submissions Policy
Company policy not to accept unsolicited
manuscripts.

GOLD CIRCLE FILMS

9420 Wilshire Boulevard Suite 250
Beverly Hills CA 90212
T   310 278 4800
F   310 278 0885
E   info@goldcirclefilms.com
W   www.goldcirclefilms.com

Founded in 2000 and has produced
films such as *My Big Fat Greek Wedding*,
White Noise (and the sequel *White
Noise 2*) and, most recently, *Because
I Said So*.

Submissions Policy
Has a policy not to accept or consider
unsolicited submissions of concepts, creative
ideas, suggestions, stories, artwork or other
potential content.

GOLDCREST FILMS

1240 N. Olive Drive Los Angeles CA 90069
T   323 650 4551
F   323 650 3581
E   mail@goldcrestfilms.com
W   www.goldcrestfilms.com

Founded in 1977. Produces, finances and
distributes motion pictures. Titles in the library
include *Chariots of Fire*, *Gandhi*, and *The
Killing Fields*.

SAMUEL GOLDWYN FILMS

9570 W Pico Boulevard Suite 400 Los Angeles
CA 90035
T   310 860 3100
F   310 860 3198
E   info@samuelgoldwyn.com
W   www.samuelgoldwynfilms.com

Develops, produces and distributes feature
films and documentaries. Titles include
The Squid and the Whale (nominated
for an Academy Award), *Raising
Victor Vargas*, *Japanese Story* and
Super Size Me.

GRACIE FILMS

10202 W. Washington Boulevard Poitier 2nd
Floor Culver City CA 90232
T   310 244 4000
W   www.graciefilms.com

Founded in 1986, producing award-winning
films and television series. Output includes
Broadcast News, *Jerry Maguire* and *The
Simpsons*.

GRB ENTERTAINMENT

13400 Riverside Drive Sherman Oaks
CA 91423
T   818 728 7600
F   818 728 7601
W   www.grbtv.com

Specializes in unscripted alternative
programming. Has produced television shows
such as *True Caribbean Pirates*, *Princes of
Malibu*, *Growing Up Gotti*, *Simply Irresistible*
and *Beauty Shop Secrets*.

GREEN DOG FILMS

2030 S. Sherbourne Drive #16 Los Angeles
CA 90034
T   310 287 0198
E   info@greendogfilm.com
W   www.greendogfilm.com

Contacts
Jason Gurvitz

Established in 1999, film production company
specializing in drama and documentaries.
Credits include *The Ungodly*.

Submissions Policy
Welcomes unsolicited manuscripts by email.

GREENESTREET FILMS INC

9 Desbrosses St 2nd Floor New York
NY 10013
T   212 609 9000
F   212 609 9099

E general@gstreet.com
w www.greenestreetfilms.com

Has produced movies including *In the Bedroom, Swimfan, Uptown Girls* and *Yes*.

HALLMARK ENTERTAINMENT

1325 Avenue of the Americas 21st Floor
New York NY 10019
T 212 977 9001
F 212 977 9049
w www.hallmarkent.com

Since 1994 Hallmark Entertainment (the successor to RHI entertainment) has been among the largest suppliers of movies and mini-series in the television industry. Its productions have received 448 Emmy Nominations, 104 Emmy Awards and 15 Golden Globe Awards. Its critically-acclaimed productions include *Animal Farm, Arabian Nights, Don Quixote, Merlin* and *Human Trafficking*.

HALLMARK HALL OF FAME

12001 Ventura Place Suite 300 Studio City
Los Angeles CA 91604

Contacts
J. Callahan *Manager of Development*

Founded in 1951, specialists in television movies and character dramas. Winner of around 80 Emmy awards. Production credits include *Magic of Ordinary Days* and *Candles on Bay Street*.

Submissions Policy
Does not accept unsolicited manuscripts.

HAMZEH MYSTIQUE FILMS

61 Blaney Street Swampscott MA 01907
E info@HamzehMystiqueFilms.com
w www.hamzehmystiquefilms.com

Has produced films such as *Blood of Eden* and *The Letter*, which won best documentary at the Boston International Film Festival.

Submissions Policy
Accepts submissions for feature films, MOWs, and television pilots for consideration as future projects. To submit material, complete a release form available on website and post the first 10 pages of material to the address provided.

HAPPY MADISON PRODUCTIONS

10202 West Washington Boulevard Judy Garland Bldg. Culver City CA 90232
T 310 244 3100
w www.adamsandler.com

Founded by Adam Sandler and has produced films such as *Deuce Bigalow, The Animal* and *The Benchwarmers*.

HARBOR LIGHTS ENTERTAINMENT

1438 North Gower Street Box 4 Building 2 Third Floor Hollywood CA 90028
T 323 462 3887
w www.harborlightentertainment.com

An independent motion picture development and production company with credits including *Mindscan* (starring Morgan Freeman), *Manjiro* and *28/6*.

HBO

1100 Avenue of the Americas New York
NY 10036
w www.hbo.com

HBO Films (part of the HBO cable television network) has its main focus on the television market, with successful mini-series such as *Band of Brothers* and *Angels in America*. It has also had success in the film industry with critically-acclaimed films such as *American Splendour* and *Elephant* (winner of the Palme D'Or at the Cannes Film Festival). HBO Films productions won the Primetime Emmy Award for 'Outstanding Made for Television Movie' every year from 1993 to 2002, except in 2000.

JIM HENSON CO.

1416 N La Brea Avenue Hollywood CA 90028
T 323 802 1500
F 323 802 1825
W www.henson.com

Founded by Jim Henson, the creator of *The Muppets*, in 1958. Other television credits include *Farscape* as well as the film *MirrorMask*. Also responsible for the creation of the Emmy Award-winning *Bear in the Big Blue House*.

HIT ENTERTAINMENT

1133 Broadway Ste 1520 New York
NY 10010
T 212 463 9623
W www.hitentertainment.com

Launched in 1989, Hit entertainment is one of the world's leading children's entertainment producers. Included in its portfolio are internationally-renowned children's properties such as *Bob the Builder*, *Thomas & Friends* and *Barney*.

Submissions Policy
It is company policy not to accept unsolicited submissions or new programme ideas. Submissions will only be accepted through agents, publishers and content providers for the entertainment industry. A submissions pack is available for downloading from their website.

HOLLYWOOD PICTURES

500 South Buena Vista Street Burbank
CA 91521
T 818 560 1000
W www.disney.go.com

Part of the Walt Disney Corporation, producing films for a more mature, adult audience than Walt Disney Pictures. Has produced films such as *Arachnophobia*, *The Sixth Sense* and, most recently, *The Invisible*.

ICON PRODUCTIONS

808 Wilshire Boulevard 4th Floor
Santa Monica CA 90401
W www.iconmovies.com

Icon Productions was founded by actor/director Mel Gibson in 1989. Has produced award-winning films such as *Braveheart* and *The Passion of the Christ*. Also produces television movies and series such as *The Three Stooges*, *Complete Savages* and *Kevin Hill*.

IMAGINE ENTERTAINMENT

9465 Wilshire Boulelvard 7th Floor
Beverly Hills CA 90212
W www.imagine-entertainment.com

A film and television production company founded in 1986 by director Ron Howard and producer Brian Grazer. Output includes the Golden Globe- and Emmy Award-winning television series *24* and *Arrested Development*, as well as the Academy Award-winning films *Apollo 13* and *A Beautiful Mind*.

IMPACT PICTURES LLC

9200 Sunset Boulevard Suite 800 Los Angeles
CA 90069
E production@impactpix.com

Major feature-film production company specializing in adapting videogames for the screen. Past projects include *Resident Evil*, *Resident Evil: Apocalypse* and *DOA: Dead or Alive*.

Submissions Policy
No unsolicited scripts. Material accepted only via an agent.

INTERMEDIA FILMS

9242 Beverley Boulevard Suite 201 Beverley Hills Los Angeles CA 90210
T 310 777 3561
F 310 550 3886

E   info@intermediafilm.com
W   www.intermediafilm.com

Contacts
Martin Schuermann CEO

Founded in 1995, producing feature films with budgets between US$4m. and US$30m. Examples of output include *Breach*, *RV*, *Alexander* and *Terminator 3*.

Submissions Policy
Does not welcome unsolicited approaches.

JERSEY FILMS

PO Box 491246 Los Angeles CA 90049
T   310 550 3200
F   310 550 3210

Founded by Danny DeVito and Rhea Perlman. Credits include *Matilda*, *Pulp Fiction*, *Erin Brockovich* and *Freedom Writers*. Also produced the television sitcom *Reno 911*.

KETTLEDRUM FILMS

4961 Agnes Avenue Valley Village CA 91607
T   818 506 7525
E   kettledrum@worldnet.att.net

Contacts
Judd Bernard *Partner*

Founded in 1967, producing films across a wide range of genres, from *Monty Python* to thrillers and westerns. Worked with actors including Michael Caine, Lee Marvin and Glenda Jackson.

Submissions Policy
Welcomes new writing, 'depending on subject matter'.

KILLER FILMS INC.

380 Lafayette Street Suite 202 New York NY 10003
T   212 473 3950
F   212 473 6152
W   www.killerfilms.com

Has produced films such as *An American Crime*, *Mrs Harris* (Primetime Emmy nominee), *Infamous* and, most recently, *Then She Found Me* (directed by Helen Hunt).

KULTUR INTERNATIONAL FILMS, INC.

195 Highway 36 West Long Branch NJ 07764
T   732 229 2343
F   732 229 0066
E   info@kultur.com
W   www.kultur.com

Contacts
Dennis Hedlund *Chairman*

Founded in 1980, independent company specializing in performing arts documentaries, including ballet, opera and music.

Submissions Policy
Accepts unsolicited proposals.

LAKESHORE ENTERTAINMENT CORP

9268 W 3rd Street Beverly Hills CA 90210
T   310 867 8000
F   310 300 3051
E   info@lakeshoreentertainment.com
W   www.lakeshoreentertainment.com

Founded by Tom Rosenberg in 1994, Lakeshore has produced over 40 films including *Runaway Bride*, *Underworld* and *The Mothman Prophecies*. Also produced the multi-award-winning *Million Dollar Baby*.

LEAUDOUCE FILMS

1626 Wilcox Avenue #424 Los Angeles CA 90028
T   323 469 3546
F   323 417 4710
E   info@leaudouce.com
W   www.leaudouce.com

Contacts
Ana Marie Laperal *President*

Founded in 2003, film production company specializing in features and international co-productions. Credits include *Seed of Contention.*

Submissions Policy
Does not accept unsolicited manuscripts.

LIONSGATE FILMS

2700 Colorado Avenue Santa Monica
CA 90404
T   310 449 9200
W www.lionsgatefilms.com

Founded in 1976, focusing on foreign and independent films. Known for distributing controversial films such as *Fahrenheit 9/11* and *American Psycho*. It received an Academy Award for Best Picture for *Crash.* It is also the producer of the popular television series the *Dead Zone* and *Weeds.*

LIVEPLANET

2644 30th Street Santa Monica CA 90405
T   310 664 2400
F   310 664 2401
E   info@liveplanet.com
W www.liveplanet.com

Produces feature films and scripted and non-scripted television programmes. Films include *Matchstick Men, American Wedding* and *The Core.*

LUCASARTS

PO Box 29908 San Francisco CA 94129-0908
W www.lucasarts.com

Established in 1982 by George Lucas, a leading publisher and developer of interactive entertainment software for videogame console systems and personal computers. Works closely with sister company Industrial Light & Magic. Among its

properties are *Star Wars, Indiana Jones* and *Mercenaries.*

LUCASFILM LTD

5858 Lucas Valley Road Nicasio
CA 94946
T   415 662 1800
F   415 448 2495
W www.lucasfilm.com

Founded in 1971 by George Lucas, the architect behind the *Starwars* and *Indiana Jones* films series. The production company has won a total of 19 Academy Awards and produced the Emmy Award-winning television series *The Young Indiana Jones Chronicles.*

M8 ENTERTAINMENT

1875 Century Park E Ste 2000 Los Angeles
CA 90067
T   310 226 8300
F   310 226 8350
E   info@media8ent.com
W www.media8ent.com

Media 8 was formed in 1993 and subsequently changed its name to M8 Entertainment in 2004. Credits include *Lovewrecked, The Upside of Anger* and the Academy Award-winning *Monster.*

MACE NEUFELD PRODUCTIONS

9100 Wilshire Boulevard Suite S17 - East Tower Beverly Hills CA 90212
T   310 401 6868

Contacts
Mace Neufeld *President*

Film and television production company with credits including *The Hunt for Red October, Patriot Games, The Saint* and *Sahara.*

Submissions Policy
Does not welcome unsolicited manuscripts.

MACGILLIVRAY FREEMAN FILMS, INC.

PO Box 205 Laguna Beach CA 92652
T   949 494 1055
F   949 494 2079
W www.macfreefilms.com

Contacts
Patty Collins *Manager, Sponsorship and Development*

Established in 1963, producers with particular reputation for large-format films for IMAX cinemas. Past credits include *The Living Sea* and *Dolphins*, both nominated for Academy Awards in the Best Documentary/Short Subject category.

MANDALAY PICTURES

4751 Wilshire Boulevard 3rd Floor
Los Angeles CA 90010
T   323 549 4300
W www.mandalay.com

Film studio founded in 1995 as part of the Mandalay Entertainment Group. Output includes *Seven Years in Tibet, Donnie Brasco, I Know What You Did Last Summer* and the sequel *I Still Know What You Did Last Summer*.

Submissions Policy
Has a company policy not to accept unsolicited materials.

MATADOR PICTURES LLC

12021 Wilshire Boulevard Suite 117
Los Angeles CA 90025
T   310 472 6220
F   310 472 6223
E   admin-la@matadorpictures.com
W www.matadorpictures.com

Founded in 1999. Has produced award-winning films across genres including *Ae Fond Kiss* (winner of two awards at the Berlin Film Festival and nominated for The Golden Bear), *Ten Minutes Older* and *The Wind that Shakes the Barley* (winner of the Palme D'Or and numerous other awards). Also has offices in London.

MATTHAU COMPANY

11661 San Vicente Boulevard #609
Los Angeles CA 90049
T   310 454 3300
E   info@matthau.com
W www.matthau.com

Founded in 1990, producing films including *Dennis the Menace, Grumpy Old Men* and *The Grass Harp*. The company focuses on stories with 'humanity, heart and humour'.

MERCHANT IVORY PRODUCTIONS

250 W 57th St Ste 1825 New York
NY 10107
T   212 582 8049
F   212 459 9201
E   contact@merchantivory.com
W www.merchantivory.com

Founded in 1961 and best known for producing period pieces such as *A Room With A View* and *Howards End*, each of which won three Academy Awards. Also received eight Academy Award nominations for *The Remains of the Day*.

MICROSOFT GAME STUDIOS (MGS)

Microsoft Corporation One Microsoft Way
Redmond WA 98052-6399
W www.microsoft.com/games

The game creation wing of the Microsoft Corp. Develops and publishes games for Windows-based PCs and Xbox consoles. Examples of output include *Combat Flight Simulator, Dungeon Siege, Halo* and *Kingdom Under Fire*.

PARAMOUNT MOTION PICTURES GROUP

5555 Melrose Avenue Hollywood
CA 90038-3197
T   323 956 5000
F   323 862 1204
W www.paramount.com

Founded in 1912 and one of the giants
of the movie world. Output in more
recent times (either producing or
co-producing) includes *Forrest Gump*,
Mission Impossible, *Ghost*, *Titanic*, *Vanilla
Sky*, *Changing Lanes*, *Team America: World
Police*, *Dreamgirls* and *Zodiac*. Their television
series include *The Brady Bunch*, *MacGyver*, the
Star Trek franchise and *Sabrina the Teenage
Witch*.

PARTICIPANT PRODUCTIONS

E   info@participantproductions.com
W www.participantproductions.com

Founded in 2004. Production credits
include *Arna's Children*, *North Country*
and *Syriana*. Won the Oscar for best
documentary for *An Inconvenient
Truth*.

Submissions Policy
Has a company policy not to accept unsolicited
manuscripts.

PATHFINDER PICTURES LLC

Ocean Front Walk Ste. 7 Venice CA 90291
T   310 664 1500
E   info@pathfinderpictures.com
W www.pathfinderpictures.com

Founded in 1998 and has produced *Double
Deception* (starring Louis Mandylor), the
sci-fi thriller *Shadow Fury* and the drama
Until The Night.

Submissions Policy
Does not accept unsolicited submissions,
concepts, creative ideas, stories or content of
any sort.

PERSISTENT ENTERTAINMENT

9107 Wilshire Boulevard Ste. 500
Beverly Hills CA 90210
T   310 777 0126
F   310 777 5259
E   info@persistent-ent.com
W www.persistent-ent.com

Founded in 1997, producing films including
The Beautiful Ordinary, *Walker Payne* and
Southland Tales (starring Dwayne 'The Rock'
Johnson, Sean William Scott and Sarah
Michelle Gellar).

Submissions Policy
Company policy not to accept unsolicited
manuscripts. Email a brief synopsis of project
ideas for consideration.

PIXAR ANIMATION STUDIOS

1200 Park Avenue Emeryville CA 94608
T   510 922 3000
F   510 922 3151
W www.pixar.com

Pixar Animation Studios, a subsidiary of
Disney (since 2006) is a seven time
Academy Award-winning computer
animation studio. It has produced such films
as *Toy Story*, *Finding Nemo*, *Cars* and *The
Incredibles*.

RAECOM PRODUCTIONS

5333 S. Genoa Way Centennial CO 80015
T   303 699 8110
F   303 317 3022
E   customerservice@RaecomProductions.com
W www.RaecomProductions.com

Contacts
Villa Rae McClure *Executive Producer*

Founded in 2003, producing across a wide
range of genres, including documentaries, music
videos, short films and feature films.

Submissions Policy
Welcomes unsolicited manuscripts.

RED STORM

3200 Gateway Ctr. Boulevard Suite 100
Morrisville NC 27560
T 919 460 1776
F 919 468 3305
W www.redstorm.com

Founded in 1996, the brainchild of Doug
Littlejohns and novelist Tom Clancy. Now
a leader in content development for
multiple-media.

REGENT ENTERTAINMENT

10990 Wilshire Boulevard Penthouse 1800
Los Angeles CA 90024
T 310 806 4288
F 310 806 4268
E info@regententertainment.com
W www.regententertainment.com

Production credits include *Tom and Viv*, *One
False Move* and *Gods and Monsters* (winner of
the 1999 Academy Award for Best Adapted
Screenplay).

REVOLUTION STUDIOS

2900 W. Olympic Boulevard Santa Monica
CA 90404
T 310 255 7000
F 310 255 7001
E info@revolutionstudios.com
W www.revolutionstudios.com

Founded in 2000. Credits include *Punch-Drunk
Love*, *13 Going on 30*, *The Animal* and *Daddy
Day Care*.

RIVER ROAD ENTERTAINMENT

1901 Avenue of the Stars 2nd Floor
Los Angeles CA 9006
T 310 860 9470
F 310 461 1490
W www.riverroadentertainment.com

Founded in 1987. Has produced the film *Old
Explorers* plus documentaries on rock star
Prince, baseball great Kirby Puckett and Irish
theater director Joe Dowling. Also produces
in-flight entertainment programming.

ROCKSTAR GAMES

622 Broadway New York NY 10012-2600
W www.rockstargames.com

Founded in 1998, publishers of titles including
Grand Theft Auto, *Midnight Club*, *Max Payne*,
Smuggler's Run, *Manhunt* and *Red Dead
Revolver*.

Submissions Policy
Welcomes input from the gaming community
but any submissions of any nature whatsoever
become the sole and exclusive property of
Rockstar Games, which shall have full right,
title and interest thereto, including under
copyright, in all media now existing or
hereafter created, and without any obligation
to account or make any payment to the
submitter for any use thereof.

ROGUE PICTURES

100 Universal City Plaza Universal City
CA 91608
T 818 777 7373
W www.roguepictures.com

Launched in 2004, Rogue Pictures is a division
of Focus Features, the speciality film division of
Universal Studios. Mainly produces and
distributes low-budget action/horror films.
Output includes *Shaun of the Dead*, *Seed of
Chucky*, *Assualt on Precinct 13* and *Hot Fuzz*.

ALEX ROSE PRODUCTIONS

8291 Presson Place Los Angeles CA 90069
T 323 654 8662
F 323 654 0196
E alexroseproductions@hotmail.com

Contacts
Alexandra Rose *Producer*

Established by Oscar nominee Alex Rose, film production company producing drama, comedy and romance. Output includes *The Other Sister* and *Exit to Eden*.

Submissions Policy
Seeking new writing that they consider 'original, gratifying and uplifting'. Must sign release form.

SCOTT RUDIN PRODUCTIONS

560 South Buena Vista Street Los Angeles CA 91521-1759

An independent film and theatre production house at Paramount Pictures. Has produced films including *The Truman Show*, *I Heart Huckabees*, *Zoolander*, the Oscar-nominated *Notes on a Scandal* and the Oscar-winning *The Queen*.

JOEL SCHUMACHER PRODUCTIONS

1149 N Gower Street Ste 247 Los Angeles CA 90038
T 323 785 2274
F 323 785 2275

Production company whose output includes *Phantom of the Opera* (based on the Andrew Lloyd Webber musical). Currently producing a movie entitled *Centricity*.

SCOTT FREE PRODUCTIONS

614 N La Peer Drive Los Angeles CA 90069
T 310 360 2250
F 310 360 2251

Film and television production company founded in 1995 by Ridley Scott and his brother Tony. Has produced films such as *Black Hawk Down*, *In Her Shoes*, *Matchstick Men*, *Kingdom of Heaven* and the multi-Academy Award-winning *Gladiator*. Has been producing the CBS crime series *Numb3rs* since 2005.

SEGA OF AMERICA

650 Townsend Street Suite 650 San Francisco CA 94103-4908
W www.sega.com

Sega of America was founded in 1986 by the Sega Corporation of Japan but can trace its roots back to the 1940s. A giant of the gaming world, its franchises include *Phantasy Star*, *Sonic the Hedgehog*, *Shining Force*, *Total War* and *Sega Rally*.

SEVEN ARTS PICTURES

9595 Wilshire Boulevard Ste 1000 Beverly Hills CA 90212
W www.7artspictures.com

Has produced films such as *An American Rhapsody* (winner of the Hollywood Discovery Award for best feature at the Hollywood Film Awards) and *Interstate 60*.

SHINEBOX MOTION PICTURES

288 E. 1090 N. Orem UT 84057
T 801 427 3638
E contact@shineboxmp.com

Contacts
Bryan Young *Producer*

Established in 1999, producing documentaries, narrative features and shorts. Recent credits include *This Divided State*, winner of Best Documentary at the 2005 Santa Cruz International Film Festival.

Submissions Policy
Welcomes unsolicited manuscripts.

SHORELINE ENTERTAINMENT, INC.

1875 Century Park East Suite 600 Los Angeles CA 90067
T 310 551 2060
F 310 201 0729
E info@shorelineentertainment.com
W www.shorelineentertainment.com

Founded in 1992. Has produced titles including *The Secret, Sidekick* and *Marilyn Hotchkiss Ballroom Dancing and Charm School,* which premiered at the Sundance Film Festival.

SIERRA ENTERTAINMENT

6060 Center Drive 5th Floor Los Angeles CA 90045
w www.sierra.com

Video games and interactive entertainment developer and publisher. Its studios include Massive Entertainment (founded in 1997; sample games: *Ground Control*); Radical Entertainment (sample games: *The Simpsons: Hit & Run, The Incredible Hulk: Ultimate Destruction* and *Scarface*); Swordfish Studios (founded in 2002; sample games: *Brian Lara International Cricket*); and High Moon Studios (sample games: *Darkwatch*).

SILVER LION FILMS

701 Santa Monica Boulevard Suite 240
Santa Monica CA 90401
T 310 393 9177
F 310 458 9372
E slf@silverlionfilms.com
w www.silverlionfilms.com

Established in 1986, an independent feature film production company which self-finances its projects. Past credits include *Man on Fire, Flipper* and *Crocodile Dundee in Los Angeles.*

Submissions Policy
Email synopsis in first instance before sending complete manuscript.

SILVERS/KOSTER PRODUCTIONS

353 S. Reeves Drive Penthouse Beverly Hills CA 90212
T 310 991 4736
F 310 284 5797
E skfilmco@aol.com
w www.silvers-koster.com

Contacts
Iren Koster *Owner*

Established in 1985 by the daughter of comedian Phil Silvers and the nephew of director Henry Koster. Film production company producing drama, comedy and family films.

Submissions Policy
Does not welcome unsolicited manuscripts. Prefers first contact by email.

SNEAK PREVIEW ENTERTAINMENT

6705 Sunset Boulevard 2nd Floor
Hollywood CA 90028
T 323 962 0295
F 323 962 0372
E indiefilm@sneakpreviewentertain.com
w www.sneakpreviewentertain.com

Produces independent films, including *Hellbent, When do we Eat?* and *The Civilization of Maxwell Bright.* Some titles focus on adult content.

SOMMERS COMPANY

204 Santa Monica Boulevard Suite A
Santa Monica CA 90401
E info@sommerscompany.com
w www.sommerscompany.com

Founded in 2004. Produced *Van Helsing,* (starring Kate Beckinsale). Projects in development include *Jason and the Argonauts* and the William Goldman-scripted epic *Flame over India.*

Submissions Policy
Does not accept unsolicited manuscripts.

SONY PICTURES ENTERTAINMENT INC

10202 W Washington Boulevard Culver City
CA 90232
T 310 244 4000
F 310 244 2626
w www.sonypictures.com

Sony Pictures Entertainment is the television and film production/distribution unit of the Sony media conglomerate. It comprises of various studios and entertainment brands including Columbia Pictures, TriStar Pictures, MGM and United Artists. In 1992 Sony created Sony Pictures Classics for art-house fare and its output includes the Academy Award-winning *Crouching Tiger, Hidden Dragon* and the Academy Award-nominee *House of Flying Daggers*.

SONY PICTURES IMAGEWORKS

9050 W. Washington Boulevard Culver City CA 90232
T   310 840 8000
F   310 840 8100
W   www.imageworks.com

An Academy Award-winning, state-of-the-art digital production studio dedicated to the art of visual effects production and character animation. Film credits include *Spider-man, The Chronicles of Narnia: The Lion, The Witch and the Wardrobe* and *Stuart Little*.

SOUTHERN SKIES/GREAT NORTHER FILM AND MUSIC

1104 South Holt Avenue Suite 302
Los Angeles CA 90035
T   310 855 9833
F   310 855 0220
E   gr8norther@hotmail.com

Contacts
Edward D. Markley *President/Director*

Founded in 1980, feature film production company with past credits including *City Slickers, Alien 3* and *Major League*. Specializes in drama and comedy features.

Submissions Policy
Welcomes unsolicited manuscripts, but 'only if they're great!'

SPYGLASS ENTERTAINMENT

10900 Wilshire Boulevard 10th Floor
Los Angeles CA 90024
T   310 443 5800
F   310 443 5912
W   www.spyglassentertainment.com

Spyglass Entertainment was founded in 1998 and has produced Academy Award-nominated films such as *The Sixth Sense, The Insider* and *Seabiscuit*. It also produced the Academy Award-winning *Memoirs of a Geisha* and the television drama series *Miracles*.

Submissions Policy
Company policy not to accept unsolicited materials.

SQUARE ENIX CO., LTD.

999 N. Sepulveda Boulevard Third Floor
El Segundo CA 90245
W   www.square-enix.com

Founded in Tokyo, Japan in 1975. Creating, publishing and distributing entertainment content including interactive entertainment software and publications in Asia, North America and Europe. Properties include *Final Fantasy, Dragon Quest* and *Kingdom Hearts*.

STAR ENTERTAINMENT GROUP, INC.

13457 Ventura Boulevard Suite 140 Sherman Oak CA 91423
T   818 988 2200
F   818 988 2202
W   www.findinghomemovie.com

Contacts
Lawrence David Foldes *Chairman*

Independent production company specializing in films 'with substance'. Recent feature film *Finding Home* won best picture awards at a number of international film festivals.

Submissions Policy
Welcomes unsolicited approaches by mail but prefers submission of character descriptions and a synopsis only. 'No mindless comedies, please!'

STORM ENTERTAINMENT

127 Broadway Ste 222 Santa Monica
CA 90401
T   310 656 2500
F   310 656 2510
E   storment95@aol.com
W   www.stormentertainment.com

Founded in 1995, Storm Entertainment has produced films such as *Hell's Kitchen* (starring Angelina Jolie), *Being Considered*, *The Criminal* and *The Shiner* (starring Michael Caine).

STRAND RELEASING

6140 Washington Boulevard Culver City
CA 90232
T   310 836 7500
F   310 836 7510
E   strand@strandreleasing.com
W   www.strandreleasing.com

Although Strand Releasing started off as a film distribution company in 1989, it has ventured into film production since 2000. Produces art-house films such as *Split*, *Wo de mei li xiang chou* and *Psycho Beach Party*.

SUMMIT ENTERTAINMENT

1630 Stewart Street Ste. 120 Santa Monica
CA 90404
T   310 309 8400
W   www.summit-ent.com

Major motion picture distributor and producer. Credits include *The Hottie and the Nottie*, *The Alibi*, *Mr. & Mrs. Smith*, *Insomnia*, *Memento*, *American Pie*, *The Loss of Sexual Innocence*, *Lock, Stock and Two Smoking Barrels* and *Evita*.

THINKFILM

23 East 22nd Street 5th Floor New York
NY 10010
T   212 444 7900
F   212 444 7901
E   info@thinkfilmcompany.com
W   www.thinkfilmcompany.com

Founded in 2001 by four former Lionsgate Films executives, producing films including *Going to Pieces: The Rise and Fall of the Slasher Film*, *When Stand Up Stood Out* and *Bloodlines*.

TIME RIVER PRODUCTIONS

Box 70615 Pasadena CA 91117
T   626 304 0080

Contacts
Eric Cloud *Assistant*

Founded in 1986, producing motion pictures and television programmes.

Submissions Policy
Develop screenplays in-house so does not welcome any unsolicited manuscripts.

TOLLIN/ROBBINS PRODUCTIONS

4130 Cahuenga Boulevard Unit 305 Toluca Lake CA 91602
T   818 755 3000
F   818 766 8488
E   info@tollinrobbins.com
W   www.tollinrobbins.com

Founded in 1993. Television output includes *Smallville* and *One Tree Hill*. Feature film productions include *Wild Hogs* (starring Tim Allen, John Travolta and Martin Lawrence) and *Norbit* (starring Eddie Murphy). Also the award-winning documentary *Hardwood Dreams*, narrated by Wesley Snipes.

TOUCHSTONE PICTURES

500 S Buena Vista St Burbank CA 91521
W   touchstone.movies.go.com

Established in 1984, a film division of the Walt Disney Company. It releases features with themes of a more mature nature than those that get released under the Walt Disney Pictures banner. Output includes *Pretty Woman*, *Sister Act*, *Armageddon*, *Hidalgo* and the Academy-nominated *Apocalypto*.

TRIBECA PRODUCTIONS

375 Greenwich Street 8th Floor New York NY 10013
T 212 941 4000
F 212 941 4044

Motion picture production company co-founded in 1989 by Robert de Niro. Output includes *36*, *The Good Shepherd*, *Meet the Fockers*, *About a Boy*, *Meet the Parents*, *Analyze This*, *A Bronx Tale* and *Cape Fear*.

TRIGGER STREET PRODUCTIONS

W www.triggerstreet.com

Founded in 1997 by Kevin Spacey. Credits include *Beyond the Sea*, *The United States of Leland* and *The Big Kahuna*. In 2002, TriggerStreet.com was established as a web-based filmmaker and screenwriter's community. Aims to assist the careers of emerging filmmakers and screenwriters.

TSG PRODUCTIONS

718 S. 22nd Street Philadelphia PA 19146
T 218 546 1448
E wd24p@hotmail.com

Contacts
Robert M. Goodman *Producer*

Established in 1989, independent film and television production company producing drama, comedy and documentaries. Recent features include *Stone Reader*.

Submissions Policy
Welcomes unsolicited manuscripts, but prefers a query letter first. Pleased to receive new writing: 'if it's good we don't care'. High budget or effects-based ideas are unsuitable.

UBISOFT ENTERTAINMENT

625 Third Street San Francisco CA 94107
T 415 547 4000
F 415 547 4001
W www.ubisoftgroup.com

Has 15 in-house production studios across 11 countries. Distributes games in over 50 countries. Examples of output include *Blazing Angels*, *Brothers in Arms* and the *Chessmaster*, *The Settlers*, *Prince of Persia*, *Rayman* and *Tom Clancy's Ghost Recon* series.

UGLY BETTY PRODUCTIONS, INC.

618 Carroll Street 2nd Flr. Brooklyn NY 11215
T 718 399 7544
F 718 399 7415
E ubp@uglybetty.com
W www.uglybetty.com

Has produced the short films *Thirsty*, *Face Value*, *Lucky* and *Ping Pong Love*.

UNITED ARTISTS ENTERTAINMENT LLC

10250 Constellation Boulevard Los Angeles CA 90067
W www.unitedartists.com

Founded in 1919 by Mary Pickford, Charles Chaplin, Douglas Fairbanks and D. W. Griffith. A subsidiary of MGM Studios. In 2006, United Artists came under the control of Tom Cruise and Paula Wagner. It is responsible for the *Rocky*, *Pink Panther* and *James Bond* franchises and has produced a number of Academy Award-winning films such as *Rebecca*, *Rain Man* and *Capote*. Other recent titles include *Coffee and Cigarettes*, *Hotel Rwanda*, *Romance & Cigarettes* and *The Woods*.

UNIVERSAL PICTURES

100 Universal City Plaza Universal City
CA 91608
w www.universalpictures.com

A subsidiary of NBC Universal and one
of the major American film studios. The
second longest-lived studio in Hollywood,
producing films for over 80 years. Has won
numerous awards for its films over the
years. A taster of its recent credits includes
*Babe, American Pie, Children of Men,
The Bourne Supremacy, Van Helsing,
The 40-Year-Old Virgin, The Interpreter,
King Kong, Serenity, Miami Vice,
United 93, Alpha Dog, Bean 2* and
Because I Said So.

Submissions Policy
Does not accept unsolicited material.

VANGUARD DOCUMENTARIES

PO Box 26635 Brooklyn NY 11202-6624
T   212 517 4333
E   charleshobson@yahoo.com
w www.vanguarddocumentaries.com

Specializes in films based on arts,
cultural affairs and politics. Co-produced
the film *Harlem in Montmartre:
Paris Jazz.*

VIEW ASKEW PRODUCTIONS, INC.

116 Broad Street Red Bank NJ 07701
T   732 842 6933
F   732 842 3772
E   viewaskew@viewaskew.com
w www.viewaskew.com

Founded in 1994 by Kevin Smith and
Scott Mosier. Has produced cult films
such as *Clerks, Chasing Amy, Dogma* and
Jersey Girl.

Submissions Policy
Does not accept submissions of
material.

VILLAGE ROADSHOW PICTURES

3400 Riverside Drive Ste 900 Burbank
CA 91505
w www.villageroadshowpictures.com

Village Roadshow Pictures is the film production
division of Australia's Village Roadshow Limited
(leading media and entertainment company). It
has been co-producing films with its principal
partner Warner Bros since the late 1990s. Some of
the titles in its library include *Charlie and the
Chocolate Factory,* the *Matrix* trilogy, *Miss
Congeniality* and the Oscar-winning *Training Day.*

VULCAN PRODUCTIONS

w www.vulcanproductions.com

Produces feature films with budgets under $1
million. Credits include *Hard Candy, Far From
Heaven, The Safety of Objects* and *Where God
Left His Shoes.* Has also produced documentaries
such as *Cracking the Code of Life, Evolution* and
Strange Days on Planet Earth.

Submissions Policy
Company policy not to accept unsolicited
manuscripts. Screenplays, treatments, and/or
pitches must be submitted through established
entertainment agents and/or attorneys.

WALT DISNEY ANIMATION STUDIOS

500 South Buena Vista Street Burbank
CA 91521
T   818 560 1000
w www.disney.go.com

Founded in 1934. Has produced Academy
Award-winning features such as *Beauty and the
Beast, The Little Mermaid* and *The Lion King.*

WALT DISNEY PICTURES

500 South Buena Vista Street Burbank
CA 91521
T   818 560 1000
w www.disney.go.com

Established in 1983 as part of Walt Disney Productions, it has produced several award-winning films. Output includes *The Pirates of the Caribbean* trilogy, *Meet the Robinsons*, *Aladdin* and *Finding Nemo*. Films produced by the company are aimed at children. Also produces television shows such as *That's So Raven* and *The Replacements*.

WARNER BROS ENTERTAINMENT, INC

4000 Warner Boulevard Bldg 5 Burbank CA 91522
w www2.warnerbros.com

Warner Bros (founded in 1923), a subsidiary of Time Warner, is one of the world's largest film and television producers. Has won numerous awards over the years and is responsible for the *Harry Potter*, *Lethal Weapon* and *Batman* franchises. Television output includes *Smallville* and *ER*.

WASHINGTON SQUARE FILMS

310 Bowery 2nd Floor New York NY 10012
T 212 253 0333
F 212 253 0330
E production@wsfilms.com
w www.wsfilms.com

Has produced films including *Sweet Flame*, *Adrift in Manhattan* and *Old Joy*, plus the television programme *Words in Your Face*.

Submissions Policy
Does not accept unsolicited scripts.

THE WEINSTEIN COMPANY

375 Greenwich Street Tribeca Film Center New York NY 10013
w www.weinsteinco.com

Founded in 2005 and includes the Dimension Films label. Has produced award-winning films including *TransAmerica* and *Mrs Henderson Presents*.

JERRY WEINTRAUB PRODUCTIONS

c/o Warner Bros 4000 Warner Boulevard Burbank CA 91522
T 818 954 2500
F 818 954 1399

Based at Warner Bros Studios. Has produced movies including *The Specialist*, *The Avengers* and *Ocean's 11* (as well as *Ocean's 12* and *13*).

WEINTRAUB/KUHN PRODUCTIONS

1452 2nd St Santa Monica CA 90401
T 310 458 3300

Weintraub/Kuhn Productions has produced films including *Amazons and Gladiators*, *Endangered Species* and *Warrior Angels*.

WINKLER FILMS

211 S Beverly Drive Ste 200 Beverly Hills CA 90212
T 310 858 5780
F 310 858 5799

Has produced films including *The Net*, *Home of the Brave* and the Golden Globe-nominated *De-Lovely*.

THE SAUL ZAENTZ COMPANY

2600 Tenth Street Berkeley CA 94710
T 510 549 1528
w www.zaentz.com

Founded in 1972, producing award-winning films such as *The Unbearable Lightness of Being*, *The English Patient* and *One Flew Over The Cuckoo's Nest*.

Submissions Policy
Does not accept unsolicited material.

UNITED KINGDOM

20TH CENTURY FOX FILM CO.

Twentieth Century House 31–32 Soho Square
London W1D 3AP
T   020 7437 7766
W   www.fox.co.uk

London office of the American giant.

Submissions Policy
Does not accept unsolicited material.

AARDMAN

Gas Ferry Road Bristol BS1 6UN
T   0117 984 8485
W   www.aardman.com

Founded in 1976, Aardman produce multi-award-winning animated feature films and TV programmes. Has won Oscars for *Creature Comforts* and the adventures of *Wallace & Gromit*. Other titles include *Chicken Run* and *Flushed Away*.

Submissions Policy
Has a policy of not reading unsolicited scripts or story ideas unless they are by established writers and come through an agent. Established writers without an agent should send a CV and a one paragraph description of their idea.

ABSOLUTELY PRODUCTIONS LTD

Unit 19 77 Beak Street London W1F 9DB
T   020 7644 5575
E   www.absolutely.biz

Formed in 1988 by a group of writer/performer/producers including Morwenna Banks, Jack Docherty, Moray Hunter, Pete Baikie, John Sparkes and Gordon Kennedy. Long-established producer for TV, has recently moved into feature films too. First major show was *Absolutely*. More recent productions include *Welcome To Strathmuir* (a new comedy pilot for BBC Scotland) and *Baggage* (BBC Radio 4).

ABSTRACT IMAGES

117 Willoughby House Barbican London EC2Y 8BL
T   020 7638 5123
E   productions@abstract-images.co.uk

Contacts
Howard Ross *Managing Director*

Television production company founded in 1990.

ACACIA PRODUCTIONS LTD

80 Weston Park London N8 9TB
T   020 8341 9392
F   020 8341 9392
E   acacia@dial.pipex.com
W   www.acaciaproductions.co.uk

Contacts
John Edward Douglas Milner *MD, Writer and Director*

Founded in 1985, specializing in 'creative documentaries' and news programmes for television. Special focus on contemporary and environmental issues and historical documentaries. Titles include *Vietnam After the Fire* and *Spirit of Trees*. Company has won the special jury prize at the Banff International TV and Film Festival and the prize for best film made for TV at the New York International Documentary Festival.

Submissions Policy
Only interested in submissions within the company's remit. Does not do drama.

ACTAEON FILMS LTD

50 Gracefield Gardens London SW16 2ST
T   020 8769 3339
F   0870 134 7980
E   info@actaeonfilms.com
W   www.actaeonfilms.com

Contacts
Daniel Cormack *Managing Director and Producer*

Production company founded in 2004 by Daniel Cormack to develop and produce feature length theatrical motion pictures. Focus is on films that use elements of established commercial genres in innovative and original ways that challenge and entertain a broad range of audiences. Recent work includes the Akira Kurosawa Memorial Prize-shortlisted drama *Amelia and Michael* (2007), starring Anthony Head, and the comedy drama *Are You Strong?* (2007).

Submissions Policy
Runs an open submissions policy and encourages unsolicited screenplays from new writers. Considers original feature length screenplays of any genre and screenplays for single drama or drama series for TV. No longer considers short film screenplays. All screenplays will be read by a professional reader but cannot provide feedback unless there is a strong potential for development and only screenplays submitted with an sae will be returned.

ADDICTIVE TV

The Old North House 39a North Road London N7 9DP
T   020 7700 0333
E   mail@addictive.com
W www.addictive.com

Launched in 1992. Devises and produces television programming. Focused on music, arts and technology. Recent credits include *Mixmasters* (ITV1), *The Web Review* (ITV1) and *Spaced Out* (Sci-Fi Channel).

AFTER IMAGE

T   020 7737 7300
W www.afterimage.co.uk

Created by Jane Thorburn and Mark Lucas in 1979. Produces arts-orientated projects for television and video. Best known for art series *After Image* (Channel 4). Now tours *After Image* seasons to arts institutions in the UK as well as in the USA, Italy and France.

ALL3MEDIA

87-91 Newman Street London W1T 3EY
T   020 7907 0177
F   020 7907 0199
E   information@all3media.com
W www.all3media.com

Contacts
Sir Robert Phillis *Non-Executive Chairman*

Production and distribution company led by Steve Morrison, David Liddiment, Jules Burns and John Pfeil. Formed following the acquisition of Chrysalis Group's TV division in September 2003. Comprised of a group of production companies from across the UK, The Netherlands, New Zealand and the USA. Members include Company Pictures, Lion Television and South Pacific Pictures. Also includes international distribution subsection to represent third-party producers and broadcasters together with its own production companies.

AMBIENT LIGHT PRODUCTIONS LTD

6 Shipquay Street Derry BT48 6DN
T   028 7136 3525
E   info@ambient-light.co.uk
W www.ambient-light.co.uk

Contacts
Tony Doherty *Managing Director*

Production company founded in 2005 and working in TV, film and corporate. Titles include the documentary *Agnes* and the short film *Peace Cubed*.

Submissions Policy
Welcomes scripts whether from Bafta-nominated writers or students fresh out of college. Approach by email in the first instance.

AMC PITCURES LTD

Pinewood Studios Iver Heath Bucks SL0 0NH
T   01753 785 843
F   01753 630 651

E   films@amcpictures.co.uk
W   www.amcpictures.co.uk

Contacts
Alistair Maclean-Clark   *Managing Director*

Production company founded in April 2005. Specializes in film and television drama; eight feature films produced to date.

Submissions Policy
Unsolicited material accepted in writing with a synopsis.

ANGLIA FACTUAL

The London Television Centre Upper Ground London SE1 9LT
T   020 7620 1620
E   sue.potter@granadamedia.com
W   www.angliafactual.co.uk

Semi-independent subsidary of ITV division Granada Media. Established in 2000. Has produced over 1,000 hours of popular documentary for the BBC, ITV, Channel 4, Five, British Sky Broadcasting and Discovery Channel International. Recent output includes *Real Families: My Skin Could Kill Me* (ITV1), *Seeing The Dead* (ITV1) and upcoming *Property Developing Abroad* (Channel 5). Now fast-developing in North America where *Animal Precinct* is one of Discovery's top rated shows.

ANGLO-FORTUNATO FILMS LTD

170 Popes Lane London W5 4NJ
T   020 8932 7676
F   020 8932 7491
E   anglofortunato@aol.com

Contacts
Luciano Celentino

Founded in 1972 for the production of film and television projects. Specializes in action-comedies and psychological thrillers, most notably *Hobo Gallan the Pinch*.

Submissions Policy
Although keen on encouraging new writing, material is only accepted via agents.

APOCALYPSO PICTURES

Bretton Lincombe Lane Boars Hill Oxfordshire OX1 5DY
T   01865 735332

Company founded by producer Tania Seghatchian and director Pawel Pawlikowski. Best known for BAFTA-winning *My Summer of Love*.

APT FILMS

Ealing Studios Ealing Green London W5 5EP
T   020 8280 9125
F   020 8280 9111
E   admin@aptfilms.com
W   www.aptfilms.com

Produces commercially driven feature films. Past titles include *Wondrous Oblivion*, *Solomon & Gaenor* (nominated for an Oscar) and *Deep Water* (Best Documentary at the Rome Film Festival). Has a policy of producing short films with new talent as part of the process of development of a feature film. Up to 2007 it had made twelve such films.

ARCANE PICTURES

60-62 Great Titchfield Street London W1W 7QG
T   020 7636 4996
F   020 7323 0661
E   info@arcanepictures.com
W   www.arcanepictures.com

Co-founded by George Duffield and Meg Thomson in 1998. Strives to produce 'intelligent, sexy, innovative and commercial films'. Interested in documentary, feature and short film projects. Best known for *dot the i* starring Gael Garcia Bernal and *MILK*, an eccentric comedy set on a dairy farm starring Dawn French and Francesca Annis.

ARCHER STREET

Studio 5 10-11 Archer Street London
W1D 7A2
T   020 7439 0540
F   020 7437 1182
E   films@archerstreet.com

Producer of feature films including *And When
Did You Last See Your Father, Beyond the Sea*
and *Girl With a Pearl Earring*.

ARLINGTON PRODUCTIONS LIMITED

Cippenham Court Cippenham Lane Cippenham
Nr. Slough Berkshire SL1 5AU
T   01753 516767
F   01753 691785

Produces popular international drama with
occasional forays into other areas, for television
and the home video market.

Submissions Policy
Prides itself on its reputation for encouraging
new writers but will only look at new material
via established agents.

ART & TRAINING FILMS LTD

PO Box 3459 Stratford upon Avon CV37 6ZJ
T   01789 294910
E   andrew.haynes@atf.org.uk
W   www.atf.org.uk

Contacts
Andrew Haynes

Producer of documentaries, drama,
commercials and corporate films and video.

Submissions Policy
Submissions via agents considered.

THE ASHFORD ENTERTAINMENT
CORPORATION LTD

20 The Chase Coulsdon Surrey CR5 2EG
T   020 8660 9609
F   08701 164142

E   info@ashford-entertainment.co.uk
W   www.ashford-entertainment.co.uk

Contacts
Frazer Ashford *Managing Director*

Founded in 1996 by award-winning producer
Frazer Ashford to produce character-led
documentaries for TV. Examples of work
include *Serial Killers, Great Little Trains*
(winner of RTS Best Regional Documentary)
and *Streetlife* (winner of bronze award at the
Flagstaff Film Festival).

Submissions Policy
Happy to look at any submissions falling
within the remit of character-led
documentaries. Send hard copy with an sae.

AV PICTURES

Caparo House 103 Baker Street London
W1U 6LN
T   020 7317 0140
F   020 7224 5149
E   info@avpictures.co.uk
W   www.avpictures.co.uk

Established in 2003 when Victor Film
Company was acquired by The Caparo
Group. Company's first production was
School for Seduction, a comedy drama
starring Kelly Brook, Emily Woof and Dervla
Kirwan.

AVALON

4a Exmoor Street London W10 6BD
T   020 7598 7280
E   mikea@avalonuk.com
W   www.avalonuk.com/tv

BAFTA-winning television company formed in
1993. Supplies TV programming to all the
British terrestrial channels and most leading
satellite channels. Best known for light
entertainment programmes such as
documentary *Frank Skinner on Frank Skinner*
(ITV1) or comedy *Fantasy Football* (BBC2).
Now broadening output to include drama,
factual and formatted shows.

Submissions Policy
Script, treatment or ideas are welcomed via email.

BABY COW PRODUCTIONS

77 Oxford Street London W1D 2ES
E   john@babycow.co.uk
W   www.babycow.co.uk

Established in 1989 by Steve Coogan and Henry Normal. Has produced for the BBC, ITV and UK digital channels, specializing in cutting edge comedy. Has divisions for animation, radio and films. Productions include *Marion and Geoff, Human Remains, The Sketch Show, 24 Hour Party People, I'm Alan Partridge, Nighty Night, The Mighty Boosh, I Am Not an Animal* and *Dating Ray Fenwick*.

Submissions Policy
Dedicated development department always on the lookout for new talent. In first instance, send a synopsis or treatment and a ten page extract, plus a DVD or video if the idea is filmed, and a covering letter. If the idea is of interest, Baby Cow will contact the writer. Include all contact details, including email.

BAKER STREET MEDIA FINANCE

96 Baker Street London W1U 6TJ
T   020 7487 3677
F   020 7487 5667
E   enquiries@bakerstreetfinance.tv
W   www.bakerstreetfinance.tv

Specializes in the co-production, financing and structuring of British feature films, and British-qualifying international co-productions.

Submissions Policy
When submitting a project, Baker Street will wish to see the latest draft of a script, sales estimates, a projected finance plan, a draft budget and schedule (even if these are preliminary documents) along with a list of any creative attachments, and any available further background material. Unless otherwise requested all initial enquiries regarding script submission should be directed to Anthony

Walters or Lucy Main. Unsolicited scripts will not be accepted without sales estimates and finance plan attached. Scripts and accompanying material cannot be returned.

BBC VISION, BBC AUDIO & MUSIC

BBC Television Centre Wood Lane London W12 7RJ
T   020 8743 8000
W   www.bbc.co.uk

Contacts
Mark Thompson *Director-General*

Reorganization of the BBC operational structure has resulted in the following groups: BBC Vision Group (which runs three main areas: production, commissioning and services and includes the terrestrial and digital television channels; Drama, Entertainment and Children's; Factual and Learning); The Audio & Music Group (responsible for TV Music Entertainment; In-house Factual, Specialist Factual and Drama Audio production); and the Journalism Group (covers News; Sport; Global News, Nations and Regions). TV and radio commissioning guidance available at bbc.co.uk/commissioning

BBC WRITERSROOM

Development Manager BBC writersroom
Grafton House 379–381 Euston Road London NW1 3AU
W   www.bbc.co.uk/writersroom

Contacts
Jane Tranter *Controller, Fiction*

Champions new writers across all BBC platforms for Drama, Comedy and Children's programmes, running targeted schemes and workshops linked directly to production. It accepts and assesses unsolicited scripts for all departments: film, TV drama, radio drama, TV narrative comedy and radio narrative comedy. The website offers a diary of events, opportunities, competitions, interviews with established writers, submission guidelines and free formatting software. BBC writersroom also has a Manchester base which focuses on new writing in the north of England.

Submissions Policy

Writers should send hard copies of original, completed scripts to the address above. Before sending in scripts, log on to the website or send an A5 sae to Writersroom at the address above for the latest guidelines on submitting unsolicited work. See also bbc.co.uk/commissioning/structure/public.shtml

BBC NEW TALENT

w www.bbc.co.uk/newtalent

The BBC's search for new talent covers a constantly changing range of outlets that has included radio producers, presenters, young storytellers, filmmakers and comedy writers. Access the website for latest information.

BBC FILMS

Grafton House 379 Euston Road London NW1 3AU
T   020 7765 0251
F   020 7765 0278
w www.bbc.co.uk/bbcfilms

The feature film-making arm of the BBC, co-producing around eight titles per year. Committed to finding and developing new talent, as well as working with established names. Also produces television dramas. Credits include *Notes on a Scandal*, *The History Boys*, *Mrs Brown*, *Billy Elliot*, *Iris*, *Dirty Pretty Things* and *The Life And Death Of Peter Sellers*. Will not consider unsolicited scripts (unsolicited scripts should be sent to the BBC Writers Room). Scripts sent via production companies and agents should be addressed to the Development Assistant, 3rd Floor, Grafton House, 379 Euston Road, London NW1 3AU.

BIG HEART MEDIA

E   info@bigheartmedia.com
w www.bigheartmedia.com

Contacts
Beth Newell

Producer of drama and documetaries for television and video. Ideas/outlines welcome by email, but not unsolicited manuscripts. Keen to enourage new writing.

BLACKWATCH PRODUCTIONS LIMITED

2/1 104 Marlboro Avenue Glasgow G11 7LE
T   0141 339 9996
E   info@blackwatchtv.com
w www.blackwatchtv.com

Contacts
Nicola Black *Company Director*

Film, television and video producer of drama and documentary programmes. Output includes *The Paranormal Peter Sellers*, *Snorting Coke with the BBC*, *When Freddie Mercury Met Kenny Everett*, *Designer Vaginas*, *Bonebreakers*, *Luv Bytes* and *Can We Carry On, Girls?* for Ch4. Also coordinates the *Mesh* animation scheme.

Submissions Policy
Does not welcome unsolicited manuscripts.

BONA BROADCASTING LIMITED

Media Suitie 1 43 Cavalry Park Drive Edinburgh EH15 3QG
T   0131 661 7550
F   0131 661 7558
E   enquiries@bonabroadcasting.com
w www.bonabroadcasting.com

Contacts
Turan Ali

Producer of award-winning drama and documentary programmes for BBC Radio, TV and film projects.

Submissions Policy
No unsolicited manuscripts but send a one-paragraph summary by email in the first instance. Runs radio and TV drama training courses in the UK and internationally.

THE BUREAU

E   mail@thebureau.co.uk
w   www.thebureau.co.uk

Aims to produce films in the crossover arthouse film sector and to identify and nurture distinctive talent.

CACTUS TV

373 Kennington Road London
SE11 4PS
T   020 7091 4900
F   020 7091 4901
E   touch.us@cactustv.co.uk
w   www.cactustv.co.uk

Founded in 1994 specializing in broad-based entertainment, features and chat shows. Produces around 300 hours of broadcast material per year. Examples of programmes include *Richard & Judy*, *Sir Cliff Richard - The Hits I Missed*, *Songs of Bond* and *The British Soap Awards*.

CALON TV

47 Marylebone Lane London W1U 2NT

3 Mount Stuart Square Butetown Cardiff
CF10 5EE
T   029 2048 8400
F   029 2048 5962
E   enquiries@calon.tv
w   www.calon.tv

Contacts
Andrew Officer *Head of Development*

Founded in 2005 to produce animation and live action TV programmes and films for children, teens and families. Titles include the Bafta-winning *SuperTed*, an animated version of *Under Milk Wood* and *Hilltop Hospital*.

Submissions Policy
Happy to view the work of new writers. Send an email or letter first.

CAPITOL FILMS

Bridge House 2nd Floor 63-65 North Wharf
Road London W2 1LA
T   020 7298 6200
F   020 7298 6201
E   films@capitolfilms.com
w   www.capitolfilms.com

Founded in the early 1990s and has since handled worldwide sales and distribution of over 100 films, the majority of which it has financed or co-financed. Notable successes include *Gosford Park*, *Jeepers Creepers* and *Lucky Number Slevin*.

CARNIVAL FILM & TELEVISION

47 Marylebone Lane London W1U 2NT
T   020 7317 1370
F   020 7317 1380
E   info@carnivalfilms.co.uk
w   www.carnivalfilms.co.uk

Contacts
Gareth Neame *Managing Director*

Founded in 1978, specializing in television drama and feature film. Titles include *Hotel Babylon* (BBC), *Sea of Souls* (BBC), *Empathy* (BBC), *Lifeline* (BBC) and *Whistleblower* (ITV).

Submissions Policy
Does not encourage unsolicited material.

CARTWN CYMRU

32 Wordsworth Avenue Roath Cardiff
CF24 3FR
T   029 2046 3556
E   production@cartwn-cymru.com

Contacts
Naomi Jones *Producer*

Animation production company. Output includes: *Toucan 'Tecs* (YTV/S4C); *Funnybones* and *Turandot: Operavox* (both for S4C/BBC); *Testament: The Bible in Animation*

(BBC2/S4C); *The Miracle Maker*
(S4C/BBC/British Screen/Icon Entertainment
International); *Faeries* (HIT Entertainment plc
for CITV); *Otherworld* (animated feature film
for S4C Films, British Screen, Arts Council of
Wales).

CELADOR FILMS

39 Long Acre London WC2E 9LG
T   020 7845 6800
F   020 7845 6980
W   www.celadorfilms.com

Production company behind titles such as
Dirty Pretty Things, *Separate Lies* and *The
Descent*. Aims to develop high quality,
commercially viable feature films across
all genres.

Submissions Policy
Will commission projects at all stages
of development from verbal pitch to
developed screenplay. Submissions should
be marked for the attention of Ivana
MacKinnon. However, will only accept
submissions from established literary and
film agents or talent already known to the
company or from third party producers
seeking possible co-production.

CELADOR PRODUCTIONS

39 Long Acre London WC2E 9LG
T   020 7845 6976
F   020 7845 6980
W   www.celadorproductions.com

Produces range of TV programmes, from
situation comedy to quizzes, game shows,
popular factual entertainment and international
co-productions. Range includes *24 Carrott
Gold*, *All About Me*, *My Blue Heaven*,
Popcorn, *Schofield's TV Gold*, *The Detectives*,
The Hypnotic World of Paul McKenna and
You Are What You Eat.

Submissions Policy
Does not accept unsolicited ideas for comedy
or entertainment television formats.

CELTIC FILMS ENTERTAINMENT LTD

Lodge House 69 Beaufort Street London
SW3 5AH
T   020 7351 0909
F   0871 264 1474
E   info@celticfilms.co.uk
W   www.celticfilms.co.uk

Contacts
Stuart Sutherland *Managing Director*

Founded in 1986 producing high-end TV
drama and mainstream feature films.
Titles include fifteen *Sharpe* TV films,
Girl from Rio and *Stefan Kiszko: A Life
for a Life*.

Submissions Policy
Does not invite unsolicited material.

CHAMELEON TELEVISION LTD

Great Minster House Lister Hill Horsforth
Leeds LS18 5DL
T   0113 205 0040
F   0113 281 9454
E   allen@chameleontv.com

Contacts
Allen Jewhurst

Film and television drama and documentary
producer. Output includes *Edge of the City*;
The Family Who Vanished; *Killing for Honour*;
College Girls; *Ken Dodd in the Dock* (all for
Ch4); *Diary of a Mother on the Edge*; *Divorces
From Hell*; *Shipman*; *Love to Shop*; *The
Marchioness* (all for ITV); *Ted & Sylvia –
Love, Loss*; *Hamas Bombers* (BBC); *Liverpool
Poets* (Ch5).

Submissions Policy
Scripts not welcome unless via agents but new
writing is encouraged.

CHANNEL 4 TELEVISION

124 Horseferry Road London SW1P 2TX
W   www.channel4.com

Transmits across all of the UK, except for some parts of Wales served by S4C. Public service remit charges the channel with 'the provision of a broad range of high quality and diverse programming'. Does not produce its own programming.

CHANNEL X

17 Dufferin Street London EC1Y 8PD
T   020 7566 8160
F   020 7566 8161
E   info@channelx.co.uk
W   info@channelx.co.uk

Over 20 years experience of producing comedy and entertainment programmes for all the major UK broadcasters. Specializes in scripted broken and narrative comedy, comedy entertainment formats and gameshows. Examples of recent shows include *Blunder*, *Modern Toss*, *Lucas and Walliams – The Early Years*, *Peter Kay – The Early Years*, *California Dreaming* and *Catterick*.

THE CHILDREN'S FILM & TELEVISION FOUNDATION LTD

E   annahome@cftf.org
W   www.cftf.org.uk

Contacts
Anna Home

Involved in the development and co-production of films for children and the family, both for the theatrical market and for TV.

CHILDREN'S FILM UNIT

South Way Leavesden Herts WD2 7LZ
T   01923 354656
E   cfilmunit@aol.com
W   www.childrensfilmunit.com

An educational charity training ten- to sixteen-year-olds in all aspects of film-making. Has also produced a series of well-received feature films for television. Now works exclusively in digital video.

CINEMA VERITY PRODUCTIONS LTD

11 Addison Avenue London W11 4QS
T   020 7460 2777
F   020 7371 3329

Contacts
Verity Lambert *Chief Executive*

Founded in 1985, producing dramas and comedies for TV.

Submissions Policy
Does not encourage unsolicited approaches as company no longer has a script development department.

CLEVELAND PRODUCTIONS

5 Rainbow Court Oxhey Watford
Hertfordshire WD19 4RP
T   01923 254000
E   michael@gosling.com

Contacts
Michael Gosling

Documentary production company founded in 1977.

COASTAL PRODUCTIONS LIMITED

25b Broad Chare Quayside Newcastle-upon-Tyne NE1 3DQ
T   0191 222 3160
F   0191 222 3169
E   coastalproductions@msn.com

Contacts
Sandra Jobling *Executive Producer*

Founded in 1996, specializing in television drama. Credits include *Wire in the Blood* (series 1–4), *Rocketman*, *Take Me* and *Grafters*. Company has won 3 RTS awards, a Gold award from the New York Television Festival and was nominated for an Edgar Award.

Submissions Policy
Always looking for new and innovative writing but accepts approaches by agents only.

CODEMASTERS

PO Box 6 Leamington Spa Warwickshire
CV47 2ZT
T 01926 814132
F 01926 817595
E business.development@codemasters.com
W www.codemasters.co.uk

Develops and publishes video games for
many major platforms. Output includes
*Colin McRae Rally, Brian Lara International
Cricket, Clive Barker's Jericho, Maelstrom,
TOCA Race Driver* and *Operation
Flashpoint.* Also maintains operations
in the US and throughout Western
Europe.

COI

Hercules Road London SE1 7DU
T 020 7928 2345

Government advertising and marketing
communications, and public information
films.

COLLINGWOOD O'HARE ENTERTAINMENT LTD

10-14 Crown Street London
W3 8SB
T 020 8993 3666
F 020 8993 9595
E info@crownstreet.co.uk
W www.collingwoodohare.com

Contacts
Helen Stroud *Head of Development*

Founded in 1988, producing award-winning
animated series and specials for UK
and overseas broadcasters. Examples of
recent titles include *The Secret Show*
(BBC and Nicktoons USA), *Gordon the
Garden Gnome* (BBC), *Yoko! Jakmoko!
Toto!* (ITV), *Dennis and Gnasher* (BBC) and
Harry and his Bucketful of Dinosaurs
(C5, Nicktoons).

Submissions Policy
Does not welcome unsolicited material.

COLUMBIA TRISTAR MOTION PICTURE GROUP

25 Golden Square London W1F 9LS
T 020 7533 1000
W www.sonypictures.co.uk

Owned by Sony Pictures Entertainment.
Releases about 25 films per year.
Encompasses one production studio
(Columbia Pictures) and three film labels (Sony
Pictures Classics, Screen Gems and TriStar
Pictures). Columbia Pictures develops, produces
and distributes main-stream feature films.
Founded in 1924. Recent credits include
*Memoirs of a Geisha, The Da Vinci Code,
Casino Royale* and *Spiderman 3.* Sony Pictures
Classics produces, acquires, finances and
distributes independent and art-house films.
Screen Gems exists to cover ground between
the latter two markets. TriStar Pictures was
re-launched in 2004 as a marketing and
acquisitions unit with a particular emphasis on
genre films. Originally founded in 1982.
Output includes *Oliver Twist* and *Running
with Scissors* (upcoming).

THE COMEDY UNIT

Park Craigmont Street Glasgow G20 9BT
T 0141 305 6666
F 0141 305 6600
E scripts@comedyunit.co.uk
W www.comedyunit.co.uk

Contacts
April Chamberlain *Managing Director*

Producers of comedy entertainment for
children's TV, radio, video and film. Output
includes: *Still Game; Karen Dunbar Show;
Offside; Chewin' the Fat; Only An Excuse; Yo!
Diary; Watson's Wind Up.*

Submissions Policy
Unsolicited manuscripts welcome by post or
email.

COMPANY PICTURES

Suffolk House 1-8 Whitfield Place
London W1T 5JU
T   020 7380 3900
F   020 7380 1166
E   enquiries@companypictures.co.uk
W   www.companypictures.co.uk

Contacts
George Faber *Founder/Executive Producer*

One of the UK's largest independent
film and television drama production
companies. Established in 1998. Won
Best Independent Production Company
at the 2005 Broadcast Awards and the
European Producers of the Year Award
at the 2004 Monte Carlo Awards.
Production highlights include *Shameless*
(Channel 4), *Life and Death of Peter
Sellers* (HBO, two Golden Globe Awards,
15 Emmies) and *Elizabeth I* starring
Helen Mirren and Jeremy Irons (Channel
4/HBO, three Golden Globe Awards,
9 Emmies).

Submissions Policy
Proposals accepted only via agent.

CONTENTFILM INTERNATIONAL

19 Heddon Street London N1B 4BG
T   0207 851 6500
F   0207 851 6506
E   london@contentfilm.com
W   www.contentfilm.com

Launched in 2002. Specializes in high
quality, commercial feature films. Past
examples include Academy Award-nominated
Transamerica and *Thank You For
Smoking.*

Submissions Policy
Only accepts unsolicited material via
email with the following criteria: film
50% funded, production company
in place, significant director and/or cast
attached.

COOLABI

48 Broadley Terrace London NW1 6LG
T   020 7258 7080
F   020 7258 7090
E   info@coolabi.com
W   www.coolabi.com

Originially founded in 1999 as Alibi
Communications, producer of prime time
television drama and children's television
drama. In 2004 merged with Coolebah
Limited, a business engaged in licensing and
animated children's television production.
Became Coolabi in 2005.

COSGROVE HALL FILMS

8 Albany Road Chorlton-cum-Hardy
Manchester M21 0AW
T   0161 882 2500
F   0161 882 2555

Producer of animated children's television
programmes, founded in 1976. Highlights
include *Andy Pandy, Bill and Ben, Count
Duckula, DangerMouse, Fifi and the
Flowertots, Roald Dahl's BFG, The Jungle
Book* and *The Wind in the Willows.*

COUGAR FILMS

Paramount House 162-170 Wardour Street
London W1F 8ZX
T   020 7292 6610
F   020 7734 7878
E   admin@cougarfilms.co.uk

Feature film production company whose credits
include *Imagine Me and You.*

COWBOY FILMS

11-29 Smiths Court London W1D 7DP
T   020 7287 3808
F   020 7287 3785
E   charles@cowboyfilms.co.uk
W   www.cowboyfilms.co.uk

Founded in the 1990s, a feature film and television production company with credits including *The Last King of Scotland* and *Hole*.

THE CREATIVE PARTNERSHIP

13 Bateman Street London W1D 3AF
T   020 7439 7762
E   sally.chapman@thecreativepartnership.co.uk
W www.thecreativepartnership.co.uk

Contacts
Christopher Fowler

'Europe's largest "one-stop shop" for advertising and marketing campaigns for the film and television industries.' Clients include most major and independent film companies.

Submissions Policy
No scripts. 'We train new writers in-house, and find them from submitted CVs. All applicants must have previous commercial writing experience.'

CROSS DAY PRODUCTIONS LTD

1st floor 130-132 Wardour Street London W1F 8ZN
T   020 7287 5773
F   020 7287 5774
E   pippacro@aol.com

Producer of feature films. Credits include the award-winning *Shooting Dogs*.

CROSSROADS FILMS

2nd Floor 87 Notting Hill Gate London W11 3JZ
W www.crossroadsfilms.com

Works across a variety of media including film, television, commercials and music video. Film credits include *A Love Song for Bobby Long* and *Snow Angels*.

CS FILMS

46 Haycroft Gardens London NW10 3BN
T   020 8838 2566
E   admin@schoenfeld.co.uk

Contacts
Carl Schoenfeld

Independent producer of feature films and documentaries, founded in 2002. Examples of productions include *The Living and the Dead*, *My Brother Tom* and *A Sarajevo Diary*, which was Bafta- and Prix Europa-nominated.

Submissions Policy
Is happy to look at unsolicited work. Writers should send a one-page synopsis by email. Their advice to new writers looking to break into the industry is: 'Don't expect much money and keep your day job.'

CUTTING EDGE PRODUCTIONS LTD

27 Erpingham Road London SW15 1BE
T   020 8780 1476
F   020 8780 0102
E   juliannorridge@btconnect.com

Contacts
Julian Norridge

Corporate and documentary video and television. Output includes a US series on evangelicalism, *Dispatches* on the US tobacco industry plus government videos.

Submissions Policy
No unsolicited manuscripts; 'we commission all our writing to order, but are open to ideas.'

DAKOTA FILMS LTD

4A Junction Mews London W2 1PN
T   020 7706 9407
F   020 7402 6111
E   info@dakota-films.demon.co.uk

Film producer whose credits include *Me Without You*, *Fade to Black* and *Head in the Clouds*.

DAN FILMS

32 Maple Street London W1T 6HB
T   020 7916 4771
F   020 7916 4773
E   enquiries@danfilms.com
W   www.danfilms.com

Has worked as main or co-producer on films such as *Creep, Severance, Summer Things, The Great Challenge, The Republic of Love* and *Villa des Roses.*

DE FACTO FILMS

30 Chamberlain Street Derry BT48 6LR
T   028 712 60714
F   028 712 60714
E   defactofilms@eircom.net

Film and video production company whose credits include *Dead Long Enough.*

DIRTY HANDS PRODUCTIONS

Contacts
Sir Alan Parker *Director*

Feature film production company founded by British director Sir Alan Parker. Produces Parker films including *The Life of David Gale* (2003), *Angela's Ashes* (1999), *Evita* (1996) and the upcoming *The Ice at the Bottom of the World* (2008).

DIVERSE PRODUCTION LIMITED

6 Gorleston Street London W14 8XS
T   020 7603 4567
F   020 7603 2148
W   www.diverse.tv

Independent production company specializing in popular prime-time formats, strong documentaries, specialist factual, historical, cultural, religious, arts, music and factual entertainment. Recent Output includes *Ballet Changed My Life: Ballet Hoo!; Mission Africa; Codex; Bear Grylls' Man vs. Wild; Tribal Wife;*

Musicality; Operatunity; Who Wrote the Bible; Who You Callin' Nigger?; In Search of Tony Blair; Britain AD; Shock Treatment; Beyond Boundaries; Escape to the Legion.

DMS FILMS LTD

189 Sevington Road London NW4 3RU
T   020 8203 5540
F   0870 762 5871
E   danny@dmsfilms.co.uk
W   www.dmsfilms.co.uk

Contacts
Daniel San *Producer*

Film producer. Output includes *Understanding Jane; Hard Edge; Popcorn.*

Submissions Policy
Unsolicited screenplays not welcome: phone, fax or email synopsis or outline in first instance.

DNA FILMS LTD

15 Greek Street London W1D 4DP
T   020 7292 8700
E   info@dnafilms.com
W   www.dnafilms.com

Production company whose credits include *The Last King of Scotland, The History Boys, Notes on a Scandal, Separate Lies, Love Actually* and *28 Days Later.*

DOUBLEBAND FILMS

3 Crescent Gardens Belfast BT7 1NS
T   028 9024 3331
F   028 9023 6980
E   info@doublebandfilms.com
W   www.doublebandfilms.com

Contacts
Michael Hewitt

Specializes in documentaries and drama. Recent productions include *Seven Days that Shook the World* and *War in Mind* (both for Ch4); *Christine's Children* (BBC Northern Ireland;

nominated for both the RTS and Celtic Film Festival); *D-Day: Triumph and Tragedy* (BBC NI).

DRAKE AV VIDEO LTD

St Fagans Road Fairwater Cardiff CF5 3AE
T   029 2056 0333
E   info@drakeav.com
W www.drakeav.com

Contacts
Helen Stewart

Specialists in corporate and educational films since 1973.

Submissions Policy
Does not accept unsolicited manuscripts. Sometimes needs writers (writing to a brief) at short notice, so a short message indicating price and availability is useful.

CHARLES DUNSTAN COMMUNICATIONS LTD

42 Wolseley Gardens London W4 3LS
T   020 8994 2328
F   020 8994 2328

Contacts
Charles Dunstan

Producer of film, video and TV for documentary and corporate material. Output includes *Renewable Energy* for broadcast worldwide in 'Inside Britain' series; *The Far Reaches* travel series; *The Electric Environment*.

Submissions Policy
No unsolicited scripts.

ECOSSE FILMS

Brigade House 8 Parsons Green London SW6 4TN
T   020 7371 0290
F   020 7736 3436
E   info@ecossefilms.com
W www.ecossefilms.com

Specializes in high-quality drama for film and TV. Titles include *Mrs Brown*, *Monarch of the Glen* and *Becoming Jane*.

EIDOS INTERACTIVE LTD

SCi Entertainment Group Wimbledon Bridge House 1 Hartfield Road Wimbledon SW19 3RU
T   020 8636 3000
F   020 8636 3001
W www.eidosinteractive.co.uk

Founded in 1990 and now part of the SCi Entertainment Group Plc. Eidos incorporates publishing operations in Europe and America, with several development studios including Crystal Dynamics, IO Interactive and Pivotal Games. Credits include *Championship Manager*, *Tomb Raider*, *Who Wants To Be A Millionaire?* and *Commandos*.

ELSTREE (PRODUCTION) COMPANY LTD

Shepperton Studios Studios Road Shepperton Middlesex TW17 0QD
T   01932 592680
F   01932 592682
E   eng@elsprod.com
W www.elsprod.com

Contacts
Greg Smith *Producer*

Founded in 1966, producing feature films and films for TV. Titles include *Agnes Brown* and *Animal Farm*.

Submissions Policy
Does not encourage unsolicited approaches.

ENDEMOL UK PRODUCTIONS

Shepherds Building Central Charecroft Way London W14 0EE
T   0870 333 1700
F   0870 333 1800
E   info@endemoluk.com
W www.endemoluk.com

Major independent producer of TV and digital media content, responsible for over 5,000 hours of programming per year. Incorporates several production brands including Brighter Pictures (factual entertainment shows, reality programming, live events and popular documentaries), Cheetah Television (factual), Initial (prime time entertainment, children's and teens, events and arts shows), Zeppotron (comedy) and Showrunner (drama). Credits include *Big Brother, Deal Or No Deal, Comic Relief Does Fame Academy, Restoration Village, Soccer Aid, Extinct, Orange Playlist, Rush Hour, Lucy: Teen Transsexual* and *34 Stone Teenager: 6 Months On.*

EON PRODUCTIONS

Eon House 138 Piccadilly London W1J 7NR
T   020 7493 7953
F   020 7408 1236

Production company responsible for the James Bond series of films.

EYE FILM AND TELEVISION

Chamberlain House 2 Dove Street Norwich
NR2 1DE
T   01603 762 551
F   01603 762 420
E   production@eyefilmandtv.co.uk
W   www.eyefilmandtv.co.uk

Independent producers of drama, documentary, corporate, commercial and educational film and television programming. Specializes in development, production and post-production. Past credits include children's drama series *The Secret of Eel Island* (Five), documentary series *Hell to Hotel* (ITV Anglia, UKTV Style) and *A Different Life* (Five, BAFTA-nominated).

FARNHAM FILM COMPANY LTD

34 Burnt Hill Road Lower Bourne Farnham
GU10 3LZ
T   012 527 10313
F   012 527 25855
W   www.farnfilm.com

Contacts
Ian Lewis

Television and film: intelligent full-length film and children's drama.

Submissions Policy
Unsolicited manuscripts usually welcome but prefers a letter or email to be sent in the first instance. Check website for current requirements.

FAST FILMS

Christmas House 213 Chester Road Castle Bromwich Solihull B36 0ET
T   0121 749 7147/4144
E   gavinprime@mac.com

Contacts
Gavin Prime

Film and television: comedy, entertainment and animation.

Submissions Policy
No unsolicited manuscripts.

FEELGOOD FICTION

49 Goldhawk Road London W12 8QP
T   020 8746 2535
F   020 8740 6177
E   feelgood@feelgoodfiction.co.uk
W   www.feelgoodfiction.co.uk

Contacts
Laurence Bowen

Production company launched in 1996. Owned and run by Laurence Bowen and Philip Clarke. Currently developing film and TV projects with, among others, Five, the BBC, ITV, RTE, Paramount Comedy, The Weinstein Company, HBO, UK Film Council and Granada Films. Focuses on drama, comedy, children's TV and feature films. Notable TV credits include co-production *Double Bill* (2002, with Working Title TV), 6 part children's comedy *My Life As A Popat* (2004, BAFTA winner for Best Children's Drama) and *Suburban Shootout* (2006). Feelgood Films, the feature film wing, was launched in 2003 with *Miranda* starring Christina Ricci and Kyle MacLachlan. Has a policy of both nurturing new writers and working with the very best established talent.

FESTIVAL FILM + TV LTD

Festival House Tranquil Passage London SE3 0BJ
T   020 8297 9999
F   020 8297 1155
E   info@festivalfilm.com
W   www.festivalfilm.com

Contacts
Ray Marshall *Managing Director*

Founded in 1992, producing TV dramas and feature films. Has produced fifteen mini series for ITV based on books by Catherine Cookson. Won an International Emmy for *The Black Velvet Gown*.

Submissions Policy
Always willing to look at professionally-presented material. Adaptations and/or original work. Send treatemnt in writing first. Particularly interested in uplifting, feel-good projects. No horror, supernatural or action thriller.

FILM AND GENERAL PRODUCTIONS LTD

4 Bradbrook House Studio Place London SW1X 8EL
T   020 7235 4495
F   020 7245 9853
E   cparsons@filmgen.co.uk

Contacts
Clive Parsons

Founded in 1971, specializing in feature films and TV drama. Films include *Gregory's Girl*, *Scum*, *Breaking Glass*, *Britannia Hospital*, *True Blue*, *The Queen's Nose*, *The Giblet Boys* and *The Greatest Store in the World*.

Submissions Policy
Open policy on new writing. Send a preliminary email.

FILM4 PRODUCTIONS

W   www.channel4.com/film/ffproductions

Submissions Policy
Unable to accept unsolicited material.

The film arm of Channel 4 Television, dedicated to the production of distinctive and contemporary feature films. Credits include *Dogma*, *East Is East*, *Enduring Love*, *Me, You and Everyone We Know*, *Sexy Beast*, *The Future is Unwritten: Joe Strummer*, *The Motorcycle Diaries*, *This Is England*, *Touching the Void*, *Trainspotting* and *Wish You Were Here*.

FIREFLY FILMS LIMITED

London W1
T   020 7193 1837
F   0870 974 1165
E   info@fireflyfilms.info
W   www.fireflyfilms.info

Contacts
Matthew Hobbs *MD/Producer*

Submissions Policy
Does not welcome unsolicited material. Approach via an agent.

THE FIRST FILM COMPANY LTD

3 Bourlet Close   London W1W 7BQ
T   020 7436 9490
F   020 7637 1290
E   info@firstfilmcompany.com

Contacts
Roger Randall-Cutler *Producer*

Founded 1984. Cinema screenplays.

Submissions Policy
All submissions should be made through an agent.

FLANNEL

21 Berwick Street London W1F 0PZ
T 020 7287 9277
F 020 7287 7785
E mail@flannel.net

Contacts
Kate Haldane

Producer of drama, documentaries and comedy for television and radio.

Submissions Policy
No unsolicited manuscripts. 'Keen to encourage new writing, but must come via an agent. Particularly interested in 45–50 minute dramas for radio. Not in a position to produce plays for stage, but very happy to consider adaptations. Welcomes comedy with some track record.'

FLASHBACK TELEVISION LTD

9-11 Bowling Green Lane London
EC1R 0BG
T 020 7490 8996
F 020 7490 5610
E mailbox@flashbacktv.co.uk
W www.flashbacktelevision.com

Contacts
Taylor Downing Managing Director

Founded in 1982, award-winning producer of drama, factual entertainment and documentaries for television. Recent credits include Beau Brummell.

Submissions Policy
Does not welcome unsolicited manuscripts.

FOCUS FILMS LTD

The Rotunda Studios Rear of 116–118 Finchley Road London NW3 5HT
T 020 7435 9004
F 020 7431 3562
E focus@focusfilms.co.uk
W www.focusfilms.co.uk

Contacts
David Pupkewitz Managing Director

Film Producer. Output: The Book of Eve (Canadian drama); The Bone Snatcher (Horror, UK/Can/SA); Julia's Ghost (German co-production); The 51st State (feature film); Secret Society (comedy drama feature film); Crimetime (feature thriller); Diary of a Sane Man; Othello. Projects in development include Heaven and Earth; Tainted Desert; The Complete History of the Breast; Triomf.

Submissions Policy
No unsolicited scripts.

FORTISSIMO FILMS (UK)

34 Tavistock Street Covent Garden London
WC2E 7PB
T   020 7836 3637
F   020 7497 1133
E   nicole@fortissimo-uk.com
W www.fortissimo-uk.com

In recent years the company has become involved in developing and co-producing films and has been involved with titles including Thomas In Love, Grimm, Springtime In a Small Town, Seven Swords, Invisible Waves and Shortbus.

Submissions Policy
Does not accept unsolicited scripts.

FORWARD FILMS

Third Floor 23 Denmark Street London
WC2H 8NH
T   020 7632 9643
F   020 7240 5647
E   office@forwardfilms.co.uk

Film production company founded in 2004.

Submissions Policy
Does not encourage unsolicited material.

FRAGILE FILMS

Ealing Studios Ealing Green London W5 5EP
T 020 8567 6655
F 020 8758 8658
E info@ealingstudios.com
W www.fragilefilms.com

Production arm of Ealing Studios. The studio returned to filmmaking after 43 years in 2002 with *The Importance of Being Earnest*. Other recent releases include the animated feature *Valiant* (co-production with Vanguard Films) and *Alien Autopsy* with Ant and Dec. Also expanding into television, most recently with *The Pilot Show* (Channel 4).

Submissions Policy

Fragile Films does not accept unsolicited material from un-represented writers. Approaches to the development department should be a one/two page synopsis via email to development@ealingstudios.com.

FREMANTLEMEDIA LTD

1 Stephen Street London W1T 1AL
T 020 7691 6000
W www.fremantlemedia.com

One of the world's leading providers of television entertainment programmes such as *The Bill*, *American Idol* and *The Price is Right*.

FUTURE FILMS LIMITED

76 Dean Street London W1D 3SQ
T 020 7009 6600
F 020 7009 6602
E info@futurefilmgroup.com
W www.futurefilmgroup.com

Formed in 2000, providing a full range of services from pre-financing to post-production. Highly experienced as both a co-producer on international productions and as executive producer on other productions.

NOEL GAY TELEVISION

Shepperton Studios Studios Road Shepperton TW17 0QD
T 01932 592569
F 01932 592172
E charles.armitage@virgin.net

Contacts

Charles Armitage CEO

Output includeds *The Fear* (BBC Choice); *Second Chance* (Ch4); *Hububb* Series 1–5 (BBC); *I-Camcorder* (Ch4); *Frank Stubbs Promotes* and *10%ers* Series 2 (both for Carlton/ITV); *Call Up the Stars* (BBC1); *Smeg Outs* (BBC video); *Red Dwarf*; *Dave Allen* (ITV); *Windrush* (BBC2). The Noel Gay Motion Picture Company has credits including *Virtual Sexuality*; *Trainspotting* (with Ch4 and Figment Films); *Killer Tongue*; *Dog Soldiers*; *Fast Sofa* and *Pasty Faces*. Associate NGTV companies are Grant Naylor Productions and Pepper Productions.

Submissions Policy

NGTV is willing to accept unsolicited material from writers but 1–2-page treatments only. No scripts.

GMTV

London Television Centre Upper Ground London SE1 9TT
T 020 7827 7000
F 020 7827 7001
E www.gmtv.com

Contacts

Terry O'Sullivan *Head of Forward Planning*

Launched in 1993, breakfast television programme aimed at housewives with children.

GOLD CIRCLE FILMS

10-11 Great Russell Street London WC1B 3NH
T 020 7631 0173
F 020 7631 0189

E amartin@goldcirclefilms.com
W www.goldcirclefilms.com

Independent film production company founded in 2000 by Norm Waitt. Subsidiary of Gold Circle Entertainment Inc. Recent features include *Because I Said So* (with Diane Keaton) and *My Big Fat Greek Wedding*.

Submissions Policy
Unsolicited material is not accepted.

GOLDCREST FILMS INTERNATIONAL LTD

65–66 Dean Street London W1D 4PL
T   020 7437 8696
F   020 7437 4448
E   info@goldcrestfilms.com
W   www.goldcrestfilms.com

Contacts
Wayne Godfrey

Since it was established in 1977, Goldcrest Films has become a leading independent film production company winning many prizes at international festivals and 19 Academy Awards and 28 Baftas. Finances, produces and distributes films and television programmes. Output includes *Chariots of Fire*, *Gandhi*, *The Killing Fields*, *A Room With a View*, *Local Hero*, *The Mission* and *To End All Wars*. 'We are currently seeking film projects to invest equity in through our Finishing Fund in return for International Sales Rights.'

Submissions Policy
Scripts via agents only.

THE GOOD FILM COMPANY

The Studio 5-6 Eton Garages Lambolle Place London NW3 4PE
T   020 7794 6222
F   020 7794 4651
E   yanina@goodfilms.co.uk
W   www.goodfilms.co.uk

Contacts
Yanina Barry *Executive Producer*

Corporate film and video production company founded in 1988. Output includes commercials, music videos, documentaries and photographic stills.

Submissions Policy
Unsolicited material not accepted.

GRANADA MEDIA

The London Television Centre Upper Ground London SE1 9LT
T   020 7620 1620
W   www.granadamedia.com

Leading commercial television production and distribution company. Part of ITV Productions (the production and resource division) and ITV Worldwide (the distribution, merchandising and international production business) of the UK media company ITV plc. ITV Productions is the largest commercial TV producer in the UK, creating over 3,500 hours of original programming each year. Established for over 50 years. Invests in projects across most genres. ITV Productions is the primary producer for ITV1. Whilst trading as Granada it produces programming for the BBC, Channel 4, five, and satellite and digital channels. Credits include *The Street* (BBC1), *Come Dine With Me*, *Countdown* (Channel 4) and *Brainiac* (Sky).

GRANITE FILM & TELEVISION PRODUCTIONS

10 Margaret Street London W1W 8RL
T   020 3008 8498
F   020 3008 6171

Contacts
Simon Welfare

Producer of television documentary programmes such as *Nicholas & Alexandra*; *Victoria & Albert* and *Arthur C. Clarke's Mysterious Universe*.

GRAPHITE FILM AND TELEVISION

31 Carnaby Street London W1F 7DL
T   020 7434 9242
E   contact@graphitefilms.com

Contacts
Stephen Taylor *Managing Director*

Production company founded in 1994, specializing in film and television drama. Productions include *Get Real*.

Submissions Policy
Submissions via agent only.

GREEN UMBRELLA LTD

59 Cotham Hill Cotham Bristol BS6 6JR
T   0117 906 4336
F   0117 923 7003
E   postmaster@umbrella.co.uk
W   www.umbrella.co.uk

Film producers specializing in science and natural history documentaries. Output includes episodes for *The Natural World*, *Wildlife on One* and original series such as *Living Europe* and *Triumph of Life*.

Submissions Policy
Unsolicited treatments relating to natural history and science subjects are welcome.

GREENPOINT FILMS

7 Denmark Street London WC2H 8LZ
T   020 7240 7066
F   020 7240 7088
E   info@greenpointfilms.co.uk
W   www.greenpointfilms.co.uk

Produces feature films alongside television and radio programming. Feature film credits include *The Only Boy For Me* starring Helen Baxendale and *Hideous Kinky* starring Kate Winslet. Recently aired on ITV was the twelve part comedy series *High Stakes*.

GREENWICH VILLAGE PRODUCTIONS

14 Greenwich Church Street London SE10 9BJ
T   020 8853 5100
F   020 8293 3001
E   tv@fictionfactory.co.uk
W   www.fictionfactory.co.uk

Contacts
John Taylor

Features, arts and educational projects, webmovies and new-media productions. Recent Output includes *The Rings of Saturn* and *Beastworlds*.

Submissions Policy
Manuscripts via agents only or from writers with a professional track record in the chosen medium.

GRUBER FILMS LTD

2 Sheraton Street London W1F 8BH
T   08703 669 313
E   richard.holmes@gruberfilms.com

Feature film production company, whose credits include *The Great Pretender*.

HAMMERWOOD FILM PRODUCTIONS

W   www.filmangel.co.uk

Film, video and TV drama. Output includes *Iceni* (film; co-production with Pan-European Film Productions and Boudicca Film Productions Ltd); *Boudicca – A Celtic Tragedy* (TV series). In preproduction: *The Black Egg* (witchcraft in 17th century England); *The Ghosthunter*; *Iceni* (documentary of the rebellion of AD61); *No Case to Answer* (legal series).

Submissions Policy
Study the website before submitting material.

HARBOUR PICTURES

6 Providence Villas Studio Brackenbury Road London W6 OBA
T   020 8749 4100
F   020 8740 1937
E   info@harbourpictures.com
W   www.harbourpictures.com

Contacts
Nicholas Barton *Producer/Chief Executive*

Originally set up as the film production arm of ABTV Ltd (now Harbour Pictures Holdings Ltd). Began feature film development and production in 1999 with *Calendar Girls* (co-produced with Buena Vista). Released in 2003/2004. Now the 7th highest grossing British film ever in the UK: over £20 million taken at the UK box office and approximately $100 million internationally. Follow-up *Kinky Boots* (co-produced with Miramax) released in 2006. Currently two other films in development for Miramax plus others for BBC Films, The UK Film Council, Pathé and Hanway Films. Previous television drama and documentary credits for ABTV/Harbour Pictures include: *Byzantium – The Lost Empire* (Discovery/Channel 4), *The Vanishing Man* (ITV, 3rd highest rated TV film in 1997), *Bye Bye Baby* (Channel 4 film by Jack Rosenthal, winner of 1992 Prix Europa and 1993 Writer's Guild Award).

HARCOURT FILMS

58 Camden Square London NW1 9XE
T 020 7266 5880
E jmarre@harcourtfilms.com
W www.harcourtfilms.com

Contacts
Jeremy Marre *Director/Writer/Producer*

Production company run by Jeremy Marre concentrating on documentary features for television. Strong links to the international market. Recent credits include *Soul Brittannia* (BBC), *Reigning in Hell* (Channel 4, Court TV in USA), *What's Going On* (BBC, PBS) and *The Real Phil Spector* (Channel 4). To date Marre has won one Grammy and two Emmies.

HARTSWOOD FILMS LTD

Twickenham Studios The Barons St Margarets Twickenham Middlesex TW1 2AW
T 020 8607 8736
F 020 8607 8744
E films.tv@hartswoodfilms.co.uk
W www.hartswoodfilms.co.uk

Established in the 1980s, an award-winning independent producer of drama, light entertainment and documentary films. Production credits include *Jekyll*, *After Thomas*, *Wonderful You*, *The English Wife*, *A Woman's Guide to Adultery*, *Men Behaving Badly*, *Coupling*, *Carrie & Barry*, *Is It Legal?* and *The Savages*. Documentaries include *The Welsh Great Escape*, *In Love With Elizabeth* and *Going to Chelsea*.

HAT TRICK PRODUCTIONS LTD

10 Livonia Street London W1F 8AF
T 020 7434 2451
F 020 7287 9791
E info@hattrick.com
W www.hattrick.com

Set up in 1986, producing TV programmes in the fields of comedy, drama and entertainment. Among its large collection of award-winning shows are *Clive Anderson Talks Back*, *Drop the Dead Donkey*, *Father Ted*, *Game On*, *Harry Enfield's Television Programme*, *Have I Got News For You*, *Room 101*, *The Kumars at No. 42*, *Trevor's World of Sport*, *Underworld* and *Whose Line Is It Anyway?*

Submissions Policy
Will not consider unsolicited scripts or treatments. Material should be sent via a recognized agent only.

HEADGEAR FILMS LIMITED

4th Floor Douglas House 3 Richmond Buildings (off Dean Street) London W1D 3HE
T 0203 230 1054
F 0203 230 1059
E maria@headgearfilms.com
W www.headgearfilms.com

Founded in 2002, the company has quickly gained a reputation for developing, producing and distributing feature films for the international market. Examples of titles include *Rabbit on the Moon*, *Chunky Monkey* and *Fingers X'D*.

HEALTHCARE PRODUCTIONS LIMITED

The Great Barn Godmersham Park Canterbury
Kent CT4 7DT
E penny@healthcareproductions.co.uk
W www.healthcareproductions.co.uk

Contacts
Penny Wilson

Established in 1989, producing health-based
dramas and documentaries for TV and the
DVD market. Has won numerous awards
from the BMA.

Submissions Policy
Happy to look at new material, which should
be submitted by email.

HERITAGE THEATRE LTD

Unit 1 8 Clanricarde Gardens London
W2 4NA
T 020 7243 2750
F 020 7792 8584
E rm@heritagetheatre.com
W www.heritagetheatre.com

Contacts
Robert Marshall

Founded in 2000 to produce and distribute
distinguished theatre productions via
DVD or broadcast TV. Titles include *Primo*
and *The Rivals*.

Submissions Policy
Does not invite unsolicited submissions.

HEYDAY

5 Denmark Street London WC2H 8LP
T 020 7836 6333
F 020 7836 6444
E office@heydayfilms.demon.co.uk

Founded in 1997, the company's first
film was *Ravenous* and it has subsequently
worked on the *Harry Potter* series of
movies.

DAVID HILL

107 Wellington Road North Stockport
SK4 2LP
T 0161 477 9090
F 0161 477 9191
E david.hill@acrobat-tv.co.uk
W www.acrobat-tv.co.uk

Contacts
David Hill

All script genres for broadcast and
corporate television, including training
and promotional scripts, comedy and
drama-based material. Output includes *Make a
Stand* (Jack Dee, Gina Bellman and John
Thompson for Video Arts); *The Customer View*
(Roy Barraclough for Air Products); *Serious
About Waves* series (Peter Hart for the Royal
Yachting Association); *Fat Face Night*series
(Extreme).

Submissions Policy
No unsolicited manuscripts.

HOLMES ASSOCIATES

The Studio 37 Redington Road London
NW3 7QY
T 020 7813 4333
E holmesassociates@blueyonder.co.uk

Contacts
Andrew Holmes

Prolific originator, producer and packager
of documentary, drama and music television
and films. Output has included *Ashes and
Sand* (Film 4); *Chunky Monkey* (J&V
Films); *Prometheus* (Ch4 'Film 4'); *The
Shadow of Hiroshima* (Ch4 'Witness'); *The
House of Bernarda Alba* (Ch4/WNET/Amaya);
Piece of Cake (LWT); *The Cormorant*
(BBC/Screen 2); *John Gielgud Looks Back*;
*Rock Steady; Well Being; Signals; Ideal
Home?* (all Ch4); *Seven Canticles of
St Francis* (BBC2).

Submissions Policy
Submissions only accepted by email in synopsis
form.

HOLY COW FILMS

222 Dalling Road London W6 OER
T   020 8735 9161
F   020 8748 1976

Feature film production company whose
credits include *Backwoods*.

HOURGLASS PRODUCTIONS

27 Princes Road Wimbledon London
SW19 8RA
T   020 8540 8786
E   productions@hourglass.co.uk
W   www.hourglass.co.uk

Contacts
Martin Chilcott *Director*

Founded in 1984, specializing in science
and medical documentaries for TV and
DVD. Recent titles include *Science from
Nature*. Has been BAFTA-nominated and
awarded a gold medal at the New York
Film Festival.

Submissions Policy
Interested in leading-edge scientific
proposals. Approach in writing.

ICON FILMS

E   info@iconfilms.co.uk
W   www.iconfilms.co.uk

Contacts
Harry Marshall

Film and TV documentaries. Output
includes *Nick Baker's Weird Creatures*
(five/Animal Planet/Granada International);
*Tom Harrisson – The Barefoot
Anthropologist* (BBC). Specializes in factual
documentaries.

Submissions Policy
Open-minded to new documentary
proposals.

THE ILLUMINATED FILM COMPANY

2 Glenthorne Mews off Glenthorne Road
London W6 0LJ
T   020 8748 3030
F   020 8748 3725
E   info@illuminatedfilms.com
W   www.illuminatedfilms.com

Contacts
Iain Harvey *Producer*

Set up in 1993. Producers of *The Very Hungry
Caterpillar and Other Stories*, *T.R.A.N.S.I.T.*,
War Game, *Christmas Carol - The Movie* and
Little Princess.

Submissions Policy
Will look at unsolicited material but contact by
email first.

IMARI ENTERTAINMENT LTD

PO Box 158 Beaconsfield HP9 1AY
T   01494 677147
F   01494 677147
E   info@imarientertainment.com

Contacts
Jonathan Fowke

TV and video producer, covering all areas of
drama, documentary and corporate
productions.

IMPACT PICTURES

3 Percy Street London W1T 1DE
T   020 7636 7716
F   020 7636 7814
E   production@impactpix.com

Established in 1989. Film production company
whose credits include *Resident Evil*, *Resident
Evil: Apocalypse* and *The Dark*.

INTERNATIONAL MEDIA

Enterprise House 59-65 Upper Ground
London SE1 9PQ
W   www.internationalmedia.de

Global, independent film company based in Munich, London and Los Angeles. Develops, finances, produces and distributes film and television projects. Intermedia Films, the company's traditional business, concentrates on high-quality motion pictures. Intermedia Cinema serves the high-budget action and horror market, while Intermedia TV provides programming for the international market. Output includes Oliver Stone's *Alexander* (starring Colin Farrell, Angelina Jolie and Sir Anthony Hopkins), *Terminator 3* (starring Arnold Schwarzenegger), *Life of David Gale* (starring Kate Winslet) and *The Wedding Planner* (starring Jennifer Lopez).

IPSO FACTO FILMS

11-13 Broad Court London WC2B 5PY
T   020 7240 6166
F   020 7240 6160
E   info@ipsofactofilms.com
W   www.ipsofactofilms.com

Founded in 1993 and has produced over 10 features and over 50 shorts and documentaries. Credits include *Irina Palm*, *School For Seduction*, *Short Order*, *Bye Bye Blackbird*, *Headrush* and *Gone For A Dance*.

ISIS PRODUCTIONS

387b King Street Hammersmith London W6 9NJ
T   020 8748 7634
F   020 8748 3046
E   isis@isis-productions.com
W   www.isisproductions.co.uk

Contacts
Nick de Grunwald *Director*

Formed in 1991, Isis Productions focuses on the production of music and documentary programmes. Output includes *Imagine – Yusuf Islam* (BBC); *Pet Shop Boys – A Life in Pop*; *Rufus Wainwright*; *Brian Ferry – The Dylan Sessions*; *Ray Davies – The World from My Window*; *James Brown – Soul Survivor*

(Ch4); *Bernie Taupin* (ITV 'South Bank Show'); *Iron Maiden, Judas Priest* (Five 'Rock Classics'); Films on *Deep Purple, Metallica, Def Leppard, Lou Reed, Elton John, Elvis Presley, Sex Pistols* (ITV 'Classic Albums 3'); *Simply Red, Nirvana, Cream, Pink Floyd, Motorhead* ('Classic Albums 4'); *England's Other Elizabeth – Elizabeth Taylor* (BBC 'Omnibus').

ISOLDE FILMS

28 Twyford Avenue London W3 9QB
T   020 8896 2860
E   isolde@btinternet.com
W   www.tonypalmer.org

Contacts
Michela Antonello

Film and TV documentaries. Output includes *Wagner; Margot; Menuhin; Maria Callas; Testimony; In From the Cold; Pushkin; England, My England* (by John Osborne).

Submissions Policy
Unsolicited material is read, but send a written outline first.

ITV PRODUCTIONS

The London Television Centre Upper Ground South Bank London SE1 9LT
T · 020 7620 1620
F   020 7261 3041
W   www.itv.com

Contacts
Michele Buck *Controller of ITV Productions (Drama), London*

ITV Productions is the largest commercial TV production company in the UK. Produces original programmes, co-productions and TV movies for ITV channels and other broadcasters, both in the UK and abroad. Output includes *Hornblower; Poirot; Miss Marple; Touching Evil; Where the Heart Is; The Last Detective; Jericho.*

JAM PICTURES AND JANE WALMSLEY PRODUCTIONS

8 Hanover Street London W1S 1YE
T   020 7290 2676
F   020 7256 6818
E   producers@jampix.com

Contacts
Jane Walmsley

JAM Pictures was founded in 1996 to produce drama for film, TV and stage. Projects include: *Hillary's Choice* (TV film, A&E Network); *Son of Pocahontas* (TV film, ABC); *Rudy: the Rudy Giuliani Story* (TV film, USA Network); *One More Kiss* (feature, directed by Vadim Jean); *Bad Blood* (UK theatre tour). Jane Walmsley Productions, formed in 1985 by TV producer, writer and broadcaster, Jane Walmsley, has completed award-winning documentaries and features such as *Hot House People* (Ch4).

Submissions Policy
No unsolicited manuscripts. 'Letters can be sent to us, asking if we wish to see manuscripts; we are very interested in quality material, from published or produced writers only, please.'

JUNIPER COMMUNICATIONS LTD

52 Lant Street London SE1 1RB
T   020 7407 9292
F   020 7407 9292
E   juniper@junipertv.co.uk
W   www.junipertv.co.uk

Contacts
Belkis Bhegani *Company Director*

Founded in the early 1980s, a TV production company which has been nominated for Baftas and won several RTS awards. Also does some radio work. Specializes in documentaries, dram-docs, studio-based discussions, political programmes, history, science, arts and popular culture. Productions include *The Trouble with Atheism*, *Aberfan: The Untold Story*, *Dispatches: What Muslims Want*, *Iraq - The Reckoning*, *The Edwardians* and *London Architecture*.

Submissions Policy
Contact by phone email or post in the first instance.

JUSTICE ENTERTAINMENT

PO Box 4377 London W1A 7SX
E   info@timwestwood.com
W   www.timwestwood.com

Television and radio production company.

KAOS FILMS

E   info@kaosfilms.co.uk
W   www.kaosfilms.co.uk

Set up to manage the annual British Short Screenplay Competition, in association with the National Film and Television School, and produce the winning scripts. Subsequently the company began feature film production as part of an on-going initiative is to find hi-concept, commercial screenplays (independent of the Short Screenplay Competition).

Submissions Policy
Unsolicited material accepted subject to guidelines detailed on the website. Email to hi-concept@kaosfilms.co.uk. All genres considered. Competition details found under 'Awards'.

KEO FILMS.COM LTD

101 St John Street London EC1M 4AS
T   020 7490 3580
F   020 7490 8419
E   keo@keofilms.com
W   www.keofilms.com

Contacts
Katherine Perry

Television documentaries and factual entertainment. Output includes *Atlantic Britain* and *Surviving Extremes* (both for Ch4/NatGeo Europe); *Beyond River Cottage; Where's Your F***ing Manners?; Road Trip; Tales From River Cottage; How To Be a Man; Running for*

God; Heavy; My Body My Business; A Dangerous Obsession; Sperm Bandits (all for Ch4); *10 Years Younger* (Discovery Health).

Submissions Policy
No unsolicited manuscripts.

KINGFISHER TELEVISION PRODUCTIONS

Martindale House The Green Ruddington Nottingham NG11 6HH
T 0115 945 6581
F 0115 921 7750

Contacts
Tony Francis

Broadcast television production.

KISMET FILM COMPANY

25A Old Compton Street London W1D 5JW
T 020 7734 0099
F 020 7734 1222
E kismetfilms@dial.pipex.com

Produces feature films. Previous titles include *Born Romantic, Hypnotic* and *The River King.*

KUDOS FILM & TELEVISION

12–14 Amwell Street London EC1R 1UQ
T 020 7812 3270
F 020 7812 3271
E info@kudosfilmandtv.com
W www.kudosfilmandtv.com

Established in 1992, producing TV programmes and feature films. Production credits include the TV series *Spooks* and *Hustle* and films such as *Pure, Comfortably Numb, Among Giants* and *Meeting People is Easy.* Has a firm belief in nurturing talented writers.

LAGAN PICTURES LTD

21 Tullaghbrow Tullaghgarley Ballymena BT42 2LY
T 028 2563 9479/077 98
F 028 2563 9479
W laganpictures@tullaghbrow.freeserve.co.uk

Contacts
Stephen Butcher *Producer/Director*

Film, video and TV: drama, documentary and corporate. Output includes *A Force Under Fire* (Ulster TV). In development: *Into the Bright Light of Day* (drama-doc); *The £10 Float* (feature film); *The Centre* (drama series).

Submissions Policy
'We are always interested in hearing from writers originating from or based in Northern Ireland or anyone with, preferably unstereotypical, projects relevant to Northern Ireland. We do not have the resources to deal with unsolicited manuscripts, so please write with a brief treatment/synopsis in the first instance.'

LANDSEER PRODUCTIONS LTD

140 Royal College Street London NW1 0TA
T 020 7485 7333
F 1 866 469 9445
E ken@landseerfilms.com
W www.landseerfilms.com

Contacts
Ken Howard *Director*

Specializes in documenatries, childrens' televion and music programmes. Recent productions include *Living the Dream* for the South Bank Show. Has won many international awards including Baftas, Emmys, Royal Television Society awards and the New York Festival Gold Medal.

Submissions Policy
Approach with ideas (not manuscripts) via email.

LILYVILLE SCREEN ENTERTAINMENT LTD

7 Lilyville Road London SW6 5DP
T 020 7471 8989
E tony.cash@btclick.com

Contacts
Tony Cash

Drama and documentaries for TV. Output includes *Poetry in Motion* (series for Ch4); *South Bank Show: Ben Elton and Vanessa*

Redgrave; *Musique Enquête* (drama-based French language series, Ch4); *Sex and Religion* (ITV); *Landscape and Memory* (arts documentary series for the BBC); Jonathan Miller's production of the *St Matthew Passion* for the BBC; major documentary on the BeeGees for the *South Bank Show*.

Submissions Policy
Scripts with an obvious application to TV may be considered. Interested in new writing for documentary programmes.

LIME PICTURES LIMITED

Campus Manor Childwall Abbey Road Childwall Liverpool L16 OJP
T   0151 722 9122
F   0151 722 1969
W www.limepictures.com

Formerly Mersey Television before changing its name in 2006. Specializes in drama productions for television. Examples of output include *Bonkers*, *Hollyoaks* and *The Outsiders*.

LIONSGATE FILMS

Ariel House 74a Charlotte Street London W1T 4QJ
T   020 7636 3935
F   020 7323 0961
W www.lionsgatefilms.co.uk

Independent producer and distributor of motion pictures, television programming, home entertainment, family entertainment and video-on-demand content. Prides itself on producing 'original, daring, quality entertainment' for an international market. Past credits include *Bend It Like Beckham* and *Good Night and Good Luck*.

LONDON SCIENTIFIC FILMS LTD

Dassels House Dassels Braughing Ware SG11 2RW
T   01763 289905
E   lsf@londonscientificfilms.co.uk

Contacts
Mike Cockburn

Film and video documentary and corporate programming.

Submissions Policy
No unsolicited manuscripts.

LUCIDA PRODUCTIONS

5 Alleyn Crescent London SE21 8BN
T   020 8761 4344
E   pj.lucida@tiscali.co.uk

Contacts
Paul Joyce

Television and cinema: arts, adventure, current affairs, documentary, drama and music. Output has included *Motion and Emotion: The Films of Wim Wenders*; *Dirk Bogarde – By Myself*; *Sam Peckinpah – Man of Iron*; *Kris Kristofferson – Pilgrim*; *Wild One: Marlon Brando*; *Stanley Kubrick: 'The Invisible Man'*; *2001: the Making of a Myth* (Ch4); *Mantrap – Straw Dogs, the final cut* (with Dustin Hoffman). Restoration of the Director's Cut of *The Devils* plus the documentary *Hell on Earth* with Ken Russell and Vanessa Redgrave. Currently in development for documentary projects.

LUMINA

3rd Floor 1A Adpar Street London W2 1DE
T   020 7535 6714
E   sales@lumina-films.com
W www.lumina-films.com

Involved in financing and producing features, series and documentaries aimed at young adults. Titles include *Straightheads*, the series *City of Men* and *Favela Rising*.

MALONE GILL PRODUCTIONS LTD

27 Campden Hill Road London W8 7DX
T   020 7937 0557
F   020 7460 3750
E   malonegill@aol.com

Contacts
Georgina Denison

Mainly documentary but also some drama. Output includes *The Face of Russia* (PBS); *Vermeer* ('South Bank Show'); *Highlanders* (ITV); *Storm Chasers; Nature Perfected* and *The Feast of Christmas* (all for Ch4); *The Buried Mirror: Reflections on Spain and the New World* by Carlos Fuentes (BBC2/Discovery Channel).

Submissions Policy
Approach by letter with proposal in the first instance.

MARCHMONT FILMS

24 Three Cups Yard Sandland Street London WC1R 4PZ
E   office@marchmontfilms.com
w   www.marchmontfilms.com

Contacts
Daniel Hayes *Development Executive*

Founded in 2002, making films across genres including drama, comedy and thriller. Titles include *Out in the Cold* and *The Green Wave*.

Submissions Policy
Recieved 2,000 script submissions in 2006. Developing slate of low budget features in syndication with producers worldwide. Welcomes new writing. Visit website for details of current schemes and policies.

MARK FORSTATER PRODUCTIONS LTD

11 Keslake Road London NW6 6DJ
T   020 8933 4375
F   020 8933 4375

Contacts
Mark Forstater

Active in the selection, development and production of material for film and TV. Output includes *Monty Python and the Holy Grail; The Odd Job; The Grass is Singing; Xtro; Forbidden; Separation; The Fantasist; Shalom Joan Collins; The Silent Touch; Grushko; The Wolves of Willoughby Chase; Between the Devil and the Deep Blue Sea; Doing Rude Things.*

Submissions Policy
No unsolicited scripts.

MATERIAL ENTERTAINMENT

3rd Floor 101-102 Jermyn Street London SW1Y 6EE
T   020 7808 3999
F   020 7839 3514
E   info@material-ent.com

Contacts
Robert Jones *President*

Joint feature film production venture between New Line Cinema in the US and Entertainment Film Distributors in the UK. Launched in 2005. Ultimately hopes to produce up to four films a year. Currently developing first film *Run Fat Boy Run* directed by David Schwimmer. Announced new children's fantasy project, *Dream Team*, in April 2007.

MAVERICK TELEVISION

Progress Works Heath Mill Lane Birmingham B9 4AL
T   0121 771 1812
F   0121 771 1550
E   mail@mavericktv.co.uk
w   www.mavericktv.co.uk

Contacts
Juliet Howell

Established in 1994, Maverick has a strong reputation for popular factual programming as well as drama. It is now one of network television's most prolific independent suppliers. Output includes *10 Years Younger; Who'll Age Worst?; Bollywood Star; Fat Chance; Born Too Soon; VeeTV; Trade Secrets; Embarrassing Illnesses; 10 Things You Didn't Know About ...; How To Live Longer; The Property Chain; Male, 33, Seeks Puberty; Extreme Engineering; Picture This: Accidental Hero; Up Your Street; The Property Chain; Motherless Daughters;*

Highland Bollywood: Black Bag; Health Alert: My Teenage Menopause; Long Haul; Learning to Love the Grey.

MAYA VISION INTERNATIONAL LTD

6 Kinghorn Street London EC1A 7HW
T   020 7796 4842
F   020 7796 4580
W   www.mayavisionint.com

Contacts
Tamsin Ranger

Film and TV: drama and documentary. Output includes *Saddam's Killing Fields* (for 'Viewpoint', Central TV); *3 Steps to Heaven* and *A Bit of Scarlet* (feature films for BFI/Ch4); *A Place in the Sun* and *North of Vortex* (dramas for Ch4/Arts Council); *The Real History Show* (Ch4); *In Search of Myths and Heroes; In Search of Shakespeare; In the Footsteps of Alexander the Great; Conquistadors* (BBC documentaries); *Hitler's Search for the Holy Grail; Once Upon a Time in Iran* (Ch4 documentaries).

Submissions Policy
Absolutely no unsolicited material; commissions only.

MBP TV

Saucelands Barn Coolham Horsham
RH13 8QG
T   01403 741620
F   01403 741647
E   info@mbptv.com
W   www.mbptv.com

Contacts
Phil Jennings

Maker of film and video specializing in programmes covering equestrianism and the countryside.

Submissions Policy
No unsolicited scripts, but always looking for new writers who are fully acquainted with the subject.

MELENDEZ FILMS

Julia House 44 Newman Street London
W1T 1QD
T   020 7323 5273
F   020 7323 5373

Contacts
Steven Melendez

Independent production company specializing in 2D animation. Also involved in production and film design for clients in England, Spain, Sweden, India and the US, plus website design and 3D animation on the web. Clients include book publishers, TV companies and advertisers. Winner of international awards for films, particularly of classic books, stories and comic characters.

Submissions Policy
Will look at unsolicited projects in outline or synopsis form only. Enclose sae.

MENDOZA FILM PRODUCTIONS

3–5 Barrett Street London W1U 1AY
T   020 7935 4674
F   020 7935 4417
E   office@mendozafilms.com
W   www.mendozafilms.com

Contacts
Wynn Wheldon

Commercials, title sequences (e.g. Alan Bleasdale's G.B.H.); party political broadcasts. Currently in pre-production on a feature-length comedy film. Involved with the Screenwriters' Workshop.

Submissions Policy
Unsolicited manuscripts welcome but 'comedies only, please'. Material will not be returned without sae.

MENTORN

43 Whitfield Street London W1T 4HA
T   020 7258 6700
F   020 7258 6888
W   www.mentorn.co.uk

Independent television producers founded in 1985, with offices in London, Oxford and Glasgow. Produces across a range of genres including drama, current affairs, factual and entertainment. Titles include *The Government Inspector, The Hamburg Cell, A Very Social Secretary* and the documentaries *The Boy Who Gave Birth to His Twin* and *Terror in Moscow.*

MERCHANT IVORY

46 Lexington Street London W1F OLP
T   020 7437 1200
F   020 7734 1579
E   contact@merchantivory.com
W   www.merchantivory.com

Production company founded in 1961 by James Ivory and Ismail Merchant. Strong reputation for producing high-quality features, short films and documentaries. The company's output includes *A Room With a View, Howards End, The Remains of the Day, Jefferson in Paris, Surviving Picasso, The Mystic Masseur, Le Divorce, Heights* and *The White Countess.*

MIDSUMMER FILMS PRODUCTIONS

33 St Lawrence Terrace London W10 5SR
T   020 8932 8870
F   020 8932 8871
E   info@midsummerfilms.com
W   www.midsummerfilms.com

Contacts
Stephen Bath *Head of Development*

Film production company founded in 1997. Specializes in action, horror and destinctive niche films. Titles include *An American Haunting.*

Submissions Policy
Email with a CV and synopsis in the first instance.

MIRAGE

Old Chapel Studios 19 Fleet Street London NW3 2QR
T   020 7284 5588
F   020 7284 5599
E   tbricknell@mirageenterprises.co.uk

Film production company whose credits include *Birthday Girl, Heaven, Cold Mountain* and *Breaking and Entering.*

MIRAGE FILMS

5 Wardor Mews London W1F 8AL
T   020 7734 3627
F   020 7734 3735
E   production@miragefilms.net
W   www.miragefilms.net

Film and video production company focusing on documentary alongside TV commercial and corporate production. Experienced in foreign adaptations.

MISSION PICTURES

23 Golden Square London W1F 9JP
T   020 7734 6303
F   020 7734 6202
E   info@missionpictures.net

Film production company whose past credits include *Thunderpants, Gladiatress, Millions* and *Piccadilly Jim.*

MOB FILM COMPANY

10–11 Great Russell Street London WC1B 3NH
T   020 7580 8142
F   020 7255 1721
E   mail@mobfilm.com
W   www.mobfilm.com

Founded in 1998 to produce commercials, documentary, television drama and film. Offices in London and Leeds. Examples of output includes: the films *One More Kiss, The Virgin of Liverpool* and *Scenes of a Sexual Nature*; the TV drama *Hogfather*; and the factual programmes *Working The Thames* and *Skin Deep*.

Submissions Policy
Scripts (with synopsis) should be emailed or posted to Andrew Boswell (andrew@mobfilm.com).

MOONSTONE FILMS

London
T 020 7870 7180
F 0870 005 6839
E info@moonstonefilms.co.uk
W www.moonstonefilms.co.uk

Contacts
Tony Stark *Executive Producer*

Founded in 1989, producing documentaries for television. Has made programmes for the BBC and Channel 4. Output includes *Arafat Investigated, Arafat's Authority, Under Pressure, The Mind of a Martyr* and *Collaborators*.

Submissions Policy
Happy to look at scripts/ideas. Approach by email.

MULHOLLAND PICTURES

19 Barnsbury Park London N1 1HQ
T 020 7607 7120
F 020 7700 4428
E dejong@mulhollandpictures.com
W www.mulhollandpictures.com

Contacts
Ate de Jong *General Manager*

Founded in 1999, a Dutch company with a London office. Productions include *Left Luggage, The Discovery of Heaven* and *Fogbound*. Also co-produced *Enigma*.

Submissions Policy
Will look at one-page synopses but does not encourage unsolicited material.

NEAL STREET PRODUCTIONS

26-28 Neal Street London WC2H 9QQ
T 020 7240 8890
F 020 7240 7099
E post@nealstreetproduction.com
W www.nealstreetproductions.com

Independent film and theatre production company established in 2003 by Sam Mendes, Pippa Harris and Caro Newling. Past productions include *Jarhead*.

Submissions Policy
Does not accept unsolicited material and will immediately return to sender, unread.

NEON

Studio Two 19 Marine Crescent Glasgow G51 1HD
T 0141 429 6366
F 0141 429 6377
E stephy@go2neon.com
W www.go2neon.com

Contacts
Stephanie Pordage

Television and radio: drama and documentary producers. Output includes *Brand New Country; Asian Overground; Peeking Past the Gates of Skibo*. Supports and encourages new writing 'at every opportunity'.

Submissions Policy
Welcomes unsolicited material but telephone in the first instance.

NUMBER 9 FILMS

Linton House 24 Wells Street London W1T 3PH
T 020 7323 4060
F 020 7323 0456
E info@number9films.co.uk

Contacts
Stephen Woolley

Leading feature film producer. Output includes *Breakfast on Pluto*; *Stoned*; *Mrs Harris*. Forthcoming productions: *And When Did You Last See Your Father?*; *How to Lose Friends and Alienate People*; *Edith and the Lonely Doll*.

Submissions Policy
No unsolicited material.

OCTOBER FILMS LTD

Spring House 10 Spring Place London NW5 3BH
T   020 7284 6868
F   020 7284 6869
E   info@octoberfilms.co.uk
W   www.octoberfilms.co.uk

Independent film and TV producer operating since 1989. Offices in London and Manchester. Produces for a range of domestic and international broadcasters. Output includes documentary, factual entertainment, popular current affairs, docu-drama, history and science. Titles include *Godless in America*, *The Fundamentalists*, *Srebrenica: Never Again?*, *The Boy Who Lived Before*, *The Fight for Ground Zero*, *The Last Slave* and *Meeting The Taleban*.

OMNIVISION LTD

Pinewood Studios Iver Heath Buckinghamshire SL0 0NH
T   01753 656 329
F   01753 631 146
E   info@omnivision.co.uk
W   www.omnivision.co.uk

Contacts
Christopher Morris *Managing Director*

A TV production and post-production company founded in 2000. Produces TV documentaries for the UK and abroad, along with news coverage and tv series. Also produces corporate DVDs for the health industry.

Submissions Policy
Welcomes approaches by letter or email. Offers quick decisions on material.

ORLANDO TV PRODUCTIONS

Up-the-Steps Little Tew Chipping Norton OX7 4JB
T   01608 683218
F   01608 683364
E   info@orlandomedia.co.uk
W   www.orlandomedia.co.uk

Contacts
Mike Tomlinson

Producer of TV documentaries and digital multimedia content, with science, health and information technology subjects as a specialization.

Submissions Policy
Approaches by established writers/journalists to discuss proposals for collaboration are welcome.

ORPHEUS PRODUCTIONS

6 Amyand Park Gardens Twickenham TW1 3HS
T   020 8892 3172
F   020 8892 4821
E   richard-taylor@blueyonder.co.uk

Contacts
Richard Taylor

Television documentaries and corporate work. Output has included programmes for the BBC, ITV and Ch4 as well as documentaries for the United Nations, the Shell Film Unit and Video Arts.

Submissions Policy
Unsolicited scripts are welcomed with caution. 'Our preference is for the more classically structured documentary that, while being hard-hitting, explores the subtleties and the paradox of an issue – and is not presented by unqualified celebrities.'

OUTCAST PRODUCTION

92 Buckhold Road London SW18 4AP
E   andythewise@aol.com

Contacts
Andreas Wisniewski

Low-budget feature films.

Submissions Policy
No unsolicited manuscripts; send synopsis or treatment only. 'We are actively searching for and encouraging new writing.'

OXFORD FILM AND TELEVISION

6 Erskine Road London NW3 3AJ
T   020 7483 3637
F   020 7483 3567
E   email@oftv.co.uk
W   www.oftv.co.uk

Contacts
Nicolas Kent *Creative Director*

Independent film and television production company. Produced over 100 hours of drama, docu-drama and documentaries for the BBC, Channel Four, ITV, PBS, Showtime, Lifetime, A&E, HBO, Bravo, ABC Australia, Discovery and The Learning Channel. Produced six feature films including the Oscar-winning *Restoration* and the Oscar and BAFTA-nominated *Hilary and Jackie*. To date has won two Oscars, four BAFTAs, two Indies, an RTS award, the Silver Hugo at the Chicago Film Festival and a Cable ACE.

PALADIN INVISION

8 Barb Mews London W6 7PA
T   020 7348 1950
F   020 7348 1961
E   pitv@pitv.com
W   www.pitv.com

Contacts
William Clan *Founder/Producer*

Co-venture between two influential British documentary-makers: William Cran and Clive Syddall. Combined 500 hours of television programming produced. Focuses on factual projects including history, current affairs,

religion, music & arts documentaries. Sold both at home and internationally. Output includes *The Age of Aids* (WGBH/PBS/Channel 4/Granada International), *Do You Speak American?* (WNET-BBC/CBCPBS), *Extreme Oil* (WNET-PBS/BBC/CBC/C4 International) and landmark six-part series *Commanding Heights: The Battle for the World Economy*. Awards received from BAFTA, Royal Television Society, the Chicago, San Francisco, and New York Television Festivals, the Peabody Award for Broadcasting and four American Emmy awards.

PAPER MOON PRODUCTIONS

Wychwood House Burchetts Green Lane
Littlewick Green Nr. Maidenhead
SL6 3QW
T   01628 829819
F   01628 829819
E   david@paper-moon.co.uk

Contacts
David Haggas

Broadcast documentaries and corporate communications. Recent output includes *Bilbo & Beyond*, an affectionate glimpse into the life and work of the dedicated philologist and fantasy writer J.R.R. Tolkien.

PARALLAX EAST LTD

Victoria Chambers St Runwald Street
Colchester CO1 1HF
T   01206 574909
F   01206 577669
E   assistant@parallaxindependent.co.uk

Contacts
Victoria May *Production Assistant*

Founded in 2005, producing films including *Almost Adult* and *Yasmin*.

Submissions Policy
Very receptive to new writing but doesn't encourage unsolicited approaches.

PASSION PICTURES

3rd Floor 33–34 Rathbone Place London
W1T 1JN
T   020 7323 9933
F   020 7323 9030
E   info@passion-pictures.com

Contacts
Andrew Ruhemann *Managing Director*

Documentary and drama includes: *One Day in
September* (Academy Award-winner for Best
Feature Documentary, 2000); also commercials
and music videos.

Submissions Policy
Unsolicited manuscripts welcome.

PATHÉ PICTURES

Kent House 14-17 Market Place Great Titchfield
Street London W1W 8AR
T   020 7323 5151
F   020 7631 5368
E   press.office@pathe-uk.com
W   www.pathe.co.uk

Feature film production company. Examples
of recent credits include *Enduring Love*,
Bride and Prejudice - A Bollywood Musical,
The Magic Roundabout, *Mrs Henderson
Presents*, *The Queen* and *Big
Nothing*.

PELICULA FILMS

59 Holland Street Glasgow G2 4NJ
T   0141 287 9522

Contacts
Mike Alexander

Television producer. Maker of drama
documentaries and music programmes for
the BBC and Ch4. Output includes *As
an Eilean* (From the Island), *The
Trans-Atlantic Sessions 1 & 2*, *Nanci
Griffith*, *Other Voices 2* and *Follow the
Moonstone*.

PHOTOPLAY PRODUCTIONS LTD

21 Princess Road London NW1 8JR
T   020 7722 2500
F   020 7722 6662
E   info@photoplay.co.uk

Contacts
Patrick Stanbury

Documentaries for film, television and video
plus restoration of silent films and their
theatrical presentation. Output includes *The
Cat and the Canary*; *Orphans of the Storm*;
Cecil B. DeMille: American Epic and the
'Channel 4 Silents' series of silent film
restoration, including *The Wedding March* and
The Iron Mask. Recently completed *Garbo* and
I'm King Kong!

Submissions Policy
No unsolicited manuscripts; 'we tend to create
and write all our own programmes.'

PICTURE PALACE FILMS

13 Egbert Street London NW1 8LJ
T   020 7586 8763
F   020 7586 9048
E   info@picturepalace.com
W   www.picturepalace.com

Contacts
Malcolm Craddock *Producer and Chief
Executive*

Founded in 1971, producing films and TV
dramas. Works include *Acid House*, the *Sharpe*
films (for ITV), *Frances Tuesday*, *A Life for a
Life* (for ITV) and *Rebel Heart* (for BBC1).

Submissions Policy
Welcomes new writing in principle (though
admits to being 'often disappointed') via agents.

PLANET24 PICTURES LTD

39 Meadow Road Trimdon Village TS29 6JN
T   0870 765 8780
E   planet24picture@aol.com
W   www.planet24pictures.co.uk

Contacts
Mercedes de Dunewíc

Producer of television and video documentaries plus community/infomercials. Output includes *Jack the Ripper: The Conspiracies*; *Truth to Tell*; *Pitmen and Politics: The County Built on Coal.*

Submissions Policy
Manuscripts, plot outlines and screenplays considered but email for information first. 'Welcome the input of new writers with radical points of view.'

PLANTAGENET FILMS LIMITED

Ard-Daraich Studio B Ardgour Nr Fort William PH33 7AB
T 01855 841384
F 01855 841384
E plantagenetfilms@aol.com

Contacts
Norrie Maclaren

Film and television: documentary and drama programming such as *Dig* (gardening series for Ch4); various *Dispatches* for Ch4 and *Omnibus* for BBC.

Submissions Policy
Keen to encourage and promote new writing; unsolicited manuscripts welcome.

PORTOBELLO PICTURES LTD

Eardey House 4 Uxbridge Street Notting Hill Gate London W8 7SY
T 020 7908 9890
F 020 7908 9899
E mail@portobellopictures.com
W www.portobellopictures.com

Contacts
Eric Abraham *Producer*

Founded in 1985, producing all kinds of drama for film, TV and theatre. Productions include Roald Dahl's *Danny the Champion of the World*, *Kolya* (which won Best Foreign

Language Oscar in 1997), *Dark Blue World* and *Dalziel and Pascoe.*

Submissions Policy
Interested in new writing and actively scouts new writing platforms at festivals, on television, in the theatre and via agents. Does not invite unsolicited material though.

POWERSTONE ENTERTAINMENT LTD

E info@powerstonefilms.com
W www.powerstonefilms.com

Develops and produces feature films and drama, aiming for universal stories with international appeal. Particular interest in films for children, youth and families but also caters for older audiences.

POZZITIVE TELEVISION

Paramount House 162–170 Wardour Street London W1F 8AB
T 020 7734 3258
F 020 7437 3130
E david@pozzitive.co.uk

Contacts
David Tyler

Producer of comedy and entertainment for television and radio. Output includes *Dinner Ladies*; *Coogan's Run*; *The 99p Challenge*; *The Comic Side of 7 Days*; *Armando Iannucci's Charm Offensive.*

Submissions Policy
Unsolicited manuscripts of TV and radio comedy welcome. 'No screenplays or stage plays or novels, please. Send hard copy of full sample script. We read everything submitted this way. Sorry, we don't return scripts unless you send an SASE.'

PRESCIENCE FILM FINANCE LTD

Marlborough House 45 Wycombe End Beaconsfield Bucks HP9 1LZ
T 01494 670737
F 01494 670740

E info@presciencefilmfinance.co.uk
w www.presciencefilmfinance.co.uk

Contacts
Paul Brett *Director*

Specialist film company founded in 2004.
Works with leading UK and international
producers, distributors and sales agents. Has
working relationships with a range of
international studios (Hollywood majrs and
mini-majors), as well as leading film and
television producers. Recent titles include
Tideland (2005), *The Ferryman* (2007) and
How About You (2007).

Submissions Policy
Welcomes unsolicited approaches.

PRINCESS PRODUCTIONS

3rd Floor Whiteley's Centre 151 Queensway
London W2 45B
T 020 7985 1985
w www.princesstv.com

TV production company established in
1996, producing entertainment programmes
across a range of genres. Titles include *The
Wright Stuff*, *Date My Mom*, *The Great
Garden Challenge*, *Secrets of the CIA* and
The Friday Night Project. Carbon Princess,
a joint venture between Princess Productions
and Carbon Media, was recently set-up to
produce high-end documentaries including
science, history, arts and contemporary
journalism.

PRIORITY PICTURES

9 Grafton Mews London W1T 5HZ
T 0207 380 3983
F 0207 380 3981
w www.prioritypictures.co.uk

Founded by Marion Pilowsky and Colin
Leventhal in 2004. Develops, finances and
produces feature films for a worldwide
audience. Credits include *The All Together*,
Nina's Heavenly Delights, *Stingray* and
upcoming *Teacher Boy*.

QWERTY FILMS

42-44 Beak Street London W1F 9RH
T 020 7440 5920
F 020 7440 5959
E info@qwertyfilms.com

Feature film producer. Production credits
include *Alien Autopsy*, *Aspects of Love*,
Severance and *Stage Beauty*.

SARAH RADCLYFFE PRODUCTIONS

5th floor 83-84 Berwick Street London
W1V 3PL
T 020 7437 3128
F 020 7437 3129

Film production company established by the
co-founder of Working Title. Credits include
Love's Brother, *Free Jimmy* and *Tara Road*.

RAGDOLL LTD

Timothy's Bridge Road Stratford-upon-Avon
Warks CV37 9NQ
T 01789 400100
F 01789 400178
E reception@ragdoll.co.uk
w www.ragdoll.co.uk

Founded by Anne Wood. Notable titles include
Teletubbies, *Brum*, *Boohbah*, *Rosie & Jim*,
BadJelly the Witch, *Pob* and *Open a Door*
(an international exchange of five minute films).
In The Night Garden and *Tronji* are to be
broadcast on the BBC.

RDF MEDIA GROUP

The Gloucester Building Kensington Village
London W14 8RF
T 020 7013 4000
F 020 7013 4111
w www.rdfmedia.com

Has several programming production
operations. RDF Television is the largest
production company within the group, with

offices in London and Bristol. Works across a range of genres. Credits include *Wife Swap, Faking It, Holiday Showdown, Scrapheap Challenge, Shipwrecked* and *How To Be A Property Developer*. Foundation TV Productions, based at The Maidstone Studios, specializes in pre-school, drama, comedy, factual and family entertainment. Output includes *Ministry of Mayhem, Globo Loco, Finger Tips* and *Brilliant Creatures*. IWC Media, with offices in Glasgow and London, produces factual, factual entertainment and drama programmes. Titles includes *Location, Location, Location, Fallen Angel, Mission Implausible* and *Crimes That Shook The World*. Presentable is based in Cardiff, producing entertainment, music, comedy, arts, history, features and documentary programmes. Particular reputation for poker programmes. Radar, based in London, specializes in original entertainment and factual entertainment programmes. Titles include *Christian O'Connell's Sunday Service* and *Banzai*. Touchpaper Television is a drama producer, with credits including *The Queen's Sister, Rocket Man, The Best Man* and *NY-LON*. The Comedy Unit, based in Glasgow, produces for radio and television. Output includes *Still Game* and *The Karen Dunbar Show*.

RECORDED PICTURE COMPANY

24 Hanway Street London W1P 9DD
T   020 7636 2251
F   020 7636 2261
E   info@recordedpicture.com
W   www.recordedpicture.com

Film production company established in 1971. Credits include *Merry Christmas, Mr. Lawrence, The Last Emperor* (winner of nine Oscars), *Crash, Sexy Beast, Tideland* and *Fast Food Nation*.

RED PRODUCTION COMPANY

c/o Granada TV Quay Street Manchester
M60 9EA
T   0161 827 2530
F   0161 827 2518

E   info@redlimited.co.uk
W   www.redproduction.com

Contacts
Nicola Shindler *Chief Executive*

Founded in 1998, aims to bring original and intersting voices to the screen in award-winning productions. Titles include *New Street Law, Clocking Off, The Second Coming, Queer as Folk, The Mark of Cain* and *Casanova*.

Submissions Policy
Welcomes new writing and reads all submissions. Keen to work with fresh, new talent. Approach with ideas via email or post.

REDWEATHER

Easton Business Centre Felix Road Easton
BS5 0HE
T   0117 941 5854
F   0117 941 5851
E   production@redweather.co.uk
W   www.redweather.co.uk

Broadcast documentaries on arts and disability, corporate video and CD-ROM.

RENAISSANCE FILMS

34/35 Berwick Street London W1F 8RP
T   020 7287 5190
F   020 7287 5191
E   info@renaissance-films.com

Film production company whose credits include *Henry V, Peter's Friends, Much Ado About Nothing, The Luzhin Defence, The Reckoning, Inbreeds, We Don't Live Here Anymore* and *Candy*.

REVOLUTION FILMS

24 Hanway Street London W1P 9DD

9a Dallington Street London EC1V 0BQ
T   020 7566 0700
F   020 7566 0701
E   email@revolution-films.com
W   www.revolution-films.com

Contacts
Michael Winterbottom *Director*

Founded by producer Andrew Eaton and director Michael Winterbottom in 1994. Focuses mostly on feature-length dramatic projects. Recent output includes *The Cock and Bull Story*, *The Road to Guantanamo* and upcoming *A Mighty Heart*.

Submissions Policy
No unsolicited material.

RICHMOND FILM & TELEVISION

PO Box 11354 London NW3 4AZ
T 020 7722 6464
E mail@richmondfilms.com

Contacts
John Calkins *Head of Development*

Founded in 1986 and has won Bafta and RTS awards. Credits include *Press Gang*, *Wavelength* and *in2minds*.

Submissions Policy
Does not welcome unsolicited material. Will look at if sent by an agent. Seeks short treatments with all info about submissions of project and reaction to it.

ROCKET PICTURES

1 Blythe Road London W14 OHE
T 020 7603 9530
F 020 7348 4830
E luke@rocketpictures.co.uk

Film and TV production company established by Elton John in 1996. Credits include *Women Talking Dirty*, *It's a Boy Girl Thing* and *Him and Us*.

ROCLIFFE

PO Box 37344 London N1 8YB
E scripts@rocliffe.com
W www.rocliffe.com

A production company that has produced the short films *Chicken Soup*, *No Deposit, No Return* and *The Welcome Committee* (commissioned by the European Commission, CICEB and The British Council to celebrate the enlargement of Europe). Currently developing its feature film slate and keen to build relationships with writers and directors.

RS PRODUCTIONS

191 Trewhitt Road Newcastle-upon-Tyne NE6 5DY
T 0191 224 4301
E enquiries@rsproductions.co.uk
W www.rsproductions.co.uk

Contacts
Mark Lavender

Feature films and television: drama series/serials and singles. TV documentaries and series. Working with established and new talent.

RUBY FILMS

12 Cleveland Row London SW1A 1DH
T 020 7925 2999
F 020 7925 2979
E ruby@rubyfilms.com
W www.rubyfilms.com

Established in 1999 by Alison Owen and Neris Thomas. Production credits include *Happy Now?*, *Love + Hate*, *Sylvia*, *Is Harry on the Boat* and *Brick Lane*.

SAMUELSON PRODUCTIONS

13 Manette Street London W1D 4AW
T 020 7439 4900
F 020 7439 4901
W www.samuelsonproductions.com

Film production company established in 1990. Titles include *Chromophobia*, *Gabriel & Me*, *Stormbreaker*, *The Gathering* and *Things To Do Before You're 30*.

SANDS FILMS

119 Rotherhithe Street London SE16 4NF
T 020 7231 2209
F 020 7231 2119
E sands@sandsfilms.co.uk
W www.sandsfilms.co.uk

Contacts
Christine Edzard

Film and TV drama. Output includes *Little Dorrit*; *The Fool*; *As You Like It*; *A Dangerous Man*; *The Long Day Closes*; *A Passage to India*; *Topsy Turvy*; *Nicholas Nickleby*; *The Gangs of New York*; *The Children's Midsummer Night's Dream.*

Submissions Policy
No unsolicited scripts.

SCALA PRODUCTIONS

2nd Floor 37 Foley Street London W1W 7TN
T 020 7637 5720
F 020 7637 5734
E scalaprods@aol.com

Contacts
Ian Prior *Head of Production*

Founded in 1992, producing feature films. Credits include the Oscar-nominated and BAFTA-winning *Little Voice*, Shane Meadows *24 7: Twenty Four Seven*, Fred Schepisi's *Last Orders*, *Backbeat*, *Leo* and *Ladies in Lavendar* (which made over US$30m).

Submissions Policy
A keen supporter of new writing through its relationships with leading talent agents, links to established and emerging academic institutions and its patronage of theatre nationwide. Does not invite unsolicited submissions.

SCOPE PRODUCTIONS LTD

180 West Regent Street Glasgow G2 4RW
T 0141 221 4312
E laurakingwell@scopeproductions.co.uk
W www.scopeproductions.co.uk

Contacts
Laura Kingwell

Corporate film and video and multimedia communications for clients across all sectors.

SCREEN FIRST LTD

The Studios Funnells Farm Down Street
Nutley East Sussex TN22 3LG
T 01825 712034

Contacts
Paul Madden *Producer/Director*

Founded in 1985 to make films and television programmes. Focus on animation, arts, children's programmes, documentary and drama. Examples of output include *Ivor the Invisible.*

Submissions Policy
Does not welcome unsolicited approaches.

SCREEN VENTURES LTD

49 Goodge Street London W1T 1TE
T 020 7580 7448
F 020 7631 1265
E info@screenventures.com
W www.screenventures.com

Contacts
Christopher Mould

Film and TV sales and production: documentary, music videos and drama. Output includes *Life and Limb* (documentary, Discovery Health Channel); *Pavement Aristocrats* (SABC); *Woodstock Diary*; *Vanessa Redgrave* and *Genet* (both for LWT 'South Bank Show'); *Mojo Working*; *Burma: Dying for Democracy* (Ch4); *Dani Dares* (Ch4 series on strong women); *Pagad* (Ch4 news report).

SCREENHOUSE PRODUCTIONS LTD

Chapel Allerton House 114 Harrogate Road
Leeds LS7 4NY
T 0113 266 8881
F 0113 266 8882

E paul.bader@screenhouse.co.uk
W www.screenhouse.co.uk

Contacts
Paul Bader

Specializes in science TV, documentary, stunts and events, including outside broadcasts. Output includes *Stardate* (BBC2 astronomy series), *Zapped* (Discovery/US/Canada), *The Man Who Invented the Aeroplane* (UKTV/BBC North); *Science Shack, Local Heroes* (BBC2, presented by Adam Hart-Davis).

Submissions Policy
'More likely to consider written up proposals.'

SCREENPROJEX.COM – A DIVISION OF SCREEN PRODUCTION ASSOCIATES LTD

T 020 7287 1170
E info@screenprojex.com
W screenprojex.com

Contacts
Doug Abbott

Feature films: *The Fourth Man; The Case; Black Badge; The Truth Game; Club Le Monde; Midnight Warriors; Strong Language; Holding On; Chunky Monkey; Sixty-three Closure.*

Submissions Policy
No unsolicited manuscripts. Send preliminary letter outlining project and CV.

SEPTEMBER FILMS LTD

Glen House 22 Glenthorne Road London England W6 0NG
T 020 8563 9393
F 020 8741 7214
E www.septemberfilms.com
W september@septemberfilms.com

Contacts
David Green *Chairman*

Founded in 1985, working in film and television. Specializes in popular factual entertainment, reality and entertainment formats, documentaries, feature films and TV movies. Offices in London and LA. Recent titles include *Beauty and the Geek, Bridezillas, Haunted Homes* and *Breathtaking*. Other highlights include *Ozzy Osbourne Uncut* (winner of Montreux Bronze Rose Award), the award-winning feature *House of America* and the Oscar-nominated *Solomon and Gaenor.*

Submissions Policy
Does not usually accept unsolicited manuscripts. Has own in-house development team.

SERENDIPITY PICTURE COMPANY

Media Cabin 11 Lyndhurst Road Westbury on Trym BS9 3QY
T 0117 908 2711
E tony@serendipitypictures.com

Contacts
Tony Yeadon *Director*

Founded in 1984. Specializes in television documentaries with focus on travel, food and history. Was awarded first runner up prize by the One World Broadcasting Trust for TV Documentaries at BAFTA.

Submissions Policy
Only interested in documentary ideas. Email in first instance.

SHINE ENTERTAINMENT

140 Kensington Church Street Notting Hill London W8 4BN
T 020 7985 7000
F 020 7985 7001
E info@shinelimited.com
W www.shinelimited.com

Founded by Elisabeth Murdoch in 2001. Makes a range of programmes for the UK, US and international markets including drama, entertainment, factual, features and format entertainment programming. Examples of titles include *Sinchronicity, Sugar Rush, The Story of Light Entertainment* and *1970s: That Was The Decade That Was.*

Submissions Policy
Does not accept unsolicited manuscripts.

SIANCO CYF

36 Y Maes Caernarfon LL55 2NN
T 01286 676100
F 01286 677616
E post@sianco.tv

Contacts
Siân Teifi

Children's, youth and education programmes, children's drama, people-based documentaries for adults.

Submissions Policy
Does not accept any unsolicited scripts.

SILENT SOUND FILMS

Cambridge Court Cambridge Road
Frinton-on-Sea CO13 9HN
T 01255 676381
E thj@silentsoundfilms.co.uk
W www.silentsoundfilms.co.uk

Contacts
Timothy Foiter *Managing Director*

Production company founded in 1998 with background in fine art and art-house films. Also involved in television arts documentaries, with co-production contacts in France, the Netherlands and Hungary.

Submissions Policy
No manuscripts. Prefer to be approached via email with 50 word soundbite. Very rarely takes up unsolicited material.

SIXTEEN FILMS

20 Great Chapel Street London W1F 8FW

187 Wardour Street London W1F 8ZB
T 020 7734 0168
F 020 7439 4196
W www.sixteenfilms.co.uk

Contacts
Ken Loach *Director*

Established by Ken Loach and Rebecca O'Brien in spring 2002 following the dissolution of Parallas Pictures. Concentrates on film and television drama. Recent production *The Wind That Shakes The Barley* won Best Film at the 2006 Cannes Film Festival.

Submissions Policy
Not currently seeking new projects. However, unsolicited submissions (treatment or screenplay) are accepted via post FAO Alistair Griggs. Responses take a minimum of six weeks.

SKYLINE PRODUCTIONS

10 Scotland Street Edinburgh EH3 6PS
T 0131 557 4580
F 0131 556 4377
E leslie@skyline.uk.com
W www.skyline.uk.com

Contacts
Leslie Hills *Producer/Writer*

Produces film and television drama and documentary.

SLATE FILMS

20 Great Chapel Street London W1F 8FW
T 020 7734 1217
F 020 7287 9622
E info@slatefilms.com
W www.slatefilms.com

Contacts
Andrea Calderwood *Executive/Producer*

International film and television production company established by Andrea Calderwood in 2000. Projects cover a range of budgets and markets, from mainstream cinema comedies to edgy first feature films, BBC1 series to Channel 4 drama serials. Notable credits include *Once Upon A Time In The Midlands* starring Robert Carlyle (Film Four) and *Last King of Scotland* (co-production feature film directed by Kevin MacDonald).

SLY FOX FILMS

The Far Barn Foxhole Lane   Cranbrook
TN18 5NJ
T   01580 752839
E   info@slyfoxfilms.com
W   www.slyfoxfilms.com

Contacts
Linda James   *Producer*

Founded in 1982 by Stephen Bayly and Linda
James, who have produced over 50 hours of
prime time drama, six TV movies and seven
feature films. Recent titles include *Slatehead*
(a rock climbing drama) and *The Icarus Girl*
(a supernatural drama).

Submissions Policy
Does not encourage unsolicited material. The
principals predominately generate projects from
their own ideas or by optioning books to
adapt.

SMG PRODUCTIONS & GINGER PRODUCTIONS

Pacific Quay   Glasgow   G3 7TG
T   0141 300 3000
W   www.smgproductions.tv@alsoadd

Contacts
Elizabeth Partyka   *Managing Director*

SMG Productions, which incorporates
Ginger Productions, makes programmes
for the national television networks, including
ITV, Ch4 and Sky. Specializes in drama,
factual entertainment and children's
programming. Output includes *Taggart; Rebus;
Our Daughter Holly; Club Reps.* (Ginger
Productions at 3 Waterhouse Square,
138–142 Holborn, London EC1N 2NY.
T 020 7882 1020 W ginger.tv)

SO TELEVISION LTD

18 Hatfields   London   SE1 8GN
T   020 7960 2000
F   020 7960 2095

E   info@sotelevision.co.uk
W   www.sotelevision.co.uk

Set up in 2000 by Graham Norton and
Graham Stuart, producing entertainment
programmes for TV. Titles include *The Graham
Norton Show, School's Out* and *Bring Back
Dallas*.

SOMETHIN ELSE

Units 1–4 1A Old Nichol Street   London
E2 7HR
T   020 7613 3211
F   020 7739 9799
E   info@somethin-else.com
W   www.somethin-else.com

Contacts
Jez Nelson

Producer of television, video and radio
documentaries, DVD and interactive content.

Submissions Policy
Ideas for TV shows welcome; send letter in the
first instance.

SPECIFIC FILMS

25 Rathbone Street   London   W1T 1NQ
T   020 7580 7476
F   020 7636 6886
E   info@specificfilms.com

Contacts
Michael Hamlyn   *Managing Director*

Film production company whose titles include
Priscilla, Queen of the Desert.

SPELLBOUND PRODUCTIONS LTD

90 Cowdenbeath Path Islington   London
N1 0LG
T   020 7713 8066
F   020 7713 8066
E   phspellbound@hotmail.com

Contacts
Paul Harris

Specializes in feature films for cinema and drama for television. Keen to support and encourage new writing.

Submissions Policy
Material will only be considered if in correct screenplay format and accompanied by sae.

SPICE FACTORY

14 Regent Hill Brighton BN1 3ED
T   01273 739182
F   01273 749122
E   info@spicefactory.co.uk
W   www.spicefactory.co.uk

Contacts
Shirine Best *Development Co-ordinator*

Established in 1994, has now produced, co-produced or co-financed more than forty films (with over US$300m. of production spend). Recent titles include *Perfect Creature* and *Merchant of Venice*.

Submissions Policy
Does not welcome unsolicited approaches.

'SPOKEN' IMAGE LTD

8 Hewitt Street M15 4GB
T   0161 236 7522
F   0161 236 0020
E   info@spoken-image.com
W   www.spoken-image.com

Contacts
Geoff Allman

Film, video and TV production for documentary and corporate material. Specializes in high-quality brochures and reports, CD-ROMs, exhibitions, conferences, film and video production for broadcast, industry and commerce.

STAGESCREEN PRODUCTIONS

12 Upper Saint Martins Lane London WC2H 9JY
T   020 7497 2510
F   020 7497 2208

E   info@stagescreenproductions.com
W   www.stagescreenproductions.com

Contacts
Jeffrey Taylor *CEO*

Founded in 1989 and has worked on a number of prestigious films and television programmes. Particular expertise in arranging international co-productions. Output includes *What's Cooking* (a comedy-drama that opened at Sundance), the adventure film *Young Alexander* and *Jekyll*, a six-hour series for the BBC.

Submissions Policy
Happy to look at ideas (not complete manuscripts) sent in via email. Welcomes new writers.

TONY STAVEACRE PRODUCTIONS

Channel View Blagdon BS40 7TP
T   01761 462161
F   01761 462161
E   newstaving@btinternet.com

Contacts
Tony Staveacre

Producer of dramas and documentaries as well as music, arts and comedy progammes. Recent Output includes *Tango Maestro* (BBC4) and *The Old Boys Band* (BBC1).

Submissions Policy
No unsolicited manuscripts.

STIRLING FILM & TV PRODUCTIONS LIMITED

137 University Street Belfast BT7 1HP
T   028 9033 3848
F   028 9043 8644
E   anne@stirlingtelevision.co.uk

Contacts
Anne Stirling

Producer of broadcast and corporate programming– documentary, sport, entertainment and lifestyle programmes.

STRAIGHT FORWARD FILM & TELEVISION

Building 2 Lesley Office Park 393 Hollywood
Road Belfast BT4 2LS
T 028 9065 1010
F 028 9065 1012
E enquiries@straightforwardltd.co.uk

Contacts
John Nicholson

Northern Ireland-based production company
specializing in documentary, feature and
lifestyle series for both regional and network
transmission. Output includes *We Shall
Overcome* (winner of Best Documentary at
1999 Celtic Television Festival for BBC);
Conquering the Normans (Ch4 Learning –
history of Normans in Ireland); *Gift of the Gab*
(Ch4 Learning – contemporary Irish writing);
Sportsweek (BBC Radio Ulster); *On Eagle's
Wing* (full stage musical/TV material; story of
the Scots/Irish in America); *Fire School;
Mission Employable; Sweet Child of Mine;
School Challenge*, 3rd series; *World Indoor
Bowls* (all for BBC NI); *Awash With Colour*
(series, BBC Daytime).

SUNSET + VINE PRODUCTIONS LTD

30 Sackville Street London W1S 3DY
T 020 7478 7300
F 020 7478 7407
E reception@sunsetvine.co.uk
W www.sunsetvine.co.uk

Established in 1983, a leading independent
supplier of sports programmes. Produces over
2,000 hours per year.

TABLE TOP PRODUCTIONS

1 The Orchard Chiswick London W4 1JZ
T 020 8742 0507
F 020 8742 0507
E alvin@tabletopproductions.com

Contacts
Alvin Rakoff

TV and film. Output includes *Paradise
Postponed; The Adventures of Don Quixote; A
Voyage Round My Father; The First Olympics
1896; Dirty Tricks; A Dance to the Music of
Time; Too Marvellous for Words.*

Submissions Policy
No unsolicited manuscripts.

TALKBACKTHAMES

20–21 Newman Street London W1T 1PG
T 020 7861 8000
F 020 7861 8001
E reception@talkbackthames.tv
W www.talkbackthames.tv

Contacts
Lorraine Heggessey *Chief Executive Officer*

talkackTHAMES Productions is a
FremantleMedia company. Works across
comedy, comedy drama, drama, entertainment,
documentary and lifestyle programmes. Output
includes *The Apprentice; Green Wing; The Bill;
The X Factor; Never Mind the Buzzcocks;
Grand Designs; Unteachables; Property Ladder.*

TALKING HEADS PRODUCTIONS

2-4 Noel Street London W1F 8SB
T 020 7292 7575
F 020 7292 7576
E johnsachs@talkingheadsproductions.com
W www.talkingheadsproductions.com

Contacts
John Sachs

Film and television production company
founded in 1993. Recently co-produced
Merchant of Venice, starring Al Pacino.

Submissions Policy
Unsolicited material accepted via email.

TANDEM TV & FILM LTD

Charleston House 13 High Street Hemel
Hempstead Herts HP1 3AA
T 01442 261576
F 01442 219250

E   info@tandemtv.com
W   www.tandemtv.com

Contacts
Terry Page   *Director*

Over twenty-five years experience of producing TV and corporate films. Examples of output include *One for the Road*, a story about an alcoholic produced for broadcast TV.

Submissions Policy
Does not invite unsolicited material.

TAYLOR MADE BROADCASTS LTD

3B Cromwell Park Chipping Norton OX7 5SR
T   01608 646444
E   post@tmtv.co.uk

Contacts
Trevor Taylor

Producer of documentaries for radio and television.

Submissions Policy
No unsolicited manuscripts.

TELEMAGINATION

Royalty House 72-74 Dean Street London W1D 3SG
T   020 7434 1551
F   020 7434 3344
E   mail@tmation.co.uk
W   www.telemagination.co.uk

Contacts
Beth Parker   *Managing Director*

Children's animation production company best known for *Animals of Farthing Wood, Little Ghosts* and *The Cramp Twins*.

Submissions Policy
Unsolicited material accepted; submission guidelines available upon request.

TERN TELEVISION PRODUCTIONS LTD

73 Crown Street Aberdeen AB11 6EX
T   01224 211123
F   01224 211199
E   aberdeen@terntv.com
W   www.terntv.com

Contacts
David Strachan

Broadcast, television and corporate video productions. Specializes in factual entertainment. Currently developing drama. Also at: 4th Floor, 114 Union Street, Glasgow G1 3QQ; T 0141 204 1717; E glasgow@terntv.com. And: 1st Floor, Cotton Court, 38–42 Waring Street, Belfast BT1 2ED; T 02890 241433; E belfast@terntv.com.

TESTIMONY FILMS

12 Great George Street Bristol BS1 5RS
T   0117 925 8589
F   0117 925 7608
E   steve.humphries@testimonyfilms.com

Contacts
Steve Humphries

TV documentary producer. Specializes in social history exploring Britain's past using living memory. Output includes *Hooked: History of Addictions; Married Love* (both Ch4 series); *A Secret World of Sex* (BBC series); *The 50s & 60s in Living Colour; Some Liked It Hot* (both ITV series).

Submissions Policy
Welcomes ideas from those working on life stories and oral history.

THIN MAN FILMS

9 Greek Street London W1D 4DQ
T   020 7734 7372
F   020 7287 5228
E   info@thinman.co.uk

Producer of feature films including *All or Nothing* and *Vera Drake*.

TIGER ASPECT PRODUCTIONS

7 Soho Street London W1D 3DQ
T 020 7434 6700
F 020 7434 1798
E general@tigeraspect.co.uk
W www.tigeraspect.co.uk

An independent television producer working across a range of genres including comedy, drama, entertainment, factual, animation, wildlife (Tigress) and feature films (Tiger Aspect Pictures). Examples of titles include *Mr. Bean*, *Lenny Henry in Pieces*, *Harry Enfield and Chums*, *Murphy's Law*, *Rescue Me*, *The Vicar of Dibley*, *Fat Friends*, *Teachers*, *Murder*, *Omagh*, *Gimme Gimme Gimme*, *A Place in France*, *Country House* and *Streetmate*.

TIGERLILY FILMS LIMITED

Studio 17 The Whitecahpel Centre Myrdle Street London E1 1HL
T 020 7247 1107
F 020 7247 2008
E info@tigerlilyfilms.com
W www.tigerlilyfilms.com

Founded in 2000, a film and television production comapny working across a range of genres including documentary, drama, feature films and children's programming. Titles include the children's drama *Patrick's Planet*, the feature film *Transit*, the documentaries *37 Uses for a Dead Sheep*, *Arte* and *Alexis Arquette: She's My Brother*.

Submissions Policy
Does not accept any unsolicited material.

TOUCH PRODUCTIONS LTD

18 Queen Square Bath BA1 2HN
T 01225 484666
F 01225 483620
E erica@touchproductions.co.uk

Contacts
Erica Wolfe-Murray

Over the last 20 years, Touch has made a wide range of programmes including award-winning investigations, popular documentaries, medical and science films, revelatory history productions as well as observational, social, religious and arts programmes. Current commissions include *The Human Footprint* (a Ch4 documentary special) and various series and documentaries for the BBC, National Geographic, TLC and Animal Planet. Other projects include *Transplanting Memories?*; *The Boy Who Couldn't Stop Running*; *Parish in the Sun*; *Revival* and *Angela's Dying Wish*.

TRANSATLANTIC FILMS PRODUCTION AND DISTRIBUTION COMPANY

Cabalva Studios Whitney-on-Wye HR3 6EX
T 01497 831428
F 01497 831677
E revel@transatlanticfilms.com
W www.transatlanticfilms.com

Contacts
Revel Guest *Executive Producer*

Producer of TV documentaries. Output includes *Belzoni* (Ch4 Schools); *Science of Sleep and Dreams*; *Science of Love* and *Extreme Body Parts* (all for Discovery Health); *Legends of the Living Dead* (Discovery Travel/S4C International); *2025* (Discovery Digital); *How Animals Tell the Time* (Discovery); *Trailblazers* (Travel Channel).

Submissions Policy
No unsolicited scripts. Interested in new writers to write 'the book of the series', e.g. for Greek Fire and History's Turning Points, but not usually drama script writers.

TRAVEL CHANNEL

64 Newman Street London W1T 3EF
T 020 7636 5401
F 020 7636 6424
E katie.isworth@travelchannel.co.uk
W www.travelchannel.co.uk

Contacts
Katie Isworth *Marketing Executive*

Founded in 1994, specializing in travel programmes.

Submissions Policy
Happy to receive unsolicited approaches by email.

TV CHOICE LTD

PO Box 597 Bromley BR2 OYB
T   020 8464 7402
F   020 8464 7845
E   tvchoiceuk@aol.com
W   www.tvchoice.uk.com

Contacts
Norman Thomas

Produces a range of educational videos for schools and colleges on subjects such as history, geography, business studies and economics.

Submissions Policy
No unsolicited manuscripts; send proposals only.

TWENTY TWENTY TELEVISION

20 Kentish Town Road London NW1 9NX
T   020 7284 2020
F   020 7284 1810
W   www.twentytwenty.tv

Contacts
Peter Casely-Hayford *Managing Director*

Large independent television production company. Concentrates on documentaries, lifestyle programmes, popular drama and living history series. Established in 1982. Broadcast internationally by networks including the BBC, CBBC, ITV, Channels 4, Five, ABC, The Discovery Channel, Turner Original Productions, Sundance Channel and CNN. Recent successes include *The Choir* (BBC2), *Bad Lads Army* (ITV1) and *How to Divorce without Screwing up your Children* (Channel 4). Both *Brat Camp* and *That'll Teach Em* have now aired a third season.

Submissions Policy
Drama enquiries and scripts should be emailed to jamieisaacs@twentytwenty.tv.

TWOFOUR BROADCAST

Twofour Studios Estover Plymouth PL6 7RG
T   01752 727 400
F   01752 727 450
E   enq@twofour.co.uk
W   www.twofour.co.uk

Contacts
Melanie Leach *Managing Director*

Television production company founded in 1987. Specializes in factual entertainment, drama and comedy.

Submissions Policy
Unsolicited material or ideas accepted via email.

TYBURN FILM PRODUCTIONS LIMITED

Cippenham Court Cippenham Lane
Cippenham Nr. Slough Berkshire SL1 5AU
T   01753 516767
F   01753 691785

A subsidiary of Arlington Productions, specializing in theatrical films and popular drama.

THE UK FILM AND TV PRODUCTION COMPANY PLC

3 Colville Place London W1T 2BH
T   020 7255 1650

Contacts
Henrietta Fudakowski *Head of Development*

In 2006 *Tsotsi*, UKFTV's first wholly-produced film, won the Oscar for best foreign language film. Other titles include *Bugs! in 3D*.

Submissions Policy
Telephone ahead of sending a submission to see if script might be suitable for the company.

VERA PRODUCTIONS

66–68 Margaret Street London
W1W 8SR
T 020 7436 6116
F 020 7436 6117

Contacts
Phoebe Wallace

Produces television comedy such as *Bremner, Bird and Fortune*.

VERTIGO FILMS

The Big Room Studios 77 Fortress Road
London NW5 1AG
T 020 7428 7555
F 020 7485 9713
E scripts@vertigofilms.com
W www.vertigofilms.com

A development, finance, production and distribution media company founded in July 2002. Major titles include *The Football Factory*, *It's All Gone Pete Tong*, *A Good Woman*, *Dirty Sanchez*, *Outlaw* and *Dogging–A Love Story*.

WADDELL MEDIA

Strand Studios 5/7 Shore Road Holywood
County Down BT18 9HX
T 028 9042 7646
F 028 9042 7922
E info@waddellmedia.com
W www.waddellmedia.com

A leading producer of factual, lifestyle and entertainment programming for the UK, Irish and international markets. Founded in 1988, producing around 50 hours of television each year for most of the leading UK broadcasters. Also has major commissions in the US for Discovery, National Geographic and A&E.

WALL TO WALL

8–9 Spring Place London NW5 3ER
T 020 7485 7424
F 020 7267 5292
W www.walltowall.co.uk

Contacts
Alex Graham *Chief Executive*

Factual and drama programming. Output includes *Who Do You Think You Are?*; *New Tricks*; *A Rather English Marriage*; *Glasgow Kiss*; *Sex, Chips & Rock 'n' Roll*; *The 1940s House*; *Body Story*; *Neanderthal*; *The Mafia*; *Not Forgotten*; *H.G. Wells*.

WALSH BROS LTD

4 The Heights London England SE7 8JH
T 020 8858 6870
E info@walshbros.co.uk
W www.walshbros.co.uk

Contacts
John Walsh *Producer/Director*

Specializes in documentaries and drama. Highlights include *Monarch* (feature film), the Bafta-nominated *Don't Make Me Angry* and *Headhunting the Homeless*. Founded in 1996, working in film, TV and computer games.

Submissions Policy
Will look at new writers but contact by email first.

WARP X

The Workstation Paternoster Row Sheffield
S1 2BX
T 0114 213 0333
F 0870 220 0652
E info@warpx.co.uk
W www.warpx.co.uk

Contacts
Kate Fewins *Co-ordinator*

A pioneering film studio, producing films using cutting-edge digital technology aiming to revitalize the low-budget sector of British film. Working with the Low Budget Feature Film Scheme set up by the UK Film Council's New Cinema Fund and Film4. Making seven digital feature films between 2006 and 2008.

Submissions Policy
Does not accept unsolicited scripts.

WARPFILMS

The Workstation Paternoster Row Sheffield
S1 2BX
T   0114 213 0333
W   www.warpfilms.com

WarpFilms was founded in 2000 and makes features, short films, music videos and TV programmes. Titles include *Dead Man's Shoes* (Bafta-nominated), *My Wrongs* (Bafta-winning) and *This is England* (named Best Film at the BIFAs).

Submissions Policy
Is open to new writing submitted via agents or personal recommendation.

WORKING TITLE FILMS LTD

Oxford House 76 Oxford Street London
W1D 1BS
T   020 7307 3000
F   020 7307 3001

Contacts
Natascha Wharton *Head of Development (Films)*

Feature film producer. Output includes *United 93; Smokin' Aces; Sixty Six; Catch a Fire; Gone; Nanny McPhee; Pride & Prejudice; The Interpreter; Wimbledon; Bridget Jones 2: Edge of Reason; Shaun of the Dead; Love Actually; Thunderbirds; Ned Kelly; Johnny English; Bridget Jones's Diary; Captain Corelli's Mandolin; Ali G Indahouse; Billy Elliot; Notting Hill; Elizabeth; Fargo; Dead Man Walking; French Kiss; Four Weddings and a Funeral; The Hudsucker Proxy; The Tall Guy;*

Wish You Were Here; My Beautiful Laundrette. Television (drama, family/children's entertainment, comedy) output: *The Robber Bride; Perfect Strangers; The Other Woman; Dr Jekyll & Mr Hyde; Ready When You Are Mr McGill; Come Together; Lucky Jim; Randall & Hopkirk (deceased) I & II; The Last of the Blonde Bombshells; Doomwatch; Tales of the City; Lano and Woodley I & II; The Baldy Man I & II; The Borrowers I & II; News Hounds.*

Submissions Policy
No unsolicited manuscripts at present.

WORLD PRODUCTIONS

16 Dufours Place London W1F 7SP
T   020 7734 3536
E   ellen@world-productions.com
W   www.world-productions.com

Contacts
Tony Harnett *Executive Producer*

Established in 1990. Has produced over 250 hours of network drama: renewable one hour series, mini-series and single films. Over 40 hours programming produced in 2006. Exists as a company of producers working across all genres. Creators of *Lilies* (BBC1), *Goldplated* (Channel 4), *Rough Diamond* (Channel 4), *This Life* and *Ballykissangel.*

Submissions Policy
Submissions via agent only.

WORTMAN UK/POLESTAR PICTURES

48 Chiswick Staithe London W4 3TP
T   020 8994 8886
E   nevillewortman@beeb.net

Contacts
Neville Wortman *Senior Producer, Development*

Founded in 1989, producing feature films and mainstream television. Specializes in drama and documentary, with examples of output including *Eruption Mount St Helena, Munich Air Crash, Murder in Paradise, Julius Caesar,*

Nuclear Spy Race and *Hitler Bomb Plot.* Programmes have been shown on BBC, Channel 4 and Discovery, among others.

Submissions Policy
Open to new writing but only through established agents. Send a synopsis and 2–6 pages of dialogue.

CANADA

100 PERCENT FILM & TELEVISION INC.

116 Spadina Avenue Suite 701 Toronto Ontario M5V 2K6
T   416 304 5225
F   416 304 1222
E   info@onehundredpercent.ca
W   www.onehunredpercent.ca

Emmy Award-winning film and TV production company. Credits include *The Newsroom* and *At The Hotel.*

AFFINITY PRODUCTIONS

2740B Queensview Drive Ottawa Ontario K2B 2A2
T   613 820 4660
F   613 820 5020
E   www.affinityproductions.tv
W   info@affinityproductions.tv

Television production company producing for domestic and international broadcasters.

AFTERDARK PRODUCTIONS INC.

Suite 303 1668 Barrington Street Halifax Nova Scotia B3J 2A2
T   902 423 3497
F   902 484 6880
E   info@afterdarktv.com
W   www.afterdarktv.com

Film and television production house specializing in the creation, development and production of popular appeal films, television and documentaries. Titles include *A Bug and a*

Bag of Weed, The Life and Times of Super 8 and *Afterdark TV.*

Submissions Policy
Does not accept unsolicited material unless accompanied by a submission release form.

ALBERTA FILMWORKS

1310-11th Street SW. Calgary Alberta T2R 1G6
T   403 777 9900
F   403 777 9914
E   mail@albertafilmworks.com
W   www.albertafilmworks.com

An independent film and television production founded in the late 1980s. Production credits include *Brokeback Mountain, The Christmas Blessing* and *The Ron Clark Story.*

ALLIANCE ATLANTIS

121 Bloor Street East Suite 1500 Toronto Ontario M4W 3M5
T   416 967 1174
F   416 960 0971
E   info@AllianceAtlantis.com
W   www.allianceatlantis.com

Formed in 1998 from the merger of two former production companies, Alliance Communications and Atlantis Communications. Principal business activities are broadcasting, entertainment and motion picture distribution. Has a controlling interest in and operates 13 speciality television channels and is a 50% co-owner and co-producer of the *CSI: Crime Scene Investigation* franchise, in partnership with CBS Productions. Does not accept and/or review unsolicited creative material of any kind. Any unsolicited materials will be returned unread and/or discarded at Alliance Atlantis' sole discretion.

AMBERWOOD ENTERTAINMENT CORP.

987 Wellington Street 2nd floor Ottawa Ontario K1Y 2Y1
T   613 238 4567
F   613 233 3857

E   info@amberwoodanimation.com
w   www.amberwoodanimation.com

Founded in 1997, specializing in, but not limited to, animation. Produces across genres and formats, including features and series. Titles include *The Secret World of Benjamin Bear*, *The Snow Queen*, *Zeroman* and *Hoze Houndz*.

ANAÏD PRODUCTIONS INC.

208 3132 Parsons Road Edmonton Alberta
T6N 1L6
T   780 413 9285
F   780 465 0580
E   anaid@anaid.com
w   www.anaid.com

Founded in 1993, an award-winning film and television production company dedicated to the development and production of quality dramatic and factual programming. Includes documentaries and lifestyle series, reality and game shows, children's and adult drama, mini series and feature/television movies. Examples of output include *Mentors*, *The Tourist*, *Taking It Off*, *The Family Restaurant* and *X-Weighted*.

Submissions Policy
Submissions guidelines and proposal submission agreement available from website. Will not accept proposals for 'one-off' or single, one-hour documentaries.

ANAGRAM PICTURES

3rd Floor 291 East 2nd Avenue Vancouver
British Columbia V5T 1B8
T   604 720 9021
F   604 730 9042
E   anagram@anagrampictures.ca
w   www.anagrampictures.ca

Contacts
Andrew Currie *Writer/Director/Producer*

Feature-film and tv movie production company. Launched in 1997. Focuses on drama and comedy.

Submissions Policy
No unsolicited material.

ANGEL ENTERTAINMENT CORPORATION

2710 Millar Avenue Saskatoon Saskatchewan
S7K 4J4
T   306 244 8691
F   306 933 3183
w   www.angelentertainment.ca

An international motion picture company producing market-driven feature films, documentaries and television programming. Examples of output include *Shadow Puppets*, a sci-fi horror-thriller, *Rabbit Fall* and the documentary series, *Spirit Creations*.

APARTMENT 11 PRODUCTIONS

828 St. Catherine Street East Suite 200
Montreal Quebec H2L 2E3
T   514 282 0776
F   514 282 0796
w   www.apartment11.tv

Children's television producer, with titles including *Prank Patrol* and *Mystery Hunters*.

AQUILA PICTURES

130 Bloor Street West Suite 600 Toronto
Ontario M5S 1N5
E   info@aquilapictures.com
w   www.aquilapictures.com

Primarily concerned with the development and production of feature films and television programmes. Recent productions include *The House*, *Gangster Exchange* and *Tomkat: Animated*.

AVANTI PICTURES CORPORATION

810-289 Alexander Street Vancouver British
Columbia V6A 4H6
T   604 609 0339
E   info@avantipics.com
w   www.avantipics.com

Founded in 1996 as a base for like-minded producers and other creative people to produce high quality dramas and documentaries for television and festivals.

Submissions Policy
Happy to receive ideas, programme suggestions and literary materials. Study company's policy and agreement on website. Will review and consider submissions only if this policy and agreement is accepted.

AVRIO FILMWORKS INC.

5865 Marine Drive West Vancouver British Columbia V7W 2S1
T   702 768 1918
F   702 877 4703
W   www.avriofilmworks.com

Founded by Michael Derbas to make and distribute feature films and participate in worldwide co-productions. Production credits include *Sub-Zero* and *Premonition*.

BARDEL ENTERTAINMENT INC.

548 Beatty Street Vancouver British Columbia V6B 2L3
T   604 669 5589
F   604 669 9079
E   info@bardel.ca
W   www.bardelentertainment.com

A leading animation production studio. Works with major US producers and video game studios.

BARNA-ALPER PRODUCTIONS INC.

366 Adelaide Street West Suite 700 Toronto Ontario M5V 1R9
T   416 979 0676
F   416 979 7476
E   info@bap.ca
W   www.bap.ca

Founded in 1980, producing dramas and documentaries. Examples of output include CBC's *DaVinci's Inquest*, *Shania: A Life In Eight Albums*, the mini-series

Whiskey Echo and *Turning Points of History*.

BIG MOTION PICTURES LIMITED

5 Pleasant Street 2nd Floor PO Box 202 Chester Nova Scotia B0J 1J0
T   902 275 1350
F   902 275 1353
E   contact@bigmotionpictures.com
W   www.bigmotionpictures.com

Independent television company founded in 1999. Their first production was *Task Force*. Other titles include the TV movie *Sleep Murder* and the series *Guy & a Girl* and *Snakes & Ladders*.

BIG SOUL PRODUCTIONS INC.

372 Richmond Street West Suite 301 Toronto Ontario M5V 1X6
T   416 598 7762
F   416 598 5392
E   comments@bigsoul.net
W   www.bigsoul.net

Established in 1999, a leader in Aboriginal content programming. Has produced three series of the award-winning *The Seventh Generation*.

BIOWARE CORP.

200 4445 Calgary Trail Edmonton Alberta T6H 5R7
T   780 430 0164
F   780 439 6374
E   contact@bioware.com
W   www.bioware.com

An electronic entertainment company specializing in creating computer and console video games, founded in 1995. Aims to 'deliver the best story-driven games in the world'. Recently part of a US$300 million merger with Pandemic Studios. Examples of output include *Jade Empire*, *Star Wars: Knights Of The Old Republic*, *Neverwinter Nights Series* and *Shattered Steel*.

BLACK WALK

99 Sudbury Street Unit 201 Toronto Ontario
M6J 3S7
T 416 533 5864
F 416 533 2016
E info@blackwalk.com
W www.blackwalk.com

Founded in the 1990s as a music video
production company. Since 2002 has focused
on movie and television production, with four
films completed.

BREAKTHROUGH FILMS & TELEVISION INC.

口

122 Sherbourne Street Toronto Ontario
M5A 2R4
T 416 766 6588
F 416 769 1436
E business@breakthroughfilms.com
W www.breakthroughfilms.com

Over twenty years experience of producing
television programmes including children's,
documentary, factual, drama and lifestyle series.

BRIGHTLIGHT PICTURES INC.

The Bridge Studios 2400 Boundary Road
Burnaby British Columbia V5M 3Z3
T 604 628 3000
F 604 628 3001
E info@brightlightpictures.com
W www.brightlightpictures.com

Founded in 2001 to develop, finance and
produce independent feature films and
television projects for domestic and
international markets. Production credits
include *White Noise*, *Dungeon Siege*, *Edison*
and *Wicker Man*.

CANADIAN ACCENTS INC.

🎥口

25 Yarmouth Road Toronto Ontario
M6G 1W6
T 416 653 0702
F 416 658 3176

E info@canadianaccents.ca
W www.canadianaccents.ca

Founded in 2003, a film and television
production company focussing on comedy.
Titles include *Women Fully Clothed: All
Dresses Up & Places to Go* and *Is it Art?*

CANAMEDIA FILM PRODUCTIONS INC.

口

381 Richmond Street East Suite #200 Toronto
Ontario M5A 1P6
T 416 483 7446
F 416 483 7529
E canamed@canamedia.com
W www.canamedia.com

Founded in 1978. Works across range of genres
including TV movies, drama series, children's
drama, documentaries, travel and lifestyle.

CAPRI FILMS INC.

259 Lakeshore Boulevard East 2nd Floor
Toronto Ontario M5A 3T7
T 416 535 1870
F 416 535 3414
E info@caprifilms.com
W www.caprifilms.com

Creates, develops and produces feature film and
television projects. Produces three to four film
and television projects per year. Examples of
output include *Tideland* and the mini-series
Karol.

CHEAP AND DIRTY PRODUCTIONS

1874 Grant Street Vancouver British
Columbia V5L 2Y8
T 604 872 7006
F 604 872 7086
E cheapanddirty@telus.net
W www.cheapanddirty.ca

Company founded in 2001 to produce film,
television, features, documentaries and video
games. Also available to assist in development.
Notable projects include *Fetching Cody* and *A
Safer Sex Trade*. Interested in all genres.

Submissions Policy
Material accepted via agent only.

CHUM LIMITED

299 Queen Street West Toronto Ontario
M5V 2Z5
T 416 591 5757
F 416 591 8457
E info@chumlimited.com
W www.chumlimited.com

A leading media company and content provider
that owns and operates 34 radio stations, 12
local television stations and 21 speciality
channels. Supports Canadian independent
production companies with early development
support for writing and research and, later on,
with pre-license commitments for production.

CINÉ QUA NON MÉDIA

445 Rue St-Pieere Bureau 402 Montréal
Québec H2Y 2M8
T 514 271 4000
F 514 271 4331
E info@cqnmedia.com

Contacts
Michel Ouellette *Producer and President*

Founded in 1982. Focuses on films made for
television. Noted for blending genres such as
documentary, performing arts and fiction. Recent
releases include *Velasquez's Little Museum* and
the feature documentary *Mary Shelley*.

Submissions Policy
Welcomes unsolicited material via email. Must
include letter of presentation, one-liner and
synopsis.

CRAWLEY FILMS LTD

PO Box 11069 Stn. H Nepean Ontario
K2H 7TB
E bstevens@crawleyfilms.ca
W www.crawleyfilms.ca

Contacts
Bill Stevens Jr *President and CEO*

One of Canada's oldest production companies,
founded in 1939. Has won an Academy Award
and over 100 awards from around the world.
Produces drama, documentary and animation,
concentrating on family values.

Submissions Policy
Welcomes unsolicited material in the form of a
one-page concept outline.

CRESCENT ENTERTAINMENT LTD

343 Railway Street Suite 304 Vancouver British
Columbia V6A 1A4
T 604 357 3606
F 604 357 3605
E crescent@crescent.ca
W www.crescent.ca

Established in 1990, an award-winning
television and film production company.
Specializes in developing and producing
original feature films, television and
documentaries. Television projects include
Terminal City, Happy Land and *Dead Zone*.
Films include *Mirage, Moving Malcolm, Naked
Frailties* and *Showdown at Williams Creek*.

Submissions Policy
Email synopses/concepts and all relevant
details for consideration.

DA DA KAMERA PICTURES

401 Richmond Street West Suite 385 Toronto
Ontario M5V 3A8
T 416 586 1503
F 416 586 1504
E ddkpictures@ca.internet
W www.dadakamera.com

Contacts
Sherrie Johnson *Producer*

Filmmaking arm of a theatrical production
company. Drama only. Best known for recent
release *Wilby Wonderful*, which opened at
Toronto International Film Festival and then
traveled the festival circuit.

Submissions Policy
No unsolicited material.

DARIUS FILMS INC.

1173 Dundas Street East Suite 235 Toronto
Ontario M4M 3P1
T 416 922 0007
F 416 406 0034
E info@dariusfilms.com
W www.dariusfilms.com

Founded in 1996, a film and television
production company. Titles include *Weirdsville*,
A Lobster's Tale, *The Limb Salesman*, *Motel*
and *Caprice*.

DECODE ENTERTAINMENT INC.

512 King Street East Suite 104 Toronto
Ontario M5A 1M1
T 416 363 8034
F 416 363 8919
E decode@decode-ent.com
W www.decode.tv

Contacts
Nancy Yeaman *Development Manager*

Children's and family production company
founded in 1997. Interested in live action
and animated television series projects. Also
extends to computer games. Output includes
Chop Socky Chooks, *Naturally Sadie* and
Franny's Feet.

Submissions Policy
No unsolicited material via post or email.
Welcomes phone calls to pitch potential
projects. Will respond accordingly.

DEVINE ENTERTAINMENT

2 Berkeley Street Suite 504 Toronto Ontario
M5A 2W3
T 416 364 2282
F 416 364 1440
E info@devine-ent.com
W www.devine-ent.com

Develops and produces children's and family
films for global television and cable markets
and the international home video markets. Has

won numerous international awards including
five Emmy Awards and five Gemini Awards.
Focus is on historical and timeless stories.
Examples of output include *Beethoven Lives
Upstairs*, *The Artists' Specials* (consiting of one
hour episodes each focusing on a famous artist)
and *Bailey's Billion$*.

DREAM STREET PICTURES INC.

75 Archibald Street Moncton New Brunswick
E1C 5J2
T   506 854 1057
F   506 382 4144
E   tammy@dreamstreetpictures.com
W www.dreamstreetpictures.com

Film and TV production company whose
credits include *Planet Luxury*, *Open Heart*,
Neutral Ground and *Record Man: the Life &
Times of Sam Sniderman*.

EPITOME PICTURES INC.

220 Bartley Drive Toronto Ontario M4A 1G1
T   416 752 7627
F   416 752 7837
E   info@epitomepictures.com
W www.epitomepictures.com

Over twenty-five years experience of television
production, including documentaries, drama
and soap operas. Output includes *Instant Star*
and *Degrassi: The Next Generation*.

FAST PRODUCTIONS LTD

515-425 Carroll Street Vancouver British
Columbia V6B 6E3
T   778 786 1628
F   778 786 1585
E   fast-productions@shaw.ca

Contacts
Cheryl-Lee Fast *Producer*

Formed in 2003. Develops, produces and
distributes documentaries and feature length
films. Film output focuses on drama, comedy,
thriller and romantic comedy. Also develops

television projects and reality series. Past work includes *The Zero Sum*, *Cries in the Dark*, *Papal Chase* and *Swimming Lessons*.

Submissions Policy
Not interested in first time writers. Prefers to be approached via email.

FLAMINGO NECK PICTURES INC.

108 Victoria Park Avenue Toronto Ontario
M4E 3R9
T   416 693 5952
F   416 693 9132
E   scarab23@sympatico.ca
W   www.creepy.tv

Contacts
Brian O'Dea *Executive Producer*

Founded in 2001, television and film production company specializing in drama and docu-dramas. Recent credits include *Creepy Canada* and *High: Confessions of a Pot Smuggler*.

Submissions Policy
Welcomes unsolicited manuscripts by email - 'if it's good, that's the only issue'.

FORCE FOUR PRODUCTIONS

#202 - 221 E. 10th Avenue Vancouver British
Columbia V5T 4V1
T   604 669 4424
F   604 669 4535
E   tv@forcefour.com
W   www.forcefour.com

Television production company set up in 1983, with an output embracing drama, lifestyle, documentary and reality series.

FREMANTLE CORPORATION

23 Lesmill Road Suite 201 Toronto Ontario
M3B 3P6
T   416 443 9204
F   416 443 8685
W   www.fremantlecorp.com

The Fremantle Corporation, founded in 1952, is a distribution company that co-producers programmes. Has an extensive library of programming including daytime drama *All My Children*, the comedy *Girls Behaving Badly* and *Candid Camera*.

FRONT STREET PRODUCTIONS

202-2339 Columbia Street Vancouver British
Columbia V5Y 3Y3
T   604 257 4720
F   604 257 4739
W   www.frontstreetpictures.com

Motion picture production company founded in 1999, specializing in independent films for worldwide distribution. Recent productions include the films *The Deal* and *We Don't Live Here Anymore*, and the television series *Her Sister's Keeper*, *The Secret of Hidden Lake* and *Trophy Wife*.

Submissions Policy
Actively seeking new creative talent for both television and film. To submit material, download and sign the submissions form on the website. This form needs to be signed and included with the submission or it will be rejected. Cannot guarantee a response or give specific feedback on any rejected material but will make contact if interested in the work. Does not keep or return material but disposes of it so that no-one has access to it anymore.

GALAFILM INC.

5643 Clark Street #300 Montreal Quebec
H2T 2V5
T   514 273 4252
F   514 273 8689
E   info@galafilm.com
W   www.galafilm.com

Founded in 1990, an independent film, television and new media production company. Works across genres including documentary series and one-offs, children's programming, television drama and feature film.

GINTY FILMS

483 Euclid Avenue Toronto Ontario M6G 2TI
T   416 992 5438
F   416 924 3229
E   rwginty@aol.com
W   www.robertginty.com

Contacts
Suzanne Depoe *Canada Representative*

Film and television production company
formed in 1982. Specializes in drama such as
the upcoming *The Young Churchill* for ITV.

Submissions Policy
Submissions only via agent.

HADDOCK ENTERTAINMENT INC.

#810-207 West Hastings Street Vancouver
British Columbia V6B 1H7
T   604 681 1516
F   604 684 3530
E   office@haddockentertainment.com
W   www.haddockentertainment.com

Specializes in popular prime time drama.
Founded by Chris Haddock, the creative
force behind the award-winning *Da Vinci's
Inquest, The Handler, Da Vinci's City
Hall* and *Intelligence*.

Submissions Policy
Does not accept or consider materials, creative
ideas or suggestions of any nature other than
those specifically commissioned or requested by
Haddock Entertainment or its affiliated
companies.

DAVID HAMILTON PRODUCTIONS

221 Lyon Street North Suite 2603 Ottawa
Ontario K1R 7X5
T   613 782 2220
F   613 782 3131
E   dch888@rogers.com

Contacts
David Hamilton

Producers of film dramas such as *Water*.

Submissions Policy
Does not welcome unsolicited approaches.

HANDEL PRODUCTIONS INC.

424 rue Guy Suite 110 Montreal Québec
H3J 1S6
T   514 487 1881
F   514 487 7796
E   info@handelproductions.ca
W   www.handelproductions.ca

Leading producer of documentaries and
factual programmes, established in 1985.
Production credits include *How William
Shatner Changed the World, Faith and
Fortune: The Reichmann Story,
Nowhere Else to Live* and *A Passage from
Burnt Islands*.

IMAGINATION FILM & TELEVISION PRODUCTIONS INC.

3rd Floor 10318-82nd Avenue
(The Griffith Block) Edmonton Alberta
T6E 1Z8
T   780 439 8755
F   780 430 1871
E   imagi@telusplanet.net
W   www.imaginationfilm.tv

Develops and produces dramatic long-form
television, theatrical movies and socio-political
documentaries. Titles include *A Kid's
View* (*I, II* and "*of the US*"), *Great
Canadian Ghost Stories* and *100 Days in
the Jungle*.

IMX COMMUNICATIONS INC.

1556 Queen Street Halifax Nova Scotia
B3J 2H8
T   902 422 4000
F   902 422 4427
E   imx@imx.ca
W   www.imxcommunications.com

Television and film production company established by Christopher Zimmer. Past productions include *Margaret's Museum, Love and Death on Long Island, The Real Howard Spitz, The Weight of Water, The River King* and *Partition*.

INFINITY FILMED ENTERTAINMENT GROUP LTD

Suite 100 873 Beatty Street Vancouver British Columbia V6B 2M6
T   604 681 5650
F   604 681 5664
E   www.infinityfilms.ca

Covers the spectrum from features and documentaries to television comedy, drama and variety. Titles include the film *Almost Heaven*, the documentaries *Comedic Genius, Love & Duty* and *Race of the Century*, and the series *Improv Comedy, The Jim Byrnes Show, Dawn Wells* and *Reel Adventures*.

INNER CITY FILMS INC.

842 King Street West Toronto Ontario M5V 1P1
T   416 368 3339
F   416 368 5234
E   info@innercityfilms.ca
W   www.innercityfilms.ca

Founded in 1987, a television and film production company with offices in Los Angeles, London and Johannesburg. Has produced more than 100 hours of prime-time television programming across a range of genres, from drama series to lifestyle programming.

INSIGHT PRODUCTION COMPANY LTD.

489 Kings Street West Suite 401 Toronto Ontario M5V 1K4
T   416 596 8118
F   416 596 8270
W   www.insighttv.com

Contacts
John Brunton *President and CEO, Executive Producer*

Large multi-faceted television production company founded in 1978. Involved in all genres of programming. Recent releases include *Falcon Beach* (drama), *Hatching, Matching and Dispatching* (comedy), *Canadian Idol* (variety), *Comedy Gold* (documentary) and *MuchMusic VJ Search* (reality).

Submissions Policy
Unsolicited material accepted when accompanied by a signed policy agreement. Further details found on the website.

INTERNATIONAL DOCUMENTARY TELEVISION CORPORATION

73 Alexander Street Vancouver British Columbia V6A 1B2
T   604 664 0450
F   604 664 0451
E   hello@doctv.com
W   www.doctv.com

Television production company specializing in full-length network documentary programming. Does biographical portraits, issue-driven documentary and topics of interest to the producers which can be programmed by network television.

INTERNATIONAL KEYSTONE ENTERTAINMENT

300-2339 Columbia Street Vancouver British Columbia V5Y 3Y3
T   604 873 9739
F   604 873 5919
E   films@keypics.com
W   www.keypics.com

Producers of feature films for worldwide markets. Keystone Family Pictures wing makes films for 5–11 year olds and their parents while Keystone Pictures focuses on drama, action and thriller titles.

KEATLEY ENTERTAINMENT LTD

718-510 West Hastings Street Vancouver
British Columbia V6B 1L8
T 604 291 9789
F 604 291 9759
W www.keatleyentertainment.com

Specializes in the development and production
of feature films and television series for
domestic and international markets. Is the
producer of the award-winning *Cold Squad*
television series.

KNIGHT ENTERPRISES INC.

307-99 Fifth Avenue Ottowa Ontario
K1S 5P5
T 613 730 1728
F 613 730 0182
E info@knight-tv.com
W www.knight-tv.com

Contacts
Kathy Doherty *Senior Producer*

Television and new media company specializing
in lifestyle programming. Launched in 1997.
Recent releases include *License to Grill*, *This
Food That Wine* and *Junk Brothers*.

Submissions Policy
Unsolicited submissions accepted by letter.
Must be accompanied by a signed Proposal
Submission Agreement (obtained by emailing
info@knight-tv.com).

LUMANITY PRODUCTIONS INC.

313 Brock Avenue Main Floor Toronto
Ontario M6K 2M6
T 416 531 9691
F 416 946 1854
E rbudreau@lumanityproductions.com
W www.lumanityproductions.com

Established in 2002 by Robert Budreau to
produce quality films for theatrical and
television release. Has worked on films,
television dramas and long-form documentaries.

Submissions Policy
Pleased to receive ideas, programme suggestions
and literary materials but study the submissions
policy and agreement on the website first.

MAKE BELIEVE MEDIA INC.

Suite 201 145 Keefer Street Vancouver British
Columbia V6A 1X3
T 604 874 9498
F 604 874 9484
E info@makebelievemedia.com
W www.makebelievemedia.com

Established by Lynn Booth in 1999 to make
documentaries and non-fiction programming.
Production credits include *The Perfect
Husband: The Life and Times of Tim Horton*,
The Whistleblower, *Mandrake the Magician*,
Portraits from the Frontier and *Paris Stories*.

MEDIA HEADQUARTERS FILM & TELEVISION INC.

760 Bathurst Street Studio 2 Toronto Ontario
M5S 2R6
T 416 537 8384
F 416 537 8602
E contact@mediahqs.net
W www.mediahqs.net

Produces documentaries and prime-time
specials for domestic and international
markets. Credits inlcude *Le Mozart Noir:
Reviving A Legend*, *Souvenir of Canada* and
Modern Love.

MILAGRO FILMS INC.

4446 St-Laurent Boulevard Suite 806
Montréal Québec H2W 1Z5
T 514 939 9969
E info@milagrofilms.ca
W www.milagrofilms.ca

Contacts
Flavie Langois *Head of Development*

Established in 1997. Concentrates on television drama and feature films, notably *Jericho Mansions*.

Submissions Policy
Unsolicited submissions via email. Must be accompanied by a signed release (available from the website).

MINDS EYE ENTERTAINMENT LTD.

480 Henderson Drive Regina Saskatchewan
S4N 6E3
T   306 359 7618
F   306 359 3466
E   mindseye@mindseyepictures.com
W www.mindseyepictures.com

Contacts
Kevin DeWalt *President and* CEO

Television and film production company founded in 1986. Concentrates on live action drama, children's and youth drama and lifestyle programming. Past releases include *The Englishman's Boy* (TV miniseries), *Just Cause* (22 x 1hr drama) and *Falling Angels* (feature film). Has won over 50 national and international awards, including both Genie and Gemini awards.

Submissions Policy
Unsolicited synopses accepted only when accompanied by signed submission releases. More information available on the website.

MORAG PRODUCTIONS/PASSAGE FILMS

Box 52 St. John's Newfoundland A1C 5H5
T   709 739 0447
F   709 739 0467
E   info@morag.ca
W www.morag.ca

Film and television production company, specializing in documentary and drama, including the Gemini Award-winning mini-series *Random Passage*.

MUSE ENTERTAINMENT ENTERPRISES

3451 Rue St-Jacques Montreal Quebec
H4C 1H1
T   514 866 6873
F   514 876 3911
W www.muse.ca

Independent film and television producer established in 1998. Has produced or co-produced over 85 TV movies and mini-series, 9 television series and 17 feature films. Credits include *Jane Doe, Chasing Cain II: Face* and *Silent Night*.

MVP ENTERTAINMENT INC.

Suite 400-1450 Creekside Drive Vancouver
British Columbia V6J 5B3
T   604 731 9194
F   604 731 7174
E   info@mvpfilm.com
W www.mvpfilm.com

Produces for television and cinema. Titles include *The Wild Guys*.

NELVANA LIMITED

42 Pardee Avenue Toronto Ontario
M6K 1X8
T   416 535 0935
F   416 530 2832
W www.nelvana.com

Major producer of animated films and programmes for the family market.

NEOPHYTE PRODUCTIONS INC.

19 Parkwood Avenue Toronto Ontario
M4V 2W9
T   416 944 9892
F   416 944 9916
E   info@neophyteproductions.com
W www.neophyteproductions.com

Specializes in film and video production, including short and feature length films.

Its first film was *The Onion* by
Sheila Heti.

NETWORK ENTERTAINMENT INC.

Suite 400-1168 Hamilton Street Vancouver
British Columbia V6B 2S2
T   604 739 8825
F   604 739 8835
E   info@networkentertainment.ca
W www.networkentertainment.ca

Specialists in sports and entertainment
broadcasts, established in 1999. Works
across genres including documentary
and film.

NIGHTINGALE COMPANY

588 Richmond Street West Toronto Ontario
M5V 1Y9
T   416 628 1355
F   416 628 1505
E   info@dnightingale.com
W www.dnightingale.com

Film and television production company
founded in 2000, producing across genres
including features, documentaries and
children's series.

NORSTAR FILMED ENTERTAINMENT INC.

148 Yorkville Avenue 2nd Floor Toronto
Ontario M5R 1C2
T   416 961 6278
F   416 961 5608
W www.norstarfilms.com

Founded in 1997, producing and distributing
feature films for domestic and international
markets. Production credits include the
supernatural thriller *The Marsh*, *Almost
Heaven* and the Gemini Award-winning
television series, *The Eleventh Hour.*

Submissions Policy
Always interested in new projects and potential
co-productions.

OMNI FILM PRODUCTIONS LTD

204-111 Water Street Vancouver British
Columbia V6B 1A7
T   604 681 6543
F   604 688 1425
E   info@omnifilm.com
W www.omnifilm.com

Contacts
Michael Chechik *President*

One of Canada's largest independent
television producers, founded in 1979.
Exists as a television production,
post-production and distribution branch
alongside sister companies Water Street
Pictures, Water Street Releasing and
Omni Post. Programmes are screened
in 175 countries and translated into over
20 languages. Specializes in drama,
comedy, documentary, and factual and
lifestyle series. Recent titles include
Make Some Noise (CBC), *Dragon
Boys* (CBC), *Robson Arms* (CTV, The
Comedy Network) and *Greenpeace: Making
a Stand* (Global).

Submissions Policy
Unsolicited pitches accepted via short
emailed introduction. If interested, the
company will request a synopsis, outline,
treatment and script. Preference given to
established writers or projects with
broadcaster interest.

ORCA PRODUCTIONS

3425 West 2nd Avenue Vancouver British
Columbia V6R 1J3
T   604 732 9387
F   604 732 3587
W www.orcaproductions.com

Over twenty years experience of producing
award-winning feature films, television
dramas and documentaries for the international
market. Recent productions include *Would Be
Kings.*

ORIGINAL PICTURES INC.

602-191 Lombard Avenue Winnipeg
Manitoba R3M 0X1
T   204 940 3310
F   204 943 5502
E   jessicak@originalpicturesinc.com
W www.originalpicturesinc.com

Contacts
Jessica Krawec *Executive Assistant*

Established in 2000. Produces drama
projects for film and television. Past
examples include *Falcon Beach* and *A Bear
Named Winnie*. Claims 7 Geminis and 26
Gemini nominations to date. Focuses
mostly on international projects with
potential for an American sale and/or
substantial European sales or
funding.

Submissions Policy
Accepts synopses of new projects via
email.

PANACEA ENTERTAINMENT

2nd Floor 9876A 33 Avenue Edmonton
Alberta T6N 1C6
T   780 490 1220
F   780 490 5255
W www.panaceaentertainment.com

Produces for television and screen. Film
credits include *Best Served Cold* and
Generation X. TV credits include *A Total
Write-Off*, *Catching the Chameleon* and
Children & War.

Submissions Policy
Interested in seeing projects at an
advanced stage of development i.e. draft
screenplay or teleplay. Before sending
a script, approach by email providing a
short description of the project and a
couple of introductory lines about the
author. If interested in idea, the company
will ask for a hard copy of the script
and a completed and signed submission
form.

PEACE ARCH MOTION PICTURES INC.

124 Merton Street Suite 407 Toronto Ontario
M4S 2Z2
T   416 487 0377
F   416 487 6141
E   mail@peacearch.com
W www.gfte.com

Production company specializing in feature film
and television projects. Credits include *Absolon*,
Crime Spree and the *Nature Unleashed* series.

PEACE POINT ENTERTAINMENT GROUP

78 Berkeley Street Toronto Ontario
M5A 2W7
T   416 365 7734
F   416 365 7739
E   info@peacepoint.tv
W www.peacepoint.tv

Mid-sized television production company with
credits including *Ed's Up!*, *Barnstormers* and
Devil's Perch.

POINT GREY PICTURES INC.

#4–1214 West 7th Avenue Vancouver British
Columbia V6H 1B6
T   604 221 4426
F   604 742 9957
E   info@pointgreypictures.com
W www.pointgreypictures.com

Produces documentaries for television and
cinema release. Headed by Oscar-winning John
Zaritsky. Output includes *Radiation Roulette*,
College Days, College Nights, *No Kidding* and
Men Don't Cry.

PRINCIPIA PRODUCTIONS LTD

2531 Bellevue Avenue W. Vancouver British
Columbia V7V 1E3
T   604 834 8084
F   614 921 9134
E   princip@shaw.ca

Producers of dramas and documentaries for television and the cinema since 2000. Credits include the movie *A Simple Curve*.

PROSPERO PICTURES

1200 Bay Street Suite 400 Toronto Ontario M5R 2A5
T   416 926 0853
F   416 920 8373
E   martin.katz@prosperopictures.com
W   www.prosperopictures.com

A one-stop world-wide productions services and financing boutique. Offers financing of Canadian film and television productions and treaty co-productions.

PROTOCOL ENTERTAINMENT INC.

80 Spadina Avenue Suite 405 Toronto Ontario M5V 2J4
T   416 966 2711
F   416 599 6100
W   www.protocolent.com

Founded in 1993 to develop, finance, produce and market films, series and mini-series for the North American market. Production credits include *Train 48*, *The Saddle Club*, *Police Academy: The Series* and *Goosebumps*.

QUEEN STREET ENTERTAINMENT

1971 Queen Street East Main Floor Toronto Ontario M4L 1H9
T   416 691 6655
F   416 691 8419
W   www.queenstreetentertainment.com

Produces live action feature films and television productions for the whole family under the Knightscove Family Films banner. Titles include *Blizzard*, *Kart Racer* and *Virginia's Run*.

Submissions Policy
Before reviewing or considering any material, the person submitting must download the release form from the website and mail it together with a hard copy of script or other

written creative material, marked for the attention of 'The Great Canadian Movie'. Cannot review materials submitted by email or fax.

RAVEN WEST FILMS LTD

701-207 West Hastings Street Vancouver British Columbia V6B 1H7
T   604 681 7121
F   604 681 7173
E   info@ravenwestfilms.com
W   www.ravenwestfilms.com

Contacts
Carl Bessai *President/Producer/Director*

Drama and documentary filmmaking company founded in 1999. Past successes include *Johnny* (Jury Prize winner at 1999 Toronto International Film Festival), *Lola* (Berlin, Sundance and Toronto film festivals, 2001), *Emile* starring Ian McKellen (Toronto, 2003) and *Unnatural and Accidental* (Toronto, 2006).

Submissions Policy
Encourages new writing. Welcomes unsolicited material via email.

REEL GIRLS MEDIA INC.

2nd Floor 9860A 33 Avenue Edmonton Alberta T6N 1C6
T   780 488 0440
F   780 452 4980
E   info@reelgirlsmedia.com
W   www.reelgirlsmedia.com

Produces factual and non-factual programmes for television and new media. Examples of titles include *WildFiles.TV*, *Booked.TV* and *Stories from the Seventh Fire*.

REMSTAR PRODUCTIONS

85 St-Paul Street West Montreal Quebec H2Y 3V4
W   www.remstarcorp.com

Produces theatrical and television programming for domestic and international markets. Credits include *No Good Deed, Dangerous Liason, The Five of Us, An American Haunting* and *Ma Fille, Mon Ange.*

RHOMBUS MEDIA INC.

99 Spadina Avenue Suite 600 Toronto Ontario M5V 3P8
T   416 971 7856
F   416 971 9647
E   rhombus@rhombusmedia.com
W   www.rhombusmedia.com

Over twenty-five years experience of producing feature films, documentaries and performing arts programmes. Has won an Oscar for *The Red Violin* and was nominated for *Making Overtures*. Other credits include the *Yo-Yo Ma -Inspired By Bach* series, *The Firebird, Slings & Arrows* and *Childstar.*

RINK RAT PRODUCTIONS, INC.

683 Water Street 2nd Floor St. John's Newfoundland and Labrador A1E 1B5
T   709 739 9055
F   709 739 9065
E   msexton@nfld.com
W   www.rinkratproductions.com

Contacts
Mary Sexton *Producer*

Formed in 1993. Produces comedy, drama, arts and documentary projects for film and television. Previously gained a Gemini Award for *Tommy... A Family Portrait* and two nominations for *Ron Hynes: The Irish Tour*. Other past productions include *To Think Like A Composer* and reality show *Canadian Idol: Audition Tour* (Seasons 1–3). Also runs Dark Flowers Productions (drama and documentary) and 2M Innovative.

Submissions Policy
Accepts unsolicited mailed proposals. No email. Previous credentials are an asset.

S & S PRODUCTIONS INC.

Dufferin Liberty Centre 219 Dufferin Street Suite 100A Toronto Ontario M6K 3J1
T   416 260 0538
F   416 260 1628
W   www.ssp.ca

Television producer for Canadian and international audiences, in business since 1980. Flagship title is the comedy series, *The Red Green Show*. Other credits include *History Bites, An American in Canada*, the animated series *Sons of Butcher* and the feature film *Red Green's Duct Tape Forever.*

Submissions Policy
Send a one-page summary of show proposal or script, copy of the proposal or script, contact name, address, phone number and email address, and a signed and dated copy of a release form. A proposal that is not accompanied with this form will not be read.

SAVI MEDIA INC.

158 Roxton Road 3rd Floor Toronto Ontario M6J 2Y5
T   416 597 8484
F   416 597 9596
E   mail@savi-media.com
W   www.savi-media.com

Founded in 2000, developing and producing feature films and television programmes. Film credits include *Crusade, Flower and Garnet* and *Society Rules*. Television productions include *Baby Game, Chinatown Diaries, Little India* and *My Tango With Porn.*

Submissions Policy
Actively seeking to expand portfolio, especially in television series and television longform.

SCREEN DOOR

18 Gloucester Lane 3rd Floor Toronto Ontario M4Y 1L5
T   416 535 7402
F   416 535 1839
W   www.screendoor.org

Independent production company founded in 1999 and specializing in award-winning dramatic films and mini-series.

SERENDIPITY POINT FILMS

9 Price Street Toronto Ontario M4W 1Z1
T   416 960 0300
F   416 960 8656

Boutique motion picture production company formed in 1998. Examples of output include *Fugitive Pieces*, *Where the Truth Lies*, *Being Julia* and *Ararat*.

Submissions Policy
Cannot consider or accept and materials, ideas or proposals other than those specifically requested or commissioned by the company.

SHAFTESBURY FILMS

163 Queen Street East Suite 100 Toronto Ontario M5A 1S1
T   416 363 1411
F   416 363 1428
E   mailbox@shaftesbury.org
W   www.shaftesbury.org

Produces feature films and movies and series for television, aimed at prime time and children's audiences. Examples of output include the films *Camilla*, *Conquest* and *Painted Angels*, and the television productions *11 Cameras*, *The Jane Show* and *ReGenesis*.

SHAVICK ENTERTAINMENT

112 West 6th Avenue Vancouver British Columbia V5Y 1K6
T   604 874 4300
F   604 874 4305
E   info@shavickentertainment.com
W   www.shavickentertainment.com

Film and television production company. Examples of output include *Young Blades* and *Third Man Out*.

SHOES FULL OF FEET

12 Edmonton Road Toronto Ontario M2N 4J2
T   416 274 3555
F   416 977 8557
E   info@shoesfulloffeet.com
W   www.shoesfulloffeet.com

Contacts
Kris Booth *President*

Feature film production company founded in 1999. Focuses on narrative projects.

Submissions Policy
No unsolicited material.

SHOWDOG PRODUCTIONS

100 Cameron Street PO Box 788 Moncton New Brunswick E1C 8N6
T   506 857 0297
F   506 959 1319
E   bob@showdogproductions.com
W   www.showdogproductions.com

Contacts
Bob Sissons *President*

Animation company founded in 2002 specializing in children's entertainment programmes and educational DVDs. Most recently produced the 2D animated children's TV series *Rugg Buggs*.

Submissions Policy
Material accepted via email or post. All submissions reviewed and responses sent within four weeks.

SIENNA FILMS

260 Spadina Avenue Suite 504 Toronto Ontario M5T 2E4
T   416 703 1126
E   siennainfo@siennafilms.com
W   www.siennafilms.com

Independent film and television production company.

Submissions Policy
Not currently accepting unsolicited material.

SOAPBOX PRODUCTIONS INC.

106-1258 Lynn Valley Road North Vancouver
British Columbia V7J 2A3
T   604 983 2555
F   604 983 2558
E   info@soapboxproductions.ca
W   www.soapboxproductions.ca

Formed in 1990, output includes drama,
comedy, documentary, music, children's and
reality series. Credits include *Northwood,
Cosmic Highway, Double Exposure, O.Com:
Cybersex Addiction* and *Shakin' All Over.*

SPIRE ENTERTAINMENT INC.

25 Isabella Street Toronto Ontario M4Y 1M7
T   416 964 3247
F   416 964 0964
E   info@spirefilms.com
W   www.spirefilms.com

Contacts
Jasbir "Jazz" Mann *President and CEO,
Executive Producer*

Film and television production company
established in 2003. Interested mainly in
drama, comedy, short film, feature film and
sitcom projects. Recent titles include *Code*
and *Sohni Sapna.*

Submissions Policy
Welcomes unsolicited material via email and
post. Any stage from treatment to script
acceptable.

STRADA FILMS INC.

9 Price Street Toronto Ontario M4W 1Z1
T   416 967 7090
F   416 960 0871
E   info@stradafilms.ca
W   www.stradafilms.ca

Feature film production company.

SUDDEN STORM PRODUCTIONS INC.

1 Deer Park Crescent Suite 703 Toronto
Ontario M4V 3C4
T   416 927 9342
E   question@suddenstorm.ca
W   www.suddenstorm.ca

Formed in 2001, a feature film and television
production, service and finance company.
Has provided financial and consulting services
to projects such as the television series *The
Newsroom* and *Whistler.* Continues to develop
features and movies-of-the-week in addition to
its other services.

SULLIVAN ENTERTAINMENT INC.

110 Davenport Road Toronto Ontario
M5R 3R3
T   416 921 7177
F   416 921 7538
E   inquire@sullivan-ent.com
W   www.sullivan-ent.com

Over 20 years experience as a developer,
producer and distributor of series, mini-series
and movies for television and international
release. Examples of output include *Anne
of Green Gables, Road to Avonlea* and
Butterbox Babies.

SUMMER PICTURES INC.

604 Edward Avenue Suite 2 Richmond Hill
Ontario L4C 9Y7
T   905 883 5561
F   905 787 1240
E   summer@summerpictures.biz
W   www.summerpictures.biz

Specializes in feature filmmaking. Also offers
in-house post-production.

TEMPLE STREET PRODUCTIONS

119 Spadina Avenue Suite 705 Toronto
Ontario M5V 2L1
T   416 591 0065
F   416 591 0075

E   info@templestreetproductions.com
W   www.templestreetproductions.com

Film and television production company with
credits including *Queer as Folk V*, *Darcy's Wild
Life II* and *Blueprint for Disaster II*.

TRICON FILMS & TELEVISION

372 Richmond Street West Suite 200   Toronto
Ontario M5V 1X6
T   416 341 9926
F   416 341 0173
E   info@triconfilms.com
W   www.triconfilms.com

Founded in 2000, developing and producing
television prgrammes for international markets.
Specializing in lifestyle and feature length
documentaries.

TRIPTYCH MEDIA INC.

788 King Street West Toronto Ontario
M5V 1N6
T   416 703 8866
F   416 703 8867
E   info@triptychmedia.ca
W   www.triptychmedia.ca

Produces film and television dramas.
Particularly know for adaptations of literary
works by Canadian writers including Carol
Shields, Barbara Gowdy, David Adams
Richards, Matt Cohen and Michel Marc
Bouchard. Examples of output include *The
Republic of Love*, *Falling Angels*, *The Hanging
Garden*, *Lucky Girl* and *The Bookfair
Murders*.

Submissions Policy
Email a one page synopsis and cover letter
detailing project history, plus relevant
attachments and details of key personnel.

TRUE WEST FILMS

2050 Scotia Street Suite 201 Vancouver British
Columbia V5T 4T1
W   www.truewestfilms.com

Contacts
Elizabeth Yake *President/Producer*

Film production company founded in
April 2002 specializing in drama, comedy
and POV documentary. Past work includes
It's All Gone Peter Tong and *Everything's
Gone Green*.

Submissions Policy
Unsolicited material accepted in one-page
pitch format. Scripts not read unless
requested.

UNIVERSAL STUDIOS CANADA INC.

4-2450 Victoria Park Avenue Willowdale
Ontario M2J 4A2
T   416 491 3000
F   416 491 2857
W   www.universalstudioscanada.com

Canadian arm of one of the world's great
film producing and distributing companies.

Submissions Policy
Policy not to accept or consider creative
materials, ideas, or suggestions other than
those specifically requested. Do not send
any original creative materials such as
screenplays, stories, original artwork, etc.
Anything sent may be used by Universal
or its affiliates for any purpose, including,
but not limited to, reproduction, disclosure,
transmission, publication, broadcast and
posting.

WHITE IRON PICTURES INC.

533 1201-5th Street SW Calgary Alberta
T2R 0Y6
T   403 298 4700
F   403 233 0528
E   info@whiteiron.tv
W   www.whiteiron.tv

Established in 1990, working with many North
American networks as well as independent
filmmakers. Works across genres, media and
disciplines. Produces television programming
and documentaries.

WIZZ FILMS INC.

418 Sherbrook Street East Suite 300 Montréal
Québec H2L 1J6
T   514 932 4191
F   514 932 7277
E   info@wizzfilms.com
W   www.wizzfilms.com

Contacts
Danny Bergeron

Feature film production company focused on
family animation and live action projects.
Founded in 2002.

Submissions Policy
Welcomes new scripts and co-production
projects via email.

XGENSTUDIOS INC.

#385 11215 Jasper Avenue Edmonton
Alberta T5K 0L5
T   888 808 XGEN
E   Games@XGenStudios.com
W   www.XGenStudios.com

Contacts
Dan Greig *PR Director*

Founded in 2003, games production company
specializing in free web browser games.

Submissions Policy
Welcomes unsolicited submissions. New writing
ideas should include mock screen shots and an
indication of how the game will work on a
technical level.

ZIJI FILM & TELEVISION PRODUCTIONS LTD

The Roy Building Suite 422 1657 Barrington
Street Halifax Nova Scotia B3J 2A1
T   902 425 5001
F   902 429 0077
E   info@ziji.ca
W   www.ziji.ca

Producers of award-winning documentaries,
feature films and television programmes. Titles
include *Words of My Perfect Teacher, Warrior
Songs* and *Regarding: Cohen.*

IRELAND

2000 AD PRODUCTIONS

Ardmore Studios Herbert Road Bray
County Wicklow
T   087 2979 131
F   01 276 9546
E   Adrian@2000adproductions.com
W   www.2000adproductions.com

Contacts
Adrian Devane *Producer*

Established in 2000 by freelance producer
Adrian Devane. Currently working on several
features with Irish writers.

Submissions Policy
Welcomes unsolicited manuscripts. Prefers to be
approached with a synopsis, then treatment,
then script.

ABÚ MEDIA

Teach Indreabháin Inverin County Galway
T   091 505100
F   091 505135
E   info@abumedia.com
W   www.abumedia.com

Established in 2000, an award-winning
television and film production company
producing a range of media content, including
drama, documentary and light entertainment
for English and Irish speaking markets. Also
specializes in co-productions and co-financing
international projects. Production credits
include the TV dramas *Teenage Cics* and *Cut
& Dry*, the documentary series *Coiscéim* and
the short film, *Lasair.*

ACCOMPLICE TELEVISION

The Barracks 76 Irishtown Road Dublin 4
T   01 660 3235
F   01 660 3238

E submit@accomplice-tv.com
W www.accomplice-tv.com

Founded in 2001, producing drama, documentary and comedy for TV. Production credits include *Dan & Becs* and *Bachelors Walk 3*.

ADARE PRODUCTIONS

Adare House 35A Patrick Street Dun Laoghaire County Dublin
T 01 284 3877
F 01 284 1814
E adare@eircom.net

Contacts
Brian Graham *Managing Director*

Adare Productions has been producing high-end television programmes since 1993. Specializing in the creation of entertainment formats, the company has it's own in-house studio directors and on-line editors as well as a creative team of producers and researchers.

Submissions Policy
Does not accept unsolicited manuscripts.

ANIMO TELEVISION

4 Windmill Lane Dublin 2
T 01 671 3004
F 01 679 7046
E info@animo.ie
W www.animo.ie

Specialists in factual television for the Irish market. Previous programmes include *Outside In* and *Do They Take Sugar?*, documentaries about people with disabilities.

ATHENA MEDIA

Digital Depot Digital Hub Thomas Street Dublin 8
T 01 4885850
E info@athenamedia.ie
W www.athenamedia.ie/www.podcastingireland.ie

Contacts
Helen Shaw *Managing Director*

Formed in 2003. Specializes in television, primarily factual documentaries but other genres including comedy and sport. Recent titles include *Headbanging to Beethoven, Last Chance Catholics* and *The Smallest Bundles* (Doc Shorts).

BARLEY FILMS

2 Rogan's Court Patrick Street Dun Laoghaire Dublin
T 01 289 9224
E info@barleyfilms.com
W www.barleyfilms.com

Founded in 2002, producing animated films. Output includes *Boys Night Out* and *Agricultural Report*, both nominated for awards by the International Animated Film Society. Its first feature length project, *Little Caribou*, is in production.

BOOTSTRAP FILMS LIMITED

Grange House 60 Beaumont Avenue Churchtown Dublin 14
T 01 298 7466
F 01 298 7472
E info@bootstrapfilms.com
W www.bootstrapfilms.com

Established in 2004 as an independent production company. Run by John Phelan who has raised over €30 million for international projects shooting in Ireland. Raises funds via the tax incentive scheme for filming in Ireland and through other international sources.

BOULDER MEDIA

Dartmouth House 1 Grand Parade Dublin 6
T 01 498 0030
E pete@bouldermedia.tv
W www.bouldermedia.tv

Major animation studio established in 2000. Produces work for clients including Cartoon

Network, Disney and Nickelodeon. Also produces its own projects, as well as short films.

BROWN BAG FILMS

65 Great Strand Street Dublin 1
T   01 872 1608
F   01 872 3834
E   gerald@brownbagfilms.com
W   www.brownbagfilms.com

Contacts
Cathal Gaffney *Producer*

Established in 1994, producing primarily pre-school animation (such as *Wobbly Land*) and television commercials. Received an Academy Award nomination in 2002.

Submissions Policy
Does not accept unsolicited manuscripts but interested in developing relationships with experienced children's writers for television.

CABOOM

10 Stephens Green Dublin 2
T   01 672 7077
F   01 672 7043
E   info@caboom.ie
W   www.caboom.ie

Contacts
Damian Farrell *Creative Director*

Produces entertainment, documentary, short film, commercials and animation programmes.

Submissions Policy
Welcomes outlines or treatments only.

CAMPBELL RYAN PRODUCTIONS LTD

8 Herbert Road Ballsbridge Dublin 4
T   01 660 8801
F   01 443 0639
E   info@campbellryanproductions.com
W   www.campbellryanproductions.com

Contacts
Triona Campbell *Manager/Director*

Established in 2000, its debut feature film, *The Crooked Mile*, won the Tribeca First Look award. Specializes in television and film dramas.

Submissions Policy
Welcomes unsolicited manuscripts and prefers to be emailed with a synopsis.

THE CARTOON SALOON

The Maltings Tilbury Place James Street
Kilkenny
T   056 7764481
E   info@cartoonsaloon.ie
W   www.cartoonsaloon.ie

An animation company producing for TV and the cinema. Output includes *Brendan & the Secret of Kells*.

CLADDAGH FILMS

Somerset Studios Aughinish (Kinvara PO)
County Clare
T   065 7078454
F   065 7078242
W   www.claddagh.ie

A small, independent film and television production company based in Galway. Previous films include *An Autumn Affair, Packy's Cousin, A Place in my Heart, A Talk in the Dark, The Lift* and *The Biscuit Eaters*.

COCO TELEVISION

49-50 Berystede Leeson Park Dublin 6
T   01 4970817
F   01 4970796
E   info@cocotelevision.ie
W   www.cocotelevision.ie

Formed in 1986, a leading cross-genre television production company serving domestic and international markets. Specialists in lifestyle, reality, documentary and event TV. Examples of output include *Treasure Island, Cabin Fever, CrimeCall, Desperate Houses, The Great Escape, House Hunters, A Gap in the*

Mountain, Any Given Sunday and *Made in America*.

CRANNOG FILMS

33 Clarendon Street Dublin 2
T   01 707 1612
F   01 707 1614
E   crannogfilms@indigo.ie

Contacts
Conor Harrington *Director*

Produces for both TV and film, as well as for the computer games market with a co-venture partner.

Submissions Policy
Approach through an agent or via referral.

DIGITAL ANIMATION MEDIA LIMITED

Digital Depot Roe Lane Thomas Street Dublin 8
T   01 489 3644
E   info@digitalanimationmedia.com
W   www.digitalanimationmedia.com

Produces animated films and series for TV, and is involved in computer game development. TerraGlyph is the wing that develops, produces and finances animated features films, television series and other niche market animation titles. Its output includes 26 episodes of *The Island of Inis Cool*, *The Wilde Stories* trilogy and the movies, *Duck Ugly*, *Help I'm a Fish* and *Carnivale*.

EARTH HORIZON PRODUCTIONS

Ħ

13 Windsor Place Dublin 2
T   01 661 7475
F   01 662 0337
E   info@earthhorizon.ie
W   www.rte.ie

Contacts
Marcus Stewart *Production Manager*

Has produced documentaries such as *Eco Eye*, *About the House* and *Return to Chernobyl*.

Submissions Policy
Does not accept unsolicited material.

ELEMENT PICTURES LTD

21 Mespil Road Dublin 4
T   01 618 5032
F   01 664 3737
E   mail@elementpictures.ie
W   www.elementpictures.ie

Contacts
Hilary Barrett *Office Manager*

Leading producers of film and television drama. UK office recently opened. Production credits include *Garage*, *Death of a President*, *The Wind that Shakes the Barley*, *The League of Gentlemen's Apocalypse*, *Omagh* and *The Magdalene Sisters*.

Submissions Policy
Does not welcome unsolicited approaches. Approaches should be through an agent. Interested in investigating writers who have had at least one production on radio, film or theatre, or a novel published

EO TEILIFÍS

An Chuasnóg Baile Ard Spiddal County Galway
T   091 558400
F   091 558470
E   laura@eoteilifis.ie
W   www.eoteilifis.ie

Contacts
Laura Ni Cheallaigh

Television production company and facilities provider established in the 1990s. Specializes in drama, factual programming and children's programming. Production credits include the long-running *Ros na Rún* for TG4, the fantasy drama *Géibheann*, the documentaries *The Rescuers* and *Dúiche* and the children's productions *Míre Mara* and *Mise agus Pangúr Bán*.

ESPERANZA PRODUCTIONS

44 Carysfort Avenue Blackrock County Dublin
T 01 288 8648
F 01 288 8649
E info@esperanza.ie
W www.esperanza.ie

Producers of television and film documentaries, as well as interactive media. Focus on human rights issues. Productions include *When Happiness is a Place for Your Child*, *We Still Want You But...*, *Dropping the Number 10 for Dili* and *Invisible Movement*.

FANTASTIC FILMS

3 Clare Street Dublin 2
T 087 255 1666
E info@fantasticfilms.ie
W www.fantasticfilms.ie

Formed in 2000 by John McDonnell to produce and develop movies and television drama. Prides itself on high production values and works with emerging and established writers and directors. Timbuktu was chosen to open the Dublin International Film Festival in 2004. Other productions include *The Making of a Prodigy*, *Burn the Bed*, *Six Shooter* and *Invisible State*.

FASTNET FILMS

1st Floor 75-76 Camden Street Lwr Dublin 2
T 01 4789566
F 01 4789567
E admin@fastnetfilms.com
W www.fastnetfilms.com

Film and television production company, working in feature films, television drama series and documentaries. Since 2000, Fastnet has produced over 160 hours of Irish network programming. Also active in international co-productions. Film credits include *An Teanga Runda*, *The Wonderful Story of Kelvin Kind*, *The Halo Effect* and *Eat The Peach*. Television

works include *September*, *Lord Haw Haw* and *Bang You're Dead*.

FEENISH PRODUCTIONS

26 South Frederick Street Dublin 2
T 01 671 1166
E info@feenish.com
W www.feenish.com

A film and media production company founded in 2001. Has produced a wide-ranging body of film work, with commissions and funding from TG4, RTE, BCI, the Arts Council, the Irish Film Board and a variety of independent clients. Has worked on documentary films, animations, promotional, corporate and educational films.

Submissions Policy
Film-makers with an idea for a project are encouraged to make contact. All correspondence handled in the strictest of confidence.

FERNDALE FILMS

Ardmore Studios Bray County Wicklow
T 01 276 9350
F 01 276 9557
E info@ferndalefilms.com
W www.ferndalefilms.com

Founded in 1987 by Noel Pearson as a film and theatre production company. Feature film credits include the Osacr-winning *My Left Foot*, *Tara Road*, *The Field*, *Dancing at Lughnasa* and *Frankie Starlight*. Has also produced documentaries including *Bram Stoker's Dracula* and *Brian Friel*.

FRONTIER FILMS

2 Northbrook Road Ranelagh Dublin 6
T 01 4977077
F 01 4977731
E info@frontierfilms.ie
W www.frontierfilms.ie

An independent television production company, set up in 1986. Works across a range of genres including music programming, factual series and documentaries, including *Big Boys Don't Cry* and *Remember Me*.

GALLOWGLASS PICTURES

5 Upper Baggot Street Dublin 4
T   01 6677050
F   01 6677051
E   eamon@gallowglasspictures.ie
W   www.gallowglasspictures.ie

International television company established in 1998 by Eamon McElwee and Tom Clinch. Makes international documentaries, series and corporate videos. Also experienced in multimedia. Output includes *From Clare to Here, Dublin City Life, Solo in South-East Asia* and *Wolves*.

GLOWWORM MEDIA

Cornmarket Square Limerick
T   061 446044
E   kieran@glowworm.ie
W   www.glowworm.ie

Produces factual programming and documentaries. Aims to treat subjects in a fair and sympathetic way, presenting their stories objectively and truthfully.

GRAND PICTURES LTD

44 Fontenoy Street Dublin 7
T   01 8602290
F   01 8602096
E   info@grandpictures.ie
W   www.grandpictures.ie

Established in 2000 by the producers Michael Garland and Paul Donovan. Recipients of multiple project development funding from the Irish Film Board and media slate funding. Currently developing a mixture of projects with emerging and experienced talent. Production credits include *Puffball, Val Falvey TD, Dead*

Long Enough, Spin The Bottle, Fergus' Wedding and *Paths To Freedom*.

Submissions Policy
Does not accept unsolicited scripts but happy to view brief (one page) synopsis of an idea.

GREAT WESTERN FILMS

28 Gardiner Place Dublin 1
T   01 889 8040
F   01 872 8280
E   info@greatwesternfilms.com
W   www.greatwesternfilms.com

Contacts
Eoin Holmes *Managing Director*

Founded in 2001, Great Western has produced shows such as *Trouble in Paradise, The Last Furlong* and *Camera Cafe*.

Submissions Policy
Willing to accept unsolicited manuscripts but prefers to be contacted with an initial email.

HAWKEYE FILMS

Killina Gort County Galway
T   091 638219
F   091 638048
E   info@hawkeyefilms.com
W   www.hawkeyefilms.com

Contacts
Donal R. Haughey *Managing Director*

Founded in 1994, a small film production company focusing on documentaries, especially social history and the arts. Credits include *Into The Valley, An Taibhdhearc, Deireadh le hAiocht, SLOTS, Bothar na Tra* and *Children Of Allah*.

HELL'S KITCHEN INTERNATIONAL LTD

21 Mespil Road Dublin 4
T   01 679 5065
F   01 664 3737
E   info@hellskitcheninternational.com
W   www.hellskitcheninternational.com

Since 2003 has acted as a co-producer, principally on US films shooting in Ireland. Previous films include *Laws of Attraction* and *The Honeymooners*.

ICEBOX FILMS

56 Temple Road Blackrock County Dublin
T 01 210 8501
F 01 210 8528
E info@iceboxfilms.ie
W www.iceboxfilms.ie

TV and film company, established in 2000 by Clíona Ní Bhuachalla and Charlie McCarthy. Dedicated to creating quality contemporary productions. Credits include the television drama *Legend*.

ILLUSION ANIMATED PRODUCTIONS

The Studio 46 Quinn's Road Shankill County Dublin
T 01 282 1458
F 01 282 1458
E info@illusionanimation.com
W www.illusionanimation.com

Formally established in 1999, specializing in the development and creation of pre-production packages for animated TV series, including scripting and storyboarding. Always interested in talking with potential co-production partners for future projects.

JAM MEDIA

40 Kevin Street Lower Dublin 8
T 01 4053484
F 01 4789376
E info@jammedia.ie
W www.jammedia.ie

Involved in the creation of entertainment brands across genres and platforms. Has been involved in creating animated shorts and TV series. Credits include the children's series, *Picme* and the short film, *Boiled Eggs + Beer*.

KAVALEER PRODUCTIONS LTD

The Digital Depot Roe Lane Dublin 8
T 01 488 5873
F 01 488 5801
E info@kavaleer.com
W www.kavaleer.com

Contacts
Andrew Kavanagh CEO

Founded in 2001, specializing in original children's animation. Has produced programmes such as *Garth* and *Dad the Impaler*.

Submissions Policy
Does not accept unsolicited manuscripts. Will look at letters of application briefly outlining past experience and suitability.

KITE ENTERTAINMENT LTD

4 Windmill Lane Dublin 2
T 01 617 4744
E info@kiteentertainment.com
W www.kiteentertainment.com

A television production company with a talent management wing. Specializes in comedy, with credits including *Just for Laughs* and *Anonymous*.

LIKE IT LOVE IT PRODUCTIONS

3/5 Carysfort Avenue Blackrock County Dublin
T 01 283 44 90
F 01 283 64 20
E andy.ruane@likeitloveit.com
W www.likeitloveit.com

Contacts
Andy Ruane *Managing Director*

Independent production company, whose own-format programmes are shown in over twenty countries. Creates programming for Irish and international markets. Credits include *The Lyrics Board*, *Perfect Match* and *Pop TV*.

LITTLE BIRD

13 Merrion Square Dublin 2
T   01 613 1710
F   01 662 4647
E   info@littlebird.ie
W   www.littlebird.ie

Independent film and television production company established in 1982. Has additional offices in London and Johannesburg. Credits include *December Bride*, *Into The West*, *A Man of No Importance*, *Croupier*, *Bridget Jones's Diary*, *Trauma* and *Marie and Bruce*.

LKF PRODUCTIONS

Production Office 89 Cherry Garth Rivervalley Swords County Dublin
T   01 8400 561
F   01 8400 561
E   info@lkf.ie
W   www.lkf.ie

Founded in 2005 by experienced producer, Liz Kenny. Aims to develop projects and emerging talent from Ireland and to work with European co-producers to make high-quality low-budget documentaries and feature films for the international market. Credits include the feature *WC* and the documentaries *Unspoken Children* and *In Living Hell*.

LOOPHEAD STUDIO

Cross Carrigaholt County Clare
T   065 905 8309
E   loopheadstudio@eircom.net
W   www.loopheadstudio.com

Contacts
Naomi Wilson

Founded in 2000, specializing in the production of animated films. Credits include *Among Strangers*, *Twilight* and *Reby Fox*. Won the award for best animation at the 2006 Aubagne International Film Festival.

Submissions Policy
Does not accept unsolicited manuscripts.

LOOPLINE FILM

9 Lad Lane Dublin 2
T   01 6676498
F   01 6676604
E   info@loopline.com
W   www.loopline.com

Contacts
Sé Merry Doyle *Managing Director*

Founded in 1992, specializing in high-quality documentaries for domestic and international markets. Also has a training wing, in association with Screen Training Ireland, which runs a residential course in 'Creative Documentary for Directors'. Examples of output include *Hidden Treasures*, *James Gandon - A Life*, *Essie's Last Stand* and *Ahead Of The Class*.

LUNAH PRODUCTIONS

Old Fintra Road Killybegs County Donegal
074 9731379
E   info@lunah-productions.com
W   www.lunah-productions.com

Established by the Hannigan family as a creative vehicle by which to focus their extensive experience of working in the media. Works on features, documentaries and corporate productions. Director Declan Hannigan has created work for the International Space Station.

MAGMA FILMS

16 Merchants Road Galway
T   091 569142
F   091 569148
E   info@magmaworld.com
W   www.magmaworld.com

Independent production company, with subsidiaries in Munich and Hamburg. Specializes in animated features, series and high-concept programmes. Also works on live action productions, including films, children's drama, event television and light entertainment. Animation credits include *Norman Normal*, *Pigs Next Door* and *The World of Tosh*. Among its live action credits are *Arte*, *Bus Driver*, *10 Years After* and *The Falcon Thieves*.

MCCAMLEY ENTERTAINMENT

103 The Woodlands Ratoath County Meath
T 01 825 7841
F 01 825 7841
E dmccamley@eircom.net
W www.davidmccamley.com

Contacts
David McCamley *Director/Producer/Writer*

Founded in 2000, McCamley Entertainment has produced the animated television series *The Island of Inis Cool*, which was nominated for an award at the Cartoons on the Bay international festival in 2005.

Submissions Policy
Does not accept unsolicited materials.

MEDIA PLATFORM

6 Clare Street Dublin 2
T 01 449 8167
E info@mediaplatform.ie

Contacts
Al Butler *Managing Director*

Founded in 2005, producing for cinema and television.

MEEM PRODUCTIONS

17a Greenmount Lawns Terenure Dublin 6
T 01 492 8156
E szaidi@oceanfree.net
W www.BollywoodIreland.com

Contacts
Siraj Zaidi *Producer*

Founded in 1989, Meem has produced two TV series and made nine film scripts acquisitions and developments. It has also set up an Indian Film distribution network. Particular focus on drama, documentaries and reality TV.

Submissions Policy
Does not accept unsolicited manuscripts. Approaches should be via a solicitor or agent.

MIDAS PRODUCTIONS

34 Lower Baggot Street Dublin 2
T 01 661 1384
F 01 676 8250
E mike@midasproductions.ie
W www.midasproductions.ie

Foundeded in 1986, producing for television and corporates. The TV division specializes in English- and Irish-language documentaries, light entertainment and format-driven programming for both the English and Irish speaking markets. Output includes *Close Encounters with Keith Barry* and *The Liffey Laugh*.

MIND THE GAP FILMS

Wilton Place Dublin 2
T 01 662 4742
F 01 662 4758
E info@mindthegapfilms.com
W www.mindthegapfilms.com

Independent TV production company set up by Bill Hughes and Bernadine Carraher in 2001. Specializes in documentaries, entertainment, arts and music programmes. Recent credits include *Happy Birthday Oscar Wilde*, *Last One Standing* and *The Songs of Mama Cass*.

MINT

205 Lower Rathmines Road Dublin 6
T 01 491 3333
F 01 491 3334
E info@mint.ie
W www.mint.ie

Documentary production company, specializing in historical and observational films. Output includes *Junior Doctors*, *Haughey*, *Our Lady's* and *Who Kidnapped Shergar*. Also has an office in Belfast (13 Fitzwilliam Street, Belfast, BT9 6AW; 028 9024 0555).

MOONDANCE PRODUCTIONS

3 Reilly's Terrace Cork Sreet Dublin 8
T   01 473 4599
F   01 473 4598
E   info@moondance.tv
W   www.moondance.tv

Established in 1994. Offers a complete service from concept to finished product for a range of corporate and broadcast clients. Production credits include *Sculpting Life*, featuring the artist Rowan Gillespie.

NEMETON TELEVISION PRODUCTIONS

An Rinn Dungarvan County Waterford
T   058 46499
F   058 46208
E   eolas@nemeton.ie
W   www.nemeton.ie

Contacts
Rupert Hall *Head of Development*

Founded in 1993. Specializes in factual documentary (singles and series), dramatized documentaries, Irish language programmes, sports coverage and corporate work. Credits include *Laochra Gael*, *Health Squad* and *Micheál O'Hehir*. Twice nominated for IFTAs for *The Brothers* (2006). Particularly interested in co-productions with the UK, Canada and Australia. Nemeton also runs a course in production for Irish speakers with the Waterford Institute of Technology and has an active area of development for Irish language programmes with TG4.

Submissions Policy
Principally develops ideas in-house. Ideas are welcome but contact via email in first instance or via an agent/professional representative before sending full proposal. Unsolicited

material will not be read, copied or stored in any way.

NEW DECADE FILM & TELEVISION

'Ullord' Brickfield Lane Killarney Road Bray County Wicklow
T   01 2765071
E   info@newdecade.ie
W   www.newdecade.ie

Over ten years' experience in film, TV and corporate production. Production credits include *Capital Letters*, *Maybe if You*, *Tales from the Big House* and *So, This is Dyoublong?*

NEWGRANGE PICTURES

49-50 Berystede Leeson Park Dublin 6
T   01 498 8028
F   01 496 6128
E   info@newgrangepictures.com
W   www.newgrangepictures.com

Contacts
Jackie Larkin *Producer*

Founded in 2005, Newgrange has produced films such as *Two Wrongs*, *Kings* and *The Year of the Dog*.

Submissions Policy
Does not accept unsolicited manuscripts or ideas.

ONE PRODUCTIONS

3 Clare Street Dublin 2
T   01 678 4077
F   01 678 4070
E   contact@oneproductions.com
W   www.oneproductions.com

Contacts
Tom Hopkins *Director*

Established in 2000, producing films including *Money, Fear & Justice* and *Close*, which were finalists at the Venice Film Festival. *Close* also received the DMA award for best Irish short in 2006.

Submissions Policy
Welcomes unsolicited manuscripts and prefers to be contacted via email.

PARADOX PICTURES

26 South Frederick Street Dublin 2
T   01 670 6883
F   01 670 6889
E   paradoxp@iol.ie

Founded in 1993, producing theatrical films, documentaries, shorts and animated films. Titles include *How Harry Became A Tree*, *Estella* (a documentary about the painter Estella Solomons), *Northern Lights* and *Pete's Meteor*.

PROMEDIA TV

10 Herbert Place Dublin 2
T   01 662 2500
F   01 662 2531
E   siobhan@promediatv.ie

Contacts
Siobhan O'Brien *Line Producer*

Established in 1985, producing films, documentaries and lifestyle programmes. Output includes the film *Joe my Friend*, lifestyle series *Christmas Cracked* and the documentary *Rainbows in their Lives*. Received the Crystal Bear award, Gold Camera award, New Year Film Festival gold medal and the Jacobs television award.

Submissions Policy
Will accept unsolicited material but contacted via phone or email in first instance.

RED PEPPER PRODUCTIONS

Shamrock Chambers 1-2 Eustace Street Dublin 2
T   01 670 7277
F   01 670 7278

E   office@redpepper.ie
W   www.redpepper.ie

Formed in 1990, producing commercials, corporates and TV programmes. TV credits include *Only fools buy horses*, *The Millionaire*, *The Builders & the Shantytown* and *Hollywood Trials*.

ROSG

An Spidéal Co. na Gaillimhe
T   091 553951
F   091 558491
E   eolas@rosg.ie
W   www.rosg.ie

A film and television production company established in 1998 by Ciarán Ó Cofaigh and Darach Ó Scolaí. Examples of output include *Cosa Nite*, *An Leabhar* and *Fíor Scéal*.

RTÉ INDEPENDENT PRODUCTIONS

Stage 7 RTÉ Donnybrook Dublin 4
T   01 208 2743
E   www.rte.ie

RTÉ is Ireland's public service broadcaster. Commissions hundreds of hours of independently-produced programmes each year. Submitting instructions available at www.rte.ie/commissioning/guidelines.html.

SAMSON FILMS

The Barracks 76 Irishtown Road Dublin 4
T   01 667 0533
F   01 667 0537
E   info@samsonfilms.com
W   www.samsonfilms.com

Contacts
David Collins *Managing Director*

Founded in 1984, specializing in feature length drama. Produced *Once*, which was written/directed by John Carney (winner of World World Cinema Audience Award,

Sundance 2007). Also produced *True North*, written/directed by Steve Hudson.

Submissions Policy
Always interested in new writing and welcomes unsolicited manuscripts, sent via the website. Over the past few years they have nurtured new writers, assisting with shorts and developing and producing first features.

SCANNAIN LUGH

Pier Head   Tory Island   County Donegal
T   074 910 0905
F   074 910 0905
E   info@lughfilm.com
W   www.lughfilm.com

Contacts
Loic Jourdain   *Producer and Director*

Founded in 2004, producing films and documentaries. Output includes *Fear na nOileán*.

Submissions Policy
Materials should be submitted via email.

SCREENTIME SHINAWIL

E   info@shinawil.ie
W   www.shinawil.ie

Independent production company, established in 1999 and specializing in entertainment, factual entertainment and live event programming.

Submissions Policy
Guarantees to read all proposals but does not commit to respond within a set time frame. Send sae if submission is to be returned. Each project submitted is subject to the Screentime ShinAwiL development policy process.

SHADOWHAWK FILMS

26 Cromlech Court   Dane Road   Poppintree
Dublin 11
T   01 862 7978
F   01 862 7978

E   shadow@shadowhawkfilms.com
W   www.shadowhawkfilms.com

Contacts
Cathal Byrne   *Chief Executive Officer*

A film and television production company founded in 1996. Recent productions include the films *Love's Delusion* and *Rules of the Game*, and the television shows *Sleep on It* and *Move over Mom*.

Submissions Policy
Unsolicited materials should be directed to the acquisitions department via email: operations@shadowhawkfilms.com.

SHORTT COMEDY THEATRE/WAREHOUSE TV

Unit D1A   Eastway Business Park   Ballysimon Road   Limerick
T   06 142 3934
F   06 142 3928
E   caroline@patshortt.com
W   www.patshortt.com

Contacts
Caroline O'Neill   *Administrator*

Founded in 2002, Short Comedy has produced television comedy series such as *Killinaskully* (series 1, 2 and 3).

Submissions Policy
Does not accept unsolicited materials.

SOL PRODUCTIONS LTD

Quarantine Hill   Wicklow Town
County Wicklow
T   0404 68645
F   0404 67153
E   sol@eircom.net

Contacts
Veronica O'Reilly   *Marketing Director*

Established in 1985, producing shorts, documentaries and dramas. Output includes *A Spiritual Journey.*

Submissions Policy
Does not accept unsolicited manuscripts.

SP FILMS

Unit F5 Riverview Business Park Nangor Road
Dublin 12
T 01 460 4760
F 01 460 4770
E spfilms@eircom.net

Production company of feature films and short movies. Previous titles include *The Ten Steps*, *The Honourable Scaffolder*, *Innocence* and *The Church of Acceptance*.

SPEERS FILM

24 Fitzwilliam Street Upper Dublin 2
T 01 6621130
E jonny@speers.ie
W www.speers.ie

Contacts
Jonny Speers

Produces commercials and features and offers range of production services. Credits include the film *Adam & Paul*.

STONEY ROAD FILMS

T 01 677 6681
E info@stoneyroadfilms.com
W www.stoneyroadfilms.com

Produces drama and documentary for the cinema and TV. Also has a distribution arm. Credits include *Wordweaver - The Legend of Benedict Kiely*, *Convention* and the horror series, *Shiver*.

TELEGAEL MEDIA GROUP

Telegael Spiddal County Galway
T 091 553460
F 091 553464
E info@telegael.com
W www.telegael.com

Specialists in animated productions but also develops live action, factual and entertainment programmes.

TG4

Baile na hAbhann Co. na Gaillimhe
T 091 505050
F 091 505021
E eolas@tg4.ie
W www.tg4.ie

Established in 1996. Has a 3.5% share of the national television market. Core service is its Irish language programme.

Submissions Policy
Welcomes submissions in the areas of documentaries, traditional music and song, comedy, drama, docu-soaps, lifestyle, travel and the arts. Submissions will only be accepted on TG4 submission forms and should be with TG4 by 16 January, 1 May or the 1 October. Unsuccessful applications will not be retained or returned. See the website for more details.

TILE FILMS

13 Windsor Place Dublin 2
T 01 611 4646
F 01 662 9715
E info@tilefilms.ie
W www.tilefilms.ie

Produces high-end factual documentaries with international appeal. Output includes *Ireland's Nazis*, *The Ghosts Of Duffy's Cut* and *The Lost Gods*. Also has an office in Manchester.

Submissions Policy
Send submissions to Rachel@tilefilms.ie

TIMESNAP LIMITED

15 Luttrell Park Drive Castleknock Dublin 15
T 353 86 127 2740
E mail@timesnap.com
W www.timesnap.com

Contacts
Declan Cassidy *Director*

Founded in 2005, producing documentaries including *War on Waste* and *Dancing Dublin*. It also produced the film *Mrs Friendly*.

Submissions Policy
Accepts script submission enquiries via email, which must contain relevant information about the writer, a sample page of the script and a project logline.

TOTALITY PICTURES LTD

12 Castleview Artane Dublin 5
E info@totalitypictures.com
W www.totalitypictures.com

Film production company offering range of services from script-writing to post-production.

TYRONE PRODUCTIONS

27 Lower Hatch Street Dublin 2
T 01 662 7200
F 01 662 7217
E pcarroll@tyrone-productions.ie
W www.tyrone-productions.ie

Contacts
Patricia Carroll *General Manager*

An independent television production company founded in 1987 and working across genres including drama, documentary and entertainment. Production credits include *Riverdance*, the dramas *Beckett on Film* and *Ros na Rún*, and the documentaries *The Land of Sex and Sinners* and *The Pope's Children*.

Submissions Policy
Submission form available from website.

VENOM

9 Sallymont Gardens Dublin 6
T 01 4911954
F 01 4911954
E info@venom.ie
W www.venom.ie

Film production company founded in 1994, developing work for broadcast, internet and theatrical distribution. Credits include the award-winning short, *Undressing my Mother*.

VICO FILMS

Unit D Glencormack Business Park
Kilmacanogue County Wicklow
T 087 6460406
F 01 2014999
E info@vicofilms.com
W www.vicofilms.com

Independent production company set up in 2003 with the aim of producing innovative and critically acclaimed films for the world market. Focus on developing feature projects, two of which have so far received development funding from the Irish Film Board. Recent titles include *CCW*, *Des Smyth*, *The Lump* and *Takeover*.

VINEGAR HILL PRODUCTIONS

Main Street Gortahork County Donegal
T 074 9180730
F 074 9180732
E info@vinegarhill.com
W www. vinegarhill.com

Founded in 1996, developing, scripting and producing feature films, documentaries, and broadcast television programmes. Production credits include the documentaries *Chiapas*, *Gods, Faeries and Misty Mountains* and *Saighdiúirí Beaga Gaelacha*, the animated works *Dick Terrapin* and *Sir Gawain and the Green Knight*, and the dramas *This Little Piggy* and *It's All in the Jeans*.

WIDE EYE FILMS

30 Herbert Street Dublin 2
T 01 678 7930
F 01 678 7930
E mail@wideeyefilms.com

Contacts
Nathalie Lichtenthaeler *Producer*

A multi-award-winning feature film production company established in 1999. Recent feature films produced include *Cowboys & Angels* and *The Front Line*.

Submissions Policy
Any screenplay submissions should be preceded by an initial contact (preferably e-mail).

WIDER VISION

West Clare
T 086 2607822
E info@widervision.ie
W www.widervision.ie

Formed in 2003, a television production company specializing in documentaries, dramas and corporate productions. Also provides camera crews and services to national and international broadcasters.

WILDFIRE FILMS & TELEVISION PRODUCTIONS LIMITED

Olympia House Suite 2B 61-63 Dame Street Dublin 2
T 01 6725553
F 01 6725573
E info@wildfirefilms.net
W www.wildfirefilms.net

Produces feature films, television drama and documentaries. Output includes *The Plays of John M. Synge, Middletown, Red Mist, Undertakers, The Sack Em Ups, When Pigs Carry Sticks* and *Sunday in Dublin.*

WORLD 2000 PRODUCTIONS

Ardmore Studios. Herbert Road Bray County Wicklow
T 01 276 9672
F 01 286 6810
E info@world2000.ie
W www.world2000.ie

Established in 1994, developing, producing and distributing feature and television entertainment for the global market. Utilizing the Irish tax incentive programme, finances and provides production services for works including *King Arthur, Veronica Guerin, Ella Enchanted, The Count of Monte Cristo, Braveheart* and other Irish co-produced projects.

XSTREAM PICTURES LIMITED

5 Coghill's Court Dame Street Dublin 2
T 01 6708923
E info@xstream-pictures.com
W www.xstream-pictures.com

Specializes in 'complex and innovative storytelling through a range of media.' Produces documentaries, short dramas, commercials and music videos. Television output includes the documentaries *Fair City, Behind the Scenes* and *RTE Philharmonic Choir.* Also the short film, *The Hall.*

YOUNG IRISH FILM MAKERS

St. Joseph's Studios Waterford Road Kilkenny
T 056 7764677
F 056 7751405
E info@yifm.com
W www.yifm.com

A film training and production company set up in 1991 to help young people aged 13 to 20 make digital feature films. Established the National Youth Film School in 2002 to allow young people to spend five weeks shooting a major feature film for television. Also runs film workshops. YIFM's first feature was *Under the Hawthorn Tree* for Channel 4 and RTE in 1998.

ZANZIBAR FILMS

12 Magennis Place Dublin 2
T 01 671 9480
F 01 671 9481
E info@zanzibarfilms.net
W www.zanzibarfilms.net

Founded in 1998, Zanzibar's most notable success is the film *Headrush,* which won the Miramax script award as well as four other international awards.

Submissions Policy
Willing to look at unsolicited treatments.

AUSTRALIA

3MONKEYFILMS PTY LTD

8/120 Cambridge Street Collingwood
VIC 3066
T   04 1221 6225
E   contact@3monkeyfilms.com

Contacts
Michael Robinson

Production company established in 2001,
focusing on feature film development and short
film production. Past credits include *The
Opposite of Velocity*, *The Hedge* and
A Kind of Hush.

Submissions Policy
Welcomes unsolicited manuscripts.

AGENDA FILM PRODUCTIONS

74 Watson Street Bondi NSW 2026
T   02 9389 4851
F   02 9389 4861
E   agendafilm@bigpond.com

Contacts
Ian Iveson *Director*

Founded in 1983, film and television
production company specializing in drama.
Credits include *Lost Things* and *Kideo!*.

Submissions Policy
Welcomes unsolicited manuscripts by email.

ARENAFILM

Level 2 270 Devonshire Street Surry Hills
NSW 2010
T   02 9319 7011
F   02 9319 6906
E   mail@arenafilm.com.au
W   www.arenafilm.com.au

Founded in 1987, producing feature films
that explore social and political themes.
Produced the films *Romulus, My Father*
(starring Eric Bana), *Three Dollars*, *The Bank*
and *The Boys*.

ASSOCIATED CREATIVE TALENTS

PO Box 328 Hawthorn VIC 3122
T   03 9855 1571
E   theproducer@associatedcreativetalents.net
W   www.associatedcreativetalents.net

Contacts
G D Bruny *Producer/Director*

Founded in 1983, production company with
credits including *Flynn's Flying Doctors*, *Sixty
and Over* and *Rescue*. Currently producing
2-part docu-drama mini-series for TV.

Submissions Policy
Unsolicited manuscripts are welcomed. 'The
first few pages will tell us a lot'.

AUS-TV INTERNATIONAL

PO Box 423 Woollahra NSW 1350
T   02 9929 9300
E   austv@tvaustralia.com
W   www.tvaustralia.com

Contacts
Bill Payne

Established in 1986, producing film and TV
dramas and documentaries.

Submissions Policy
Welcomes unsolicited manuscripts. Cautious
policy on new writing, 'but open to new
concepts and ideas'.

AUSTRALIAN CHILDREN'S TELEVISION FOUNDATION

3rd Floor 145 Smith Street Fitzroy VIC 3065
T   03 9419 8800
F   03 9419 0660
E   info@actf.com.au
W   www.actf.com.au

A national non-profit organization, committed
to providing Australian children with
entertaining media made especially for them.
Has created over 150 hours of high quality
children's content, screened in over

100 countries and winning over 95 local and international awards. Titles include *Round the Twist* and *Crash Zone*. Also acts as a funding body for other children's television producers, offering both script development funding and production investment.

AUSTRALIAN INTERNATIONAL PICTURES PTY LTD

4/305 North Terrace Adelaide SA 5000
T 08 8227 0681
E austinpic@hotmail.com
W www.austinpic.com

Contacts
Wayne Grom *Producer*

Established in 1981, production company focusing on feature films, television and documentaries. Recent productions include *Maslin Beach* and *The Dreaming*, which was nominated for an Australian Film Institute award.

Submissions Policy
Welcomes unsolicited manuscripts and ideas.

AVALON FILM CORPORATION

Ultima 6/30 Garfield Terrace Surfers Paradise
QLD 4217
T 07 5526 7932
F 07 5526 7932
E avalonfilms@bigpond.com

Contacts
Phil Avalon *Director*

Founded in 1976, producing 'good stories that can transfer to film or television'. Past credits include *Liquid Bridge* and *The Pact*.

Submissions Policy
Submissions only accepted through agents.

BANKSIA PRODUCTIONS

L62-80 Wellington Square North Adelaide
SA 5006
T 08 8334 5300
F 08 8334 5334

E info@banksia.com
W www.banksia.com

Founded in 1987, producing children's programmes and documentaries. Credits include *Humphrey*, the series *Great Australian Train Journeys* and the documentary *Pub Crawl With Altitude*. Has received numerous industry awards including the Prix Jeunesse (Germany) and several Logies.

BECKER ENTERTAINMENT

Level 1 11 Waltham Street Artarmon
NSW 2064
T 02 9438 3377
F 02 9439 1827
E info@beckers.com.au
W www.beckers.com.au

Integrated screen entertainment company, founded in 1965 by Russell Becker, one of the pioneers of commercial television in Australia. A leader in television and film production, distribution and exhibition. Produces TV programming across a range of genres including documentaries, entertainment shows, children's programmes, live sports and drama. Produces local language programmes for Asian markets, operating out of Singapore and Jakarta. Also has a long track record of producing feature films in Australia and the US and is a major independent film distributor in Australia and New Zealand.

BIG AND LITTLE FILMS PTY LTD

PO Box 1271 St Kilda South VIC 3182
T 03 9527 8299
F 03 9527 8266
E info@bigandlittlefilms.com
W www.bigandlittlefilms.com

Award-winning independent production company working in feature films, documentary and television drama. Develops and finances a slate of projects for domestic and international markets, working with a range of writers and directors.

BLINK FILMS PTY LTD

PO Box 1315 Crows Nest NSW 1585
T   02 9439 9900
F   02 9439 8099
E   mail@blinkfilms.com
W   www.blinkfilms.com

Contacts
Michael Bourchier *Managing Director*

Television and film production company
established in 1984, specializing in drama for
children and adults. Recent output includes *The
Upside Down Show* for childrens' TV and a
feature film, *Lucky Miles.*

Submissions Policy
Does not welcome unsolicited manuscripts, but
writers can 'pitch a genre and broad idea by
email'.

RICHARD BRADLEY PRODUCTIONS PTY LTD

PO Box 1417 Bondi Junction NSW 1355
T   02 9959 3588
E   rbproductions@bigpond.com

Contacts
Richard Bradley *CEO*

Founded in 1981, film and television company
that has since produced over 100 films
including documentaries, TV specials, TV
drama and features.

Submissions Policy
Welcomes unsolicited approaches by email.

BURBERRY PRODUCTIONS PTY LTD

Level 1 462 City Road South Melbourne
VIC 3205
T   03 9693 0600
F   03 9693 0633
E   info@burberry.com.au
W   www.burberry.com.au

Founded in 2000, producing television drama
series and children's programmes. Output

includes *Eugénie Sandler PI, The Farm, Short
Cuts* and *Last Man Standing.*

CAAMA (CENTRAL AUSTRALIAN ABORIGINAL MEDIA ASSOCIATION)

101 Todd Street Alice Springs NT 0870
T   08 8951 9778
F   08 8951 9717
E   productions@caama.com.au
W   www.caama.com.au

Contacts
Rachel Clements *Executive Producer*

Founded in 1980, indigenous media company
producing drama and documentaries. Past titles
include *Double Trouble* and *Yellow Fella.*
Produced the first aboriginal documentary
entered at Cannes Film Festival.

Submissions Policy
Welcomes unsolicited manuscripts by email, but
need to be stories with indigenous content.

CAPITOL PRODUCTIONS

PO Box 734 North Sydney NSW 2059
T   02 9966 0422
F   02 9966 0522
E   info@capitolproductions.com
W   www.capitolproductions.com

Contacts
Donna Svanberg *Executive Producer*

Founded in 1992, specializing in films and
commercials.

MATT CARROLL FILMS PTY LTD

12 Sloane Street Newtown NSW 2042
T   02 9516 2400
F   02 9516 2099
E   mcfilms@bigpond.com.au

Contacts
Matt Carroll

Film and TV production company focusing on
feature films, TV movies and drama series.

Founded in 1995, the company produced *Murder in the Outback* for ITV.

Submissions Policy
Does not welcome unsolicited manuscripts - submissions 'only via agent or log lines'.

CASCADE FILMS

117 Rouse Street Port Melbourne VIC 3207
T   03 9646 4022
F   03 9646 6336
E   info@cascadefilms.com.au
W   www.cascadefilms.com.au

Production company founded in 1983 and owned by filmmakers Nadia Tass and David Parker. Has produced a series of acclaimed feature films, starting with *Malcolm* in 1985. which won 8 Australian Film Institute awards including Best Picture, Best Script and Best Director. While continuing to produce films by the Tass/Parker writing/directing team, the company is also interested in engaging writers and directors who will develop their projects under the Cascade Films banner. Also owns and operates the Melbourne Film Studio. More recent credits include *Samantha: An American Girl Holiday, Undercover Christmas* and *The Lion, The Witch And The Wardrobe.*

CENTAUR ENTERPRISES PTY LTD

PO Box 1264 Mona Vale Sydney NSW 1660
T   04 1032 4911
E   centaurfilms@bigpond.com

Contacts
John Meagher CEO

Founded in 1975, involved in writing, producing and directing feature films and TV programmes, specializing in drama and documentaries. Output includes *Fantasy Man, The Rival* and *Australian Cotton,* which won a Gold Medal at the New York Film and TV Festival.

Submissions Policy
Welcomes new submissions but prefers introductory email first.

JAN CHAPMAN FILMS PTY LTD

PO Box 476 Woollahra NSW 2025
T   02 9331 2666
F   02 9331 2011
E   chapman@optusnet.com.au

Contacts
Jan Chapman *Producer*

Film and TV production company founded in 1989 by producer Jan Chapman. Past credits include *The Piano, Holy Smoke* and *Somersault.*

Submissions Policy
Does not welcome unsolicited manuscripts.

CINETEL PRODUCTIONS PTY LTD

15 Fifth Avenue Cremorne Sydney NSW 2090
T   02 9953 8071
E   cinetel@bigpond.net.au
W   www.cinetel.com.au

Contacts
Frank Heimans

Founded in 1976, producing documentaries and some drama for television and theatrical release. Has won 3 Gold awards from the International Film & TV Festival of New York, 2 Blue Ribbons from the American Film & Video Festival, and a Gold award at Berlin. Credits include the documentary, *Battle for Sydney Harbour.*

Submissions Policy
Welcomes new writing but not unsolicited approaches. Contact by phone in first instance.

CRACKERJACK

75 Chandos Street St Leonards NSW 2065
T   02 9438 4255
F   02 9438 4275
W   www.fremantlemedia.com

A leading boutique production company, owned by FreMantle. Preference for original ideas and formats. Specializes in light entertainment, comedy, factual and reality.

CRAWFORD PRODUCTIONS PTY LTD

Level 10 575 Bourke Street Melbourne
VIC 3000
T   03 8613 8250
F   03 8613 8262
E   admin@crawfords.com.au
W   www.crawfords.com.au

Founded in 1945 as a radio production facility, it has produced a string of domestic prime time drama successes such as *Consider Your Verdict*, *The Henderson Kids* and *The Violent Earth*.

EATON ENTERPRISES PTY LTD

18 Plateau Road Avalon Sydney NSW 2107
T   02 9918 7722
E   eatent@aapt.net.au

Contacts
Barry Eaton *Producer/Writer*

Founded in 1980, specializing in drama, documentary, internet programmes and corporate/training films. A feature, *Direct Action*, currently in production.

Submissions Policy
Happy to look at ideas via email. Prefers to develop new ideas and concepts 'from the ground up'.

ELECTRIC PICTURES

33 Canning Highway East Fremantle WA 6158
T   08 9339 1133
F   08 9339 1183
E   enquiries@electricpictures.com.au
W   www.electricpictures.com.au

Founded in 1992, producing award-winning documentaries on a range of themes including history, science, human interest, international affairs, arts and adventure. Output includes *Bom Bali*, *The Black Road* and *Tug of Love*.

Submissions Policy
Welcomes written submission of strong documentary concepts with international market potential. As a minimum, a submission should consist of a one-page synopsis outlining the idea and any supporting documentation such as character or background notes.

EMBRYO FILMS

PO Box 300 Artarmon Sydney NSW 1570
T   02 8011 3533
F   02 8915 1533
W   www.embryo-films.com

Produces drama, comedy, sci-fi and thrillers written or set in Australia or New Zealand, targeting the international TV and film markets.

Submissions Policy
Welcomes contact with new writers but submissions accepted only via the website submission form with no exceptions. See website for further details.

EMPIRE ACTION PTY LTD

Morstone Chilcott Road Berrilee Sydney
NSW 2159
T   02 9655 1067
E   mho59125@bigpond.net.au
W   www.empireaction.com.au

Contacts
Mick Hodge *Writer/Director*

Established in 2000, film and television production company creating shorts, documentaries and feature films.

Submissions Policy
Welcomes unsolicited manuscripts. Responds to new writing with 'straightforward honesty which can sometimes appear to be frightfully harsh'.

ENCHANTER PTY LTD

113/1 Marian Street Redfern NSW 2016
T   02 9699 4341
E   info@enchanter.com.au
W   www.enchanter.com.au

Contacts
Matt Carter *Producer*

Established in 1998, film, television and media production company focusing on science-fiction and fantasy genres. Limited involvement with computer games. Aims to produce films for the worldwide market utilizing local talent. Recent output includes *Perdition* and *Memory of Breathing*.

Submissions Policy
Welcomes unsolicited manuscripts by email.

ESSENTIAL VIEWING

PO Box 283 Annandale NSW 2038
T   02 85683100
F   02 95192326
W www.rbfilms.com.au

Established in 2005 by leading independent Australian feature film and television producers including Rosemary Blight and Chris Hilton (joint CEOs), Kylie du Fresne, Sonja Armstrong, Ben Grant and Ian Collie. Works across dramas, documentaries, drama-docs and factual entertainment and has first look development deals with London based RDF International and Channel Four International. Essential Pictures is the company's feature films production arm.

FEATHERSTONE PRODUCTIONS

Ḍ

68 Denison Street Bondi Junction NSW 2022
T   02 9389 1199
F   02 9369 1432
E   don@featherstoneproductions.com
W www.featherstoneproductions.com

Founded in 1985. Has produced over forty documentaries across genres including history, music and arts, science, sports and current affairs. Credits include *The Beach*, *An Imaginary Life* and the seminal TV drama, *Babakuieria*. Notable achievements include Best Documentary (Hot Docs), a Banff Rockie, Best Arts Documentary (San Francisco), Special Jury Prize (San Francisco), a UN Media Peace Prize, a BAFTA nomination and an International Emmy nomination.

FRONTIER FILMS PTY LTD

PO Box 294 Harbord NSW 2096
T   02 9938 5762
F   02 9938 5762
E   frontier@oceanguard.com

Contacts
Frank Shields

Founded in 1970, specializing in drama, animation and documentary. Credits include *Hurrah* and *The Finder*. Has shown extensively at festivals throughout the world, picking up several awards.

Submissions Policy
Approach with idea or single-page synopsis in first instance, via mail or email. If interested enough, the company will approach the sender for further material (a treatment or screenplay). At this stage, sender will be required to sign a submission release document.

GECKO FILMS PTY LTD

PO Box 1320 North Fitzroy VIC 3068
E   geckofilms@ozemail.com.au

Contacts
Sue Brooks *Screenwriter/Director*

Founded in 1992, film production company specializing in drama. Recent credits include *Road to Nhill* and *Japanese Story*, which was selected for 'Un Certain Regard' category at the Cannes Film Festival.

Submissions Policy
Not actively seeking manuscripts or new writing; generates scripts within the company.

GENERATION FILMS

367 Beaconsfield Parade St Kilda VIC 3182
T   03 9537 1963
F   03 9923 6388
E   bob@weisfilms.com
W www.weisfilms.com

Contacts
Bob Weis *CEO*

Established in 1981, production company working across a range of media including film, television and computer games. Winner of awards including the UN Media Peace Prize and AFI awards. Output includes *Women of the Sun: 25 Years Later.*

Submissions Policy
Wants 'subject driven', not 'market driven', films. Welcomes unsolicited manuscripts but prefers synopsis first.

GRANADA PRODUCTIONS

Fox Studios Australia Level 1 Building #61 Driver Avenue Moore Park NSW 1363
T   02 9383 4360
F   02 8353 3494
W www.granadaproductions.com.au

Founded in 1998, producing shows including *Australia's Next Top Model, An Aussie Goes Barmy, Teen Fat Camp* and the Logie award-winning show *Dancing with the Stars.*

GREAT WESTERN ENTERTAINMENT PTY LTD

140 Stirling Highway North Fremantle WA 6159
T   08 9 433 6899
F   08 9 433 6922
E   annem@gwe.net.au

Contacts
Paul Barron *Producer*

Established in 1983, producing for television and starting to develop computer games. Particular focus on children's television but currently developing adult drama and documentaries. Credits include *Parallax* and *Streetsmartz,* which was awarded a 2006 Screen Producers' Association of Australia award for children's projects.

Submissions Policy
Always on the lookout for fresh new talent. Email a synopsis only in first instance.

GRUNDY

FremantleMedia Australia 110-112 Christie Street St Leonards Sydney NSW 2065
T   02 9434 0666
F   02 9434 0700
W www.fremantlemedia.com

Formed out of Grundy Television, the company founded by George Grundy in 1959. Went on to become Australia's most important producer and distributor, with titles including *Sons and Daughters, Prisoner Cell Block H* and *Neighbours.* Was acquired by Fremantle (then called Pearson Television) in 1995.

HOODLUM ACTIVE PTY LTD

PO Box 38 Paddington QLD 4064
T   07 3367 2965
E   info@hoodlum.com.au
W www.hoodlumactive.com

Contacts
Tracey Robertson *CEO*

Founded in 2000, producing multi-platform drama and documentary projects. Output includes *Fat Cow Motel* and *Emmerdale Online,* an online narrative synchronised with the television serial.

Submissions Policy
Unsolicited manuscripts welcome. 'We prefer people to have an understanding and experience of the industry, not necessarily as a writer.'

INSTINCT ENTERTAINMENT

Level 1 111 Nott Street Port Melbourne VIC 3207
T   03 9646 0955
F   03 9646 1588
E   admin@instinctentertainment.com.au
W www.instinctentertainment.com.au

Founded in 1999, producing documentaries, shorts and feature films. Produced documentaries such as *To be Frank* and *SALUTE - The Peter Norman Story.* Feature film output includes *Torn, Strange Bedfellows* and *Takeaway.*

Submissions Policy
In order to submit material for consideration, include a completed application form together with a signed submission agreement, a one-page synopsis of the project and a CV.

JIGSAW ENTERTAINMENT

Development Office 1st Floor 129 Cathedral Street Woolloomooloo NSW 2011
T   02 9326 9922
F   02 9326 9277
E   thefolks@jigsaw.tv
W   www.jigsaw.tv

Established in 1999, an indie production company specializing in light entertainment, comedy and drama production. Produced the *BlackJack Trilogy* (telemovie) and the sitcom *Welcher & Welcher.*

Submissions Policy
Company policy not to accept unsolicited material.

KAPOW PICTURES

Studio 33 Technopark 2a Herbert Street St Leonards Sydney NSW 2065
T   02 9439 0399
F   02 9439 0398
E   info@kapowpictures.com.au
W   www.kapowpictures.com.au

Independent animation company founded in 1997. Works on feature films, TV series, long form TV productions and short films. Titles include *CJ the DJ* and *Here Comes Peter Cottontail.*

KOJO PICTURES

31 Fullarton Road Kent Town SA 5067
T   08 8363 8300
F   08 8363 8329
E   dean@kojo.com.au
W   www.kojo.com.au

Formed in 2004 to develop and produce feature length movies, short films and television drama. Full service from script development through to full production. Outputs include *Elise,* 2:37 and *Wolf Creek.*

LIFESIZE FILM AND TELEVISION PTY LTD

212 Punt Road Prahran Melbourne VIC 3181
T   03 9510 3027
F   03 9524 2777
E   lipscombejames@hotmail.com

Contacts
James Lipscombe *Director*

Founded in 1993, an independent production company specializing in documentaries and lifestyle programmes.

Submissions Policy
Happy to look at ideas via email.

LONELY PLANET TELEVISION

90 Maribyrnong Street Footscray Melbourne VIC 3011
T   03 8379 8000
F   03 8379 8111
E   info@lonelyplanet.tv
W   www.lonelyplanet.tv

Contacts
Laurence Billiet *Executive Producer*

The television production section of Lonely Planet Publishing, producing travel documentaries and factual entertainment. Recent titles include *The Sport Traveller* and *Going Bush.*

Submissions Policy
Welcomes one-page submissions by email.

J MCELROY HOLDINGS PTY LTD

FSA#48 Fox Studios Australia Driver Avenue Moore Park NSW 1363
T   02 9383 4475
F   02 9383 4471
E   jmcelroy@msn.com.au

Contacts
Jim McElroy *Director*

Film production company established in 1991, producing feature films in a wide range of genres. Credits include *The Year of Living Dangerously, Mr Reliable* and *Picnic at Hanging Rock.*

Submissions Policy
Unsolicited manuscripts are welcomed by mail but prefers to read synopsis first.

MEDIA WORLD PICTURES

PO Box 90 Carlton South VIC 3053
w www.mediaworld.com.au

Founded in 1982. Has produced the television programmes *The Circuit* and *Dogstar.* Films include *Zone 39, Beware of Greeks Bearing Guns* and the award-winning children's feature, *The Silver Brumby* (starring Russell Crowe).

Submissions Policy
Has a company policy not to accept unsolicited material.

MELODRAMA PICTURES PTY LTD

179 Johnston Street Fitzroy VIC 3065
T   03 9416 3566
F   03 9417 7336
E   info@melodramapictures.com
w www.melodramapictures.com

Contacts
Melanie Coombs *Producer/Company Director*

Film production company specializing in features and animation. Founded in 1999, output includes *The Glenmoore Job* and *Harvie Krumpet,* winner of Oscar for Best Animated Short.

Submissions Policy
Does not welcome unsolicited manuscripts, but 'open to genuine collaboration'.

MIDAS FILMS (DAVID DOUGLAS PRODUCTIONS PTY LTD)

Farm Dogs Bite 13B Lytton Road Moss Vale
NSW 2577
T   02 4869 5150
E   midaslectures@bigpond.com

Contacts
David Douglas *Producer/MD*

Founded in 1978, specializing in documentaries, commercials and features for domestic and international markets.

Submissions Policy
Does not welcome unsolicited approaches.

MOVING TARGETS

14/41 Broughton Road Artarmon
NSW 2064
T   02 9413 3932
F   02 9413 3931
E   rodhay@bigpond.com.au

Contacts
Rod Hay *Writer/Producer/Director*

Established in 1986, film and television production company focusing on documentaries and feature films. Output includes TV series *Height of Passion.* Documentaries are often a mixture of drama and sport.

Submissions Policy
Welcomes unsolicited manuscripts, prefers to be approached first by telephone. 'Must be able to understand the theme and characterisation as soon as possible, but also must push the envelope'.

MUSHROOM PICTURES

135 Forbes Street Woolloomooloo Sydney
NSW 2011
T   02 9360 6255
F   02 9360 7307
E   info@mushroompictures.com.au
w www.mushroompictures.com.au

Produces television shows such as *Tribal Voice* (based on the Australian band Yothu Yindi) and the series *Greatest Australian Albums*. Co-produced the film *Chopper*, and produced the films *Cut, Gettin' Square* and *Wolf Creek*.

Submissions Policy
Does not accept unsolicited scripts.

MUSIC ARTS DANCE FILMS PTY LTD

PO Box 7 Elwood VIC 3184
E   info@musicartsdance.com
W   www.musicartsdance.com

Contacts
Kevin Lucas *Director/Executive Producer*

Founded in 1986, independent production company making drama, features and documentaries for TV and film. Selections in Sundance, Berlin, London and many other film festivals. Projects focus particularly on arts in all areas, including music, dance and theatre.

Submissions Policy
Welcomes unsolicited ideas but prefers to receive a letter and synopsis first.

NEW MUSIC THEATRE

PO Box 128 Petersham NSW 2049
T   02 9558 3645
F   02 9558 3645
E   dstrahan@revolve.com.au
W   www.revolve.com.au

Contacts
Derek Strahan *Director*

Founded in 1972. Has provided scripts for projects produced by the company and third parties. Also involved in production of music. Credits include *Leonora, Fantasy* and the *Inspector Shanahan Mysteries*.

Submissions Policy
Does not welcome unsolicited approaches.

NOMAD FILMS INTERNATIONAL PTY LTD

PO Box 176 Prahran Melbourne VIC 3181
T   03 9819 3350
F   03 9819 3395
E   nomfil@rabbit.com.au
W   www.nomadfilmsinternational.com

Contacts
Douglas Stanley *Executive Producer*

Established in 1976, film and TV production company mostly concentrating on feature films and TV drama. Past credits include a drama miniseries, *Shadow of the Osprey*, and *The Promise*, a feature film.

Submissions Policy
Welcomes unsolicited manuscripts but prefers a treatment of the story first. Encourages new writing but not funding new scripts at this stage.

PERPETUAL MOTION PICTURES

PO Box 1161 Crows Nest NSW 1585
T   02 9966 0555
F   02 9877 6610
E   jo@perpetualmotionpictures.com.au
W   www.perpetualmotionpictures.com.au

Contacts
Jo Cadman *Producer*

Television production company founded in 1990, specializing in documentary and lifestyle programmes.

Submissions Policy
Happy to read all new writing, particularly within the company's genre.

PORCHLIGHT FILMS

Suite 31 94 Oxford Street Darlinghurst NSW 2010
T   02 9326 9916
F   02 9357 1479
W   www.porchlightfilms.com.au

Founded in 1996. Has produced award-winning short films, documentaries, television programmes and feature films including the independent box office hit *Mullet*, *Walking on Water* (winner of 5 AFI Awards) and the critically-acclaimed *Little Fish* (starring Cate Blanchett, Sam Neill and Hugo Weaving).

RADHART PICTURES PTY LTD

LVL 1 479 Crown Street Surry Hills NSW 2034
T   02 9699 7622
E   jason@radhart.com

Contacts
Jason Harty *Producer*

Film and television production company founded in 2001. Recent credits include *Clutch* and *Charmed Robbery*.

Submissions Policy
Welcomes unsolicited manuscripts by email.

RED CARPET PRODUCTIONS PTY LTD

PO Box 1199 Potts Point NSW 1335
T   02 9356 8677
F   02 9360 2421
E   info@redcarpetfilms.com.au
W   www.redcarpetfilms.com.au

Independent feature film production company, whose debut feature is *Somersault*. Is developing several more features and has a catalogue of award-winning short films. Offers additional services including script editing and script analysis.

SEVEN DIMENSIONS

Unit 19 156 Beaconsfield Parade Albert Park VIC 3206
E   info@7dimensions.com.au
W   www.7dimensions.com.au

Contacts
Eve Cash *CEO*

Founded in 1979, with a back catalogue of over 500 training, business and educational films and over 140 awards. Produces for television, DVD and electronic delivery. Drama, documentary and interview-based. Examples of titles include the *Take Away Training Series*, *Feedback Solutions*, *People Skills Series* and *Boomerang*.

Submissions Policy
No real capacity to accept unsolicited ideas or material. Normally uses internal team of writers.

JOHN SEXTON PRODUCTIONS

The Pavilion 3 Courallie Road Northbridge NSW 2063
T   02 9967 2222
F   02 9967 2234
E   sextonfilms@spin.net.au

Contacts
John Sexton *Managing Director*

Founded in 1972. Has produced 8 feature films focusing primarily on drama.

Submissions Policy
Submissions accepted only via recognized literary agents.

SHOOTING STAR PICTURE COMPANY PTY LTD

Suite 60 Upper Deck Jones Bay Wharf Pirrama Road Pyrmont NSW 2009
T   02 9660 6969
F   02 9660 8989
E   janelle@shootingstar.com.au
W   www.shootingstar.com.au

Contacts
Janelle Mason *Executive Producer*

Established in 1992, television production company specializing in drama and entertainment shows. Recent output includes police drama *Stingers*.

Submissions Policy
Welcomes unsolicited ideas in relevant genres.

SOUTHERN STAR ENTERTAINMENT

Level 9 8 West Street North Sydney
NSW 2060
T   02 9202 8555
F   02 9955 8302
E   general@sstar.com.au
W   www.sstar.com.au

One of Australia's largest independent creators and producers of television programming, including prime-time drama (*Blue Heelers, The Secret Life of Us, Water Rats*); children's and family television programming (*The Sleepover Club, Tracey McBean, The Adventures of Bottle Top Bill*) and factual (*Forensic Investigators*). Endemol Southern Star is a joint venture with Europe's Endemol, working on programmes such as *Big Brother* and *Deal or No Deal*.

STACEY TESTRO INTERNATIONAL PRODUCTION

26a Dow Street South Melbourne VIC 3205
T   03 9645 9181
E   info@ztudio.com
W   www.ztudio.com

Production arm of Stacey Testro International, producing film, theatre and television for a global market.

TRIMAX FILMS

Unit 3 5 Mockridge Avenue Newington
NSW 2127
T   04 1435 2410
F   02 8572 6088
E   info@trimaxfilms.com

Contacts
Lester Crombie *Producer/Director*

Established in 1982, film production company focusing on thrillers, action films and drama features.

Submissions Policy
Does not welcome unsolicited manuscripts.

VILLAGE ROADSHOW LIMITED

206 Bourke Street Melbourne VIC 3000
T   03 9667 6666
F   03 9639 1540
W   www.villageroadshow.com.au

A leading international media and entertainment company. Incorporates a major movie production business operating out of Los Angeles.

VITASCOPE FILMED ENTERTAINMENT

GPO Box 1193 Sydney NSW 2001
T   02 9590 7666
F   02 6337 5239
E   sydney@vfe.com.au
W   vfe.com.au

Independent company with a remit to develop, finance, produce and distribute feature films and television for the domestic and international markets. Work spans a range of genres from documentary and adventurous art house releases to international commercial features. Credits include *Hemispheres, Luv Sux, Romance of the Rose, The Grandfather Chest, The Song They Sing in Heaven* and *Wild Country*.

ZOOT FILM TASMANIA

PO Box 3105 West Hobartt Tasmania
TAS 7000
T   03 6236 9057
E   andy@zoot.net.au
W   www.zoot.net.au

Contacts
Andrew Wilson *Producer*

Founded in 2004, providing casting, crewing and location management services. Currently extending into computer game production. Examples of recent credits include *Race Through Time* for the BBC, the docu-drama *Exile in Hell, Kaleidoscope, The Barn, Dark Decisions* and *Cable*.

Submissions Policy
Happy to receive unsolicited submissions but reserves the right not to reply or accept any material offered. Approach by email with all relevant contact details and a one-page synopsis. Full manuscripts will not be considered. Accepts scripts of all genres but especially interested in Art House, contemporary stories. Particualrly interested in new media, cross media and trans media stories that have life beyond the box office and are suited to online distribution.

NEW ZEALAND

AJ FILMS

PO Box 37024 Halswell Christchurch
T   03 322 9279
F   03 322 9280
E   info@ajfilms.co.nz
W   www.ajfilms.co.nz

Recently established, working particularly on short films, television drama and commercials. Examples of output include the short films *Closer*, *A Quiet Night* and *Kicken*, an action adventure for Dutch television.

GEORGE ANDREWS PRODUCTIONS LTD

5H/5 Parliament Street Auckland
T   09 307 9196
E   george@aqua.co.nz

Produces documentaries and feature films. Examples of output includes *The Game of Our Lives*, *Out of the Dark*, *Nuclear Reaction* and *Nga Tohu Signatures*.

BITESIZE PRODUCTIONS LTD

62 Rame Road Greenhithe Auckland
T   09 413 9791
E   Laurence@bitesize.co.nz

Contacts
Laurence Belcher

Producers specializing in documentaries and series for television. Past titles include *Taste NZ*, *Garden Show*, *5.30 With Jude* and *Need for Speed*.

BLUESKIN FILMS LTD

PO Box 27261 Marion Square Wellington
T   04 8017176
E   catherinef@blueskinfilms.co.nz
W   www.blueskinfilms.co.nz

Contacts
Catherine Fitzgerald

Film producer established in 2002, with particular focus on short drama. Also offers script consultancy services for emerging writers for stage and screen. Examples of output include *Kerosene Creek*, *The Little Things*, *Two Cars, One Night* and *Turangawaewae: a Place to Stand*.

BORDERLESS PRODUCTIONS LIMITED

Studio 4 2A New North Road Eden Terrace Auckland
T   09 302 3103
E   qiujing@borderlessproductions.com
W   www.borderlessproductions.com

Contacts
Qiujing Wong *Principal*

Produces programmes for a range of clients including not-for-profits, television and internet broadcasters, corporations and individuals. Specialists in documentaries and factual programming. Output includes *Postcards from China*, *Nepal: Caught up in the people's war* and *A World of Kindness*.

CONBRIO MEDIA LTD

PO Box 34367 Birkenhead Auckland 0746
T   027 470 6895
E   christina@conbrio.co.nz
W   www.conbrio.co.nz

Company run by producer/writer Christina Milligan and post-producer/editor Roger Grant. Currently developing several projects for cinema, television and mobile phones. Also working with actor/writer Rawiri Paratene on short films under the banner Shorts Conbrio. Production credits include *Pet Detectives* (a children's TV drama series) and the documentary *Te Whanau a Putiputi*.

DAYBREAK PACIFIC

PO Box 91642 Auckland 1030
T   09 530 9416
E   dale@daybreakpacific.com

Feature film production company whose credits include *Treasure Island Kids 1, 2* and *3, Terror Peak, Cupid's Prey* and *Ozzie*.

DIVA PRODUCTIONS

PO Box 5986 Wellesley Street Auckland
T   09 376 5239
E   arani@ihug.co.nz

Production company with focus on film, documentaries and television comedy. Examples of previous productions include three series of *Topp Twins* and *Mr and Mrs*, co-produced with Ninox Films.

DRUM PRODUCTIONS

PO Box 91782 AMC Auckland
T   09 376 2919
E   stan@drumproductions.co.nz

Works across range of genres include films (features and shorts) and dramas, comedy and documentaries for television.

EMMANUEL PRODUCTIONS

PO Box 25736 St Heliers Auckland
T   09 575 3030
E   emmanuelproductions@xtra.co.nz

Produces short films as well as corporate videos. Its short film, *Rice*, won several awards at the 2003 Wanganui Film Festival.

EVOKE PICTURES

E   info@evokepictures.co.nz
W   www.evokepictures.co.nz

Independent film company with strong focus on the art of story-telling. Credits include *Death to the Premonition* and *Make Evelyn Smile*. Currently 'in hibernation, as we look to develop our stories and establish international contacts in the film industry'.

EXECAM TELEVISION AND VIDEO PRODUCTION

Level 2 Katipo House 195 Victoria Street PO Box 6577 Wellington
T   04 801 5600
F   04 801 5558
E   info@execam.co.nz
W   www.execam.co.nz

Works across a range of genres from television programmes to corporate video to streaming video for the internet. Involved in every stage of television production from concept through to finished show. Has worked with all three major New Zealand networks. Credits include the documentary series, *Extraordinary Kiwis*.

EXPOSURE

PO Box 99350 Newmarket Auckland
T   09 302 4031
F   09 302 4037
W   www.exposure.org

A communications company making human interest programmes for commercial, documentary and humanitarian purposes. Titles include *Journey of Hope* and *Tragedy of Child Labour*.

EYEWORKS TOUCHDOWN

PO Box 90018 Auckland Mail Centre
Auckland 1142
T   09 379 7867
F   09 379 7868
E   tv@touchdowntv.com
W   www.touchdowntv.com

A leading entertainment television production company founded in 1991. The country's market leader in broad appeal entertainment programmes, specializing in entertainment, lifestyle, sport and factual series. Examples of output include *Mountain Dew On The Edge*, *Police Stop!*, *In The Face of Fear*, *Profilers*, *Going Straight* and *Game of Two Halves*. Is also expanding into drama and film.

Submissions Policy
To submit an idea, see the online ideas submission form on the website. Automatically respects individual's intellectual property rights but has policy not to sign non-disclosure or confidentiality agreements.

FLUX ANIMATION STUDIO LTD

Private Bag MBE P280 Auckland
T   09 360 6003
F   09 360 6004
E   flux@fluxmedia.co.nz
W   www.fluxmedia.co.nz

Award-winning character animation specialist able to take a project from script to completion. Founded in 1997.

FRONT PAGE LIMITED

PO Box 90 361 Auckland Mail Centre
Auckland
T   09 377 4433
F   09 377 4434
E   harman@frontpage.co.nz
W   www.frontpage.co.nz

Contacts
Richard Harman *Executive Producer*

A leading independent producer of television current affairs and documentaries, working in both broadcast and non broadcast TV. Titles include *Agenda* and the *TV One Insight* debates.

RACHEL GARDNER

21 Picton Street Ponsonby
T   021 765 405
E   Rachel@rachelgardner.co.nz

Pursues production interests across feature films, short films, television dramas, fact-based series and documentaries. Credits include *The Pretender*, *Fog*, *Russia's Forgotten Children*, *Truant* and *The Lion Man*.

THE GIBSON GROUP LIMITED

PO Box 6185 Te Aro Wellington
T   04 384 7789
F   04 384 4727
E   info@gibson.co.nz
W   www.gibson.co.nz

Founded by Dave Gibson in 1977 and now among New Zealand's most significant independent film and television production companies. Specializes in high-end television drama for both primetime and children's audiences, along with documentary, comedy, arts magazine and factual programming. Programmes are shown in 80 countries around the world. Also works in new media. Recent credits include *The Insiders Guide to Love*, *The Insiders Guide to Happiness*, *The Strip* and *Holly's Heroes*.

GODZONE PICTURES LTD

PO Box 78-186 Grey Lynn Auckland
T   025 974 025
F   09 378 7333
E   liz@godzone.co.nz
W   www.godzone.co.nz

Produces films, TV series and documentaries. Output includes *The Creakers, Playing Possum* and *Letters about the Weather.*

GREEN STONE PICTURES

Private Bag 56 909 Dominion Road
Auckland
T 09 630 7333
F 09 623 7764
W www.greenstonepictures.com

Award-winning film and television production company, established in 1994 and specializing in factual series and documentaries. Also produces some entertainment and studio shows and children's drama. Credits include the children's drama series *Secret Agent Men Series II*, the feature film *Bella* and documentaries, *Cave Creek - The full story of a national tragedy, Back from the Dead - the Saga of the Rose Noelle* and *Whanau.*

HAWKE FILMS

PO Box 505 Nelson
T 03 547 8262
E khawke@paradise.net.nz
W www.valiantpoint.com

Produces television series, documentaries and programmes for children.

HUNTAWAY FILMS

Level 1 Steamer Wharf Lower Beach Street
Queenstown
T 03 441 1441
F 03 441 1451
E cassells@huntawayfilms.co.nz
W www.huntawayfilms.co.nz

Contacts
Jay Cassells

Operates in New Zealand and Australia, and has an office in Melbourne. Develops and produces content for film, television, DVD and new media.

Submissions Policy
Works with New Zealand and Australian writers and filmmakers in a bid 'to record and tell good New Zealand and Australian yarns'.

ISOLA PRODUCTIONS LTD

PO Box 90-781 AMC Auckland
T 09 815 1225
F 09 815 1224
E info@isola-productions.co.nz
W www.isola-productions.co.nz

Established by Rachel Jean in 2001, specializing in drama and documentary. Credits include the documentaries *Bird Flu, High Times* and *Dawn Raids*, the films *Karma* and *Minefield*, and the television series, *The Market.*

JOYRIDE FILMS LTD

120 Williamson Avenue Grey Lynn
Auckland 1021
T 09 360 5380
F 09 360 5386
E info@joyridefilms.com
W www.joyridefilms.com

Contacts
Anzak Tindall *Executive Producer*

Founded in 2003. Offers production services to international clients. Also about to make a short film and has a feature film and documentaries in development.

Submissions Policy
Happy to read new material. Email in first instance.

KIWA MEDIA

PO Box 41136 St Lukes Auckland
T 09 377 7674
F 09 375 2868
E chelsea@kiwafilm.com
W www.kiwafilm.com

Produces feature films, shorts and documentaries for domestic and international television and film markets. Specialists in dubbing programmes into indigenous languages. Production credits include *Buzz and Poppy, Stickmen, Pakeha Maori, The Natives of New Zealand* and *Gang Kids*.

Submissions Policy

Welcomes ideas from novice, intermediate and experienced screenwriters. Assesses all unsolicited scripts, novels, treatments, screenplays and pitches sent in. See website for a submissions guide.

LA LUNA STUDIOS LTD.

PO Box 525 Warkworth
T   09 974 2283
F   09 420 5703
E   cris@lalunastudios.com
W   www.lalunastudios.com

Contacts

Film and TV production company founded in 2005. Extends to computer games. Focuses on family and children's entertainment. Work includes the 3D animated short film *Kea* and upcoming 3D animated feature *The Magic Shoes*.

Submissions Policy

Welcomes unsolicited material by mail. Keen to see entertaining writing with a good moral message.

LEGGE WORK

PO Box 32 576 Devonport
T   09 445 0110
E   gordon@leggework.co.nz
W   www.leggework.co.nz

Over ten years' experience of producing sports-based programmes. Titles include *Speedweek, World of Motorsport* and *Coast to Coast*.

LITTLE ED FILMS LTD

PO Box 41152 Eastbourne Wellington
T   04 384 6385
E   angelalittlejohn@xtra.co.nz

Produces films as well as dramas, children's programmes and documentaries for television. Production credits include *Redial, They're Gone, They Ain't No Moa* and *Not Only But Always*.

LIVINGSTONE PRODUCTIONS LTD

PO Box 7896 Symonds Street Auckland 1150
T   09 636 5826
F   09 636 5825
E   info@livingstoneprods.co.nz
W   www.livingstoneprods.co.nz

Television production company founded in 1989 by John A Givins. Develops programmes from ideas generated internally and also for network operators and funded scriptwriters. Works across genres including documentaries, situation-comedy series, entertainment series, drama and television specials. Has worked with the Maori Television Service on projects in both Maori and English. Output includes *B&B, Queer Nation, Captain's Log* and *Nga Wahine Mauri Ora*.

M F FILMS LTD

23 Curran Street Herne Bay Auckland
T   09 376 0876
E   michele@mffilms.co.nz

Produces features, TV dramas, documentaries and commercials. Past credits include *One of Them, When Love Comes, 50 Ways of Saying Fabulous, The Big OE* and *God, Sreenu and Me*.

NATURAL HISTORY NEW ZEALAND

8 Dowling Street PO Box 474 Dunedin 9016
T   03 479 9799
F   03 479 9917
E   info@nhnz.tv
W   www.nhnz.tv

A leading producer of factual television, creating over 60 hours of programmes each year on the subjects of the natural world, health, science, adventure and people. Also has offices in Beijing and Washington DC. Examples of recent output include *Spider Power, World's Biggest Baddest Bugs, Nature's Warzone, Equator 2: Rivers of the Sun, Wild Horses - Return to China* and *The Curse of the Elephant Man*.

NEW ZEALAND GREENROOM PRODUCTIONS LIMITED

68 Harbour Village Drive Gulf Harbour
Whangaparaoa Auckland
T   021 888 665
E   info@nzgreen.tv
W www.nzgreen.tv

Television company founded in 1997. Leading player in surf/snow/alpine extreme sports and adventure programming. Output includes *NZ National Surf Champs* and *Arctic Challenge*.

NINOX TELEVISION LTD

PO Box 9839 Marion Square
Wellington 6141
T   04 801 6546
F   04 801 6573
E   ninox@ninox.co.nz
W www.ninoxtv.com

Contacts
David Harry Baldock *Managing Director*

Television production company formed in 1988. Over 300 hours of broadcast programming to date. Focuses on documentary, reality, and dramatized documentary formats. Past credits include *Sensing Murder, Dream Home* and *Location, Location, Location.*

Submissions Policy
Open to unsolicited material via email with letter of introduction.

ORIGIN ONE FILMS

PO Box 33-223 Petone Lower Hubb
Wellington 5046
T   04 970 9039
F   04 970 9039
E   originone@paradise.net.nz

Contacts
Brendon Hornell *Producer*

Wellington-based production company focused on drama, bio-pic and comedy film. Founded in 1999. has produced four short films to date.

Submissions Policy
Encourages unsolicited submissions by email. Keen to find an inspiring script from any writer, unknown or not.

POINT OF VIEW PRODUCTIONS

PO Box 78084 Grey Lynn Auckland
T   09 630 9222
E   s.horrocks@xtra.co.nz

Contacts
Shirley Horrocks

Producing short films and documentaries. Examples of output include *Flip and Two Twisters* (a documentary about Len Lye), the short film, *Stay in Touch* and the drama, *Managing Diversity.*

GAYLENE PRESTON PRODUCTIONS

59 Austin Street Mount Victoria Wellington
T   04 384 4242
E   the1@gaylenepreston.com
W www.gaylenepreston.com

Gaylene Preston is a leading New Zealand filmmaker and in 2001 was made New Zealand's first Filmmaker Laureate by the New Zealand Arts Foundation. Output includes the films *Perfect Strangers* and *Bread and Roses* and the mini-series, *Ruby and Rata.* Documentaries include *Earthquake!, Coffee Tea or Me?, Titless Wonders* and *Lands of our Fathers.*

RACONTEUR

PO Box 1051 Christchurch
T   03 3777 266
F   03 3777 268
E   info@raconteur.co.nz
W   www.raconteur.co.nz

Founded in 1996 by Veronica McCarthy and
Bill de Friez. Produces high-quality film and
television productions across genres including
documentaries, children's series and drama.
Output includes *The Crossing* (drama),
Mum Can I Drive? and *Animation Station*
(children's series), and *Between the Lines -
Dennis Glover* and *Madame Morison*
(documentaries).

Submissions Policy
Has an active development slate and always
willing to consider new ideas. Send an email to
development@raconteur.co.nz or contact Kim
on 03 3777 268.

RAYNBIRD PRODUCTIONS

PO Box 19-817 Woolston Christchurch
T   03 365 5323
F   03 365 1510
E   gaylene@raynbird.com
W   www.raynbird.com

Works across media including films and
documentaries, as well as educational and
corporate projects. Involved at all stages from
inception to completion.

SEVERE FEATURES

44 Francis Street Grey Lynn Auckland 1245
T   021 764198
E   severe@paradise.net.nz

Contacts
Leanne Saunders *Company Director*

Founded in 2000, a television and film
production company, specializing in drama.
Examples of output include *Christmas* (2003)
and *Nature's Way* (2006).

Submissions Policy
Welcomes unsolicited manuscripts and ideas.
Approach by email with a brief synopsis only.

SHOOTING STARS PRODUCTIONS

Apartment 8 20 Central Road Kingsland
Auckland 1021
T   09 815 8277
F   09 815 8377
E   gavin.butler@xtra.co.nz

Contacts
Gavin Butler *Director*

Film production company founded in 2001.
Develops screenplays and directs; specialized
interest in drama.

Submissions Policy
Always keen to look over new material.
Unsolicited submissions via email.

SHOTZ FILM AND VIDEO PRODUCTION LTD

49 Archmillen Avenue Pakuranga
Auckland 2010
T   09 576 8890
F   09 577 5343
E   ronel@shotzproductions.co.uk
W   www.shotzproductions.co.nz

Contacts
Ronel Schodt *Producer*

Television production company founded in
October 2002. Specializes in TVC and
documentary.

Submissions Policy
Welcomes unsolicited manuscripts and ideas via
email.

SOUTH PACIFIC PICTURES

PO Box 104-124 Lincoln North Henderson
Auckland
T   09 839 0999
F   09 839 0990
E   jjohnson@spp.co.nz
W   www.spp.co.nz

Contacts
Development Executive

Over the last 20 years South Pacific Pictures has produced over 3,000 hours of programming, both for television and cinema. Encompasses drama, entertainment, reality programming and documentaries. Has undertaken work for broadcasters in New Zealand, Australia, Canada and the UK. Believes that 'great writing is the foundation of good television [and] great execution is the realisation of that writing.' Recent production credits include the films *We're Here to Help* and *Sione's Wedding*, the documentary series *Cook - Obsession and Betrayal in the New World*, a telefeature *The Man Who Lost His Head* and the drama series *Shortland Street*, *Outrageous Fortune* and *Interrogation*.

Submissions Policy
Development department reviews all scripts, novels, screenplays and treatments submitted. Commissions writers to work on original film and television projects. See the website for the submissions guide and to download a submission release form.

SPROUT PRODUCTIONS

62 Church Street Onehunga Auckland
T   021 775 224
E   pclews@hotmail.com

Specializing in TV comedy, drama, documentary and corporate productions. Credits include *House Call 2*, *Last Laugh* and *Going Straight*.

STICKY PICTURES

PO Box 27440 Wellington
T   04 8025511
F   04 8025522
E   mhairead@stickypictures.co.nz
W   www.stickypictures.co.nz

Established in 2000, an independent producer of film and TV programmes. Produces across a range of genres including animation, documentary, drama and sports. Has a second office in Auckland. Credits include the arts show *The Living Room*, the documentaries *War of the Words* (about spelling bees), *The Magical World of Misery* (about a graffiti artist) and the short film *Dead End*.

TE ARATAI FILM & TV PRODUCTION

PO Box 3717 Shortland Street Auckland
T   09 378 7833
E   paora.tahi@xtra.co.nz

Produces programmes for television, specializing in documentaries and children's. Credits include *Tikitiki, Tu Te Puehu, Ka Hao te Rangatahi* and *Mika Live*.

TIMELINE PRODUCTIONS

PO Box 90943 AMSC Auckland 1142
T   09 309 2613
F   09 309 4048
E   info@timelineprods.com
W   www.timelineprods.com

Specializes in short and feature documentaries for broadcasters and film festivals around the world.

TOP SHELF PRODUCTIONS LTD

PO Box 9101 Wellington
T   04 382-8364
F   04 801-6920
E   topshelf@topshelfproductions.co.nz
W   www.topshelfproductions.co.nz

Founded in 1988 by Vincent Burke, producing for film and television. Specializes in documentaries, drama-documentaries, factual, information and education, arts programmes, television drama, features and short films. Has co-produced and co-financed ventures with companies from Australia, North America and Europe.

THE TV SET LTD

PO Box 91189 AMC Auckland
T   09 360 3214
E   megan@thetvset.co.nz
W   www.thetvset.co.nz

An independent documentary production company established in 2000. Company aims to tell strong personal stories that explore the human condition. Titles include 3 *Chord's & The Truth: The Anika Moa Story, Back for Good, Big Tahuna, Death on the Beach* and *One for the Road: The Michael Utting Story.*

I suppose you know the story of the writer who racked his brains how to show, very shortly, that a middle-aged man and his wife were no longer in love with each other. Finally he licked it. The man and his wife got into a lift and he kept his hat on. At the next stop a lady got into the lift and he immediately removed his hat. That is proper film writing. Me, I'd have done a four page scene about it. What this chap did took a few seconds.

A schoolmaster of mine long ago said, 'You can only learn from the second-raters. The first-raters are out of range; you can't see how they get their effects.' There is a lot of truth in this.

Raymond Chandler, 30.4.1957 (from *The Raymond Chandler Papers, Selected Letters and Non-Fiction, 1909–1959*, edited by Tom Hiney and Frank MacShane)

TEACHING GRANNY TO SUCK EGGS

Pete Daly's guide to what every screenwriter should know

OK – a lot of this you will know; some of it you will know even if you don't realize that you know it. But it really is worth rehashing. Many scripts fail because of very simplistic flaws.

Writers love to eschew the rules and avoid being formulaic. That's fine, but you need to understand the basics first. (Tarantino achieves distorted narrative paths and offbeat characters because of his in-depth knowledge of film and, especially, his understanding of genre rules.) Too many writers now fail to watch and learn. It really is essential to view as many films as possible – good and bad – to see what aspects worked and what didn't. The established classics are not top of the best-ever lists for nothing, and it is extremely difficult to be original when you don't know what went before.

European writers in particular are also prone to showing off – trying to make their work look complex and clever. As Kevin Spacey's *Verbal* says in *The Usual Suspects*, 'The greatest trick the Devil ever pulled was convincing the world he did not exist.' The major skill in screenwriting is making the complex seem simple and accessible. Look at *Shrek*. Just a kids' movie, a piece of fun? Don't make me laugh – this is a work of near genius that simultaneously plays to every level of age, background and nationality. There is hardly a wasted word in the whole screenplay, and that really takes talent!

So…where do we start? Well, every script has to have a beginning, a middle and an end. Sounds simple, but you'd be amazed how many people overlook this simple law of storytelling. Once you remember this you can play with it. Coming back to Tarantino, *Pulp Fiction* started in the middle, worked through to the conventional ending and then went round to the start for the conclusion. He knew the rule, and had the talent then to use it for his own purposes.

Talking generally, one page of screenplay will take up a minute of on-screen time (as long as you have kept your stage instructions to the basics). A movie should be 90 minutes. This is the perfect length for someone to sit in a darkened cinema with a group of strangers. If your script is over 100 pages there had better be a good reason for it (*Gandhi* was an epic deserving of three hours; many others are not). Apart from the audience attention span and the length of the drama, commercially you must remember that if you go much above 100 minutes the cinemas will lose one showing a day, which makes your project less attractive to all concerned.

Usually the opening of the story should take roughly a quarter of the running time to set up character, situation and story, although opening acts are becoming shorter and shorter in the desire to immediately capture the attention of the MTV generation. The finale should also take up 25 per cent, leaving half of the film for a middle section. Stories come in all different forms and shapes, but they need an 'inciting incident' to kick off the narrative and lead to act two. Basically something (preferably interesting) has to happen to someone (or somewhere). This then leads to a plan of action to try to overcome this change or restore the status quo. Like it or not you auteurs, the story has to be about something, with a goal at the end, or it lacks interest.

During the middle section we have to see the narrative progress, with extra layers of complexity added to increase the stakes and maintain audience interest. A baby that stays as a baby starts to become boring (to everyone except the medical profession). An audience want to see development and a route to a goal.

Movies have to have a protagonist – again, if they don't the writer should have considered this and there should be a good reason why not. This can be more than one person, and for the more experimental amongst you it could even be an inanimate object. But we must know whose story this is. They do not always have to be sympathetic, but they do have to be intriguing. The protagonist should want to do something, and there should be some force of antagonism trying to prevent this, to provide the conflict that makes the drama.

A film has to have some impact on the audience – emotionally it should make us laugh, cry, feel sad, romantic, amorous, whatever – but you need to make that connection. There also has to be some form of intellectual bond (the genre basically states whether this is more important than the emotional clout). We must be prepared to go with the story and, at times, it should make us think. There has to be some suspension of disbelief for a film to work. This is easier for some stories than others but if in doubt, think *Groundhog Day*. This was a truly preposterous premise, but it was logical at every step so we went along with it.

Movies on the whole benefit from having at least two contributory subplots to help vary tone and pace. You should also know what you're writing, and what effect you want to have on the audience. It is very useful to have a broad range of movie references to your fingertips, but be yourself and be original: no one likes copies.

Oh – and you also need talent. Talent to write dialogue that doesn't feel wooden when spoken, to know when to increase the pace or slow the momentum down, to enter the story at the right time and leave it at the right moment. But if you're not aware of the basics all the talent in the world cannot save you. You can't break rules without knowing what they are. Happy writing!

Pete Daly has worked in the film industry for over 15 years. He currently assesses and develops scripts for a wide range of producers, sales agents, distributors and public funding bodies.

WHAT MAKES A SCRIPT SELL INTERNATIONALLY?

Richard Wright says you have to think globally

Anyone who claims to know, unequivocally and specifically, what makes a script sell internationally is either a fool or a liar – sadly the film world is full of both!

Nevertheless, there are some rules of thumb that can still be helpful, such as:

(1) Avoid sports, like baseball or American football, that aren't popular outside North America. Exceptions come to mind, but can anyone actually say that *Field of Dreams* was a movie about baseball? This works the other way too: *Bend it Like Beckham* was a success not because it was a picture about soccer, but thanks to its having universal themes like ambition, love and exclusion.

(2) Avoid ethnic settings and themes that won't find sympathetic populations elsewhere in the world. *My Big Fat Greek Wedding* hit a nerve with all women who felt ugly or unloved, and who could recognize embarrassing eccentricities in their own extended family. Writing about volatile situations can cause all sorts of problems both commercially (you risk being banned or excluded in many markets) and artistically (events move much quicker than the production process and your freedom fighter may not be so enthusiastically accepted should an atrocity occur between writing and distribution).

(3) Avoid stories which require historical familiarities that international audiences won't have. Take Mel Gibson's *Apocalypto* for instance. While an in-depth knowledge of Mayan culture would make you feel a little privileged, the film itself worked because of the basic emotions of love and fear that ran through it. If you have to refer to the history books before going to the movie theatre (as many would claim of George Clooney's *Good Night and Good Luck*), the chances are you won't bother.

It may seem surprising given the US's love of fame, but it is international sales that are actually more star-driven than script-driven. It is easier to sell a bad script with a globally recognized star attached than a good script with an unknown lead. Therefore, when penning a screenplay that is going to 'travel' remember to write a great part that a major star would kill to have. This generally means having a strong leading role that is going to stretch their acting muscles and show off skills that have not been on display previously. (Cynical I know, but it perhaps also helps to have a setting or political cause that a star might find attractive.)

Many – but not all – scripts that have found international success in recent years share some general characteristics. Often they have some relation to the classic hero/quest model. They are usually longer on action and shorter on dialogue and philosophical musings. They deal with universal themes: good versus evil, conflict among a family or group, etc. Simply looking at the international box office in the last few years will give you a good idea of the types of films that are being made and achieving a degree of success at the box office – although simply 'knocking off' recent successful films is not usually a sure-fire recipe for a hit either.

Take Lakeshore's *Underworld* as a model. This is a movie with lots of fantastic action, the story is basically a traditional hero (or heroine in this case) on a quest, and it has a great lead role for an actress who wants to restyle herself (in this case making Kate Beckinsale into a kick-ass action lead when previously she was viewed chiefly as a dramatic romantic interest). Werewolf/vampire stories are genre staples, and therefore no education is required for international audiences. But the novel take on the subject – in essence it is a gang war film with vampires and werewolves – makes the story fresh and unique, so it doesn't just seem a rehash. In fact *Underworld* is a great example to writers to show that just because their script is action-led does not mean that complexity and originality have to go out of the window.

But the most important thing to bear in mind when writing a script, for the international or any other market, is: would I go to see this film if it was playing at my local cinema? If your script can't pass this simple test, you shouldn't be writing it, no matter which market it is intended for.

Richard Wright is Executive Vice President and Head of Production for Lakeshore Entertainment.

To make a fine film, you need three things: a great script, a great script and a great script.

Alfred Hitchcock

REPRESENTATION

UNITED STATES OF AMERICA

ABRAMS ARTISTS

275 Seventh Avenue 26th Floor New York
NY 10001
T   646 486 4600
F   646 486 2358
W www.abramsartists.com

Operating since 1977, with offices in New York
and Los Angeles. The literary division represents
writers and directors for film, TV and theatre.

ACME TALENT AND LITERARY AGENCY

4727 Wiltshire Boulevard Suite #333
Los Angeles CA 90010
T   323 954 2263
W www.acmetalentagents.com

A full service talent and literary agency.
Includes a literary division representing writers
of feature films, television series, TV movies
and novels.

Submissions Policy
Submission accepted by mail only.
Recommendations highly advised. Do not send
original material and include sae for a reply
and a submission release form (if necessary).

AGENCY FOR THE PERFORMING ARTS (APA)

405 S. Beverly Drive Beverly Hills CA 90212
T   310 888 4200
F   310 888 4242
W www.apa-agency.com

The agency's literary department has an
expansive roster of established screenwriters,
directors, show creators and novelists. Clients
work across both cinema and television. Also
offices in Nashville and New York.

LEE ALLAN AGENCY

7464 North 107 Street Milwaukee
WI 53224-3706
T   414 357 7708

Particular focus on screenplays, film and TV
rights. No reading fee.

Submissions Policy
Call or email in first instance before sending
script. Not currently looking for new clients.

THE ALPERN GROUP

15645 Royal Oak Road Encino CA 91436
T   818 528 1111
F   818 528 1110

Represents writers for both film and
television.

ARTIST INTERNATIONAL

9595 Wilshire Boulevard 9th Floor
Beverly Hills CA 90212
T   310 358 9239
W www.artistint.com

Provides professional representation to actors,
models, writers, directors, athletes, music
performers, artists, and other entertainment
properties. Divided into four divisions, of
which one is literary. Also offices in New York,
Miami and Dubai.

THE ARTISTS AGENCY

1180 S Beverly Drive Suite 400 Los Angeles
CA 90035
T   310 277 7779
F   310 785 9338

Specializes in representing screenwriters and
directors for film and television. Has affiliated
contacts in New York and the UK.

THE BOHRMAN AGENCY

8899 Beverly Boulevard West Hollywood
CA 90048
T   310 550 5444

Offers representation to screenwriters.

BRANT ROSE AGENCY

6671 Sunset Boulevard Ste 1584 B Los Angeles
CA 90028
T   323 460 6464

Provides representation for screenwriters.

BRILLSTEIN-GREY ENTERTAINMENT

9150 Wilshire Boulevard Ste 350 Beverly Hills
CA 90212
T   310 275 6135
F   310 275 6180

Established by Bernie Brillstein in 1969.
Manages a number of major stars along with a
roster of high profile writers and producers.

DON BUCHWALD AND ASSOCIATES, INC.

10 East 44th Street New York NY 10017
E   info@buchwald.com
W   www.buchwald.com

A full service talent agency, founded in 1977.
Offers representation across all sectors of the
entertainment industry, including a literary
department and television and film packaging
departments.

CAMBRIDGE LITERARY ASSOCIATES

135 Beach Road Unit C-3 Salisbury MA 01952
T   978 499 0374
W   www.cambridgeliterary.com

Represents books and screenplays.

Submissions Policy
Approach by mail (including a synopsis and an
sae) before sending in a manuscript. Only
interested in 'well-published authors'. No
reading fees.

MARIA CARVAINIS AGENCY, INC.

1350 Avenue of the Americas Suite 2905
New York NY 10019
T   212 245 6365
F   212 245 7196
E   mca@mariacarvainisagency.com

Contacts
Maria Carvainis *President*

Founded 1977. Handles fiction:
literary and mainstream, contemporary
women's, mystery, suspense, historical,
young adult novels; non-fiction: business,
women's issues, memoirs, health,
biography, medicine. No film scripts unless
from writers with established credits. No

science fiction. Commission: Domestic &
Dramatic 15%.

Submissions Policy
No faxed or emailed queries. No unsolicited
manuscripts; they will be returned unread.
Queries only, with IRCs for response. No
reading fee.

THE CHASIN AGENCY, INC.

8899 Beverly Boulevard #716 Los Angeles
CA 90048
T   323 278 7505

Offers representation to screenwriters.

CREATIVE ARTISTS AGENCY

2000 Avenue of the Stars Los Angeles
CA 90067
T   424 288 2000
F   424 288 2900
W   www.caa.com

Founded in 1975, one of Hollywood's most
prestigious talent and literary agencies. Also
offices in New York, Beijing, Calgary, Kansas
City, London, Nashville, St. Louis and
Stockholm.

CURTIS BROWN LTD

10 Astor Place New York NY 10003
T   212 473 5400

Contacts
Edwin Wintle *Film & TV Rights*

Founded 1914. Handles general fiction and
non-fiction. Also some scripts for film, TV and
theatre. Representatives in all major foreign
countries.

Submissions Policy
No unsolicited manuscripts; queries only, with
IRCs for reply. No reading fee.

LIZA DAWSON ASSOCIATES

240 West 35th Street Suite 500 New York
NY 10001
T   212 465 9071.
E   ldawson@lizadawsonassociates.com

General literary agency, dealing with some scripts.

DIVERSE TALENT GROUP

1875 Century Park East Suite 2250
Los Angeles CA 90067
T 310 201 6565
F 310 201 6572
W www.diversetalentgroup.com

Talent and literary agency, founded and run by Christopher Nassif.

THE ENDEAVOR TALENT AGENCY

9601 Wilshire Boulevard 10th Floor
Beverly Hills CA 90210
T 310 248 2000
F 310 248 2020

Talent and literary agency, formed in 1995. Provides representation for writers, directors and actors, working across TV, film and video games. Also has an office in New York.

ROBERT A. FREEDMAN DRAMATIC AGENCY, INC.

Suite 2310 1501 Broadway New York
NY 10036
T 212 840 5760

Founded 1928 as Brandt & Brandt Dramatic Department, Inc. Took its present name in 1984. Works mostly with established authors. Send letter of enquiry first with sae. Specializes in plays, film and TV scripts. Commission: Dramatic 10%.

Submissions Policy
Unsolicited mss not read.

THE GEDDES AGENCY

8430 Santa Monica Boulevard Ste 200
West Hollywood CA 90069
T 323 848 2700

Represents writers, actors and voice-over artists. (Also has an office at 1633 North Halsted Street, Ste 300, Chicago, Illinois 60614. T 312 787 8333)

Submissions Policy
Submissions accepted by mail only.
In first instance, send letter of inquiry with a brief description of project (either to address above or to lit@geddes.net). Will only respond if there is an interest in further investigating the project for representation.

THE GERSH AGENCY (TGA)

41 Madison Avenue Floor 33 New York
NY 10010
T 212 997 1818
F 212 997 1978
E info@gershla.com
W www.gershagency.com

Established as the Phil Gersh Agency in the 1950s and now represents many of the world's leading writing, directing and acting talents. Includes a dedicated TV literary and packaging division and a feature literary division (led by David Gersh, Richard Arlook and Abram Nalibotsky). Also has an LA office (232 North Canon Drive, Suite 201, Beverly Hills, CA 90210; T 310 274 6611).

Submissions Policy
Does not accept or consider unsolicited material, ideas or suggestions of any nature whatsoever.

ICM (INTERNATIONAL CREATIVE MANAGEMENT)

10250 Constellation Boulevard Los Angeles
CA 90067
T 310 550 4000
W www.icmtalent.com

A wide-ranging talent and literary agency. Represents directors and writers responsible for many major motion pictures and televison series. Recently acquired boutique agency Broder Webb Chervin Silbermann. Also has offices in New York and London.

Submissions Policy
Will not accept or consider any unsolicited material, ideas or suggestions of any nature whatsoever. Unsolicited materials will not be

forwarded to or discussed with any third parties.

CAROLYN JENKS AGENCY

69 Aberdeen Avenue Cambridge MA 02138
T 617 354 5099
E cbjenks@att.net

Submissions Policy
Represents screenwriters but do not send unsolicited manuscripts. Approach first by email or letter with outline of project, a short author biography and an sae. Does not charge reading fee.

KAPLAN STAHLER GUMER BRAUN

8383 Wilshire Boulevard Suite 923
Beverly Hills CA 90211
T 323 653 4483
F 323 653 4506
E info@ksgbagency.com
w www.ksgbagency.com

Established in 1981 by Elliot Stahler and Mitch Kaplan. Now one of Hollywood's most prestigious agencies, representing writers, directors and producers for cinema and television.

KNEERIM & WILLIAMS

c/o Fish & Richardson PC 225 Franklin Street
Boston MA 02110
w www.fr.com

Founded in 1990 to deal with books, screenplays, and film and TV rights.

Submissions Policy
Before sending in manuscript, contact in writing with cover letter, outline of project, a two-page synopsis, a CV and an sae. No fees charged. Not currently seeking new original screenplays.

LENHOFF & LENHOFF

830 Palm Avenue West Hollywood CA 90069
T 310 855 2411
F 310 855 2412
E charles@lenhoff.com
w www.lenhoff.com

Management company founded in 1991. Represents writers, directors, producers and cinematographers.

Submissions Policy
Unable to accept unsolicited materials.

STERLING LORD LITERISTIC, INC.

65 Bleecker Street New York NY 10012
T 212 780 6050
F 212 780 6095
w www.sll.com

Founded 1979. Handles all genres, fiction and non-fiction, plus scripts for TV and film. Commission: Home 15%; UK & Translation 20%.

Submissions Policy
No unsolicited manuscripts. Prefers letter outlining all non-fiction. No reading fee.

METROPOLITAN TALENT AGENCY

4500 Wilshire Boulevard Second Floor
Los Angeles CA 90010
T 323 857 4500
w www.mta.com

Well-established talent agency, representing numerous screenwriters.

MONTEIRO ROSE AGENCY

17514 Ventura Boulevard Suite 205 Encino
CA 91316
T 818 501 1177
F 818 501 1194
E monrose@monteiro-rose.com
w www.monteiro-rose.com

Over fifteen-years experience representing live-action and animation writers for children's television, features, home video, and interactive markets.

WILLIAM MORRIS AGENCY (WMA)

1325 Avenue of the Americas New York
NY 10019
T 212 586 5100
F 212 246 3583
w www.wma.com

One of the world's most famous talent and literary agencies, founded in 1898. Works

Founded 1989. Handles theatre, film and TV scripts. No books. Commission: Home 10%; Overseas 15%.

Submissions Policy
Preliminary letter plus professional recommendation and CV essential. No reading fee but sae required.

BRIE BURKEMAN

14 Neville Court Abbey Road London NW8 9DD
T 0870 199 5002
F 0870 199 1029
E brie.burkeman@mail.com

Contacts
Brie Burkeman

Begun in 2000 and now representing an average of 10–25 clients. Clients include Philip Gawthorne of *Dream Team* and Jean Pasley of *How About You*. Interested primarily in film scripts. Does not deal in short film or musicals.

Submissions Policy
Sample material accepted by post only with return postage and by letter. Email attachments will be deleted. No reading fee. 15% commission charged.

CAPEL & LAND LTD

29 Wardour Street London W1D 6PS
T 020 7734 2414
F 020 7734 8101
E robert@capelland.co.uk
W www.capelland.com

Contacts
Georgina Capel

Handles fiction and non-fiction. Also film and TV. Clients include Kunal Basu, John Gimlette, Andrew Greig, Dr Tristram Hunt, Liz Jones, Andrew Roberts, Simon Sebag Montefiore, Stella Rimington, Diana Souhami, Louis Theroux, Fay Weldon. Commission: Home, US & Translation 15%.

Submissions Policy
Send sample chapters and synopsis with covering letter and sae (if return required) in the first instance. No reading fee.

CASAROTTO RAMSAY AND ASSOCIATES LTD

Waverley House 7–12 Noel Street London W1F 8GQ
T 020 7287 4450
F 020 7287 9128
E agents@casarotto.co.uk
W www.casarotto.uk.com

Handles scripts for TV, theatre, film and radio. Clients include: (film) Laura Jones, Neil Jordan, Nick Hornby, Shane Meadows, Purvis & Wade, Lynne Ramsay; (TV) Howard Brenton, Amy Jenkins, Susan Nickson, Jessica Stevenson. Commission: Home 10%. Overseas associates worldwide.

Submissions Policy
No unsolicited material without preliminary letter.

MIC CHEETHAM LITERARY AGENCY

11–12 Dover Street London W1S 4LJ
T 020 7495 2002
F 020 7399 2801

Contacts
Mic Cheetham

Established 1994. Handles general and literary fiction, crime and science fiction, and some specific non-fiction. Film/TV scripts from existing clients only. Clients include Iain Banks, Simon Beckett, Carol Birch, Anita Burgh, Laurie Graham, M. John Harrison, Toby Litt, Ken MacLeod, China Miéville, Antony Sher, Janette Turner Hospital. Commission: Home 15%; US & Translation 20%. Works with The Marsh Agency for all translation rights.

Submissions Policy
No unsolicited manuscripts. Approach in writing with publishing history, first two chapters and return postage. No reading fee.

MARY CLEMMEY LITERARY AGENCY

6 Dunollie Road London NW5 2XP
T 020 7267 1290
F 020 7482 7360

Contacts
Mary Clemmey

Founded 1992. Handles fiction and non-fiction
– high-quality work with an international
market. TV, film, radio and theatre scripts
from existing clients only. US clients:
Frederick Hill Bonnie Nadell Inc., Lynn C.
Franklin Associates Ltd, The Miller Agency,
Roslyn Targ, Weingel- Fidel Agency Inc,
Betsy Amster Literary. Commission: Home
10%; US & Translation 20%. Overseas
associate Elaine Markson Literary Agency,
New York.

Submissions Policy
No unsolicited manuscripts. Approach by letter
only in the first instance giving a description of
the work (include sae). No reading fee.

JONATHAN CLOWES LTD

10 Iron Bridge House Bridge Approach
London NW1 8BD
T   020 7722 7674
F   020 7722 7677

Contacts
Ann Evans

Founded 1960. Pronounced 'clewes'. Now one
of the biggest fish in the pond, and not really
for the untried unless they are true high-flyers.
Fiction and non-fiction, plus scripts. Special
interests: situation comedy, film and television
rights. Clients include David Bellamy, Len
Deighton, Elizabeth Jane Howard, Doris
Lessing, David Nobbs, Gillian White and the
estate of Kingsley Amis. Commission: Home &
US 15%; Translation 19%. Overseas associates
Andrew Nurnberg Associates; Sane Töregard
Agency.

Submissions Policy
No unsolicited manuscripts; authors come by
recommendation or by successful follow-ups to
preliminary letters.

ELSPETH COCHRANE AGENCY

11 Orlando Road London SW4 0LE
T   020 7622 0314
E   info@elspethcochrane.co.uk

Founded in 1960, representing some
screenwriters. Commission is a negotiable
12.5%.

ROSICA COLIN LTD

1 Clareville Grove Mews London SW7 5AH
T   020 7370 1080
F   020 7244 6441

Contacts
Joanna Marston

Founded 1949. Handles all full-length
manuscripts, plus theatre, film, television
and sound broadcasting but few new writers
being accepted. Commission: Home 10%;
US & Translation 20%.

Submissions Policy
Preliminary letter with return postage
essential; writers should outline their writing
credits and whether their manuscripts have
previously been submitted elsewhere.
May take 3–4 months to consider full
manuscripts; synopsis preferred in the first
instance. No reading fee.

CURTIS BROWN GROUP

Haymarket House 28-29 Haymarket London
SW1Y 4SP
T   020 7393 4400
W   www.curtisbrown.co.uk

Established in 1899 and one of Europe's oldest
literary agencies. Interested in all forms of
fiction; rarely deals in factual formats.

Submissions Policy
Accepts unsolicited material only by post.
Requires synopsis, covering letter and CV. No
reading fee.

JUDY DAISH ASSOCIATES LTD

2 St Charles Place London W10 6EG
T   020 8964 8811
F   020 8964 8966

Contacts
Judy Daish

Founded 1978. Theatrical literary agent.
Handles scripts for film, TV, theatre and radio.
No books.

Submissions Policy
Preliminary letter essential. No unsolicited
manuscripts.

FELIX DE WOLFE

Kingsway House 103 Kingsway London
WC2B 6QX
T 020 7242 5066
F 020 7242 8119
E info@felixdewolfe.com

Contacts
Felix de Wolfe

Founded 1938. Handles quality fiction only,
and scripts. Clients include Jan Butlin, Jeff
Dowson, Brian Glover, Sheila Goff, Aileen
Gonsalves, John Kershaw, Ray Kilby, Bill
MacIlwraith, Angus Mackay, Gerard
McLarnon, Malcolm Taylor, David Thompson,
Paul Todd, Dolores Walshe. Commission:
Home $12\frac{1}{2}$%; US 20%.

Submissions Policy
No unsolicited mss. No reading fee.

THE DENCH ARNOLD AGENCY

10 Newburgh Street London W1F 7RN
T 020 7437 4551
F 020 7439 1355
E contact@den007437charnold.co.uk
W www.dencharnold.co.uk

Contacts
Elizabeth Dench

Founded 1972. Handles scripts for TV and film.
Clients include Peter Chelsom. Commission:
Home 10–15%. Overseas associates include
William Morris/Sanford Gross and C.A.A.,
Los Angeles.

Submissions Policy
Unsolicited manuscripts will be read, but a
letter with sample of work and CV (plus sae)
is required.

JANET FILLINGHAM ASSOCIATES

52 Lowther Road London SW13 9NU
T 020 8748 5594
F 020 8748 7374
E info@janetfillingham.com
W www.janetfillingham.com

Founded in 1992, representing a select list of
writers and directors working in television and
feature films in the adult and family markets.

Submissions Policy
Not currently seeking new clients but will
accept CVs sent by email. Promises to read
every CV but any other correspondence will
not be read.

FILM RIGHTS LTD/LAURENCE FITCH LTD

Quadrant House 80-82 Regent Street London
W1B 5AU
T 020 7734 9911
F 020 7734 0044
E information@filmrights.ltd.uk
W www.filmrights.ltd.uk

Agency established in 1932. Now
representing around 20 clients such as
Ray Coovey and John Chapman. Handles
most genres of film and TV projects,
particularly drama. Little interest in
historical scripts.

Submissions Policy
Reads new material mostly on recommendation
only. Commission charged: 10% domestic,
15% overseas.

JILL FOSTER LTD

9 Barb Mews Brook Green London W6 7PA
T 020 7602 1263
F 020 7602 9336
E agents@jflagency.com
W www.jflagency.com

Contacts
Jill Foster *Managing Director*

Established in 1976 to represent film and
television screenwriters. Specialists in comedy
and drama. Accepts no unsolicited manuscripts.
Charges 12.5% domestic commission, 15%
overseas.

FRA

17 Deanhill Road London SW14 7DQ
T 020 8255 7755
F 020 8286 4860
E guy@futermanrose.co.uk
W www.futermanrose.co.uk

Contacts
Guy Rose *Biography/Non-Fiction/Screenplays*

Founded 1984. Handles fiction; scripts for film and TV; biography; show business; current affairs and teenage fiction. Clients include Larry Barker, Christian Piers Betley, Shirley Clarkson, Iain Duncan Smith, Royston Ellis, Sir Martin Ewans, Yvette Fielding, Susan George, Stephen Griffin, Anita Harris, Brian Harvey, Paul Hendy, Russell Warren Howe, Keith R. Lindsay, Stephen Lowe, Eric MacInnes, Paul Marx, Max Morgan-Witts, Ciarán O'Keeffe, Erin Pizzey, John Repsch, Liz Rettig, Peter Sallis, Pat Silver-Lasky, Paul Stinchcombe, Gordon Thomas, Bill Tidy, Mark White, Toyah Willcox, Simon Woodham, Tappy Wright, Allen Zeleski.

Submissions Policy
No unsolicited manuscripts. Send preliminary letter with brief resumé, detailed synopsis, first 20 pages (approx.) and sae.

FRENCH'S

78 Loudoun Road London NW8 0NA
T   020 7483 4269

Founded in 1973. Handles scripts for all media with particular focus on screenplays. Write in first instance before sending in manuscript. Charged reading service for first-time writers. Commission charged at 10% for home market.

ERIC GLASS LTD

25 Ladbroke Crescent London W11 1PS
T   020 7229 9500
F   020 7229 6220
E   eglassltd@aol.com

Contacts
Janet Glass

Founded 1934. Handles fiction, non-fiction and scripts for publication or production in all media. Overseas associates in the US, Australia, Czech Republic, France, Germany, Greece, Holland, Italy, Japan, Poland, Scandinavia, Slovakia, South Africa, Spain.

Submissions Policy
No unsolicited manuscripts. Return postage required. No reading fee.

THE ROD HALL AGENCY LIMITED

6th Floor Fairgate House 78 New Oxford Street London W1A 1HB
T   020 7079 7987
F   0845 638 4094
E   www.rodhallagency.com
W   www.rodhallagency.com

Contacts
Charlotte Knight

Founded 1997. Handles drama for film, TV and theatre and writers-directors. Does not represent writers of episodes for TV series where the format is provided but represents originators of series. Clients include Simon Beaufoy (*The Full Monty*), Jeremy Brock (*Mrs Brown*), Liz Lochhead (*Perfect Days*), Martin McDonagh (*The Pillowman*), Simon Nye (*Men Behaving Badly*). Commission: Home 10%; US & Translation 15%. No reading fee.

ROGER HANCOCK LTD

4 Water Lane London NW1 8NZ
T   020 7267 4418
F   020 7267 0705
E   info@rogerhancock.com

Founded 1960. Special interests: comedy drama and light entertainment. Commission: Home 10%; Overseas 15%.

Submissions Policy
Unsolicited manuscripts not welcome. Initial phone call required.

DAVID HIGHAM ASSOCIATES LTD

5–8 Lower John Street Golden Square London W1F 9HA
T   020 7434 5900
F   020 7437 1072
E   dha@davidhigham.co.uk
W   www.davidhigham.co.uk

Contacts
Nicky Lund

Founded 1935. Handles fiction, general non-fiction (biography, history, current affairs, etc.) and children's books. Also scripts. Clients include John le Carré,

J.M. Coetzee, Stephen Fry, Jane Green, James Herbert, Alexander McCall Smith, Lynne Truss, Jacqueline Wilson. Commission: Home 15%; US & Translation 20%; Scripts 10%.

Submissions Policy
Preliminary letter with synopsis essential in first instance. No email submissions. No reading fee. See website for further information.

VALERIE HOSKINS ASSOCIATES LIMITED
20 Charlotte Street London W1T 2NA
T   020 7637 4490
F   020 7637 4493
E   vha@vhassociates.co.uk

Contacts
Valerie Hoskins

Founded 1983. Handles scripts for film, TV and radio. Special interests: feature films, animation and TV. Commission: Home $12\frac{1}{2}$%; US 20% (maximum).

Submissions Policy
No unsolicited scripts; preliminary letter of introduction essential. No reading fee.

ICM
Oxford House 76 Oxford Street London W1D 1BS
T   020 7636 6565
F   020 7323 0101

Founded 1973. Specializes in scripts for film, theatre, TV and radio. No reading fee.

INTERNATIONAL SCRIPTS
1A Kidbrooke Park Road London SE3 0LR
T   020 8319 8666
F   020 8319 0801
E   internationalscripts@btinternet.com

Contacts
Bob Tanner

Founded 1979 by Bob Tanner. Handles most types of books (non-fiction and fiction) and scripts for most media. No poetry, articles or short stories. Clients include

Jane Adams, Zita Adamson, Ashleigh Bingham, Simon Clark, Ann Cliff, Dr James Fleming, June Gadsby, Julie Harris, Robert A. Heinlein, Anna Jacobs, Anne Jones, Richard Laymon, Trevor Lummis, Margaret Muir, Nick Oldham, Chris Pascoe, Christine Poulson, John and Anne Spencer, Janet Woods. Commission: Home 15%; US & Translation 20%. Overseas associates include Ralph Vicinanza, USA; Thomas Schlück, Germany.

Submissions Policy
Preliminary letter, one-page synopsis, wordage, plus sae required. No unsolicited manuscripts by post or email accepted.

MICHELLE KASS ASSOCIATES
85 Charing Cross Road London WC2H 0AA
T   020 7439 1624
F   020 7734 3394
E   office@michellekass.co.uk

Contacts
Michelle Kass

Founded 1991. Handles literary fiction, film and television primarily. Commission: Home 10%; US & Translation 15–20%.

Submissions Policy
No manuscripts accepted without preliminary phone call. No reading fee.

LAW
14 Vernon Street London W14 0RJ
T   020 7471 7900
F   020 7471 7910

Founded 1996. Handles full-length commercial and literary fiction, non-fiction and children's books. Film and TV scripts handled for established clients only. Commission: Home 15%; US & Translation 20%. Overseas associates worldwide.

Submissions Policy
Unsolicited manuscripts considered; send brief covering letter, short synopsis

and two sample chapters. Sae essential.
No emailed or disk submissions.

THE CHRISTOPHER LITTLE LITERARY AGENCY

Eel Brook Studios 125 Moore Park Road
London SW6 4PS
T   020 7736 4455
F   020 7736 4490
E   info@christopherlittle.net or firstname@
W   www.christopherlittle.net

Contacts
Christopher Little

Founded 1979. Handles commercial and
literary full-length fiction and non-fiction. Film
scripts from established clients only. Authors
include Steve Barlow and Steve Skidmore, Paul
Bajoria, Andrew Butcher, Janet Gleeson, Carol
Hughes, Alastair MacNeill, Robert Mawson,
Haydn Middleton, Andrew Quinnell,
Christopher Matthew, Robert Radcliffe,
J.K. Rowling, Darren Shan, Wladyslaw
Szpilman, John Watson, Pip Vaughan-Hughes,
Gorillaz, Christopher Hale, Peter Howells, Gen.
Sir Mike Jackson, Lauren Liebenberg, Shiromi
Pinto, Dr Nicholas Reeves, Shayne Ward,
Angela Woolfe, Anne Zouroudi. Commission:
Home 15%; US, Canada, Translation,
Audio & Motion Picture 20%.

Submissions Policy
Send detailed preliminary letter in the first
instance with synopsis, first 2–3 chapters and
sae. No reading fee.

ANDREW MANN LTD

Third Floor 1 Old Compton Street London
W1D 5TA
T   020 7734 4751
F   020 7287 9264
E   info@manuscript.co.uk
W   www.andrewmann.co.uk

Contacts
Tina Betts *Literary Agent*

Agency founded in 1968, now representing
about 80 clients. Handles film and television
comedy and drama. Also interested in children's
scripts. Does not deal in horror, sci-fi, fantasy
or sitcoms.

Submissions Policy
Unsolicited material accepted as a letter, short
synopsis and 30 pages of text. No reading fee.
15% commission charged.

MARJACQ SCRIPTS LTD

34 Devonshire Place London W1G 6JW
T   020 7935 9499
F   020 7935 9115
E   subs@marjacq.com
W   www.marjacq.com

Contacts
Philip Patterson *Books*

Handles fiction and non-fiction, literary and
commercial as well as film, TV, radio scripts.
No poetry. Commission: Home 10%;
Overseas 20%.

Submissions Policy
New work welcome; send brief letter, synopsis
and approx. first 50 pages plus sae. No
reading fee.

MBA LITERARY AGENTS LTD

62 Grafton Way London W1T 5DW
T   020 7387 2076
F   020 7387 2042
E   agent@mbalit.co.uk
W   www.mbalit.co.uk

Contacts
Diana Tyler

Film and television agency founded in 1971.
Submission guidelines for unsolicited material
on the website. 10% commission charged for
television, and 10–15% for film.

MCKERNAN AGENCY

5 Gayfield Square Edinburgh EH1 3NW
T   0131 557 1771
E   maggie@mckernanagency.co.uk
W   www.mckernanagency.co.uk

Contacts
Maggie McKernan

Founded 2005. Works in conjunction with
Capel & Land Ltd. Handles fiction, both
literary and commercial; also TV, film, radio

and theatre scripts. Commission: Home 15%; US & Translation 15%.

Submissions Policy
Send sae for return of manuscripts. No reading fee.

BILL MCLEAN PERSONAL MANAGEMENT

23b Deodar Road Putney London SW15 2NP
T 020 8789 8191

Contacts
Bill McLean

Established in 1972 to represent talent from film, TV, radio and stage. No unsolicited material.

WILLIAM MORRIS AGENCY (UK) LTD

CentrePoint Tower 103 Oxford Street London WC1A 1DD
T 020 7534 6800
F 020 7534 6900
W www.wma.com

Contacts
Caroline Michel *Managing Director*

London office founded in 1965. Worldwide talent and literary agency with offices in New York, Beverly Hills, Nashville, Miami and Shanghai. Handles fiction, general non-fiction, TV and film scripts. Commission: TV 10%; UK Books 15%; US Books & Translation 20%.

Submissions Policy
Telephone in the first instance for screenplay and TV submissions. No reading fee.

THE NARROW ROAD COMPANY

182 Brighton Road Coulsdon Surrey CR5 2NF
T 020 8703 9895
F 020 8703 2558
E richardireson

Contacts
Richard Ireson *Managing Director*

Agency founded in 1986, dealing mainly in drama across theatre, film, tv and radio.

Submissions Policy
Unsolicited manuscripts should be sent with CV and return postage. The agency advises that first time writers need not apply.

PFD

Drury House 34–43 Russell Street London WC2B 5HA
T 020 7344 1000
F 020 7836 9539/9541
E postmaster@pfd.co.uk
W www.pfd.co.uk

PFD represents authors of fiction and non-fiction, children's writers, screenwriters, playwrights, documentary makers, technicians, presenters and actors throughout the world.

Submissions Policy
Consult the website for submission guidelines.

POLLINGER LIMITED

9 Staple Inn Holborn London WC1V 7QH
T 020 7404 0342
F 020 7242 5737
E info@pollingerltd.com
W www.pollingerltd.com

Contacts
Lesley Pollinger *Managing Director*

Established in 1935, interested in scripts for film and television, predominantly drama. Existing clients are in the main novellists but currently developing the dramatic rights and screenwriters lists.

RDF MANAGEMENT

RDF Management The Gloucester Building Kensington Village Avonmore Road London W14 8RF
T 020 7013 4103
E info@rdfmanagement.com
W www.rdfmanagement.com

A specialist talent agency representing actors, writers, presenters and stand-up comedians.

REAL CREATIVES WORLDWIDE

14 Dean Street London W1D 3RS
T 020 7437 4188
E business@realcreatives.com
W www.realcreatives.com

Contacts
Mark Maco

Founded in 1984 and now has 420 clients.
Interested in scripts for film and television,
especially dramas, documentaries and
action films.

Submissions Policy
Email in first instance, before mailing
or posting manuscript/idea. Charges
commission of 10–20% but no
reading fee.

REDHAMMER MANAGEMENT LTD

186 Bickenhall Mansions Bickenhall Street
London W1U 6BX
T 020 7486 3465
F 020 7000 1249
E info@redhammer.info
W www.redhammer.info

Contacts
Peter Cox *Vice President*

'Provides in-depth management for a
small number of highly talented authors.'
Willing to take on unpublished authors
who are professional in their approach
and who have major international
potential, ideally for, book, film and/or
tv. Clients: Martin Bell OBE,
John Brindley, Brian Clegg, Joe Donnelly,
Audrey Eyton, Maria Harris, Senator Orrin
Hatch, Amanda Lees, David McIntee,
Hon. Nicholas Monson, Michelle Paver,
Carolyn Soutar, Carole Stone,
Donald Trelford, Justin Wintle,
David Yelland.

Submissions Policy
Submissions considered only if the
guidelines given on the website
have been followed. Do not send
unsolicited manuscripts by post.
No radio or theatre scripts.
No reading fee.

SAYLE SCREEN LTD

11 Jubilee Place London SW3 3TD
T 020 7823 3883
E info@saylescreen.com
W www.saylescreen.com

Contacts
Jane Villiers *Agent*

Agency specializing in writers and directors
for film and television. Particularly
interested in drama, documentary and
comedy writing. Represents around
60–70 clients including Andrea Arnold
and Marc Evans.

Submissions Policy
Welcomes unsolicited sample material
with CV, cover letter and return postage.
No reading fee.

THE SHARLAND ORGANISATION LTD

The Manor House Manor Street Raunds
Northants NN9 6JW
T 01833 626 600
F 01933 624 860
E tsoshar@aol.com
W www.sharlandorganisation.co.uk

Contacts
Mike Sharland *Director*

Agency founded in 1988 concentrating on
drama, comedy and documentary work. No
manuscripts accepted unless requested;
letter/email of introduction required first. 15%
commission charged in the UK, 20% overseas.
No reading fee.

SHEIL LAND ASSOCIATES

52 Doughty Street London WC1N 2LS
T 020 7405 9351
F 020 7831 2127
E info@sheilland.co.uk

Contacts
Sophie Janson *Film, TV and Theatrical Agent*

Film, television and theatrical agents interested
to see scripts of all genres. Contact with
reception advised before sending letters and
sample writing. No reading fee. 15%
commission charged.

ELAINE STEEL

110 Gloucester Avenue London NW1 8HX
T   020 8348 0918
F   020 8341 9807
E   ecmsteel@aol.com

Contacts
Elaine Steel

Founded 1986. Handles scripts, screenplays and books. No technical or academic. Clients include Les Blair, Anna Campion, Michael Eaton, Pearse Elliott, Gwyneth Hughes, Brian Keenan, Troy Kennedy Martin, James Lovelock, Rob Ritchie, Albie Sachs, Ben Steiner. Commission: Home 10%; US & Translation 20%.

Submissions Policy
Initial phone call preferred.

MICHELINE STEINBERG ASSOCIATES

104 Great Portland Street London W1W 6PE
T   020 7631 1310
E   info@steinplays.com
W   www.steinplays.com

Contacts
MIcheline Steinberg *Agent*

Founded in 1987, dealing in drama and comedy for film, television, theatre and radio.

Submissions Policy
Does not welcome unsolicited approaches. Industry recommendation preferred. Commission charged at 10% for home and 10–20% for overseas.

THE TENNYSON AGENCY

10 Cleveland Avenue Wimbledon Chase London SW20 9EW
T   020 8543 5939
E   submissions@tenagy.co.uk
W   www.tenagy.co.uk

Contacts
Christopher Oxford *Partner*

Agency founded in 2002 with 16 clients including Julian Howell, Tony Bagley and Steve MacGregor. Interested in any fictional material for both film and television except fantasy, science fiction, children's animation or foreign language projects.

Submissions Policy
Letters of introduction encouraged at first by post or email. No reading fee. 15% domestic commission charged, 20% overseas.

CECILY WARE LITERARY AGENTS

19C John Spencer Square London
London N1 2LZ
T   020 7359 3787
F   020 7226 9828
E   info@cecilyware.com

Contacts
Cecily Ware

Founded 1972. Primarily a film and TV script agency representing work in all areas: drama, children's, series/serials, adaptations, comedies, etc. Commission: Home 10%; US 10–20% by arrangement.

Submissions Policy
No unsolicited manuscripts or phone calls. Approach in writing only. No reading fee.

AP WATT LTD

20 John Street London WC1N 2DR
T   0207 405 6774
F   0207 831 2154
E   apw@apwatt.co.uk
W   www.apwatt.co.uk

Agency founded in 1875. Film and television specialists. Interested in drama, comedy and documentary.

Submissions Policy
No unsolicited material. Approach via agent by letter FAO Media Department.

CANADA

AGENCE OMADA

451 rue Ste-Catherine Ouest bur. 201
Montréal Québec H3B 1B1
T   514 287 1246
F   514 287 7694
E   info@omada.ca
W   www.omada.ca

Represents variety of 'behind the camera' artists including screenwriters and directors.

THE ALPERN GROUP
585 Bloor Street West 2nd Floor Toronto Ontario M6G 1K5
T   416 907 5845
F   416 531 4961

Represents writers for both film and television.

AMBITION
70 High Park Avenue # 2003 Toronto Ontario M6P 1A1
T   416 629 3023
E   info@ambitiontalent.com

Contacts
David Ritchie *Owner*

Founded in 2006. Represents talent from the film and television industries. Interested in all types of material.

Submissions Policy
Material read only upon recommendation. No unsolicited emails or calls. Commission: 10–15% for clients.

AURORA ARTISTS
19 Wroxeter Avenue Toronto Ontario M4K 1J5
T   416 463 4634
E   aurora.artists@sympatico.ca

Represents writers for film and TV.

CHRISTOPHER BANKS & ASSOCIATES
Suite 410 6 Adelaide Street East Toronto Ontario M5C 1H6
T   416 214 1155
F   416 214 1150
E   info@chrisbanks.com
W   www.chrisbanks.com

Founded in 1983, a talent agency for professionals in the film, television and performing arts.

Submissions Policy
Accepts submissions for representation by referral only.

THE CHARACTERS
8 Elm Street Toronto Ontario M5G 1G7
T   416 964 8522
F   416 964 8206

Founded in 1969, a full service agency with offices in Toronto and Vancouver. Represents editors and writers, among others.

Submissions Policy
Submit a package including a resume, approximately 30-word logline, and a 1-page synopsis or a resume and demo reel or portfolio. Label "Attn: Literary Department" and include sae for return of materials. Will not consider unsolicited scripts.

GREAT NORTH ARTISTS MANAGEMENT INC.
350 Dupont Street Toronto Ontario M5R 1V9
T   416 925 2051
F   416 925 3904
E   info@gnaminc.com

Contacts
Ralph Zimmerman *President*

Represents literary talent from film, television and theatre. Founded in 1972.

Submissions Policy
No unsolicited material.

GREEN LIGHT ARTIST MANAGEMENT INC.
1240 Bay Street Suite 804 Toronto Ontario M5R 2A7
T   416 920 5110
F   416 920 4113
E   info@glam.on.ca
W   www.glam.on.ca

Represents people working across creative disciplines in the film and television industry, including directors, editors and writers.

LOWENBE HOLDINGS
680 Indian Point Road Glen Haven Nova Scotia B3Z 2TZ
T   902 823 1409
E   jmiller@loweba.ca
W   www.lowenbe.ca

Contacts
Jan Miller *President*

Development consultant company founded in 1997. Specializes in drama and documentary projects for film and television. Also produces "Pitcher Perfect" workshops presented at the Toronto International Film Festival, Hot Docs, the Banff Television Festival, the Atlantic Film Festival and training facilities across Canada.

LUCAS TALENT

7th Floor 100 West Pender Street Vancouver British Columbia V6B 1R8
T   604 685 0345
F   604 685 0341
W   www.lucastalent.com

Contacts
Anna Archer *Literary Agent*

Agency for screen talent only. Founded in 1986. Handles all genres of writing; adults and children's.

Submissions Policy
Unsolicited material only accepted following introduction via email/phone. Copy read only when requested. Process outlined on website. Only represents writers from western Canada. 10% commission charged to clients.

MENSOUR AGENCY

41 Springfield Road Ottawa Ontario K1M 1C8
W   www.mensour.ca

Roster of clients including writers working in the entertainment and advertising industries.

MERIDIAN ARTISTS INC.

207-2 College Street Toronto Ontario M5G 1K3
T   416 961 2777
E   info@meridianartists.com
W   www.meridianartists.com

Contacts
Glenn Cockburn *Agent/Owner*

Film and television literary agency founded in October 2005. Interested in all genres except documentary.

Submissions Policy
Welcomes unsolicited submissions via email. No reading fee. 10% commission charged to clients.

PANGARYK PRODUCTIONS, INC.

Script Services Division 14885 Alpine Boulevard Hope British Columbia V0X 1L5
T   604 202 5400
E   scriptservices@pangarykproductions.com
W   www.pangarykproductions.com

Contacts
Tihemme Gagnon *President*

Creative development and script services company for film and television projects. Provides story editing, script analysis, proofreading and pitch packaging services to production companies, agencies and independent screenwriters on a contractual basis.

Submissions Policy
Material accepted via emails. Non-disclosure agreements mandatory for all submissions.

VANGUARDE ARTISTS MANAGEMENT

2 Bloor Street East Suite 2902 Toronto Ontario M4W 1A8

A boutique literary film and television agency.

Submissions Policy
Does not accept unsolicited submissions.

WESTWOOD CREATIVE ARTISTS

94 Harbord Street Toronto Ontario M5S 1G6
T   416 964 3302 ext. 22
F   416 975 9209
W   www.wcaltd.com

Literary agency with a dedicated film and television department.

IRELAND

THE LISA RICHARDS AGENCY

108 Upper Leeson Street Dublin 4
T   01 637 5000
F   01 667 1256

E   info@lisarichards.ie
W   www.lisarichards.ie

Contacts
Faith O'Grady

Founded in 1989. Accepts screen and stage plays. No reading fee. Authors should submit first 2–3 scenes, a short synopsis and an sae for return of material if necessary.

AUSTRALIA

CAMERON CRESWELL AGENCY

7th Floor 61 Marlborough Street (Locked Bag 848) Surry Hills NSW 2010
T   02 9319 7199
F   02 9319 6866
E   info@cameronsmanagement.com.au
W   www.cameronsmanagement.com.au

Founded in 1976, with clients including screenwriters, directors, film editors, playwrights and a distinguished list of authors.

HLA MANAGEMENT PTY LTD

87 Pitt Street Redfern NSW 2232
T   02 9310 4948
F   02 9310 4113
E   hla@hlamgt.com.au
W   www.hlamanagement.com.au

Contacts
Kate Richter *Managing Director*

Founded in 1973. Roster of 115 clients including screenwriters, playwrights and directors. No reading fee. Commission charged at 15%.

Submissions Policy
Prefers an initial approach prior to receiving work for consideration.

STACEY TESTRO INTERNATIONAL MANAGEMENT

26a Dow Street South Melbourne VIC 3205
T   03 9645 9181
E   info@ztudio.com
W   www.ztudio.com

Literary and talent agency representing writers, directors, producers, composers, directors of photography and actors.

NEW ZEALAND

JOHNSON & LAIRD AND RACHEL GARDNER MANAGEMENTS

PO Box 78340 Grey Lynn Auckland 1002
T   09 378 9800
F   09 378 9801
E   info@rachelgardner.co.nz
W   www.rachelgardner.co.nz

Formed in 2002 representing actors, directors, presenters, voice-over artists and writers. Affiliated with agencies in Sydney, London and LA.

RICHARDS LITERARY AGENCY

PO Box 31 240 Milford
North Shore City 074
T   09 410 0209
F   09 410 0209
E   rla.richards@clear.net.nz

Contacts
Ray Richards *Agent*

Large agency founded in 1977. Currently representing over 100 clients including novelists Maurice Gee and Joy Cowley. Not interested in original screenplays. Only seeks adaptations of published books.

Submissions Policy
No unsolicited manuscripts.

SCRIPTEASE

PO Box 10251 Dominion Road
Auckland
T   027 300 6481
E   scripts@scriptease.info
W   www.scriptease.info

Established in 2000 to represent writers and assist with script development, editing and assessing.

PITCH YOUR CAT

Daryl G. Nickens has some tips for selling that great idea

In Hollywood, you can beat death and taxes. Think about it: what writer is hotter than Shakespeare and further out of the reach of the IRS? But sooner or later, everybody has to pitch. And if you're going to survive, you have to find a way to do it well.

Like getting to Carnegie Hall, the secret of a great pitch is practice, practice, practice. At a recent Writers on Genre conference sponsored by the Writers Guild Foundation, Michael Miner, co-author of *Robocop*, advised writers to hone their pitches by pitching to anyone who'll listen. If need be, 'tell it to your cat'.

The brilliance of this idea is staggering because cats are very much like many executives (and agents): self-absorbed creatures with short attention spans and sushi breath. Moreover, pitching to a cat requires the same delicate balance that must be maintained when pitching to an executive (or agent): if you're uninteresting, the cat's eyes will glaze over and it will either leave, fall asleep or start licking itself – which is the human equivalent of leaving, falling asleep or taking a cell phone call. Get hyper; not only will the cat become skittish and try everything in its power not to be in the same room with you now or ever again, but the memory of your insanity will pervade the collective cat unconscious, and other cats will avoid you like a cold fleabath.

How do you structure a good pitch?

Ron Bass says the inspiration for *My Best Friend's Wedding* was the notion of doing a Julia Roberts movie in which Julia Roberts doesn't get the guy. Sounds like a great opening line to me. This strategy of announcing a clever summary of the story – in this case, one that goes against type in a provocative way – can be especially effective in pitching episodes of TV shows, where the characters and their universe are a given (and essentially not malleable) and the goal of the pitch is to repurpose the familiar in a surprising and satisfying way.

Another effective way to start a pitch is with an epiphany: a Raymond Chandler two-guys-come-through-the-door-with-guns-aimed-at-your-hero moment from your movie. This is starting the pitch on the central dramatic question. For example, a kindly waitress lets an obviously mentally unbalanced man in out of the rain. The man sits at the piano and plays like a virtuoso. Who is he – and how did he wind up here? He would be pianist David Helfgott and this would be a great way to begin to pitch *Shine*. (And was also a great way to open the movie.) Beginning with a bang forces you to get quickly to the point: who's your protagonist, how did she get in this jam and, most importantly, how is she going to get out? Remember, cats like to toy with things that move.

Wherever you start your pitch, you end up in the same ballpark: trying to tell a compelling story about a character with a problem who makes a choice. That's the essence of drama. If you can make the audience feel something, that's great drama. If you're pitching a comedy, then you have to tell a funny story about a funny character with a funny problem that becomes really funny because the funny character makes a really funny choice. If the audience laughs, that's comedy. If they laugh a lot, that's a miracle. As the punchline to the old showbiz joke goes: dying is easy; comedy is hard.

Knowing what to pitch, however, is pretty simple. To paraphrase Karen Lutz, co-author of *Legally Blonde*, don't pitch the movie you think the studio wants to buy; pitch the movie you want to see. Put it this way: if they knew what they wanted, they wouldn't be asking you to tell them what it is.

But above all, when you pitch, remember who you're pitching to. If your pitch is just the externalization of your ordeal of pitching, it's gonna be nappy time or 'exit, stage right'; but if it's a nice fat mouse, the cat may just pounce.

HOW TO CHOOSE A SCREENWRITING COURSE

Phil Parker on where to go for screenwriting courses

The screenplay is the foundation of everything from short films to feature films and long-running soap operas, and for many people writing the screenplay is the first step in a career, or maybe just an attempt to see if you can do better than some 'awful' drama you have just watched. However, for anyone who has attempted to write a screenplay it soon becomes obvious that perhaps it is not as easy as it may first appear, and the question of attending a course comes into focus.

The question is then – which one? With over 115 listed on the Skillset website (see below), over 78,000 screenwriting course websites in the UK alone, and over 1 million sites worldwide, the choice is bewildering. Add to this situation the tales of writers who have attended courses which did not work for them, and the scale of the problem – which course is right for me? – can appear as daunting as actually writing the screenplay.

To crack the problem, start with a few simple questions.

The first question is not about the course but about you. What do you hope to gain from the course? Do you just want to see what screenwriting is all about, perhaps have a go, are you an experienced writer who wants to adapt a work for the screen or a screenwriter who just needs inspiration for a new project? Knowing what you need will indicate the level and type of course that will suit you best.

If you are a beginner then there are several introductory courses available both on the web, and as weekend or evening classes. These will provide you with an overview of the various skills you need to write a screenplay, and an introduction to the world of screenwriting. The good courses also provide you with the chance to write a short film screenplay or television drama/sitcom, and provide constructive feedback on your work. A list of UK courses can be found in his Handbook and on www.skillset.org/careers/.

The more experienced writer is better served by the short intensive courses often provided via national and international training organizations. In Europe, many of these courses are supported by MEDIA (www.c.europa.eu/information_society/ media/index_en.htm) and regional film funds, while many universities throughout the world provide short courses as part of their film school programmes.

The 'Guru' courses provided by recognized screenwriting tutors/experts such as Robert McKee and Andy Horton, now run regularly in the English-speaking world. These short, often weekend-long, courses focus mainly on feature-length dramas. These are often too specific for beginners but regularly provide inspiration, and focus, for even the most experienced writers.

The next major question is – what is your level of commitment to a course? If you only have a couple of hours a week, or the odd weekend, then a full-time college-based course is not really an option but an evening class or a part-time degree course may work for you. Equally, screenwriting is about rewriting and dealing with a very industrial process in order to see your work, realized so if you do not have the commitment to see this through then another form of creative writing course may suit you best.

Next, who are the course tutors? As with all courses it is the quality of the tutors that ultimately makes it a good course. There are two key areas to concentrate on when reviewing the tutors of a course.

Obviously, there is their own track record – are they screenwriters, have they worked professionally with screenplays e.g. script editing, or have they published books on screenwriting etc.? However, be warned, not everyone who has been a screenwriter can teach, and equally some teachers are brilliant at inspiring others, while having no track record themselves.

The second area is the track record of the course itself. What are the views of past students, and what has been the success rate of the course? The latter is particularly relevant for full-time or professional entry-level courses. Consistency in a course's outcomes suggests it is a well-run programme, which is adapted by different tutors.

This information on tutors may usually be found via the publicity for the course, or the organization providing the course. Skillset provides a professional accreditation system for masters level degree courses in the UK – see www.skillset.org/film/ training_and_events/accreditation/article_3785_1.asp

The final question is – what is the course content? Obtaining a detailed breakdown of what will be taught or offered on the course is vital in making an assessment of its quality, and whether it will work for you. For instance, if a course provides an introduction to writing for radio, theatre and television, it is unlikely to provide you with enough information to write a good screenplay. Equally, if a course is oriented towards feature film writing it will not really solve the problems you are having with your short film project or television sitcom.

However, there are some key areas a course must provide if it will really help you write a good screenplay:

- Visual and dialogue writing
- Dramatic structures
- Genre
- Writing screen characters
- The distinctions between radio, theatre, television, and cinema writing
- The process of screenwriting from outline to rewrites
- The challenges of adaptation
- How the film and television industries work with respect to screenwriters
- Screenings and screenplay extracts
- Constructive feedback on your writing.

The teaching of screenwriting is still a young art, and there are no established quality criteria that can be applied to all courses. However, there are courses to meet most needs, and the key is to ask the right questions before signing up. As with screenwriting itself, research will not only provide you with a better platform on which to make a choice but also help focus the creative desires on those areas that really need attention.

Phil Parker is the author of The Art and Science of Screenwriting, *created the UK Film Council's* Introduction to Screenwriting *course, and is a freelance consultant whose clients include Aardman Animations and Skillset.*

We had a sort of session here, with some young writers doing pitches for ideas for scripts they either had written or were intending to write, and what was interesting about the exercise was that one couldn't imagine why anyone would want to see about three quarters of the films they were pitching.

Julian Fellowes at the 2006 Cheltenham Screenwriters' Festival

COURSES

COURSES

UNITED STATES OF AMERICA

AMERICAN FILM INSTITUTE (AFI)

2021 N. Western Avenue Los Angeles
CA 90027
T   323 856 7600
F   323 467 4578
W www.afi.com

The AFI Conservatory offers a 2-year Master
of Fine Arts degree. Topics covered
in the first year include: cycle production,
screenwriting and narrative
workshops, writing the thriller,
and American approaches to film.
In the second year, issues covered
include writing for television and world
approaches to film.

AMERICAN UNIVERSITY

4400 Massachusetts Avenue NW
Washington, D.C. 200
T   202 885 2060
F   202 885 2019
E   communication@american.edu
W www.soc.american.edu

Offers a two-week screenwriting
workshop. The course demonstrates
how to develop the right idea, create
interesting characters and manage the
plot in the development of a short
dramatic film.

BOSTON UNIVERSITY

1 Sherborn Street Boston MA 02215
T   617 353 4636
E   script@bu.edu
W www.bu.edu

The School of Communication offers a 2-year
Master of Fine Arts degree in screenwriting.
The course consists of 64 credit hours of an
intensive combination of writing and film and
television classes. Students are required to write
at least three original feature-length
screenplays.

BROOKLYN COLLEGE

2900 Bedford Avenue 0314 Plaza Building
Brooklyn NY 11210
T   718 951 5664
F   718 951 4733
E   film@brooklyn.cuny.edu
W depthome.brooklyn.cuny.edu

The Department offers an undergraduate
Bachelor of Arts in Film with a concentration
in film production, film studies, screenwriting
or film marketing. Also offers a 2-year
Certificate Programme in Film with a
concentration in film production or
screenwriting.

UNIVERSITY OF CALIFORNIA (BERKELEY)

Program in Film Studies Dwinelle Hall #2670
Berkeley CA 94720
T   510 642 1415
F   510 642 8881
E   rfa@berkeley.edu
W filmstudies.berkeley.edu

Offers both undergraduate and postgraduate
degrees in films studies, with courses in
screenwriting.

UNIVERSITY OF CALIFORNIA (LOS ANGELES)–UCLA

UCLA Department of Film TV and Digital
Media Los Angeles CA 90095
T   310 825 7891
F   310 825 3383
E   smoore@tft.ucla.edu
W www.tft.ucla.edu

Contacts
Hal Ackerman Co-*chairman*

Offers courses on screenwriting fundamentals,
advanced screenwriting and creating
TV pilots. Also runs a professional
screenwriting programme. Alumni have
been involved in films including *Sideways*,
Little Miss Sunshine, *War of the Worlds* and
Forrest Gump.

Application Criteria
Applicants should have an undergraduate
degree and provide writing samples.
Applications 'should be made carefully'.

UNIVERSITY OF CALIFORNIA (SANTA BARBARA)

Santa Barbara Ellison Hall 1720
Santa Barbara CA 93106
T   805 893 2347
F   805 893 8630
E   admin@filmandmedia.ucsb.edu
W   www.filmandmedia.ucsb.edu

Offers both undergraduate and graduate Arts
degrees in Film and Media Studies.
Undergraduate students interested in
screenwriting are advised to take on additional
screenwriting courses. The graduate course
allows students the opportunity to explore the
creative process in autobiographical screenplay
construction.

UNIVERSITY OF CENTRAL FLORIDA

School of Film & Digital Media PO Box
163120 Orlando FL 32816-3120
T   407 823 4285
F   407 823 3659
E   film@mail.ucf.edu
W   film.ucf.edu

Offers a Bachelor of Fine Arts degree in
production. Students take courses in Directing,
Editing, Screenwriting and Production
Management.

CHAPMAN UNIVERSITY

1 University Drive Orange CA 92866
T   714 628 7293
F   714 997 6885
E   dodgecollege@chapman.edu
W   www.ftv.chapman.edu

Contacts
Joseph Slowensky *Associate Professor and
Chair*

Graduate courses on screenwriting offered at
the Dodge College of Film and Media Arts'
specialist Conservatory of Motion Pictures.
Course includes tuition on writing for both film

and television. The programme is led by David
S. Ward, writer of *The Sting*.

Application Criteria
Graduate programme is open to anyone with a
bachelor's degree. Screenwriting course costs
approximately $41,000 for 2 years.

COGSWELL POLYTECHNICAL COLLEGE

1175 Bordeaux Drive Sunnyvale CA 94089
T   408 541 0100
F   408 747 0764
E   info@cogswell.edu
W   www.cogswell.edu

Offers courses in producing motion
picture ideas, scriptwriting and advanced
scriptwriting. The scriptwriting course
demonstrates the fundamentals of writing a
script for animation, television, commercials,
films, and digital games, whilst the advanced
course explores the manipulation of time and
space, in-depth application of conflict and
resolution, and the application of alternative
writing formats.

COLUMBIA UNIVERSITY SCHOOL OF THE ARTS

305 Dodge Hall Mail Code 1808 2960
Broadway New York NY 10027
T   212 854 2134
E   admissions-arts@columbia.edu
W   wwwapp.cc.columbia.edu

The Film division offers a Master of Fine Arts
degree with concentrations in screenwriting,
producing and directing. Aside from the courses
in screenwriting, they also offer a course on
writing for television which concentrates on
dramas primarily based on non-fictional
material.

EMERSON COLLEGE

Department of Writing Literature & Publishing
120 Boylston Street Boston MA 02116-4624
T   617 824 8500
W   www.emerson.edu

Offers a Master of Fine Arts in creative
writing. Courses aimed at students interested in
pursuing careers in writing fiction, poetry,
nonfiction, plays or screenplays.

FLORIDA STATE UNIVERSITY FILM SCHOOL

University Center 3100A Tallahassee
FL 32306-2350
T   850 644 7728
F   850 644 2626
E   mfainfo@film.fsu.edu
W   film.fsu.edu

Offers a Master of Fine Arts in
professional writing. The programme
covers screen- and playwriting,
screenplay craft, story conceptualization,
and adaptation of a novel for both
stage and screen.

HOLLINS UNIVERSITY

PO Box 9603 Roanoke Virginia VA 24020
T   540 362 6575
F   540 362 6288
E   hugrad@hollins.edu
W   www.hollins.edu

Contacts
Klaus Phillips *Director, MA in Screenwriting
and Film Studies*

Founded in 1842. Offers range of film and
scriptwriting courses including: Screenwriting;
Advanced Screenwriting; Narrative Theory and
Practice for Screenwriters; Writing Short
Scripts; Television Sitcom Writing;
Incorporating Folklore and Myths into your
Screenplays.

Application Criteria
Applications invited from students
who can demonstrate their suitability
for the courses by submission of
undergraduate transcripts, writing
samples and letters of recommendation.
See website for details.

INSTITUTE OF SCREENWRITING

1754 Cadiz Road Wintersville OH 43953
T   888 659 3897
F   215 794 0384
W   www.inst.org

Founded in 1998, the Institute offers a
Screenwriting Diploma Course accredited by
the Open and Distance Learning Quality
Council.

UNIVERSITY OF IOWA

425 English-Philosophy Building Iowa City
IA 52242
T   319 335 0330
F   319 335 3446
E   cinema-complit@uiowa.edu

Offers both undergraduate and graduate
degrees in film studies. Also short-form and
long-form screenwriting courses. In the short-
form course, students are involved in exercises
and projects in writing, developing, and work-
shopping screenplays for short film or video, as
well as budgeting, location scouting, and other
preproduction activities. The long-form course
deals with topics such as visualization,
sequencing, dialogue, preparation of treatment,
screenplay for fiction film, and script problems.

JOHNS HOPKINS UNIVERSITY

1717 Massachusetts Avenue Suite 101
Washington, D.C. 200
T   202 452 1940
E   aapadmissions@jhu.edu
W   advanced.jhu.edu

Offers an elective Film and Screenwriting
course as part of the Master of Arts
programme. Students view and analyze classic
films, such as *Chinatown* and *Psycho*, that
illustrate screenwriting techniques, and use a
successful major film script as text to examine
storyline and structure from concept to
synopsis. The focus is on dialogue,
characterization, plot development, pacing, text
and subtext, and visual storytelling.

UNIVERSITY OF KANSAS

The Department of Theatre and Film 356
Murphy Hall Lawrence KS 66045
T   785 864 3511
W   www2.ku.edu

Offers undergraduate and graduate degrees in
theatre and film studies. In the undergraduate
basic screenwriting course the emphasis is on
the creation of a treatment and a screenplay,
whilst the intermediate course explores genre,
character, dialogue, and the development of a
personal writing style. In the graduate
programme students are exposed to dramatic

scriptwriting and explore the problems with basic screenwriting.

LOS ANGELES FILM SCHOOL

6363 Sunset Boulevard Hollywood CA 90028
T   323 860 0789
E   info@lafilm.com
W www.lafilm.com

Offers a 1-year Immersion Filmmaking Programme, which includes a course on screenwriting.

LOUISIANA STATE UNIVERSITY

The Department of English 260 Allen Hall
Baton Rouge LA 70803
T   225 578 4086
F   225 578 4129
W www.english.lsu.edu

The department of English offers a Master of Fine Arts in creative writing, which includes courses on screenwriting. Students usually complete the degree within $2\frac{1}{2}$ to 3 years.

LOYOLA MARYMOUNT UNIVERSITY

Film Studies 1 LMU Drive Los Angeles
CA 90045-2659
T   310 338 3033
E   SFTV-INFO@lmu.edu
W www.lmu.edu

Offers a Bachelor of Arts in screenwriting, and a Master of Fine Arts in screenwriting. In the undergraduate programme, students are introduced to the basic elements of screenwriting, learning about character, dialogue, plotting, visual writing, and classic and alternative structures. In intermediate and advanced courses, students write and rewrite feature length screenplays, study genres, take classes in sitcom and dramatic television writing, and learn how to adapt stories to suit different mediums.

UNIVERSITY OF MIAMI

Frances L. Wolfson Communication Building
5100 Brunson Drive Coral Gables FL 33146
T   305 284 2265
E   communication@miami.edu

Offers both undergraduate and graduate degrees in their Motion Picture programme. In the undergraduate programme, students are given an introduction to scriptwriting, which involves the creation and formatting of narrative material for motion pictures. Also offers a Master of Fine Arts in screenwriting.

UNIVERSITY OF MICHIGAN

6525 Haven Hall 505 S. State Street
Ann Arbor MI 48109
T   734 763 4087
F   734 936 1846
E   mlouisa@umich.edu
W www.lsa.umich.edu/sac

Contacts
Mary Lou Chlipala *Program Co-ordinator*

Offering undergraduate screenwriting courses taught in the Department of Screen Arts and Culture. Courses are taught by working screenwriters. Notable alumni include Arthur Miller, Jim Burnstein, Meg Kasdan and Richard Friedenberg.

Application Criteria
Tuition for in state pupils is $9,724 per semester, $29,132 out of state.

MIDDLEBURY COLLEGE

Film/Video Studies Wright Theatre
Middlebury VT 05753
T   802 443 3190
E   fdrexel@middlebury.edu
W www.middlebury.edu

Department of Film and Media Studies offers workshops in screenwriting. The first workshop is a creative writing course which explores key dramatic elements such as character, setting, point of view, plot, and theme set in a narrative medium. In the second workshop, students are exposed to the various purposes of film treatments, character backstories, synopses, sequence outlines, master scene scripts, and shooting scripts.

MINNESOTA STATE UNIVERSITY

Department of Communication Studies Film
Studies and Theatre Arts   1104 7th Avenue
South Moorhead MN 56563
T   218 477 2126
W   www.mnstate.edu

The Department offers evening courses in
writing for film and television as part of their
film studies major programme.

MOUNT HOLYOKE COLLEGE

Film Studies Program Art Building Mount
Holyoke College South Hadley ME 01075
T   413 538 2000
E   filmstudies@mtholyoke.edu
W   www.mtholyoke.edu

Offers an intensive screenwriting course with
an emphasis on structure and character, which
prepares the student for the step outline of a
feature-length film.

UNIVERSITY OF NEVADA (LAS VEGAS)–UNLV

Film Department 4505 Maryland Pkwy.
Las Vegas NV 89154
T   702 895 3320
W   www.unlv.edu

Offer a 3-year Master of Fine Arts degree in
screenwriting. The degree focuses specifically
on the art and craft of writing for screen.

UNIVERSITY OF NEW ORLEANS

Department of Drama and Communications
Performing Arts Center New Orleans
LA 70148
T   504 280 6000
W   www.uno.edu

Offers a Master of Fine Arts degree in film
production, with the option to specialize in
creative writing (including fiction writing,
non-fiction writing, playwriting, poetry
writing and screenwriting).

NEW YORK FILM ACADEMY

100 E. 17th St. New York NY 10003
T   212 674 4300
F   212 477 1414

E   film@nyfa.com
W   www.nyfa.com

Offers a comprehensive range of
screenwriting courses from an 8-week
(or 12-week evening) workshop to a
one-year programme. In addition to writing
classes, students also study film craft,
acting, pitching, and cinema studies as
they apply to screenwriting. They will
also write, direct and edit a short digital
film or scene from a feature script.

NEW YORK UNIVERSITY

School of Continuing and Professional Studies
Office of Admissions 145 4th Avenue Room
201 New York NY 10003
T   212 998 7200
W   www.scps.nyu.edu

Offers wide range of screenwriting
certificates including: Screenwriting I:
An Introduction; Screenwriting II: A
Workshop; Master Class for Screenwriting
Certificate Students; Adapting True
Stories Into Screen Stories; Advanced
Storyboarding and Storytelling; Marketing
Your Screenplay; Writing a Screenplay
in 10 Weeks; Rewriting a Screenplay
in 10 Weeks; Screenwriting Technique,
Theory, and Practice; The Screenwriter's
Craft; Writing for Prime-Time Television;
Writing the Sundance Movie.

UNIVERSITY OF NORTH CAROLINA AT GREENSBORO

Department of Broadcasting and Cinema 321
McIver Bldg. UNCG PO Box 26170
Greensboro NC 27402-6170
T   336 334 5360
F   336 334 5039
W   www.uncg.edu

Offers a Master of Fine Arts in drama with a
concentration in film and video production,
with the option to specialize in screenwriting.
Aside from a screenwriting course, they also
offer a media writing course which gives the
student practice in television script writing,
with emphasis given to development of
concepts and proposals for episodic television.

NORTH CAROLINA SCHOOL OF THE ARTS

1533 South Main Street Winston-Salem
NC 27127-2188
T   336 770 3399
E   thompsona@ncarts.edu
W   www.ncarts.edu

Offers a 4-year Bachelor of Fine Arts degree
with the option to specialize in screenwriting.
In the first year the course covers topics
such as character, conflict, visual storytelling,
setting, dialogue, emotional tone, stage
directions, and professional format. In the
second year students explore genre, climaxes
and resolutions, the controlling idea
and an introduction to traditional three-act
structure.

OHIO UNIVERSITY SCHOOL OF FILM

Lindley Hall 378 Athens OH 45701
T   740 593 1323
F   740 593 1328
E   filmdept@www.ohiou.edu
W   www.finearts.ohio.edu

Offers a Master of Fine Arts degree with
courses in screenwriting. The focus is on the
narrative screenplay.

UNIVERSITY OF OKLAHOMA

640 Parrington Oval Norman OK 73019
T   405 325 3020
F   405 325 7135
E   fvs@ou.edu
W   www.ou.edu/fvs

The College of Arts and Sciences offers an
interdisciplinary programme in film and video
studies. The feature screenwriting course within
the programme is an introduction to writing for
the screen which includes a variety of
assignments leading up to developing and
writing a feature screenplay.

PENNSYLVANIA STATE UNIVERSITY

Department of Film/Video and Media Studies
129 Carnegie University Park PA 16802
T   814 863 1484
E   sws102@psu.edu
W   www.comm.psu.edu

Runs an undergraduate programme which has
film-video as a major. It involves the in-depth
study of film and video production and
incorporates idea development, writing,
production craft and production management.

PURCHASE COLLEGE

State University of New York Conservatory of
Theatre Arts & Film 735 Anderson Hill Road
Purchase NY 10577
T   914 251 6830
W   www.purchase.edu

Offers a dramatic writing course as part of the
Bachelor of Fine Arts programme. The
introduction to screenwriting course involves
exercises in writing short stories and scenes.

REGENT UNIVERSITY

School of Communication and the Arts 1000
Regent University Drive Virginia Beach
VA 23464
T   888 777 7729
F   757 226 4394
W   www.regent.edu

Offers a Master of Fine Arts with the option to
major in script and screenwriting. Some of the
courses covered include story structure for stage
and screen, playwriting, writing for television,
feature film scriptwriting, and writing Christian
drama for stage and screen.

SAN DIEGO STATE UNIVERSITY

5500 Campanile Drive San Diego
CA 92182-4561
T   619 594 1375
F   619 594 1391
E   kzaccari@mail.sdsu.edu
W   www.sdsu.edu

They offer an undergraduate BS degree in
Television, Film, and New Media Production
(TFM), with courses in screenwriting.

SAN FRANCISCO STATE UNIVERSITY

1600 Holloway Avenue San Francisco
CA 94132
T   415 338 1629
F   415 338 0906

E cinedept@sfsu.edu
W www.cinema.sfsu.edu

Offers a Bachelor of Arts degree in cinema which includes courses in screenwriting. The course involves practice in film writing, emphasizing story and plot dynamics, characterization, narration, dialogue and script forms.

SCOTTSDALE COMMUNITY COLLEGE

9000 E. Chaparral Road Scottsdale AZ 85256
T 480 423 6000
E kate.herbert@sccmail.maricopa.edu
W www.scottsdalecc.edu

The Motion Picture/Television department offers Certificates of Completion and Associate of Applied Science degrees, with the option to specialize in screenwriting (2-year programme). It also offers classes in the hour-long television drama, sitcom writing, and short script writing which includes writing training films, promotional pieces, 30 and 60 second advertising spots, infomercials and other corporate materials.

UNIVERSITY OF SOUTHERN CALIFORNIA (USC)

USC School of Cinema-Television CTV-G130
Los Angeles CA 90089-2211
T 213 740 3303
F 213 740 8035
E writing@cinema.usc.edu
W cinema.usc.edu

The school offers both an undergraduate degree in Fine Arts and a Master of Fine Arts degree. Their philosophy in storytelling is a combination of compelling characters and three-act structure. Also teaches experimental narratives, television pilot writing and writing for growing media like mobisodes, internet series and gaming.

SYRACUSE UNIVERSITY

201 Tolley Administration Building Syracuse
NY 13244-1100
T 315 443 1870
E orange@syr.edu
W www.syr.edu

Department of Transmedia offers a 2-year Master of Fine Art in Film, with courses in scriptwriting. The introductory scriptwriting course explores the basic elements of film scripting: dramatic fundamentals, screenplay format, narrative strategies, character creation and dialogue development.

TEMPLE UNIVERSITY

344 Annenberg Hall School of Communications
& Theater 2020 North 13th Street
Philadelphia PA 19122
T 215 204 8421
E dlannon@vm.temple.edu
W www.temple.edu

The school offers a Bachelor of Arts in Film and Media Arts. Includes a seminar- and workshop-based 'writing for media' course. Other elements include scene analysis for writers and directors.

UNIVERSITY OF TEXAS

Austin Department of Radio-TV-Film CMA
6.118 TX 78712-1091
T 512 471 4071
F 512 471 4077
W rtf.utexas.edu

Offers a Master of Fine Arts degree with the option to specialize in screenwriting. The objective of the 2-year programme is to provide a foundation of skills that will enable writers to achieve success either in features or television and in either Hollywood or independent arenas.

UCLA EXTENSION WRITERS' PROGRAM

10995 LeConte Avenue Suite 440 Los Angeles
CA 90024
T 310 825 9415
F 310 206 7382
E writers@uclaextension.edu
W uclaextension.edu/writers

Contacts
Leigh-Michil George *Program Representative in Screenwriting*

Programme offers almost 150 onsite and online film and television courses each year. Also certificates in feature film and television, an annual Writers' Studio, a screenplay competition and a nine-month 'masterclass'. Alumni include Iris Yamashita (Oscar nominee for *Letters from Iwo Jima*) and Gavin Hood (Oscar winner for *Tsotsi*).

Application Criteria
Open admission policy. Courses cost between $95 and $535.

UNIVERSITY OF UTAH

Division of Film Studies 375 S 1530 E RM 257b Salt Lake City UT 84112-0380
T   801 581 5127
E   info@film.utah.edu
W   www.film.utah.edu

Offers both a Bachelor of Arts and a Master of Fine Arts in Film Studies. The screenwriting course involves the development of a narrative screenplay, script format, character development, dramatic construction, dialogue and other storytelling skills.

WESTERN MICHIGAN UNIVERSITY

School of Communication Kalamazoo MI 49008
T   269 387 3130
F   269 387 3990
E   eric.mcconnell@wmich.edu
W   www.wmich.edu

Offers a Bachelor of Arts degree in Film, Video and Media studies, with courses in film and television scripting and playwriting.

WRITERS GUILD OF AMERICA EAST FOUNDATION/COLUMBIA SCHOOL OF THE ART SCREENWRITING WORKSHOP

555 West 57th Street Suite 1230 New York NY 10019
T   212 767 7800
F   212 582 1909
W   www.wgaeast.org

The workshop is an intense 10-week course. The 3-hour Saturday workshops at Columbia University are followed by one-on-one mentoring sessions. In addition, workshop participants attend master classes taught by renowned screenwriters.

WRITERS GUILD TRAINING PROGRAMME

7000 West Third Street Los Angeles CA 90048
T   323 951 4000
F   323 782 4800
W   www.wga.org

6-week training programme that allows novice writers to train with professional writers on episodic (comedy or drama) TV series in their second or subsequent year of production.

UNITED KINGDOM

ARISTA DEVELOPMENT

11 Wells Mews London W1T 3HD
T   020 7323 1775
F   020 7323 1772
E   arista@aristotle.co.uk
W   www.aristadevelopment.co.uk

Created in 1996 by Stephen Cleary, then Head of Development at British Screen, to provide script development skills training for European-based development executives, producers and writers. Provides long term training for writers, such as the Adept 3 programme programme for MA screenwriter graduates, supported by Skillset's Film Skills Fund, The Media Programme of the EU and Arista's own Writer Scholarship Fund. Also offers an international consultancy service to create bespoke training around the globe.

ARVON FOUNDATION

National Administration: 2nd Floor 42A Buckingham Palace Road London SW1W 0RE
T   020 7931 7611
F   020 7963 0961
W   www.arvonfoundation.org

Contacts
Terry Hands *Joint President*

Founded 1968. Offers people of any age (over 16) and any background the opportunity to live and work with professional writers. Four-and-a-half-day residential courses are held throughout the year at Arvon's four centres, covering poetry, fiction, drama, writing for children, songwriting and the performing arts.

Bursaries towards the cost of course fees are available for those on low incomes, the unemployed, students and pensioners. Runs a biennial international poetry competition.
Campuses at:
Devon: Totleigh Barton, Sheepwash, Beaworthy EX21 5NS; T 01409 231338; F 01409 231144; E t-barton@arvonfoundation.org
Yorkshire: Lumb Bank, Heptonstall, Hebden Bridge HX7 6DF; T 01422 843714; F 01422 843714; E l-bank@arvonfoundation.org
Inverness shire: Moniack Mhor, Teavarran, Kiltarlity, Beauly IV4 7HT; T 01463 741675; E m-mhor@arvonfoundation.org
Shropshire: The Hurst, Clunton, Craven Arms SY7 0JA; T 01588 640658; F 01588 640509; E hurst@arvonfoundation.org

UNIVERSITY OF WALES, BANGOR

Bangor Gwynedd LL57 2DG
T   01248 383561
E   prospectus@bangor.ac.uk
W www.bangor.ac.uk

Offers an MA in creative writing, allowing students to develop their specific interests in their preferred genre and style.

BATH SPA UNIVERSITY

Newton Park Bath BA2 9BN
T   01225 875573
F   01225 875503
E   r.kerridge@bathspa.ac.uk
W www.bathspa.ac.uk

MA in Creative Writing. A course for creative writers wanting to develop their work.
Teaching is by published writers in the novel, poetry, short stories and scriptwriting. In recent years, several students from this course have received contracts from publishers for novels, awards for poetry and short stories and have had work produced on BBC Radio.

UNIVERSITY OF BIRMINGHAM

Department of Drama and Theatre Arts
Edgbaston Birmingham B15 2TT
T   0121 414 3344
F   0121 414 3971
E   e.m.braekkanpayne@bham.ac.uk

The MPhil in Playwriting Studies, established by playwright David Edgar in 1970, was the UK's first postgraduate course in playwriting. An intensive course which encourages students to think critically about dramatic writing, assisting them to put these insights into practice in their own plays.

UNIVERSITY OF BOLTON

Chadwick Campus Chadwick Street Bolton Lancashire BL2 1JW
T   01204 900600
E   ngd1@bolton.ac.uk
W www.bolton.ac.uk

Contacts
Jenny Shepherd *Course Leader, Media, Writing and Production*

Founded in 2005, the university offers an undergraduate degree in Media, Writing and Production. Students may specialize in screenwriting, digital filmmaking or film studies strands. Creative Writing degree also offers screenwriting options. The best student scripts are produced by filmmaking students.

Application Criteria
Applications should be made through UCAS (240 points required).

BOURNEMOUTH UNIVERSITY

The Media School Weymouth House Talbot Campus Fern Barrow Poole BH12 5BB
T   01202 965553
F   01202 965099

Contacts
Katrina King *Programme Administrator*

Three-year, full-time BA (Hons) course in Scriptwriting for Film and Television.
Graduates emerge with the ability to write TV and film scripts across genres – movies, sitcoms, TV drama series, soaps, short comedies, TV screenplays, etc. The programme is designed to suit both school leavers and those of mature years wishing to prepare themselves for new career opportunities. Was the UK's first undergraduate screenwriting programme and is one of only two undergraduate screenwriting

programmes in the UK to be accredited by Skillset.

BRIDGEND COLLEGE

Cowbridge Road Bridgend CF31 3DF
T 01656 302302
F 01656 663912
E enquiries@bridgend.ac.uk
W www.bridgend.ac.uk

Runs course teaching scriptwriting for TV and film. Aims to develop skills in character analysis, narrative, storytelling and script layout. Areas of script writing covered include drama, factual and documentary. Costs £90 for 30 weeks teaching.

BURTON MANOR

The Village Burton Neston CH64 5SJ
T 0151 336 5172
F 0151 336 6586
E enquiry@burtonmanor.com
W www.burtonmanor.com

Wide variety of short courses, residential and non-residential, on writing and literature. Full details in brochure.

CARDIFF UNIVERSITY CENTRE FOR LIFELONG LEARNING

Senghennydd Road Cardiff CF24 4AG
T 029 2087 0000
F 029 2066 8935
E learn@cardiff.ac.uk

Contacts
Ian Spring *Coordinating Lecturer for English, Media and Creat*

University founded by royal charter in 1883. Course availability detailed in *Choices* brochure, published twice yearly. Normally a range of 10–20 week courses in Media and Creative Writing. Approximately £65 for a 10-week course (reduced fees available).

UNIVERSITY OF CENTRAL LANCASHIRE

Preston Lancashire PR1 2HE
E cenquiries@uclan.ac.uk
W www.uclan.ac.uk

Offers a modular BA in screenwriting. Provides opportunity to study both screenwriting and film-making up until the second year.

THE CENTRAL SCHOOL OF SPEECH AND DRAMA

The Embassy Theatre Eton Avenue London NW3 3HY
T 020 7722 8183
F 020 7722 4132
E enquiries@cssd.ac.uk

Contacts
Dymphna Callery *Course Leader*

MA in Writing for Stage & Broadcast.

CITY LIT

Keeley Street Covent Garden London WC2B 4BA
T 020 7492 2652
F 020 7492 8256
E humanities@citylit.ac.uk

The Writing School offers a wide range of courses: Ways Into Creative Writing; Writing for Children; Playwriting; Screenwriting; Comedy Writing. Various lengths of course available. The Department offers information and advice during term time.

CITY UNIVERSITY

Northampton Square London EC1 0HB
T 020 7040 8268
F 020 7040 8256
E ell@city.ac.uk
W www.city.ac.uk/ell/cfa/write

Contacts
Alison Burns *Courses Co-ordinator, Writing and Journalism*

Courses for adults offered by the Department of Education and Lifelong Learning include Writing for Children, Writing Comedy, Writing Situation Comedy and Writing TV Drama. Open-access evening classes with expert tutors. Alumni include Catherine Tate and Rachel Zadok.

COMMUNITY CREATIVE WRITING AND PUBLISHING

'Sea Winds' 2 St Helens Terrace Spittal Berwick-upon-Tweed Northumberland TO15 1RJ

T 01289 305213

E mavismaureen@aol.com

Contacts

Maureen Raper *Author/Tutor/Moderator*

Offering writing courses for all ability levels, including Writing for Radio and Television. Courses run for 10 weeks, with competitions and prizes available at the end. Costs £2.50 per lesson.

DARTINGTON COLLEGE OF ARTS

Totnes TQ9 6EJ

T 01803 862224

F 01803 861666

E registry@dartington.ac.uk

W www.dartington.ac.uk

Contacts

Mark Leahy *Director of Writing*

BA (Hons) Writing or Writing (Contemporary Practices) or Writing (Scripted Media); Textual Practices minor award; MA Performance Writing: exploratory approaches to writing as it relates to performance, visual arts, sound arts and contemporary culture. Encourages the interdisciplinary, with minor awards and electives at BA level in arts and cultural management, choreography, music, theatre, visual performance.

DE MONTFORT UNIVERSITY

The Gateway Leicester LE1 9BH

T 0116 250 6470

F 0116 257 7199

E pghums@dmu.ac.uk

W www.dmu.ac.uk

MA offered in television scriptwriting. Offers direct links and networking opportunities within the industry by introducing the students to professional writers, script editors, agents and producers through a regular programme of guest lectures, workshops and location visits. By writing 'shadow' scripts of existing television shows, the students learn the disciplines of writing to a brief and experience the demands of writing for a popular soap opera or multi-episodic television drama. Guest writers have included Jimmy McGovern (*Cracker/Gunpowder Treason & Plot*), Peter Berry (*Silent Witness*), Ellie Barker (*Tracy Beaker*), Rob Gittins (*EastEnders*), Andy Hamilton (*Drop the Dead Donkey/Trevor's World of Sport*), Lizzie Mickery (*Messiah*), Tony Marchant (*Take Me Home/Mark of Cain*) and Sarah Bagshaw (*Emmerdale/Heartbeat/The Royal*).

UNIVERSITY OF DERBY

Kedleston Road Derby DE22 1GB

T 01332 591736

E adtenquiry@derby.ac.uk

W www.derby.ac.uk

Offers a course in media writing, providing broad coverage. Options to specialize in scriptwriting for radio, television and film in later stages.

DOCUMENTARY FILMMAKERS GROUP

4th Floor Shacklewell Studios 28 Shacklewell Lane London E8 2EZ

T 020 7249 6600

E info@dfgdocs.com

W www.dfgdocs.com

A non-profit, comprehensive resource for documentary filming, established in 2001. Offers training and hosts screenings, festivals and forums.

UNIVERSITY OF EAST ANGLIA

School of Literature and Creative Writing University Plain Norwich Norfolk NR4 7TJ

T 01603 456161

E j.camplin@uea.ac.uk

W www.uea.ac.uk/eas/admissions/courseprofiles/w800tb

Contacts

Val Taylor *Director of Scriptwriting*

School of Literature and Creative Writing offers masters degree in Creative Writing: Scriptwriting. Explores writing for stage, screen and radio through series of workshops and seminar modules, culminating in the writing of a full-length script. Classes are supplemented with regular masterclasses with industry professionals. Alumni include Ian McEwan, Tracy Chevalier and Bill Gallagher.

Application Criteria
Applicants should hold a first degree or relevant experience. Courses cost £3,168 (full-time) or £1,584 (part-time) per year.

UNIVERSITY OF EDINBURGH

Graduate School of Literatures Languages and Cultures 19 George Square Edinburgh EH1 1JZ
T   0131 650 3068
E   rjamieso@staffmail.ed.ac.uk
W   www.ed.ac.uk

Contacts
R Alan Jamieson *MSc Convenor*

Masters in Creative Writing. Aims to develop creative and reflective understanding of the chosen genre of writing via creative and literary-critical courses.

EUROSCRIPT

PO Box 3117 Gloucester GL4 0WW
T   0780 336 9414
E   enquiries@euroscript.co.uk
W   www.euroscript.co.uk

An independent, script development organization. Aims to facilitate the production of high-quality marketable screenplays for film and television via a process of on-going creative collaboration with writers and producers/directors. The Advanced Screenwriting Workshop costs £595 (concessions) and £950 for writer/producer or writer/director teams.

UNIVERSITY OF EXETER

Room 206 Department of English Queen's Building Queen's Drive Exeter EX4 4QH
T   01392 264263
F   01392 264361
E   soe.pgoffice@ex.ac.uk
W   www.ex.ac.uk/english

Offers BA (Hons) in English with 2nd and 3rd year options in creative writing, poetry, short

fiction, screenwriting and creative non-fiction. MA English; MA Creative Writing: poetry, novella, screenwriting, life writing and novel. PhD Creative Writing.

FIRST TAKE

13 Hope Street Liverpool L37 7DD
T   0151 708 5767
F   0151 709 2613
E   all@first-take.org
W   www.first-take.org

Contacts
Lynne Harwood *Director*

An independent television and film production and training organization. Offers courses such as Distinct Voices: Diverse Lives, a talent development scheme aimed at groups who are under-represented in the industry, and From Scratch to Screen, a short film writing course. Schemes include some of the scripts being produced.

Application Criteria
Only open to writers living in the North West. Participation is free.

UNIVERSITY OF GLAMORGAN

Department of English Treforest Pontypridd CF37 1DL
T   01443 654292
E   wmason@glam.ac.uk
W   www.glam.ac.uk

Contacts
Wyn Mason

MA in Scriptwriting (Theatre, Film, TV or Radio): a two-year part-time Masters degree for scriptwriters (held at the Cardiff School for Creative and Cultural Industries).

GOLDSMITHS, UNIVERSITY OF LONDON

New Cross London SE14 6NW
T   020 7919 7060
F   020 7919 7509
E   admissions@gold.ac.uk
W   www.goldsmiths.ac.uk

Contacts
Jennifer New *Corporate Publicity Assistant*

Founded in 1891, the institution offers masters courses in Script Writing, Filmmaking, Feature Film, Screen Documentary and Screen Studies. Script Writing course focuses on developing professional skills such as pitching for employment and production funding. During the programme students produce a short fiction script and a feature film or equivalent length TV or radio script.

Application Criteria
Applicants to all MA courses should have a first degree or relevant professional experience.

MARK GRINDLE ASSOCIATES LTD

15 Gladstone Square Ashfield Dunblane Perthshire FK15 0JN
T   01786 825 789
E   mga@markgrindle.com
W   www.markgrindle.com

Contacts
M. Grindle *Director*

Founded in 2003, offering bespoke training for screenwriters in Scotland wanting to embrace gaming and interactive media. Courses include a 2-day boot camp, a 10-week design documents course and one-to-one mentoring. Open to screenwriters with at least 2 years of experience.

UNIVERSITY OF HULL

Scarborough Campus Filey Road Scarborough YO11 3AZ
T   01723 362392
F   01723 370815
E   s.andrews@hull.ac.uk
W   www.hull.ac.uk

Contacts
Stuart Andrews *Director of Studies*

BA Single Honours in Theatre and Performance Studies incorporates opportunities in writing and other media across each level of the programme. Works closely with the Stephen Joseph Theatre and its artistic director Alan Ayckbourn. The theatre sustains a policy for staging new writers. The campus hosts the annual National Student Drama Festival which includes the International Student Playscript Competition (details from The National Information Centre for Student Drama; nsdf@hull.ac.uk).

INITIALIZE FILMS

15 Southampton Place London WC1V 6QA
T   0207 404 1053
E   info@initialize-films.co.uk
W   www.initialize-films.co.uk

Contacts
Marion Simon *Co-ordinator*

Consultancy to producers and film funds that has run courses since 2005 on writing for TV, soaps and features, development money and marketing scripts. Also available are courses for developing new talent and for women screenwriters.

Application Criteria
Anyone is eligible to apply. Fees from £70 upwards.

INSTITUTE OF SCREENWRITING

Overbrook Business Centre Poolbridge Road Blackford Wedmore Somerset BS28 4PA
T   0800 781 1715
E   screenwriting@inst.org
W   www.inst.org/screenwriting-course

Contacts
Alan Asbridge *Customer Services Co-ordinator*

Institution providing courses run by active screenwriters 'not armchair theorists'. Offering Distance Learning Diploma in Screenwriting. Accredited by the Open and Distance Learning Quality Council.

INTERNATIONAL FILM SCHOOL WALES

University of Wales Newport Caerleon Campus PO Box 101 Newport NP18 3YG
T   01633 432432
F   01633 432046
E   uic@newport.ac.uk
W   artschool.newport.ac.uk/filmschool.html

The leading institution for the promotion and development of the audiovisual culture of Wales, accredited as a Screen Academy by Skillset. Currently over 500 undergraduate and postgraduate students. Excellent links with industry. Many courses involve a screenwriting component.

JIM ELDRIDGE WRITING WORKSHOPS

Pear Tree Farm Bowness on Solway Wigton Cumbria CA7 5AF
T 01697 352246
E jimeldridge@jimeldridge/force9.co.uk
W www.jimeldridge.com

Contacts
Jim Eldridge *Director and Workshop Tutor*

Courses run by a professional screenwriter since 2004, showing how to write for film, TV and radio. Workshops deal with the business side as well as the creative side of writing. Workshops take place twice a year, in spring and autumn. Costs £29 per workshop.

LANCASTER UNIVERSITY

Department of English and Creative Writing Bowland College Lancaster LA1 4YT
T 01524 594169
F 01524 594247
E L.Kellett@lancaster.ac.uk
W www.lancs.ac.uk/depts/english/crew

Contacts
Lyn Kellett *Course Officer in Creative Writing*

Department of English and Creative Writing offers both campus-based and distance learning masters degrees in creative writing. First degree in any subject is required. Applicants should send samples of their writing along with application form.

LEEDS METROPOLITAN UNIVERSITY

School of Film Television & Performing Arts H505 Civic Quarter Calverley Street Leeds LS1 3HE
T 0113 283 2600 ext 38
E screenwriting@leedsmet.ac.uk
W www.leedsmet.ac.uk

Contacts
Chris Pugh *Administrator*

Offers a Diploma/MA in Screenwriting (Fiction). Based firmly upon the traditional crafts of storytelling and screen narrative the course emphasizes the development of the student's individual voice and creativity, with originality and innovation at the heart of the course. Graduates will have a thorough understanding of the creative and business processes involved in development, commissioning and writing for both television and film, and will have a strong portfolio of work, and contacts, to enable them to develop their careers in their chosen area/s. Skillset-accredited.

UNIVERSITY OF LEEDS, BRETTON HALL CAMPUS

School of Performance and Cultural Industries Bretton Hall Campus West Bretton Wakefield WF4 4LG
T 0113 343 9109
F 0113 343 9186
E enquiries-pci@leeds.ac.uk
W www.leeds.ac.uk/paci

Contacts
Garry Lyons *Course Director*

MA in Writing for Performance and Publication. This postgraduate programme (launched in September 2006) is particularly relevant to aspiring writers with professional ambitions, especially in the areas of theatre, film, television and radio drama, as well as the published novel and other culturally significant genres. Studies are offered over one-year full-time and two-years part-time and the tutors are established authors in their chosen fields. The course director is award-winning playwright and screenwriter Garry Lyons (*The Bill*, *The Worst Witch*, *Leah's Trials*). The MA is one of a new portfolio of post-graduate degrees to be offered by Leeds University's School of Performance and Cultural Industries, which will relocate to a new £4 million theatre complex on the main Leeds campus in the autumn of 2007. Students are not only given the opportunity to work on their own writing projects but are also encouraged to collaborate with colleagues on other MAs such as Performance Studies, with a view to seeing their work staged.

LIGHTHOUSE ARTS AND TRAINING

28 Kensington Street Brighton East Sussex
BN1 4AJ
T 01273 647197
E info@lighthouse.org.uk
W www.lighthouse.org.uk

Contacts
Emma Bassett *Administrator*

Founded in 1986, offering professional
development courses for aspiring and practicing
filmmakers, screenwriters, animators and artists
working with digital and moving image media.
Courses include Introduction to Screenwriting
and The Craft of Writing TV Drama. Offers a
wide range of initiatives such as production
schemes, masterclasses, networking events
and bursaries.

UNIVERSITY OF LIVERPOOL

Continuing Education 126 Mount Pleasant
Liverpool L69 3GR
T 0151 794 6900/6952
F 0151 794 2544
E conted@liverpool.ac.uk
W www.liv.ac.uk/conted

Contacts
John Redmond *Course Organiser*

Courses include: Introduction to Creative
Writing; Scriptwriting; Journalism; Writing for
Children; Writing Your Life Story and a series
of Saturday courses on aspects of writing. Most
courses take place on one evening or daytime
meeting weekly, with some Saturdays and
linked days. Courses may be taken to pursue a
personal interest or to gain university credit
towards an award. CE offers a Certificate in
Higher Education (Creative Writing) – 120
credits. For most courses no previous
knowledge is required. There are fee
concessions for those who are receiving certain
benefits or are retired. Free prospectus on
request or see the website.

LONDON COLLEGE OF COMMUNICATION

School of Media Elephant and Castle London
SE1 6SB
T 0207 514 6858
F 0207 514 6843

E k.marshall@lcc.arts.ac.uk
W www.lcc.arts.ac.uk

Contacts
Kelly Marshall *Course Director*

Since 1992 the college has offered a part-time
MA in screenwriting. Develops screenwriting
skills through a series of lectures, seminars
and tutorials. Students build up a portfolio
of work, including a full-length film or
television series. The college is part of the
University of the Arts.

Application Criteria
Requires a first degree or proven experience.
Annual fees are £1,584 for EU students and
£4,900 overseas.

THE LONDON FILM SCHOOL

24 Shelton Street Covent Garden London
WC2H 9UB
T 020 7836 9642
F 020 7497 3718
E b.dunnigan@lfs.org.uk
W www.lfs.org.uk

Contacts
Brian Dunnigan *MA Screenwriting Course
Leader*

Founded in 1956, offers Masters courses
in Screenwriting and Filmmaking.
One-year screenwriting course includes
one-to-one mentoring with industry
professionals and tuition in small groups.
Alumni include Michael Mann, Mike Leigh,
Tak Fujimoto and Roger Pratt. Degree courses
are validated by London Metropolitan
University.

METROPOLITAN FILM SCHOOL

Ealing Studios Ealing Green London W5 5EP
T 020 8280 9112
F 020 8280 9111
E jonathan@metfilmschool.co.uk
W www.metfilmschool.co.uk

Contacts
Jonathan Peake *Marketing Director*

Founded in 2003, courses are taught by a
professional script development executive.

Offers 6-month part-time Write a Feature Film course, in which students write a synopsis, treatment and first draft of a script. Admission is open to all. Course costs £1,400.

MIDDLESEX UNIVERSITY

Trent Park Bramley Road London N14 4YZ
T   020 8411 5000
F   020 8411 6652
E   tpadmissions@mdx.ac.uk
W   www.mdx.ac.uk

The UK's longest established writing degree offers a Single or Joint Honours programme in Creative and Media Writing (full or part-time). This modular programme gives an opportunity to explore journalism, poetry, prose fiction and dramatic writing for a wide range of genres and audiences. Option for work experience in the media and publishing industries. Contact Admissions or David Rain (d.rain@mdx.ac.uk). MA in Writing (full-time, part-time; day and evening classes) includes writing workshops; critical seminars; lectures and workshops from established writers; introduction to agents and publishers. Options available: Fiction, Poetry or Scriptwriting. Contact: Sue Gee, 020 8411 5941 (s.gee@mdx.ac.uk). Also offers research degrees M.Phil/PhD in Creative Writing. Contact: Maggie Butt (m.butt@ mdx.ac.uk). The University has a thriving Writing Centre running an annual literary festival, weekly talks, community projects and writers in residence.

MOONSTONE INTERNATIONAL SCREEN LABS

67 George Street Edinburgh EH2 2JG
T   0131 220 2080
F   0131 220 2081
W   www.moonstone.org.uk

Founded in 1997 in consultation with the Sundance Institute. Supports the work of European independent screenwriters and directors through a programme of advanced project-based development and training. Two Screenwriters' Labs held each year for a week each, giving participants the opportunity to develop their screenplays with the assistance of leading screenwriters.

Application Criteria
The Labs are open to feature film writers and directors from throughout Europe. Applicants must have a proven extensive track record.

MORLEY COLLEGE

61 Westminster Bridge Road London SE1 7HT
T   020 7450 1889
F   020 7928 4074
E   enquiries@morleycollege.ac.uk
W   www.morleycollege.ac.uk

Offers a one-term screenwriting course. Aims to teach students how to develop feature script outlines and complete a script for a short film. Concentration on mainstream and independent world cinema, with an emphasis on narrative and story structure.

NAPIER UNIVERSITY

Craiglockhart Campus Edinburgh EH14 1DJ
T   08452 60 60 40
W   www.napier.ac.uk

Full- or part-time MA in screenwriting. Taught modules cover the history of screenwriting and the cinema; the theory and practice of story forms and structure; the craft of screenwriting for film, television and new media; and the professional skills and business contexts of writing in the creative industries.

NATIONAL FILM AND TELEVISION SCHOOL

Beaconsfield Studios Station Road
Beaconsfield Buckinghamshire HP9 1LG
T   01494 671234
F   01494 674042
E   info@nfts.co.uk
W   www.nfts.co.uk

Contacts
Corinne Cartier *Head of Screenwriting*

Founded in 1971, the Skillset Screen Academy offers a 2-year MA in Screenwriting and an 18-month Diploma in Script Development. The masters course is based in a working film studio to familiarize students with the production process. All courses are 90% or more practical work. Alumni include Ashley Pharoah, Sandy Welch and Shawn Slovo.

Application Criteria
Previous degree is not essential, but relevant experience is an advantage. Applicants should send a screenplay or other writing sample. 'Dedication and a prolific output are expected'.

NEW YORK FILM ACADEMY

23 Southampton Place London WC1A 2BP
T   020 7430 2227
F   020 7430 2772
E   filmuk@nyfa.com
W   www.nyfa.com

Screenwriting workshops presented by the US-based New York Film Academy. Students can develop an idea into a feature length screenplay in an eight-week course or enter a one-year programme.

NORTHERN VISIONS MEDIA CENTRE

23 Donegall Street Belfast BT1 2FF
T   028 9024 5495
F   028 9032 6608
E   info@northernvisions.org
W   www.northernvisions.org

Self-contained two-day intensive script writing workshop, taught by filmmaker Laurence Henson.

OXFORD FILM AND VIDEO MAKERS

54 Catherine Street Oxford OX4 3AH
T   01865 792 731
E   office@ofvm.org
W   www.ofvm.org

Contacts
Richard Duriez

Founded in 1987 to offer screenwriting courses at introductory and advanced levels. Part-time 22-week programmes designed by the UK Film Council as a first step for aspiring talent. £225 per module. Applications online.

PANICO @ THE LONDON FILM ACADEMY

PO Box 496 London WC1A 2WZ
T   020 7386 7711
E   info@londonfilmacademy.com
W   www.panicofilms.com

Offers a film foundation course and range of short courses for filmmakers and scriptwriters.

PERFORMING ARTS LABS

6 Flitcroft Street London WC2H 8DJ
T   020 7240 8040
E   screenwriters@pallabs.org
W   www.pallabs.org

PAL's screenwriters labs are among the longest-established screenwriters' programmes in the UK. Over 200 alumni since 1989.

UNIVERSITY OF PORTSMOUTH

School of Creative Arts Film and Media Portsmouth PO1 2EG
T   023 9284 5138
F   023 9284 5152
E   creative@port.ac.uk
W   www.port.ac.uk/departments/academic/scafm

Offers creative writing and combined creative writing degrees across a wide range of undergraduate programmes, and in all genres. BA, MA and PhD study is available. The School is a key partner in a national AHRC Research training project in Creative Writing. Staff include a number of national and/or international award-winning writers, short story writers/novelists, playwrights, screenwriters, new-media writers and poets. The School runs regular national and international creative writing events.

RAINDANCE LTD

81 Berwick Street London W1F 8TW
T   0207 287 3833
F   0207 439 2243
E   courses@raindance.co.uk
W   www.raindance.co.uk

Offers array of courses for aspiring filmmakers and writers. Taught by industry professionals and aims to give students an insight into the realities of the filmmaking world. Also offers script registration service.

ROYAL HOLLOWAY UNIVERSITY OF LONDON

Media Arts Centre Arts Building Egham
Surrey TW20 0EX
T   01784 443734
F   01784 443832
E   MediaArts@rhul.ac.uk
W   www.rhul.ac.uk/media-arts

Offers an MA Feature Film Screenwriting (MAFFS). Devised in 1999 with input from many people working in the film industry. Aimed at people already employed in the business, writers in other media with an interest in writing for film and those following an educational path. Part-time over two years or full time over one year. For those wishing to write for film and television, there is an MA in Screenwriting for TV and Film (Retreat Programme). Starts in January each year (two years part-time, taught in six one-week residential blocks. Two blocks held at writers' retreats in Yorkshire and Shropshire). Students work on film and television ideas, outlines, and then drafts for one of a variety of televisual or cinematic genres.

UNIVERSITY OF SALFORD

Postgraduate Admissions School of Media Music & Performance Adelphi Building Peru Street Salford M3 6EQ
T   0161 295 6026
F   0161 295 6023
E   r.humphrey@salford.ac.uk
W   www.smmp.salford.ac.uk

MA in Television and Radio Scriptwriting. Two-year, part-time course taught by professional writers and producers. Also offers masterclasses with leading figures in the radio and television industry.

SCREENLAB

Diorama Arts Centre 3-7 Euston Centre Regents Place London NW1 3JG
E   enquiries@screen-lab.co.uk
W   www.screen-lab.co.uk

Offers workshops and personal tuition to help students in all aspects of screenwriting.

THE SCRIPT FACTORY

66–67 Wells Street London W1T 3PY
T   020 7323 1414
E   general@scriptfactory.co.uk
W   www.scriptfactory.co.uk

Established in 1996, The Script Factory is a screenwriter and script developer organization set up to bridge the gap between writers and the industry, and to promote excellence in screenwriting. Specializing in training, screenings, masterclasses and various services from its base in central London, The Script Factory operates throughout the UK and internationally. For the best source of information on upcoming activities, courses and latest news, and to join the free mailing list, check the website.

UNIVERSITY OF SHEFFIELD

Institute for Lifelong Learning 196–198 West Street Sheffield S1 4ET
T   0114 222 7000
F   0114 222 7001
W   www.shef.ac.uk/till

Certificate in Creative Writing (Degree Level 1) and a wide range of courses, from foundation level to specialist writing areas, open to all. Courses in poetry, journalism, scriptwriting, comedy, short story writing, travel writing. Brochures and information available from the address above.

SIGNALS MEDIA ARTS

Advanced Screenwriting Victoria Chambers St Runwald Street Colchester CO1 1HF
T   01206 560255
F   01206 369086
E   anitabelli@signals.org.uk
W   www.signals.org.uk

Open access course lasting ten weeks. Students work on a piece of their own work, from pitch to developed script. Some basic knowledge of screenwriting and understanding of writing for a visual medium is expected.

SOUTH THAMES COLLEGE

Wandsworth High Street Wandsworth London
SW18 2PP
T   020 8918 7777
E   studentservices@south-thames.ac.uk
W www.south-thames.ac.uk

Offers an introductory course teaching the
skills and techniques needed to create an
effective script for film and television. Focus is
on feature films.

SOUTHAMPTON SOLENT UNIVERSITY

East Park Terrace Southampton Hampshire
SO14 0YN
T   023 8031 9000
E   Richard.Hudson@solent.ac.uk
W www.solent.ac.uk

Contacts
Rich Hudson *Senior Lecturer*

Offers a BA in screenwriting, designed in
collaboration with working screenwriters.
Specializes in writing for all major screen
formats, including drama documentary, soap
opera, comedy and feature film. Entry Level:
180 points, with at least 160 points from 6 or
12-unit awards. Particularly welcomes mature
students, and those who may have relevant
experience.

UNIVERSITY OF SURREY, ROEHAMPTON

Erasmus House Roehampton Lane London
SW15 5PU
T   020 8392 3000
E   enquiries@roehampton.ac.uk
W www.roehampton.ac.uk

Offers undergraduate and postgraduate degrees
in creative writing, including components in
screenwriting.

TAPS (TRAINING AND PERFORMANCE SHOWCASE)

Shepperton Studios Studios Road Shepperton
Middlesex TW17 0QD
T   01932 592 151
F   01932 592 233
E   admin@tapsnet.org
W www.tapsnet.org

Contacts
Jill James *Executive Director*

Founded in 1993, offering workshops and
masterclasses on writing for comedy, continuing
drama and games, as well as script editing.
Alumni have worked on series including
Coronation Street, *EastEnders* and *The Bill*,
and received commissions for their own
original series ideas.

THAMES VALLEY UNIVERSITY

Ealing Campus St Mary's Road Ealing London
W5 5RF
T   020 8579 5000
E   learning.advice@tvu.ac.uk
W www.tvu.ac.uk

MA in creative screenwriting. Designed to
help writers find a personal voice as
well as understand the requirements of
the industry.

Application Criteria
Applicants will typically have at least an upper
second-class honours degree in Literature,
Theatre or Media or related discipline, or an
equivalent overseas qualification.

TY NEWYDD WRITERS' CENTRE

Llanystumdwy Cricieth LL52 0LW
T   01766 522811
F   01766 523095
E   post@tynewydd.org
W www.tynewydd.org

Residential writers' centre set up by the Taliesin
Trust with the support of the Arts Council of
Wales to encourage and promote writing in
both English and Welsh. Most courses run from
Monday evening to Saturday morning. Each
course has two tutors and a maximum of 16
participants. A wide range of courses for all
levels of experience. Early booking essential.
Fees from £400 inclusive. People on low
incomes may be eligible for a grant or bursary.
Course leaflet available.

UNIVERSITY COLLEGE FALMOUTH

Woodlane Falmouth TR11 4RH
W www.falmouth.ac.uk

PgDip/MA professional writing programme. An intensive vocational writing programme developing skills in fiction, magazine journalism/features, screenwriting. Students work on an extended writing project and form links with other PgDips such as television production and broadcast journalism.

UNIVERSITY OF WEST OF ENGLAND

Faculty of Creative Arts Bower Ashton Campus Kennel Lodge Road Bristol BS3 2JT
T   0117 32 84716
F   0117 32 84745
E   eileen.elsey@uwe.ac.uk
W   www.uwe.ac.uk/amd

Contacts
Eileen Elsey *Programme Leader, MA Media*

Faculty established as the Bristol School of Practical Art in 1853. Became Faculty of Creative Arts within UWE in 1992. Offers MA in Media (Screenwriting) which seeks to teach a professional approach to screenwriting including how to pitch ideas to the industry. Full- or part-time.

Application Criteria
Applicants should have skill and experience in creative writing and critical analysis. Will normally have an honours degree but applicants with other qualifications or professional experienced are encouraged to apply. Application forms available via website, phone or post. Applicants should also include a 10-page script. Course made up of four 30-point modules (£609 each) and one 60-credit module (£1218).

UNIVERSITY OF WESTMINSTER

Harrow Campus Watford Road Northwick Park Harrow Middlesex HA1 3TP
T   020 7911 5903
F   020 7911 5955
E   haradm@wmin.ac.uk
W   www.wmin.ac.uk

Contacts
Dave Haddock *Campus Admissions and Marketing Office Manager*

Founded in 1838 as the Polytechnic Institution; showed the first public moving-picture show in 1896. Offering MA courses in Film and TV: Theory, Culture and Industry and Screenwriting and Producing for Film and TV. Also undergraduate courses on Contemporary Media Practice and Film and Television Production. Alumni include Michael Jackson (Channel 4 and BBC), Asif Kapadia and Seamus McGarvey.

Application Criteria
Applications for undergraduate courses through UCAS; MA courses direct to the institution.

WESTMINSTER ADULT EDUCATION SERVICE

Ebury Bridge Centre Sutherland Street London SW1V 4LH
T   020 7297 7297
F   020 7641 8140
E   info@waes.ac.uk
W   www.waes.ac.uk

Contacts
Karen Fraser *Course Team Leader for Video and Make-up*

Offering courses on scriptwriting for short and feature films. Scriptwriting for Film incorporates script analysis of short films, screenings, group discussions and individual written work. Scriptwriting for Feature Films offers an introduction to screenwriting, examing structure, character and genre.

Application Criteria
Beginners and those with previous experience are eligible.

UNIVERSITY OF WINCHESTER

Winchester Hampshire SO22 4NR
T   01962 841515
F   01962 842280
E   course.enquiries@winchester.ac.uk
W   www.winchester.ac.uk

The university was founded in 1840. It offers BA courses in creative writing and media production and MA courses in writing for children and creative and critical writing.

Application Criteria
Application criteria and other course-specific information available in the university prospectus.

THE WRITERS BUREAU

Sevendale House 7 Dale Street Manchester M1 1JB
T   0161 228 2362
F   0161 228 3533
E   studentservices@writersbureau.com
W   www.writersbureau.com

Contacts
Diana Nadin *Director of Studies*

Founded in 1989, offering a comprehensive writing course covering scriptwriting for TV, radio and theatre. Accredited by the Open and Distance Learning Quality Council. Admission is open to anyone. Courses cost £274.

WRITERS' HOLIDAY AT CAERLEON

School Bungalow Church Road Pontnewydd Cwmbran NP44 1AT
T   01633 489438
E   writersholiday@lineone.net
W   www.writersholiday.net

Contacts
Anne Hobbs

Annual six-day comprehensive conference including 12 courses for writers of all standards held in the summer at the University of Wales' Caerleon Campus. Courses, lectures, concert and excursion all included in the fee. Private, single and en-suite, full board accommodation. Courses have included Writing for Publication and Writing for the Radio.

WYE VALLEY ARTS CENTRE

Hephzibah Gallery Llandogo NP25 4TW
T   01594 530214
F   01594 530321
E   wyeart@cwcom.net
W   www.wyeart.cwc.net

Courses (held at Hephzibah Gallery, Llandogo in the Wye Valley and 'at our house in Cornwall') include Creative Writing and Fiction Workshop. All styles and abilities.

YORKSHIRE ART CIRCUS

School Lane Glasshoughton Castleford Yorkshire WF10 4QH
T   01977 550 401
E   admin@artcircus.org.uk
W   www.artcircus.org.uk

Contacts
Lesley Wilkinson *Manager of Core Activities*

Community arts charity organizing creative writing courses and a professional writer development programme which offers masterclasses, workshops and peer analysis. All tutors are working writers and artists, and include Bafta award winners and Orange Prize nominees.

Application Criteria
Day courses in writing cost from £37; 63-hour writers development programme costs £450.

CANADA

CANADIAN FILM CENTRE

Windfields 2489 Bayview Avenue Toronto Ontario M2L 1A8
T   416 445 1446
F   416 445 9481
W   www.cfccreates.com

Originally a film training centre, now offering a wide range of programmes and funding opportunities for practitioners of television, film and interactive media. Also involved in production across a wide range of media.

THE CANADIAN SCREEN TRAINING CENTRE

61A York Street Ottawa Ontario K1N 5T2
T   613 789 4720
F   613 789 4724
E   info@cstc.ca
W   www.cstc.ca

A non-profit organization dedicated to advancing the development of the Canadian film, television and New Media industry. Provides intensive, short-duration workshops to develop the skills demanded by the screen industry. Screenwriting courses include: An Introduction to Screenwriting; Polishing Your Craft: Developing Your Script; The Next Big Thing: Writing for Television; The Feature Screenplay: Writing for the Big and Small Screen.

PRAXIS CENTRE FOR SCREENWRITERS

School for the Contemporary Arts Simon Fraser University Suite 3120 515 W. Hastings Street Vancouver British Columbia V6B 5K3
T 604 268 7880
F 604 268 7882
E praxis@sfu.ca
W www.praxisfilm.com

Non-profit organization devoted to the professional development of Canadian screenwriters and filmmakers. As well as offering courses, the centre runs competitions and a scripts for option service.

UNIVERSITY OF REGINA

Faculty of Fine Arts Department of Media Production & Studies Room ED243 Education Building Regina Saskatchewan S4S 0A2
T 306 585 4796
F 306 585 4439
E film@uregina.ca
W www.uregina.ca/finearts

Offers a 4-year Bachelor of Fine Arts degree in Film and Video production, which includes course options on scriptwriting.

UNIVERSITY OF TORONTO

School of Continuing Studies 158 St George Street Toronto Ontario M5S 2V8
T 416 978 2400
F 416 978 6666
E learn@utoronto.ca
W learn.utoronto.ca

Offers screenwriting courses which can be used towards the SCS Certificate(s) in Creative Writing. Students develop the practical skills necessary to write good screenplays, using a hands-on workshop format. Students are expected to participate

in class discussions, produce work for each class and develop a good portion of a screenplay. Suitable for both beginners and more experienced screenwriters.

VANCOUVER FILM SCHOOL

2nd Floor 198 West Hastings Street Vancouver British Columbia V6B 1H2
T 604 685 5808
F 604 685 5830
W www.vfs.com

The school offers a one-year comprehensive programme in screenwriting. Topics covered in the programme include writing a TV spec, comedy sketch, features, shorts and documentaries. The course also covers pitching and story editing.

YORK UNIVERSITY (GRADUATE PROGRAM IN FILM)

224 Centre For Film And Theatre 4700 Keele Street Toronto Ontario M3J 1P3
T 416 736 2100
W www.yorku.ca

The Centre offers a Master of Fine Arts degree with the option to specialize in screenwriting.

IRELAND

FÁS SCREEN TRAINING IRELAND

Adelaide Chambers Peter Street Dublin
T 01 483 0840
F 01 483 0842
E film@fas.ie
W www.screentrainingireland.ie

Aims to provide continuing training for professionals in film, television, animation and digital media. Runs a bursary award scheme.

HUSTON SCHOOL OF FILM & DIGITAL MEDIA

University College Galway Galway
T 091 495076
W www.filmschool.ie

Based at the National University of Ireland, Galway, the Schools inaugural programme was an MA in screenwriting. Offers advanced training in screenplay writing integrated with courses in film history and analysis. Supported by regular film screenings and workshops. The School seeks to make a virtue of the West of Ireland's special position as a potential 'contact zone' between the disparate traditions of American and European cinema. Activities are intended to foster a critical awareness of both mainstream and alternative film traditions.

BILL KEATING CENTRE

Milltown Park Sandford Road Ranelagh Dublin 6
T 01 219 6510
W www.bilkeatingcentre.com

Provides comprehensive training and practical studio experience in all aspects of television, with an emphasis on presentation, production and direction. Also offers a programme development service.

NATIONAL FILM SCHOOL

School of Creative Art Dun Laoghaire Institute of Art Design and Technology Kill Avenue Dun Laoghaire County Dublin
T 01 214 4600
F 01 214 4700
E info@iadt.ie
W www.iadt.ie

The National Film School (NFS) at IADT was launched in 2003 as a centre of excellence for education and training in film, animation, broadcasting and digital media. Courses are full- or part-time. The MA in Screenwriting provides writers with the opportunity to learn the craft of screenwriting while producing a full-length (90-minute) screenplay. The programme is delivered over thirty weeks and study is supported by lectures and seminars from prominent writers, directors and producers.

Application Criteria
Students are required to have an existing portfolio of work that is relevant to their chosen course. Applicants can either apply through the CAO (Central Application Office) system or directly to IADT. Application forms are available on the website.

NATIONAL YOUTH FILM SCHOOL

St Joseph's Studios Waterford Road Kilkenny
T 056 7764677
F 056 7751504
E info@yifm.com
W www.yifm.com

Founded in 2001, a film school for young Irish people aged 13 to 20. A residential school for 20 film makers run over five weeks during the summer holidays.

Application Criteria
Students applying for this programme should be able to show some previous involvement or interest in film making. Application forms available from website. Costs €800 (excluding accommodation).

UCD SCHOOL OF FILM

Room 109 Arts Annexe University College Dublin Belfield Dublin 4
T 01 716 8301
F 01 716 8684
E film.studies@ucd.ie
W www.ucd.ie/film

Contacts
Rowena Kelly *Administrator*

Conducts practical courses in film production and screenwriting. Set up in 1992 on the initiative of actor Gregory Peck, film producer Noel Pearson, former UCD President Patrick Masterson and UCD Professor Richard Kearney. Aims to cater for the changing demands of an expanding Irish film industry. The School conducts film production and screenwriting components on the M.A. degree programme on behalf of its academic sister body, the O'Kane Centre for Film Studies.

Application Criteria
Early application is advised. Normal qualification for admission is a First Class Honours or Second Class Honours, Grade I Primary Degree. Applications from graduates in a wide range of disciplines and subjects

encouraged. Candidates with other equivalent qualifications or experience also welcome to apply. Industry experience may be taken into account when assessing applications.

WRITING MOVIES

T   01 239 0410
E   writingmovies@ireland.com
W   www.writingmovies.net

An intensive two-day course in screenwriting by award-winning Scottish film-maker Laurence Henson, given regularly in Dublin since 1998. Costs €195.

AUSTRALIA

AUSTRALIAN COLLEGE QED

PO Box 730 Bondi Junction NSW 1355
T   02 9386 2500
W   www.acq.edu.au

The school of Journalism, Media, and Photography offers a course on film and television that involves working on scripts, screenwriting and television production. Students learn how to write for television, film and video, develop their own screenplay and how to market it.

AUSTRALIAN FILM, TELEVISION AND RADIO SCHOOL

PO Box 126 North Ryde NSW 1670
T   02 9805 6611
F   02 9887 1030
E   infonsw@aftrs.edu.au
W   www.aftrs.edu.au

Offers both full-time and short courses in screenwriting. In the graduate diploma in film and television, screenwriting students develop dramatic and visual storytelling craft skills through a series of production workshops and a three-day film shoot which develops short comedy, serious drama and genre-based scripts. Students in the Master of Arts degree write and co-produce series television drama, complete at least one industry-ready feature-length screenplay and/or

a long- or short-form digital or interactive media project.

BOND UNIVERSITY

University Drive Robina QLD 4226
T   07 5595 1024
E   information@bond.edu.au
W   www.bond.edu.au

Offers a 2-year full-time Bachelors degree in Film and Television with courses in screenwriting. Also offers a Master of Creative Arts in screenwriting.

CURTIN UNIVERSITY OF TECHNOLOGY

GPO Box U1987 Perth WA 6845
T   08 9266 9266
F   08 9266 2255
W   www.curtin.edu.au

Offers a 1-year Graduate Diploma in Film and Television with courses in screenwriting. The screenwriting courses focus on writing for documentaries and dramas.

FILM AND TELEVISION INSTITUTE

PO Box 579 Fremantle WA 6959
T   08 9431 6700
F   08 9335 1283
E   fti@fti.asn.au
W   www.fti.asn.au

Offers an introductory course on the basic principles of writing short drama scripts. Over the four sessions, participants will write 3–5 minute scripts and explore character development, point of view, plot, the script editing process and other techniques.

FILMMAKING SUMMER SCHOOL AT MELBOURNE UNIVERSITY

605 Rathdowne Street Carlton North VIC 3054
T   03 9347 5035
F   03 9349 4443
E   info@summerfilmschool.com
W   www.summerfilmschool.com

Contacts
Sharon Peers *Co-ordinator*

Run since 1994 as part of the university's summer programme, all courses are taught by film practitioners in their area of expertise. Specialized workshops on adaptation, writing for television, comedy writing and writing for children.

Application Criteria
Anyone can apply. Cost varies from daily rate of AUS$95 to discounted full course fees.

THE INTERNATIONAL FILM SCHOOL SYDNEY

27 Rosebery Avenue Rosebery NSW 2018
T   02 9663 3789
F   02 9663 0816
E   Katrina@ifss.edu.au
W   www.ifss.edu.au

Offers a 2-year intensive filmmaking training course. In the first year, students attend the screenwriting programme, studying the moment-to-moment construction of cinema. Also offers a 6-day short course on screenwriting.

LA TROBE UNIVERSITY

VIC 3086
T   03 9479 2499
F   03 9479 3638
E   cinema@latrobe.edu.au
W   www.latrobe.edu.au

Offers a Bachelor of Creative Arts degree with courses in screenwriting. Students learn various industry-accepted screenwriting formats used for fiction film and television drama, including film treatments and television 'bibles'.

UNIVERSITY OF MELBOURNE

Faculty of the Victorian College of the Arts 234 St Kilda Road Southbank VIC 3006
T   03 9685 9300
F   03 9682 1841
W   www.vca.unimelb.edu.au

Offers both undergraduate and postgraduate degrees in film and television with courses in screenwriting. In the Masters degree the screenwriting course involves the study of

characterization and dramatic form at an advanced level. Each Masters student is expected to develop a script that they will take into production.

METRO SCREEN

PO Box 299 Paddington NSW 2021
T   02 9361 5318
F   02 9361 5320
E   training@metroscreen.org.au
W   www.metroscreen.com.au

Offers a 5-month full-time certificate in Screen, covering screenwriting, producing, directing, camera, lighting, sound and editing. Also offers short courses in screenwriting. The introductory course for beginners covers topics such as plot, structure, dialogue, character and industry standard formatting. The advanced course focuses on how to rewrite and progress through successive drafts of a script as well as how to ask for feedback and collaborate with other writers and filmmakers.

OPEN CHANNEL

Victoria Harbour Shed 4 North Wharf Road Docklands VIC 3008
T   03 8610 9300
E   info@openchannel.org.au

Offers a short course on screenwriting where sessions cover script formatting, structure and narrative development. Also offers a scriptwriting workshop where learners develop and write a script over a four-month period under the support and guidance of industry professionals. Learners will be trained in script conventions, techniques and format.

QUEENSLAND SCHOOL OF FILM & TELEVISION

PO Box 380 Fortitude Valley QLD 4006
T   07 3262 5022
F   07 3262 5655
W   www.qsft.qld.edu.au

Offers a short-course in screenwriting, and covers topics such as script formatting, creating ideas, developing narrative, characters, and three-act structure.

RMIT UNIVERSITY

GPO Box 2476V Melbourne VIC 3001
T   03 9925 2000
F   03 9663 2764
W   www.rmit.edu.au

Contacts
Brendan Lee *Programme Administrator*

Offers Advanced Diploma of Arts in
Professional Screenwriting, providing
specialist training in writing for film,
television and digital media across all
genres. Aims to encourage students to
develop their own creative strengths but
also expose them to professional contexts
and practices.

Application Criteria
Mature applicants should have relevant
experience or 'evidence of ability to meet the
demands of the programme'.

SCREENPLAY.COM.AU

PO Box 300 Artarmon NSW 1570
T   02 8011 3533
W   www.screenplay.com.au

Contacts
Jeff Bollow

Established in 2000, offering a 2-day
weekend course, plus Pro-Series: Down
Under, a 6-month online workshop.
Courses run by a production company
seeking screenplays with local content to
be produced locally.

Application Criteria
Costs AUS$350; Pro Series: Down Under
$1,299.

SYDNEY FILM SCHOOL

82 Cope Street Waterloo NSW 2017
T   02 9698 2244
F   02 9698 2246
W   www.sydneyfilmschool.com

Offers a Diploma course in screenwriting,
which covers topics such as the nature
of a screenplay, formatting a script,
creating characters, and structuring
a story.

UNIVERSITY OF TECHNOLOGY, SYDNEY

PO Box 123 Broadway Sydney NSW 2007
T   02 9514 1593
F   02 9514 2778
E   Margot.Nash@uts.edu.au
W   www.uts.edu.au

Contacts
Margot Nash *Senior Lecturer, Screenwriting,
Writing and Cultur*

Founded in 1988, offering 1-year Graduate
Certificate in Screenwriting, as well as
screenwriting streams in Masters writing
courses. 3-year Master of Arts: Writing course
gives screenwriters the opportunity to focus on
a major project under supervision.

Application Criteria
Application is open to anyone through the
website.

NEW ZEALAND

AUCKLAND UNIVERSITY

Film Television and Media Studies Private Bag
92019 Auckland Mail Centre Auckland 1142
T   09 373 7599 Ext. 874
F   09 373 8764
E   media@auckland.ac.nz
W   www.arts.auckland.ac.nz

Offers courses in film and TV production,
including screenwriting elements.

MASSEY UNIVERSITY

School of English & Media Studies Private Bag
11 222 Palmerston North
T   06 356 9099 ext 7311
F   06 350 5672
W   ems.massey.ac.nz

Offers various undergraduate and graduate
creative writing and performance papers
including media script writing.

NEW ZEALAND FILM ACADEMY

PO Box 10-222 Dominion Road
Auckland 1030
T   09 374 5709
F   09 309 8136

E info@nzfilmacademy.com
W www.nzfilmacademy.com

Offers range of 6- to 18-week courses underpinned by principles of education through experience and the importance of storytelling.

SOUTH SEAS FILM AND TELEVISION SCHOOL

PO Box 34-579 Birkenhead Auckland 1310
T 09 444 3253
F 09 444 7821
E info@southseas.tv
W www.southseas.co.nz

Leading film, television, onscreen acting and animation training institution.

UNITEC NEW ZEALAND

School of Performing and Screen Arts Private Bag 92025 Carrington Road Mt Albert Auckland
T 09 849 4180
W www.unitec.ac.nz

Offers three-year full-time Bachelor of Performing and Screen Arts (Directing and Writing for Screen and Theatre) for those interested in a career as a writer or director for film, TV or theatre.

VICTORIA UNIVERSITY

IIML Victoria University PO Box 600 Wellington
T 04 463 6854
F 04 463 6865

E modernletters@vuw.ac.nz
W www.vuw.ac.nz

Taught from the International Institute of Modern Letters at Glenn Schaeffer House on the Kelburn Campus, offering internationally-respected creative writing programmes. Applications should be made directly to the International Institute of Modern Letters.

UNIVERSITY OF WAIKATO

Department of Screen and Media Studies
T 07 838 4543
F 07 838 4767
E screenandmedia@waikato.ac.nz
W www.waikato.ac.nz

Aims to provide students with the skills to work within the rapidly-evolving media environment. Includes modules on screenwriting.

WHITIREIA COMMUNITY POLYTECHNIC

Private Bag 50 910 Porirua 5240
T 0800 944 847
F 04 237 3101
E info@whitireia.ac.nz
W www.whitireia.ac.nz

Year-long online creative courses with options in scriptwriting.

There is a story of Billy Wilder's later years when the legendary director pitched an idea for a movie to a young producer. The power broker opened the conversation. 'Tell me about your career, Mr Wilder.' 'You first,' said Wilder.

STORYTELLING AROUND THE WORLD

Lucy Scher, co-director of The Script Factory, discusses techniques of storytelling

Picture the scene:
A group of young Macedonian writers are at a Script Factory workshop in Skopje, looking through the morning newspaper as instructed. It is in Cyrillic so I can't read it but one by one they stop and laugh at the same story. One of them translates the headline: *200 Macedonian students are to be given the opportunity to work in Disneyworld, Florida, for the summer to improve their English and their relationships.*

What a great idea, and this is one of the stories that developed: A Macedonian grandma finds out she is dying and despite the fearful tales of America and Americans, decides she must visit her grandson who is working for the summer at Disneyworld in Florida. She has never left the country before, but manages to secure a visa and a ticket. She sets off from Skopje airport (the size of a bus stop in Camden Town) and arrives at Los Angeles International. You know and I know that she has gone to the wrong Disney theme park and thus begins a heart-warming Road Movie from LA to Florida, undertaken by the most unlikely heroine, with time running out. Without much experience, money or language she learns the fundamental humanity of all people at the time she most needs it.

Stories emerge from our emotional experiences, or rather from our need to make sense of those experiences. We all create stories, tell them, absorb them and generally have a very sophisticated appreciation of story, even if our understanding is at the subconscious level.

I have, perhaps, one of the most enjoyable jobs imaginable in that I run screenwriting workshops all over the world where the central purpose is to listen to writers telling me their stories. Some five years and twenty countries later, this seems a good opportunity to reflect on this unique experience in the hope that I can turn it into useful observation for new screenwriters picking up this book and embarking on the journey.

A good first question is, what are those things that can motivate writers to write, that have emotional importance? This is my list gathered from stories I have heard around the world:

- The big life-changing events like births, deaths, marriages and divorces
- Our hopes and dreams
- The moments when, if we had had our time again, we would have done things differently
- Moving, whether by choice or force – but a significant change in our environment
- Fears about the repercussions of our actions and decisions as well as the fear of never being able to know everything
- The things we observe about people, or about the zeitgeist
- Frustrations of modern living; either comic or tragic
- Mythology – what happened before we arrived somewhere and how that affects us
- The things that happened to us as children/adults that remain inexplicable
- The things that happened to us as children that we have interpreted a number of ways over our lives or the things that are ripe with complex meaning
- Secrets – the stuff we are hiding in ourselves and the stuff we're hiding for other people
- Broken rituals – the habitual events that only become meaningful when they stop being what they always were

All of these triggers can suggest a change in our character or a change in our point of view about *being* that has an impact on our lives. And, fundamentally, this is what a screenplay explores for a created character in an invented or part-invented situation, in a contained period of time.

My working definition of story development for screenplays is this: the developer seeks to find what is meaningful in the story to the writer and assists her to make that meaningful to an audience. This is a useful definition because it requires that one part of my job is a forensic investigation of the material and the writer to find that meaning; the second is that I have an understanding of how the audience responds to the story. I have written quite a lot on how the audience responds to the story, but this is the first time I have written down the process of extracting meaning.

My underlying assumption here is that to write down a story, unpaid – to spend the time and effort required – is undertaken only because it means something to the author. To illustrate: whoever at that Skopje workshop picks up the Macedonian grandma story idea and takes it right through the necessary treatments, scripts and rewrites will do so because they have connected with something in the material. A bell has gone off that resonates and won't keep quiet.

It is that meaning that should be sacred in a story and script development process, whether formal or not. However, the choices about how to tell the story are not sacred. Once the meaning is agreed, the characters, events and scenes should be created, developed, rewritten and selected according to their expediency in the telling of the story, for the purpose of story is to convey meaning. Easy...

Except why is this so hard? Probably because it matters.

Also, perhaps, because it is hard to separate what happens from what it means, when it is personal. If the writer writes out of an emotional need to process something that he has experienced and is trying to make sense of, the steps that have to be mounted in developing it as a screenplay are those that take that specific personal experience and make it universal. In other words, new writers are well served in knowing the source of their idea throughout the writing process and being able to define the meaning. Keep that meaning sacred but let expediency and good sense guide the other choices.

An exercise that I encourage writers to do is to 'break a ritual' to try to generate ideas and images *that didn't happen*, but that still conjure the emotional meaning that the writer is hoping to convey. From this...

INT. CHURCH a funeral in progress

Came this...

On the first day of the long school summer holiday each year, Tom and Ben would wake up earlier than usual and race to get washed, dressed and grab a spanner so they could tinker on the old car with their father, while their mother effortlessly fitted everything into two suitcases. Once the luggage was loaded and the oil and tyres checked the family set off for the Lakes to enjoy each other at leisure.

The year their mother died the boys tried to bring enthusiasm to the task of car fixing, but it became clear that they hadn't really known what they were doing and the joy had, of course, gone. They tried, they smiled, they packed their fishing rods, they said 'we can't wait', but as the car pulled into the road it was the overfull plastic carrier bags stuffed in the boot that really betrayed the loss.

The mother dying is important. The way we understand the impact and the chaos of loss may be better conveyed in the snapshot of a car boot full of carrier bags, where once it had been two orderly suitcases, than in a funeral scene.

In workshops in the countries of the former Soviet bloc the disappointment in the post-1989 freedoms is a very common theme in stories. In a group of twenty-five Polish writers last year at least twenty explored the idea of a character leaving Poland for the UK, Ireland or Scandinavia and encountering horrific hostility, abuse, exploitation, even death. Certainly not living the dream they felt they had been sold. This is hard territory to negotiate with these writers, who *want* to co-produce in western Europe. We already know that capitalism is not the answer to everything, that money doesn't buy happiness, that we don't always get what we deserve. The question is, how do these writers say it so that we are happy to hear it again? And I reiterate, preserve the meaning but find a story to tell it in such a way that feels innovative.

I was fortunate to go to Palestine just before the recent change of government to work with eleven writers on their film treatments. Story is conflict; I think I was expecting some quite high-octane stuff in this most conflicted region on earth. Yet the stories were singularly without it.

The Key is the story of an eight-year-old boy from Bethlehem who wants to go to the cinema, but his father won't let him. One night he steals his father's key and sneaks out by himself. At the cinema he attaches himself to a large family group and slips in unnoticed; he marvels at the screen with eyes popping. Suddenly he is tapped on the shoulder. He turns in fright, but it is his teacher sitting behind him, who walks him home safely. He returns the key to its hook behind the door and gets back into bed, happy.

I think there is something quite magical about the simplicity of this story and even while I heard myself saying, on auto-pilot, to the writer, *what if he gets caught...what if he gets lost...what about conflict*...I hoped it may be possible to make it as it was; the hopes and dreams of Palestine made manifest in a trouble-free trip to the cinema. Not yet, though.

Writing is rarely schematic. It is unlikely that anyone sits down and thinks, 'I will write about the importance of trust, or the value of justice.' So the process of discovering and defining meaning is a process and a really important one. Find it, write it down and remember to protect it, while remaining open to the world of possibilities about how to tell it.

The Script Factory's international training is supported by the British Council.

SOCIETIES AND
ORGANIZATIONS

UNITED STATES OF AMERICA

ACADEMY OF MOTION PICTURE ARTS AND SCIENCES

8949 Wilshire Boulevard Beverly Hills
CA 90211
T   310 247 3000
W www.oscars.org

Founded in 1927, the Academy is a professional honorary organization composed of over 6,500 filmmakers. The purpose of the organization is: to foster cooperation among creative leaders; recognize outstanding achievements; cooperate on technical research and improvement of methods and equipment; and provide a common forum and meeting ground for various film-related crafts. Hosts of the Oscars.

ACADEMY OF TELEVISION ARTS & SCIENCES (ATAS)

5220 Lankershim Boulevard North Hollywood CA 91601
T   818 754 2800
F   818 761 2827
W www.emmys.org

Founded in 1946, ATAS awards the Primetime Emmys and is the creator of the Television Hall of Fame, whilst its East Coast counterpart, the National Academy of Television Arts & Sciences (NATAS), distributes Emmy Awards in various categories including Daytime, Sports, News and Documentary and Public Service.

Membership/Registration Policy
Membership can be either active status or associate status subject to requirements (see website for further details).

ALLIANCE OF MOTION PICTURE & TELEVISION PRODUCERS

15503 Ventura Boulevard Encino CA 91436
T   818 995 3600
W www.amptp.org

Founded in 1982, the primary trade association with respect to labour issues in the motion picture and television industry. The association negotiates 80 industry-wide collective bargaining agreements on behalf of over 350 motion picture and television producers.

AMERICAN FILM INSTITUTE (AFI)

2021 N. Western Avenue Los Angeles
CA 90027
T   323 856 7600
F   323 467 4578
W www.afi.com

Founded in 1967, a non-profit organization established to train the next generation of filmmakers and to preserve the American film heritage. The AFI Conservatory trains filmmakers by focusing on hands-on experience with established figures, and maintains America's film heritage through the AFI Catalogue of Feature Films.

AMERICAN SCREENWRITERS ASSOCIATION

269 S. Beverly Drive Ste. 2600 Beverly Hills
CA 90212-3807
T   866 265 9091
E   asa@goasa.com
W www.asascreenwriters.com

This non-profit organization provides writers with practical resources, networking opportunities, and services and programmes. It has an international membership of more than 40,000 members from 40 countries located throughout North America, Europe, the Pacific and the Middle East. The association works with many leading screenwriters such as Gary Ross (*Seabiscuit, Pleasantville, Big*), Aaron Sorkin (*The West Wing, An American President*) and Shane Black (*Lethal Weapon, The Last Boy Scout*). Also offers script registration service.

Membership/Registration Policy
In order to become a member, a membership application must be completed and annual fees

paid (there is no set criteria on becoming a member).

ATLANTA SCREENWRITERS GROUP

E info@atlscript.org
W www.atlscript.org/group.shtml

Founded in 1998 to help local screenwriters develop their ideas, swap industry stories and give constructive feedback.

Membership/Registration Policy
Membership is open to all. An email should be sent to notify attendance prior to the meeting and an idea for discussion is mandatory (a complete script is not necessary).

THE AUTHORS GUILD

31 East 32nd Street 7th Floor NY 10016
T 212 563 5904
F 212 564 8363
E staff@authorsguild.org
W www.authorsguild.org

Founded in 1912 by a group of writers, the Guild now represents more than 8,000 authors. Provides web services, seminars on subjects of professional interest and legal advice on contracts and publishing disputes.

Membership/Registration Policy
Writers can qualify for 'Regular Membership' if they have been published by an established American publisher or had three works published in a periodical of general circulation in the last 18 months. 'Associate Membership' is available to those with a contract for a work not yet published.

CINESTORY

PO Box 3736 Idyllwild CA 92549
T 909 659 1180
F 909 659 1176
E cinestory@cinestory.com
W www.cinestory.com

Founded in 1995, it has developed a 3-day Retreat where aspiring writers have the

opportunity to have one-on-one meetings, informal hook-ups, and movie clip discussions with industry leaders. Every writer meets with three Retreat mentors each to discuss their script submissions and careers.

CLICK & COPYRIGHT

21 Dorset Road Saint Paul MN 55118
T 651 552 9663
F 651 552 9663
E info@clickandinc.com
W www.clickandcopyright.com

Founded in 1999, assisting independent artists to protect their work by drafting and preparing the correct US Copyright Office forms. Copyright registration of a screenplay with the US Copyright Office protects the screenplay for the author's entire life and for a further 70 years, and it is also the only way to protect a screenplay from infringement in Federal Court.

DRAMATISTS GUILD OF AMERICA

1501 Broadway Suite 701 New York NY 10036
T 212 398 9366
F 212 944 0420
W www.dramatistsguild.com

Established over 80 years ago, a professional organization for playwrights, composers and lyricists working in the American theatre market. Its business affairs division provides model contracts and agreements, and advice in negotiating contracts with theatres, collaborators, publishers and others.

Membership/Registration Policy
There are three categories of membership. Membership as a student is available for those who are enrolled in a dramatic writing course. Membership as an Associate is open to those who have written at least one stage play and Active membership is available to those playwrights who have had at least one play produced in a Broadway, Off-Broadway, or LORT theatre.

FILM INDEPENDENT

9911 West Pico Boulevard 11th Floor
Los Angeles CA 90035
T 310 432 1200
F 310 432 1203
W www.filmindependent.org

Established over 25 years ago, a
non-profit organization dedicated to
independent film and independent
filmmakers. Members have access to
discounted equipment, editing suites,
casting rooms, a valuable resource library,
over 120 free screenings and 150 educational
events every year. Film Independent
also produces the Los Angeles Film
Festival and the Independent Spirit
Awards.

Membership/Registration Policy
Membership costs a nominal fee and is open
to all.

INDEPENDENT FILM & TELEVISION ALLIANCE

10850 Wilshire Boulevard 9th Fl. Los Angeles
CA 90024-4321
T 310 446 1000
F 310 446 1600
E info@ifta-online.org
W www.ifta-online.org

Founded in 1980 as the American
Film Marketing Association, the trade
association for the independent film
and television industry worldwide. Its
members include 160 companies from
22 countries, spanning production,
distribution and financing of independent
film and television programming.

NORTHWEST SCREENWRITERS' GUILD

4616 25th Avenue NE PMB #439 Seattle
WA 98105
T 206 760 0462
E illovox@comcast.net
W www.nwsg.org

Dedicated to helping screenwriters in the
Northwest further their craft and careers.
Provides workshops and opportunities for
direct interface with industry professionals.

Membership/Registration Policy
Membership open to anyone. Those who have
completed screenplays can apply for
professional 'compendium' standing
(see website for details).

ORGANIZATION OF BLACK SCREENWRITERS

1968 West Adams Boulevard Los Angeles
CA 90018
T 323 735 2050
F 323 735 2051
E obswriter@sbcglobal.net
W www.obswriter.com

Founded in 1986 to address the lack
of black writers represented in the
entertainment industry. Provides members
with intense training, hands-on experience,
expansive resources and extensive industry
exposure.

Membership/Registration Policy
There are various levels of membership,
including student, general (emerging writers)
and professional (writers who have been
accepted into a writing fellowship).

PROTECTRITE

Nat'l Creative Registry 1106 Second Street
CA 92024
T 800 368 9748
W www.protectrite.com

Founded in 1994, a leader in online intellectual
property registration. Establishes the
completion date of registered materials and
offers long-term storage if original is lost or
destroyed.

SAN FRANCISCO SCREENWRITERS

2443 Fillmore Street #365 San Francisco
CA 94115
T 415 386 8668
F 415 386 8668
E scribner@sfscreenwriters.com
W www.sfscreenwriters.com

The San Francisco Screenwriters is an
organization of writers living in the Bay Area
who help each other with their scripts, ideas
and marketing strategies.

SCREENWRITERS FEDERATION OF AMERICA

4337 Marina City Drive Suite 1141 Marina del Rey CA 90292
w www.screenwritersfederation.org

Formerly known as Screenwriters Guild of America, a federation of industry professionals including screenwriters, directors, producers, literary agents, managers, educators, authors and studio executives. Aims to assist screenwriters in personal and professional development, build a networking community for professional screenwriters, and to administer a Federation-sanctioned, industry-standard, free marketplace for greenlit scripts. Also offers a script registration service.

SUNDANCE INSTITUTE

8530 Wilshire Boulevard 3rd Floor Beverly Hills CA 90211-3114
T   310 360 1981
F   310 360 1969
E   Institute@sundance.org
w www2.sundance.org

Founded in 1981 by Robert Redford, a non-profit organization which runs highly competitive programmes for emerging and aspiring producers, directors, writers and film composers. Runs a Screenwriters Lab focusing entirely on script and story development every January. Also owns and runs the annual Sundance Film Festival.

US COPYRIGHT OFFICE

101 Independence Avenue S.E.
Washington, D.C. 205
T   202 707 3000
w www.copyright.gov

Allows for copyright protection of manuscripts.

WRITERS GUILD OF AMERICA, EAST

555 West 57th Street Suite 1230 New York NY 10019
T   212 767 7800
F   212 582 1909
w www.wgaeast.org

WRITERS GUILD OF AMERICA, WEST

7000 West Third Street Los Angeles CA 90048
T   323 951 4000
F   323 782 4800
E   website@wga.org
w www.wga.org

In 1951, the Writers Guild of America, East and the Writers Guild of America, West were formed to represent writers in motion pictures, television and radio. Since 1954 they have negotiated and administered minimum basic agreements with major film producers, networks and stations. Offers range of other services and support to writers. The total membership of the Guild (East and West) is approximately 11,000. It also offers script registration which protects the writers work for a period of 10 years.

Membership/Registration Policy
Membership of the Guild works on a unit system basis. In order to be eligible for current membership a writer must acquire a minimum of 24 units in the three years preceding application. A writer may be eligible for Associate membership if he or she has had writing employment and/or sales within the Guild's jurisdiction and with a signatory company but has acquired less than 24 units in the three years preceding application. For full details regarding the unit system see organization's website.

UNITED KINGDOM

FEDERATION OF SCREENWRITERS IN EUROPE

C/O UNI-Europa Box 9 31 rue de l'Hopital Brussels B-1000
E   manager@scenaristes.org
w www.scenaristes.org

Contacts
Christina Kallas *Chair*

A non-profit organization which aims to defend freedom of artistic expression and to promote the work and rights of scriptwriters. Represents 21 national guilds and 9,000 writers. Membership is open to any organization representing screenwriters in a European country. A yearly contribution is payable.

THE EUROPEAN SCREENWRITERS MANIFESTO

Spearheaded by the Federation of Screenwriters in Europe, the following manifesto was initially signed by 125 writers from 22 European countries at the European Conference on Screenwriting in November 2006. It was officially presented at the Berlin International Film Festival in February 2007, where the number of signatories passed 1,000. To add your name to the list, visit scenaristes.org.

Stories are at the heart of humanity and are the repository of our diverse cultural heritage. They are told, retold and reinterpreted for new times by storytellers. Screenwriters are the storytellers of our time. European writing talent should be trusted, encouraged and supported. The European film industries need to find ways to attract and keep its screenwriters in the cinema and in their craft. We assert that:

1. The screenwriter is an author of the film, a primary creator of the audiovisual work.
2. The indiscriminate use of the possessory credit is unacceptable.
3. The moral rights of the screenwriter, especially the right to maintain the integrity of a work and to protect it from any distortion or misuse should be inalienable and should be fully honored in practice.
4. The screenwriter should receive fair payment for every form of exploitation of his work.
5. As author the screenwriter should be entitled to an involvement in the production process as well as in the promotion of the film and to be compensated for such work. As author he should be named in any publication accordingly, including festival catalogues, TV listing magazines and reviews. We call on:
6. National governments and funding agencies to support screenwriters by focusing more energy and resources, whether in form of subsidy, tax breaks or investment schemes, on the development stage of film and television production and by funding writers directly.
7. Scholars and film critics to acknowledge the role of screenwriters, and universities, academies and training programmes to educate the next generations in accordance to the collaborative art of the medium and with respect towards the art and craft of screenwriting.
8. Festivals, film museums and other institutions to name the screenwriters in their programs and plan and screen film tributes to screenwriters just as they do to directors, actors and countries.
9. National and European law should acknowledge that the writer is an author of the film.
10. National and European law should ensure that screenwriters can organise, negotiate and contract collectively, in order to encourage and maintain the distinct cultural identities of each country and to seek means to facilitate the free movement of writers in and between all nations.

We will: Distribute this manifesto to industry members and the press in our respective countries. Campaign for the implementation of the agenda defined by this manifesto. Seek the transition into national and European law of the legal changes demanded by this manifesto.

BECTU SCRIPT REGISTRATION SERVICE

373-377 Clapham Road London SW9 9BT
T   020 7346 0900
F   020 7346 0901
E   info@bectu.org.uk
W www.bectu.org.uk

Enables members to register scripts to provide proof that a script was in existence by a given date. Members send their script to BECTU Head Office. The union logs the script, seals it and returns it to the member concerned for safekeeping. Does not archive such scripts or keep copies. Submissions information available on the website.

BRISTOL SCREENWRITERS

E   contact@bristolscreenwriters.org
W www.bristolscreenwriters.org

Membership organization that gives writers of film screenplays the opportunity to have their work read to an audience for feedback and comment. Also runs events that give writers the opportunity to explore different aspects of the film industry. Supported by Watershed Media Centre.

THE BRITISH ACADEMY OF FILM & TELEVISION ARTS (BAFTA)

195 Piccadilly London W1J 9LN
T   020 77340022
F   020 77341792
E   info@bafta.org
W   www.bafta.org

Supports, develops and promotes the moving image industry, including film, TV and video games. Membership of 6,500 individuals professionals around the world. Hosts high-profile annual industry awards.

BRITISH FILM INSTITUTE

Stephen Street Office / bfi National Library 21 Stephen Street London W1T 1LN
T   020 7255 1444
W   www.bfi.org.uk

Founded in 1933 to promote understanding and appreciation of Britain's film and television heritage and culture. BFI Southbank (formerly the National Film Theatre) hosts over 1,000 screenings per year as well as many special events. The BFI also runs the IMAX cinema on London's South Bank as well as publishing extensively on the industry, playing a key role in the Times bfi London Film Festival and the London Lesbian and Gay Film Festival, administering the national archive of the moving image and the national film library. It oversees a programme of cinema, video and DVD releases and publishes *Sight & Sound*, a monthly film magazine.

CHANNEL 4 BRITISH DOCUMENTARY FILM FOUNDATION

E   help@britdoc.org
W   www.britdoc.org

Aims to promote and develop the British documentary by looking beyond television to develop, fund and distribute the work of the next generation of UK documentary filmmakers. Offers grants for short films, particularly by new filmmakers, feature-length projects with the potential to break through, experimental films, passion projects by established filmmakers, documentaries by artists from other mediums such as photography or art and ambitious development projects. Main fund is worth over £500,000 per annum to fund one-off documentary films. Also administers a competition for four emerging filmmakers to make totally unique three minute films for Channel 4, Studio Artois and the BRITDOC festival.

Membership/Registration Policy
Easiest way to make contact is to sign up and explain how you want to work with the organization. Potential filmmakers can then be emailed when the Foundation is accepting submissions, with details of how to apply.

EUROSCRIPT

PO Box 3117 Gloucester GL4 OWW
T   0780 336 9414
E   enquiries@euroscript.co.uk
W   www.euroscript.co.uk

Contacts
Anne Woods *Director*

Founded in 1996 as part of the EU Media programme, the organization has been an independent development company since 2000. Aims to develop high quality screenplays with writers and producers from around the world. Offers weekend and residential workshops, individual consultancy and an annual screenplay competition.

Membership/Registration Policy
No membership required, courses and services available at a variety of prices.

FILM AGENCY FOR WALES

Suite 7 33-35 West Bute Street Cardiff CF10 5LH
T   029 2046 7480
F   029 2046 7481
E   enquiries@filmagencywales.com
W   www.filmagencywales.com

The national development agency for the film industry in Wales, established in July 2006. Aims to increase the range and number of films being produced by new, emerging and established Welsh talent. A particular interest in supporting Welsh writers, writer-directors, directors and producers. Funding available.

FILM EDUCATION

21-22 Poland Street London W1F 8QQ
T   020 7851 9450
F   020 7439 3218
W www.filmeducation.org

Founded in 1985, a registered charity funded by the UK film industry and the BFI. Aims to meet the increasing demand by teachers for current educational material on film and film making. Organizes training courses, conferences, workshops, seminars and events including National Schools Film Week.

FILM LONDON

Suite 6 10 The Tea Building 56 Shoreditch High Street London E1 6JJ
T   020 7613 7676
F   020 7613 7677
E   info@filmlondon.org.uk
W www.filmlondon.org.uk

Promotes and develops London as an international filmmaking capital. Includes all film, television, commercials and new interactive media based in London. The organization has a long history of supporting film productions, from experimental work to narrative fiction, animation and documentaries. Funding awards include the Pulse Digital Shorts scheme, London Production Fund, Microwave Micro-Budget Feature Film Fund, Borough Production Funds and London Artists' Film and Video Awards.

FIRST LIGHT MOVIES

Unit 6 Third Floor The Bond 180-182 Fazeley Street Birmingham B5 5SE
T   0121 753 4866
E   clare@firstlightmovies.com
W www.firstlightmovies.com

Contacts
Pip Eldridge CEO

Launched in 2001, First Light provides funding and expertise for 5- to 18-year-olds from all backgrounds to make short digital films with professional filmmakers. Distributes National Lottery money through UK Film Council funding. Enabled more than 10,000 young people to make more than 750 films.

Membership/Registration Policy
Funding is given through an application process 3 times a year. There are 3 funding awards available worth a total of £25,000.

ISLE OF MAN FILM

Hamilton House Peel Road Douglas Isle of Man IM1 5EP
T   01624 687173
F   01624 687171
E   iomfilm@dti.gov.im
W www.isleofmanfilm.com

Contacts
Hilary Dugdale *Development Manager*

Founded in 1995, the organization (formerly known as The Isle of Man Film Commission) promotes the activities of the island's film industry and actively markets the Isle of Man as a film location. Helped produce and finance over 80 productions to date. The Isle of Man Media Development Fund offers to assist films with up to 25% of their budget as direct equity investment if the project is largely filmed on the Isle of Man and benefits local service providers.

Membership/Registration Policy
Full application details can be found on the organization's website.

NEW PRODUCERS ALLIANCE

NPA Film Centre 7.03 Tea Building 56 Shoreditch High Street London E1 6JJ
T   020 7613 0440
F   020 7729 1852
E   queries@npa.org.uk
W www.npa.org.uk

Founded in 1993, a national membership organization offering training and networking opportunities to filmmakers.

NEW WRITING NORTH

Culture Lab Grand Assembly Rooms Newcastle University King's Walk Newcastle-upon-Tyne NE1 7RU
T   0191 222 1332
F   0191 222 1372
W   www.newwritingnorth.com

The writing development agency for the north-east of England. Works with writers across genres to develop career opportunities, new commissions, projects, residencies, publications and live events.

NEW WRITING SOUTH

9 Jew Street Brighton BN1 1UT
T   01273 735353
E   chris@newwritingsouth.com
W   www.newwritingsouth.com

Contacts
Chris Taylor *Director*

Founded in 1998, aims to encourage and develop creative writing in southeast England and offer practical resources to writers. Builds partnerships between writers and those who may produce their work and encourages new writing opportunities.

Membership/Registration Policy
Membership is open to all creative writers in the region. Annual subscription fee of £35 (concessions £20).

NORTHERN IRELAND SCREEN

Alfred House 21 Alfred Street Belfast BT2 8ED
T   028 9023 2444
F   028 9023 9918
E   info@niftc.co.uk
W   www.northernirelandscreen.co.uk

Incorporated in 1997 as the Northern Ireland Film and Television Commission. Involved in many aspects of promotion and development of screen-based industries. Allocates various funds for the development and production of the moving image, including feature film, shorts, animation, documentaries, television drama series and new media.

NORTHERN SCREENWRITERS

E   info@northernscreenwriters.co.uk
W   www.northernscreenwriters.co.uk

A non-profit organization based in Manchester. Membership of film-makers and scriptwriters based in the North West. Core activities are a script development programme, script workshops and groups and a searchable script database.

PACT (PRODUCERS ALLIANCE FOR CINEMA AND TELEVISION)

Procter House 1 Procter Street Holborn London WC1V 6DW
T   020 7067 4367
F   020 7067 4377
W   www.pact.co.uk

Trade association representing the commercial interests of independent feature film, television, animation and interactive media companies. Also has an office in Glasgow.

PLAYER–PLAYWRIGHTS

The Secretary 9 Hillfield Park London N10 3QT
E   P-P@dial.pipex.com
W   dspace.dial.pipex.com/town/plaza/gen87/main.html

Established in 1948 as a writers' co-operative. Meets upstairs at the Horse and Groom in Great Portland Street, W1. Membership of 100–150, mostly writers or aspiring writers but also actors (professional and amateur) who perform members' works. Current presidents are Laurence Marks and Maurice Gran.

REGIONAL SCREEN AGENCIES

Nine self-governing regional development agencies to support and develop the media sectors throughout England and to promote public access to film culture. They are:
EM Media – East Midlands (35-37 St Mary's Gate, Nottingham, NG1 1PU. T: 0115 934 9090. F: 0115 950 0988. Web: www.em-media.org.uk. Email: info@em-media.org.uk)
Film London (Suite 6.10, The Tea Building, 56 Shoreditch High Street, London, E1 6JJ. T: 020 7613 7676. F: 020 7613 7677.

Web: www.filmlondon.org.uk.
Email: info@filmlondon.org.uk)
North West Vision (Manchester Film Office,
Ground Floor, BBC New Broadcasting House,
Oxford Road, Manchester, M60 1SJ. T: 0870
609 4481. Web: www.northwestvision.co.uk)
Northern Film and Media (Central Square,
Forth Street, Newcastle-upon-Tyne, NE1 3PJ.
T: 0191 269 9200. F: 0191 269 9213.
Web: www.northernmedia.org.
Email: info@northernmedia.org)
Screen East (2 Millennium Plain, Norwich,
NR2 1TF. T: 01603 776 920. F: 01603
767191. Web: www.screeneast.co.uk.
Email: info@screeneast.co.uk)
Screen South (The Wedge, 75–81 Tontine
Street, Folkestone, Kent, CT20 1JR. T: 01303
259777. F: 01303 259786. Web:
www.screensouth.org. Email:
info@screensouth.org)
Screen West Midlands (9 Regent Place,
Birmingham, B1 3NJ. T: 0121 265 7120. F:
0121 265 7180. Web: www.screenwm.co.uk.
Email: info@screenwm.co.uk)
Screen Yorkshire (Studio 22, 46 The Calls,
Leeds, LS2 7EY. T: 0113 294 4410. F: 0113
294 4989. Web: www.screenyorkshire.co.uk.
Email: info@screenyorkshire.co.uk)
South West Screen (St Bartholomews Court,
Lewins Mead, Bristol, BS1 5BT. T: 0117 952
9977. F: 0117 952 9988. Web:
www.swscreen.co.uk. Email:
info@swscreen.co.uk)

ROCLIFFE FORUM

Rocliffe PO Box 37344 London N1 8YB
E   scripts@rocliffe.com
W   www.rocliffe.com

A production company that runs New Film
Forums and monthly New Writing Forums.
Established by Farah Abushwesha in 2000 and
run by Pippa Mitchell, Kerry Appleyard and
Abushwesha. Now has over 6,000 members.
The Writing Forum is a monthly platform for
new writing and a networking event. Three 7–8
minute script extracts (any genre) are cast
in-house and rehearsed by professional actors
and directors on the evening. A narrator sets
the piece in context and the extracts are then
performed to an audience of producers,
development executives, directors, actors and
literary agents. The writer then receives
feedback and answers questions from the
audience. Attendance is by reservation only.

ROYAL TELEVISION SOCIETY

5th Floor Kildare House 3 Dorset Rise London
EC4Y 8EN
T   020 7822 2810
F   020 7822 2811
E   info@rts.org.uk
W   www.rts.org.uk

Founded in 1927. A leading forum for
discussion and debate on all aspects of the
television community, providing opportunities
for making contact with people at all levels
across the industry. Hosts a high-profile annual
industry awards ceremony, as well as talks,
lectures and conferences. Society archive (going
back to its foundation) open to members and
academic researchers by appointment.

SCOTTISH SCREEN

249 West George Street Glasgow G2 4QE
T   0845 300 7300
E   info@scottishscreen.com
W   www.scottishscreen.com

Formed in 1997, the national screen agency for
Scotland with responsibility for developing all
aspects of screen culture and industry across
the country. Acts as a government advisor as
well as an advocate for the industry and a
development agency.

THE SCRIPT FACTORY

Welbeck House 66/67 Wells Street London
W1T 3PY
T   020 7323 1414
F   020 7323 9464
E   general@scriptfactory.co.uk
W   www.scriptfactory.co.uk

Founded in 1996 and now one of Europe's
leading development organizations for
screenwriters. Aims to identify and develop
new talent, to support the people who work
with screenwriters and to present live
screenwriting events. Has an in-house staff of
ten plus a large pool of freelancers to deliver an

annual training programme catering for in excess of 1,000 people per year. The board includes Daniel Battsek (president of Miramax Films), Andrew Cripps (president of United International Pictures), Mike Figgis, Anthony Minghella and Meera Syal. Also offers a script registration service.

THE SCRIPT VAULT

w www.thescriptvault.com

Offers a script registration and deposit service that safeguards copyright by registering the author of a piece of work and also establishing the date it was written. Costs £10 per script for ten years.

SKILLSET

Prospect House 80-110 New Oxford Street London WC1A 1HB
T 020 7520 5757
E info@skillset.org
w www.skillset.org

The sector skills council for the audio visual industries (broadcast, film, video, interactive media and photo imaging). Jointly funded by industry and government. Aims to ensure that the UK's audio-visual industries have people with the right skills, in the right place, at the right time. Conducts consultation work with industry, publishes research and strategic documents, runs funding schemes and project work, and provides information. Also provides careers advice for aspiring new entrants and established industry professionals.

THE SOCIETY OF AUTHORS

84 Drayton Gardens London SW10 9SB
T 020 7373 6642
F 020 7373 5768
E info@societyofauthors.org
w www.societyofauthors.org

Contacts
Mark Le Fanu *General Secretary*

An independent trade union with more than 8,000 members. As well as campaigning for the profession, the society advises members on negotiations with publishers, agents and other organizations, and offers guidance on business aspects of their writing. Also assists with complaints and legal disputes. Among the society's publications are *The Author*, published quarterly, and the *Quick Guide* series on various aspects of writing (free to members). Groups within the organization for different genres and types of writing.

Membership/Registration Policy
Membership is open to all published authors. Annual subscription costs £85, with some concessions available.

SOUTHWEST SCRIPTWRITERS

15 Quarry Steps Clifton Bristol BS8 2UD
T 0117 909 5522
E info@southwest-scriptwriters.co.uk
w www.southwest-scriptwriters.co.uk

Contacts
John Colborn *Secretary*

Organization founded in 1994 for keen writers of stage, screen and radio. Members must be over 18. Workshop meetings take place weekly at Bristol Old Vic theatre. Discussion events with established professionals, rehearsed readings and occasional productions of new work also take place. Meetings cost £1 plus a £6 annual subscription fee.

TALENT CIRCLE

w www.talentcircle.co.uk

Online network founded in 2003. Caters for the independent film industry including screenwriters, filmmakers or production staff. Provides access to jobs, industry news and resources online. Other activites include seminars, screenings and networking events. Free registration gives full access to the site.

UK FILM COUNCIL

10 Little Portland Street London W1W 7JG
T 020 7861 7861
F 020 7861 7862
E info@ukfilmcouncil.org.uk
w www.ukfilmcouncil.org.uk

The government-backed strategic agency for film in the UK, aiming to promote the UK industry and increase enjoyment and understanding of it. Runs a development fund with £12 million over three years to support the development of high quality and commercially-viable screenplays. There is also a premiere fund with £24 million over three years to facilitate the production of more mainstream films. The new cinema fund has £15 million over three years to back innovative filmmakers, especially new talent, and to explore new production technologies. Its short film schemes have produced over 450 films.

UK MEDIA DESK

c/o UK Film Council 10 Little Portland Street London W1W 7JG
T   020 7861 7511
F   020 7861 7950
E   england@mediadesk.co.uk
W www.mediadesk.co.uk

Contacts
Agnieszka Moody *Director of UK MEDIA Desk*

Exists to promote and administer the EU's MEDIA Programme in the UK. Originally formed in 1991. The MEDIA 2007 initiative commenced on 1 January 2007 and runs until 31 December 2013. Budget totals €755 million to support professional training (screenwriting, business and new tecnologies), project development and the international circulation of European productions. Funding is available for film and television productions, new media companies, sales agents, distributors, festival and market organisers, training providers and exhibitors.

Membership/Registration Policy
Applications are sent to the Executive Agency in Brussels. See website for more information.

WOMEN IN FILM AND TELEVISION UK (WFTV)

6 Langley Street London WC2H 9JA
T   020 7240 4875
E   info@wftv.org.uk
W www.wftv.org.uk

Founded in 1990. A membership association open to women with at least one year's professional experience in the television, film and/or digital media industries. Currently over 800 members. Seeks to protect and enhance the status, interests and diversity of women working across the media.

WRITERNET

Cabin V Clarendon Buildings 25 Horsell Road London N5 1XL
T   020 7609 7474
E   info@writernet.org.uk
W www.writernet.org.uk

Contacts
Jonathan Meth *Director*

Founded in 1985, the organization works with new writing in all performance contexts. Formerly known as the New Playwrights Trust. Provides industry networking opportunities, advice, guidance and career development training.

WRITERS COPYRIGHT ASSOCIATION

Ealing Film Studios Ealing London
E   mail@wcauk.com
W www.wcauk.com

Contacts
Jon Newman *Managing Director*

Founded in 2000, offering copyright protection of literary material and intellectual property.

Membership/Registration Policy
Registration fees: £25 for 5 years (UK), £99 for 10 years (worldwide).

WRITERS' GUILD OF GREAT BRITAIN

15-17 Britannia Street London WC1X 9JN
T   020 7833 0777
F   020 7833 4777
E   admin@writersguild.org.uk
W www.writersguild.org.uk

Contacts
Bernie Corbett *General Secretary*

The TUC-affiliated union for professional writers. Established in 1958, the Guild represents writers working in TV, film, radio, theatre, books, poetry and videogames. Negotiates minimum fees, royalties and other terms with all major UK production groups. The organization offers its members: legal advice and contract-vetting; a pension scheme for screen and radio writers; weekly email bulletin and quarterly *UK Writer* magazine; and regular events.

Membership/Registration Policy
Full membership is available to anyone who has received payment for a piece of written work under a contract with terms not less than those negotiated by the Guild. Writers who do not qualify can join as Candidate Members and those on accredited writing courses or theatre attachments can become Student Members.

CANADA

ACADEMY OF CANADIAN CINEMA AND TELEVISION

172 King Street East Toronto Ontario
M5A 1J3
T   416 366 2227
F   416 366 8454
E   info@academy.ca
W www.academy.ca

Contacts
Jeanette Slinger *Managing Director*

Non-profit body to promote Canadian cinema and television mostly through the Genie Awards, Gemini Awards and Les Prix Gemeaux. Other activities include the Academy Speaker Series, Kodak Soirees, Screening Series and industry-partnered events. Created in 1979. Now over 4,000 members. Four types of membership with varying eligibility requirements: voting membership (annual fee CA$150), friend of the Academy (CA$100), alumni membership (CA$75), student membership (CA$25).

ALLIANCE FOR CHILDREN AND TELEVISION (ACT)

1400 René-Lévesque Boulevard East Office 713
Montreal Quebec H2L 2M2
E   info@act-aet.tv
W www.act-aet.tv

Seeks to enrich the screen-based media children experience by providing ongoing professional training, rewarding high-quality programmes and ensuring that children and youth have regular access to high-quality programming.

CANADIAN FILM AND TELEVISION PRODUCTION ASSOCIATION (CFTPA)

151 Slater Street Suite 902 Ottawa Ontario
K1P 5H3
T   613 233 1444
F   613 233 0073
E   ottawa@cftpa.ca
W www.cftpa.ca

Aims to promote and stimulate the Canadian production industry. A non-profit trade association representing almost 400 film, television and interactive media companies across the country. Runs a national mentorship programme to train young people in the demands of the industry. Offices in Ottawa, Toronto and Vancouver.

CANADIAN FILM INSTITUTE

2 Daly Avenue Suite 120 Ottawa Ontario
K1N 6E2
T   613 232 6727
F   613 232 6315
E   cfi-icf@magma.ca
W www.cfi-icf.ca

Incorporated in 1935 as a federally-chartered, non-governmental, non-profit cultural organization. Merged with the Conservatory of Cinematographic Art (Montreal) to form Cinematheque Canada in 1988 but retains its autonomous programming, budgetary, and administrative activities in Ottawa. Aims to encourage and promote the production, diffusion, study, appreciation, and use of moving images for cultural and educational purposes in Canada and abroad. Runs an ongoing public film programme, distributes a small collection of films, and publishes books and monographs on Canadian cinema.

CANADIAN SCREENWRITER COLLECTION SOCIETY (CSCS)

366 Adelaide Street West Suite 401   Toronto Ontario M5V 1R9
T   416 979 7907
F   416 979 9273
E   info@wgc.ca
W   www.writersguildofcanada.com/cscs/

Created by the Writers Guild of Canada to claim, collect, administer and distribute secondary authors' levies that film and television writers are entitled to under the national copyright legislation of several European countries and other jurisdictions.

Membership/Registration Policy
Membership open to writers with a writing credit on a produced Canadian feature film or television programme.

CANADIAN WOMEN IN COMMUNICATIONS

67 Yonge Street Suite 804   Toronto   Ontario M5E 1J8
T   416 363 1880
F   416 363 1882
E   cwcafc@cwc-afc.com
W   www.cwc-afc.com

Founded in 1991, a national, bilingual organization dedicated to the advancement of women in the communications sector through strategic networking and targeted professional development.

Membership/Registration Policy
Membership open to women and men currently working in the communications industry, a student in the field or any person who supports CWC's mandate.

DOCUMENTARY ORGANIZATION OF CANADA

215 Spadina Avenue Suite 126   Toronto Ontario M5T 2C7
T   416 599 3844 x1
F   416 979 3936
E   execdir@docorg.ca
W   www.docorg.ca

Contacts
Samantha Hodder *Executive Director*

A national non-profit professional and advocacy organization dedicated to supporting the art of independent documentary filmmaking and filmmakers in Canada. Represents over 500 directors, producers, and craftspeople in six regional chapters (Atlantic, Quebec, Toronto, British Columbia, Newfoundland and Ottawa-Gatineau).

NATIONAL FILM BOARD OF CANADA

PO Box 6100 Station Centre-ville   Montreal Quebec H3C 3H5
T   1 800 267 7710
F   514 283 7564
W   www.nfb.ca

A federal cultural agency created in 1939. Its mandate is to produce and distribute distinctive, culturally diverse, challenging and relevant audiovisual works that 'provide Canada and the world with a unique Canadian perspective'. There is a French Program to produce films of importance to Francophones in Quebec and the rest of Canada and an English Program that works with documentary directors in every region of Canada.

SOCIÉTÉ DES AUTEURS DE RADIO, TÉLÉVISION ET CINÉMA

1229 rue Panet   Montréal   Québec   H2L 2Y6
T   514 526 9196
E   information@sartec.qc.ca
W   www.sartec.qc.ca

Founded in 1949 to represent writers of radio, television and cinema works in the French language. Around 800 members.

WOMEN IN FILM & VIDEO VANCOUVER

1815 Pine Street Unit #102   Vancouver   British Columbia V6J 3C8
T   604 685 1152
F   604 685 1124
E   info@womeninfilm.ca
W   www.womeninfilm.ca

A non-profit society of professional women founded to support, advance, promote and celebrate the professional development and achievements of women involved in British Columbia's film, video and television industry.

224   SOCIETIES AND ORGANIZATIONS

WOMEN IN FILM AND TELEVISION TORONTO

110 Eglinton Avenue East Suite 601 Toronto
Ontario M4P 2Y1
T   416 322 3430 ext. 22
F   416 322 3703
E   wift@wift.com
W   www.wift.com

Dedicated to the advancement of women
and under-represented groups in screen-based
media. Offers year-round training and
business skills development through its
Centre for Media Professionals, networking
events and industry awards. Represents
over 3,000 women and men in Canadian
screen-based media. Offers much useful
advice on filmmaking on the affiliated
canadianfilmmaker.com

WRITERS GUILD OF CANADA

366 Adelaide Street West Suite 401 Toronto
Ontario M5V 1R9
T   419 979 7907
F   416 979 9273
E   info@wgc.ca
W   www.wgc.ca

Contacts
Maureen Parker *Executive Director*

Originally part of the Association of
Canadian Television and Radio Artists
(ACTRA). Independent as of 1995.
Represents 1,800 professional screenwriters
across Canada. Activities include:
negotiating, administering and enforcing
collective agreements with producers and
broadcasters; working with government
agencies to improve support; and increasing
the profile of screenwriters. Produces
Canadian Screenwriter Awards and the
Canadian Screenwriter Magazine. Also
offers script registration services.

Membership/Registration Policy
Qualification is one writing contract in
WGC jurisdiction. Occasionally offers
membership incentives. Total
membership fees CA$500 (CA$350
initiation fee and CA$150 annual
basic dues).

IRELAND

ARTS COUNCIL IRELAND

70 Merrion Square Dublin 2
T   01 618 0200
F   01 676 1302
E   www.artscouncil.ie

Established in 1951, the state's development
agency for the arts aims to promote the
appreciation and practice of the arts. Provides
range of awards and bursaries to individuals
and organizations, worth €72.3m. in 2006.

CORK FILM CENTRE

20-21 Anglesea Street Cork
T   021 431 6033
F   021 431 6125
E   info@corkfilmcentre.com
W   www.corkfilmcentre.com

Resource-based organization providing for
people working in the medium of the moving
image.

FÁS SCREEN TRAINING IRELAND

Adelaide Chambers Peter Street Dublin
T   01 483 0840
F   01 483 0842
E   film@fas.ie
W   www.screentrainingireland.ie

Aims to provide continuing training for
professionals in film, television, animation and
digital media. Runs a bursary award scheme.

FILM BASE

Curved Street Building Temple Bar Dublin 2
T   01 679 6716
F   01 679 6717
E   info@filmbase.ie
W   www.filmbase.ie

Founded in 1986 as a support organization
for Ireland's independent film and video
sector. Runs training and development
programmes, hires equipment and editing
suites, provides an information service and
lobbies for the low budget film sector.
Publishes *Film Ireland* magazine and the
Ireland on Screen directory and administers
a short film award scheme.

GALWAY FILM CENTRE

Cluain Mhuire Monivea Road Galway
T 091 770748
F 091 770746
E info@galwayfilmcentre.ie
W www.galwayfilmcentre.ie

Offers range of services and facilities to
independent filmmakers, artists and community
groups.

IRISH FILM AND TELEVISION ACADEMY

First Floor Palmerstown Centre Kennelsfort
Road Palmerstown Dublin 20
T 01 620 0811
F 01 620 0810
E info@ifta.ie
W www.ifta.ie

A not-for-profit all-Ireland organization to
promote, encourage and reward creative
excellence in film and television. Does this
through screenings, educational events, awards,
archiving and the production of a quarterly
magazine.

IRISH FILM BOARD/BORD SCANNÁN NA HÉIREANN

Queensgate 23 Dock Road Galway
T 091 561 398
F 091 561 405
E info@filmboard.ie
W www.irishfilmboard.ie

Contacts
Louise Ryan *Marketing and Communications Executive*

Ireland's national film agency, founded in
1993. Funds the development and production
of Irish films aimed at domestic and
international audiences, and promotes
Ireland as a location for international
production.

IRISH FILM INSTITUTE

Irish Film Centre 6 Eustace Street Temple Bar
Dublin 2
T 01 679 5744
E info@irishfilm.ie
W www.irishfilm.ie

Founded as the National Film Institute of
Ireland in 1945 with mission to promote and
preserve film culture in Ireland. Maintains the
Irish Film Archive, the Irish Film Centre and a
travelling cinema, Cinemobile.

IRISH PLAYWRIGHTS AND SCREENWRITERS GUILD

Art House Curved Street Temple Bar Dublin 2
T 01 670 9970
E info@script.ie
W www.script.ie

Contacts
David Kavanagh *Chief Executive*

Formerly the Society of Irish Playwrights,
which was founded in 1969, the Irish
Playwrights' and Screenwriters' Guild is the
representative body in Ireland for writers for
the stage, screen, radio and new media.

Membership/Registration Policy
Full membership of the Guild is available to
any writer resident in Ireland who has
contracted to write for payment in Ireland for
the stage or screen (including radio and the
new media). They also have an associate
membership open to aspiring writers.

IRISH WRITERS CENTRE

19 Parnell Square Dublin 1
T 01 872 1302
F 01 872 6282
E info@writerscentre.ie
W www.writerscentre.ie

Founded in 1991 to foster writing and an
audience for literature in Ireland. Runs a
year-round programme of readings, workshops,
lectures and seminars as well as a range of
support and information services. Grant-aided
by the Arts Councils of Ireland.

SCREEN PRODUCERS IRELAND

77 Merrion Square Dublin 2
T 01 662 1114
F 01 661 9949
E info@screenproducersireland.com
W www.screenproducersireland.com

Representative body for independent film,
television and animation producers in Ireland.

AUSTRALIA

AUSTRALIAN FILM COMMISSION

Level 4 150 William Street Woolloomooloo
NSW 2011
T   02 9321 6444
F   02 9357 3737
W www.afc.gov.au

The commission ensures the creation,
preservation and availability of Australian
audiovisual content. Through the
National Film and Sound Archive, the
AFC collects, documents, preserves and
provides access to Australia's screen and
sound heritage. Also has offices in Melbourne,
Brisbane and Canberra.

AUSTRALIAN FILM INSTITUTE

236 Dorcas Street South Melbourne VIC 3205
T   03 9696 1844
F   03 9696 7972
W www.afi.org.au

Contacts
Justine Beltrame *Awards Manager*

Established in 1958, not-for-profit organization
for industry professionals and general members.
Activities include running annual AFI awards
and film festival.

Membership/Registration Policy
Professional membership or general
membership, 1 year costs AUS$55, 2 years
AUS$95.

AUSTRALIAN SCRIPT CENTRE

77 Salamanca Place Hobart Tasmania
T   03 6223 4675
E   info@ozscript.org
W www.ozscript.org

Offers a script registration service. Prices and
submission guidelines available in the website.

THE AUSTRALIAN WRITERS' GUILD

8/50 Reservoir Street Surry Hills NSW 2010
T   02 9281 1554
F   02 9281 4321
E   admin@awg.com.au
W www.awg.com.au

Contacts
Joel Naoum *Admin and Project Officer*

Professional body representing film, theatre,
television, radio and new media writers
throughout Australia. Founded in 1962, the
organization provides script assessment and
registration services, along with free industrial
and legal advice for members. Aims to help
authors protect their creative rights and
improve professional standards.

Membership/Registration Policy
Membership is open to writers or 'any person
in sympathy with the AWG's aims and
objectives'.

FILM AUSTRALIA

101 Eton Road Lindfield NSW 2070
T   02 9413 8777
F   02 9416 5672
W www.filmaust.com.au

Founded in 1946, a government-owned
company producing television documentaries
and educational programmes. Provides support
to the Australian documentary sector through a
range of services and facilities.

FILM FINANCE CORPORATION

Level 12 130 Elizabeth Street Sydney
NSW 2000
T   02 9268 2555
F   02 9264 8551
E   ffc@ffc.gov.au
W www.ffc.gov.au

Wholly-owned government company
funding only projects with high levels
of creative and technical contribution
by Australians, or projects certified
under Australia's Official Co-Production
Programme. Funds expensive programme
formats such as feature films,
mini-series, telemovies and documentaries,
and does not normally fund cheaper
formats such as current affairs, serial
drama and 'infotainment'. Since its
establishment, it has invested in 1,056
projects including *Strictly Ballroom*,
*The Adventures of Priscilla: Queen of
the Desert* and *Muriel's Wedding*.

NEW ZEALAND

FILM NEW ZEALAND

23 Frederick Street PO Box 24142
Wellington 6142
T   04 385 0766
F   04 384 5840
E   info@filmnz.org.nz
W   www.filmnz.com

Contacts
Judith McCann *Chief Executive Officer*

Founded in 1994 by the screen production
industry. Constituted as a charitable trust with
governance by a board of trustees. Provides
information, introductions and support to
national and international filmmakers interested
in using New Zealand as a filming location.

THE NEW ZEALAND FILM ARCHIVE

84 Taranaki Street Wellington 6011
T   04 384 7647
F   04 382 9595
E   info@nzfa.org.nz
W   www.filmarchive.org.nz

Contacts
Virginia Callanan *Registrar*

Independent charitable trust established in
1981. Strives to collect, protect and project
New Zealand's moving image history. Regular
events include weekly screenings, community
programmes, education initiatives and a
research library.

NEW ZEALAND FILM COMMISSION

Level 2 The Film Centre 119 Jervois Quay PO
Box 11 546 Wellington
T   04 382 7680
F   04 384 9719
E   info@nzfilm.co.nz
W   www.nzfilm.co.nz

Established in 1978 by act of parliament. Has
the statutory responsibility 'to encourage and
participate and assist in the making, promotion,
distribution and exhibition of films' made in
New Zealand by New Zealanders on New
Zealand subjects. Provides loans and equity
financing to film-makers to assist in the

development and production of feature films
and short films. Also active in the sales and
marketing of New Zealand films, and with
training and professional development.

NEW ZEALAND WRITERS GUILD

PO Box 47 886 Ponsonby Auckland 1144
T   09 360 1408
F   09 360 1409
E   info@nzwg.org.nz
W   www.nzwritersguild.org.nz

A professional association of script writers
and a registered trade union, founded
in 1975. Represents the interests of
writers in the fields of film, television,
theatre, radio, comedy and new media.
Membership encompasses most of the
professional script writers working in
New Zealand. Activities include: publishing
and providing information and advice;
lobbying government; representing
writers to funding bodies and other
industry organizations; providing template
contracts and agreements; providing
opportunities for skill development;
registering intellectual property; arbitrating
on script credits.

NGA AHO WHAKAARI MĀORI IN FILM, VIDEO AND TELEVISION INCORPORATION

PO Box 68 626 Nexton Auckland 1145
T   09 368 4430
F   09 368 4431
E   ngaahowhakaari@xtra.co.nz
W   www.ngaahowhakaari.com

Contacts
Kelvin McDonald *Executive Officer*

National representative body for Māori
working in film, video and television in New
Zealand. Established in 1996. Focuses on the
advancement of Māori moving images, culture
and language, and supports the development of
Māori film and television production.

SCREEN DIRECTORS GUILD OF NEW ZEALAND

PO Box 47-294 Ponsonby Auckland 1011
T   09 360 2102
F   09 360 2107

E   office@sdgnz.co.nz
W   www.sdgnz.co.nz

Contacts
Anna Cahill *Executive Director*

Has its genesis in 1995 when 18 directors
met for an annual conference in Wellington
and discussed the need for a representative
organization. Promotes the New Zealand
film and television industries as well as
lobbying for better working conditions
for members. Also administers a royalty
payment scheme.

Membership/Registration Policy
Full membership open to any screen
director, editor or independent producer
with a minimum of twenty minutes
of credited screen time. Also offers
secondary, associate, student and
temporary memberships.

SCREEN PRODUCTION AND DEVELOPMENT ASSOCIATION OF NEW ZEALAND (SPADA)

Level 2 170 Cuba Street PO Box 9567
Te Aro Wellington
T   04 939 6934
F   04 939 6935
E   info@spada.co.nz
W   www.spada.co.nz

Membership-based organization, established in
the 1980s and now with over 350 members.
Represents the collective interests of
independent producers and production
companies on all issues that affect the business
and creative aspects of independent screen
production in New Zealand. Activities include
professional development, lobbying, an
e-newsletter and hosting of industry
networking events.

SCRIPT TO SCREEN

PO Box 147 263 Ponsonby Auckland
T   09 360 5400
F   09 360 1409
W   www.script-to-screen.co.nz

An independent, industry-wide initiative,
established to develop the culture of
screenwriting in New Zealand. Formerly called
The New Zealand Writers Foundation, a joint
initiative of the New Zealand Writers Guild
and the NZ Film Commission, conceived in
2001. Works in partnership with other sectors
of the film and television industries. Each
month the Writer's Room hosts leading
screenwriters to discuss their craft. Also runs a
Script Read-Through Workshop series, where
scripts are performed by professional actors,
and writing workshops. Administers an
international scholarship in conjunction with
the British Council New Zealand, under the
terms of which a New Zealand screenwriter
spends several months developing a script with
a major production company.

WOMEN IN FILM & TELEVISION

PO Box 6652 Wellington
T   04 389 3862
E   info@wiftwellington.org.nz
W   www.wgtn.wift.org.nz

Contacts
Zelda Edwards

An organization offering support to women in
the film and television industries via an
informal network. Part of WIFT International.
Men are welcome to belong as Friends of
WIFT. Also runs a chapter in Auckland
(PO Box 90-415, Auckland Mail Center;
T 09 378 7271; W www.wiftauckland.org.nz;
E office@wiftauckland.org.nz)

PAGE TO SCREEN

Barry Turner on the journey from novel to screenplay

From novelist to screenwriter used to be a natural progression. Maybe progression is the wrong word. There was and is more money to be made from putting words into actors' mouths but the frustration of working with the oddballs of the screen trade can be hard for writers who are used to doing their own thing. Too many of them have wound up with a bottle as their best friend. Whether this has acted as a dreadful warning or whether producers have got wise to the fact that books and movies are two different products needing different skills, it is true that fewer novelists now set their rose-tinted sights on Hollywood. They still want the money but are happiest when their books are optioned by a major studio. They can then get back to doing what they do best while leaving others to translate their work into moving images.

But, of course, nothing is ever that simple. For a start, the seven-figure book to movie offers that attract press headlines are misleading. The typical option, giving exclusive rights for one or two years, is hedged about with conditions which let the production company off the hook if it proves too hard or too expensive to attract a marketable director and actors. Less than one in ten options is 'exercised'. For the rest, the author banks an up-front payment, on average ten to twenty thousand dollars, and learns to live with disappointment.

On a more optimistic note, a third of the movies produced in Hollywood are based on books and plays. It is easy to see why. A successful novel will have a fan base attached, a promise, if not a surefire guarantee, that it will translate into profitable cinema. In effect the author provides a cheap means of testing the market. The money paid for the film rights to a novel, even if sizeable in publishing terms, is as nothing compared to the cost of creating a screenplay from scratch.

For the author, the trick is not to lose this initial advantage. Unless you happen to be a trained lawyer and a financial whiz combined, the first step is to get on the right side of an agent who is immersed in the business. Only a specialist knows who, if anyone, to take seriously from a crowd of chancers. The film industry attracts more con artists than an estate agents' convention. Moreover, the complexity of making a deal barely needs elaborating when film contracts run to fifty pages or more.

Producers come in all guises. The independent with a shared desk may have the backup of a major studio but then again he may simply be gambling on hitting the jackpot. An offer may come from an actor chasing a meaty role or from a scriptwriter short on ideas of his own. As a general rule, an eagerness to produce is in inverse proportion to the capacity to deliver.

Writing in a recent edition of *The Author*, Giles Foden, whose novel *The Last King of Scotland* became a much lauded movie, warned of the contentious issues that can arise when filming is about to start. The buyout fee or purchase price will almost certainly tantalize with the offer of a two or three per cent share of the profits. The production sums involved make this sound like a lottery win. But as Giles Foden points out, 'Hollywood accountants like spinning profits into deficits by constantly introducing costs after the fact'. The two to three per cent may well end up worthless.

The best advice is to try for a purchase price tied to a percentage of the budget. Producers will usually insist that there is a cap on the amount paid but authors, or their agents, can be equally tough on setting a minimum.

Other Foden tips include an insistence on the film having the title of the book and on the right to an image from the movie for the cover of a new edition. Don't dispose carelessly of associated rights that might turn out to be lucrative – the stage adaptation, for example. And if you expect or hope for anything like visits to the set, tickets and first-class travel to premieres across the Atlantic, make sure they are in the contract.

Even the success stories have their downside. Authors who sell out to the film industry must know that they have surrendered all proprietorial claims. Any resemblance between an original book and the screen adaptation will be entirely coincidental and there is nothing the author can do about it. Tom Clancy, whose box-office hits include *The Hunt for Red October* and *Patriot Games* compares selling the film rights to pimping your daughter. A more optimistic view is taken by Nick Hornby. 'The way I see it, selling the film rights to a book is a no-lose situation for a writer. Someone gives you money for work you have already done; if the film is bad, you will attract a few more readers, and if it is good (or failing that, successful), chances are that your readership will increase.'

But suppose the ambitions of an author go further than simply selling a project on the best terms. Success brings huge rewards. In Hollywood, there is even a decent living to be made out of failure, the scripts that fail to make it on to screen. The downside is a work ethic that requires writers to submerge their identities. Big studios are liable to engage three or more writers on any single production. Often the rewrites are so extensive as to lose even a hint of the original work.

Faced with demands to amend and adapt, sensitive writers can be forgiven their occasional outbursts. There is the story of Dorothy Parker throwing a typewriter through her office window. A party of tourists on their round of the Paramount Studios looked up to see a distraught Miss Parker peering through the broken glass. 'Let us out,' she shrieked. 'We're as sane as you are!' That was in 1938 and though writers are no longer herded together and told to get on with it, nothing else has changed. During his days in Writers' Block, David Mamet commented that 'film is a collaborative business; bend over'.

Movie-writing takes time, which is the other big drawback to the screen trade. While an author might expect to spend a year on a novel, a screenwriter should not be too surprised if his words are still unspoken after a decade of toing and froing. He will be on to other work by then but the frustration of non-fulfilment can be hard.

Normally the film-going experience for most people is they want to go out, they want something entertaining, and your job, I think, is to make it an interesting good time, to make it a grown-up good time, to make it complicated to make things linger in their brain... but that doesn't mean giving them a terrible time.

Julian Fellowes at the 2006 Cheltenham Screenwriters' Festival

FESTIVALS

UNITED STATES OF AMERICA

AFI FESTIVAL

2021 N. Western Avenue Los Angeles
CA 90027-1657
T   323 856 7600
F   323 467 4578
W www.afi.com

Established in 1987, the festival features a rich
slate of films from emerging filmmakers. The
American Film Market (largest motion picture
trade event in the world) runs concurrently
with the festival. Held over 10 days in
November.

AFRICAN DIASPORA FILM FESTIVAL

T   212 864 1760
E   info@nyadff.org
W www.nyadff.org

Founded in 1993 to offer a platform for
conveying African Diaspora artistic styles and
craft in film. Held annually for about two
weeks during November/December. There is no
submission fee but, owing to volume, tapes and
DVDs will not be sent back.

AMERICAN BLACK FILM FESTIVAL

E   abff@thefilmlife.com
W www.abff.com

Established in 1997, the aim of this 5-day
festival is to strengthen the black filmmaking
community through resource sharing,
education, artistic collaboration and
development. Held annually.

Submissions Policy
There are four categories of film for
consideration at the Festival, each with its own
submission criteria (see website for further
information).

ANGELUS STUDENT FILM FESTIVAL

7201 Sunset Boulevard Los Angeles CA 90046
T   800 874 0999
F   323 874 1168

E   info@angelus.org
W www.angelus.org

Contacts
Monika Moreno *Director*

Founded in 1996 for student films up to 90
minutes. Screenings/awards ceremony held at
the Directors' Guild of America, Hollywood.
Also runs workshops and hosts a lunch for
finalists. Held annually (October in 2008). Past
honorary chairs include Gary Oldman, Sean
Astin, Jim Caveziel and Lynn Redgrave.

Submissions Policy
Submissions welcome via website. Free
admission to festival events.

ANTELOPE VALLEY INDEPENDENT FILM FESTIVAL

W www.aviff.com

Established in 1997 and has developed a
reputation as a filmmaker-friendly festival with
standing-room-only crowds and lively
post-screening discussions. While the festival
welcomes the work of first-time filmmakers, it
also consistently features highlights from a
variety of international festivals including
Cannes, Sundance, and the Academy of Motion
Picture Arts & Sciences Student Academy
Awards. Held annually.

Submissions Policy
Submission of material is subject to an
application fee.

ASIAN AMERICAN INTERNATIONAL FILM FESTIVAL

145 Ninth Street STE 350 San Francisco
CA 94103
T   415 863 0814
F   415 863 7428
W www.asianamericanmedia.org

Established in 1982, an important launching
point for Asian American independent
filmmakers as well as a vital source for new
Asian cinema. The festival is the largest

presenter of Asian American film in the world, screening over 130 films and attracting an audience of almost 30,000 people. Held annually in March.

Submissions Policy
Submission of material is subject to an application fee and films and videos must be made by or about Asian Americans and Asians of any nationality. All lengths and genres will be considered.

ASIAN CINEVISION

T   212 989 1422
F   212 727 3584
E   info@asiancinevision.org
W   www.asiancinevision.org

Established in 1978, the country's first festival dedicated to screening works by media artists of Asian descent. The festival has many categories that showcase the best of Asian and Asian American cinema, including features, shorts competition, screenplay competition, music video competition, works-in-progress and 'for youth by youth'. Held annually.

Submissions Policy
Only accepts material submitted by people of Asian descent.

ASPEN FILMFEST

Aspen Film 110 E. Hallam Street Suite 102 Aspen CO 81611
T   970 925 6882
F   970 925 1967
E   filmfest@aspenfilm.org
W   www.aspenfilm.org

Contacts
Laura Thielen *Executive Director*

Established in 1979, festival for full-length features and documentaries, with events including screenings and the annual 'Independent by Nature' award. Recent films featured included *Capote* and *Shut Up and Sing*. Held annually in September/October, typically lasting 5 days.

Submissions Policy
Does not welcome unsolicited applications.

ASPEN SHORTSFEST

Aspen Film 110 E. Hallam Street Aspen CO 81611
T   970 925 6882
F   970 925 1967
E   shortsfest@aspenfilm.org
W   www.aspenfilm.org

Contacts
Laura Thielen *Executive Director*

Events include competition screenings, free roundtable discussions, special presentations and an awards ceremony. Live action, documentary and animated shorts. Previous films entered include *The Danish Poet* and *Eramos Pocos*. Aspen Shortsfest is an Oscars qualifying event. Held annually, typically lasting 5 days in April.

Submissions Policy
Welcomes unsolicited applications. Website has details of entry guidelines and procedures.

ATLANTA FILM FESTIVAL

IMAGE Film & Video Center 535 Means Street NW Suite C Atlanta GA 30318
T   404 352 4225
F   404 352 0173
E   aff@imagefv.org
W   www.atlantafilmfestival.com

Established in 1976, an annual festival featuring narrative, documentary, animation, and student films. Over ten days, showing more than 150 films. The festival provides filmmakers with the opportunity to attend panels and workshops.

AUSTIN FILM FESTIVAL

PO Box 13006 Austin TX 78711
T   800 310 FEST
E   info@austinfilmfestival.com
W   www.austinfilmfestival.com

Contacts
Mary P. Hansell *Screenplay/Teleplay Competition Director*

Founded in 1994, festival and conference focusing on screenwriters' contribution to the film and television industries. Includes screenplay awards for television and film across genres such as drama, comedy and science-fiction, with prizes of between $2,500 and $5,000. Previous recipients of awards include Shane Black, Harold Ramis and Barry Levinson. Held annually in October.

Submissions Policy
Screenplay and teleplay awards are open only to writers who do not earn a living from television or film. Scripts must not have been optioned or sold.

AUSTIN GAY AND LESBIAN INTERNATIONAL FILM FESTIVAL

T 512 302 9889
F 512 302 1088
E info@agliff.org
W www.agliff.org

Established in 1987, the oldest and largest gay and lesbian film festival in the southwest. Showcases features and shorts, mainstream and avant-garde. Held annually for 9 days during the months of September and October.

Submissions Policy
Films and videos should be of interest to lesbians, gay men, bisexual, intersex and/or transgendered people, and is subject to a submission fee.

AVIGNON/NEW YORK FILM FESTIVAL

T 212 650 3083
W www.avignonfilmfest.com

Established in 1994, this 5-day festival is the American version of the Avignon Film Festival. The festival screens a selection of features and documentaries. Held annually.

Submissions Policy
Submission of material is subject to an administrative fee.

BIG BEAR LAKE INTERNATIONAL FILM FESTIVAL

PO Box 1981 Big Bear Lake CA 92315
T 909 866 3433
E bigbearfilmfest@aol.com
W www.bigbearfilmfestival.com

Contacts
Sandy Steers *Vice President/Screenwriting Director*

Established in 2000, activities include a screenwriting competition, as well as screenings, networking events, seminars and a film awards ceremony. The festival is a 3-day event held annually in September.

Submissions Policy
Unsolicited entries of films or screenplays are welcomed by email.

BRONX INDEPENDENT FILM FESTIVAL

The Lovinger Theatre at Lehman College The City University of New York 250 Bedford Park Boulevard West Bronx NY 10468
E film@bronxstage.com
W www.bronxstage.com

Founded in 2003 to celebrate the history of film in The Bronx by showcasing emerging filmmakers while promoting The Bronx as a cultural destination. The 2-day festival is held annually. Accepts narrative, documentary, animation and experimental films. Short Films should be 29 minutes or less and feature films should run for 30 minutes or more.

BROOKLYN INTERNATIONAL FILM FESTIVAL

BiFF 180 South 4th Street Suite 2 S Brooklyn NY 11211
T 718 486 8181
F 718 599 5039
E submit07@wbff.org
W www.wbff.org

Held annually since 2002, the successor to the Williamsburg Brooklyn Film Festival. For and by independent film makers.

CAROLINA FILM AND VIDEO FESTIVAL

T 336 334 4197
E cfvf@uncg.edu
W www.carolinafilmandvideofestival.org

Founded in 1978, this festival focuses on works of student and/or independent filmmakers. It is a competitive festival and offers awards in the following categories: documentary, narrative, and experimental or animated film.

Submissions Policy
Works of any length from students and independent filmmakers.

CHICAGO CITY LIMITS COMEDY FILM FESTIVAL

T   212 888 5233
E   film@chicagocitylimits.com
W   www.firstsundays.com

The festival takes place on the first Sunday of every month and features short comedy films.

Submissions Policy
Submission of material is subject to an administrative fee. Accepts films that are under 1 minute and up to 30 minutes.

CHICAGO INTERNATIONAL FILM FESTIVAL

T   312 683 0121
F   312 683 0122
E   info@chicagofilmfestival.com
W   www.chicagofilmfestival.org

Founded in 1964 by award-winning filmmaker and graphic designer Michael Kutza. The festival is a competitive event with categories for feature films, documentaries and short films (including animation and student productions). Held annually.

Submissions Policy
Submission of material is subject to an application fee, and entries that have been screened publicly in Chicago or aired on US television prior to the festival are not eligible for screening. Entries must be either in English or contain English subtitles and must be accompanied by a 25–30 word summary of the production's content.

CHICAGO UNDERGROUND FILM FESTIVAL

E   info@cuff.org
W   www.cuff.org

Running since 1994 and aims to showcase independent, experimental and documentary films from around the world that dissent radically in form, technique, or content from the indie mainstream. Held annually for one week.

Submissions Policy
Submission of material is subject to an administrative fee. Foreign language work must be dubbed or subtitled in English and a written description or synopsis must be enclosed with the entry form.

CINEQUEST SAN JOSE FILM FESTIVAL

T   408 995 5033
F   408 995 5713
E   info@cinequest.org
W   www.cinequest.org

Contacts
Mike Rabehl

Founded in 1991, showcasing independent films. Also hosts the Maverick film competition. Held annually for about 12 days.

Submissions Policy
Submission of material is subject to an administrative fee and films of all running lengths are accepted.

CLEVELAND INTERNATIONAL FILM FESTIVAL

2510 Market Avenue Cleveland
OH 44113-3434
T   216 623 3456
W   www.clevelandfilm.org

Founded in 1977, the festival screens films in a variety of categories including American Independents, Gay, Lesbian, Bisexual and Transgender interest films, and Spanish language films.

CONEY ISLAND SHORT FILM FESTIVAL

532 La Guardia Place #638 New York
NY 10012
E   info@coneyislandfilmfestival.com
W   www.coneyislandfilmfestival.com

Founded in 2001. Jury presents awards for best feature, short, documentary feature, documentary short, experimental, animation, music video and "Made in Coney Island". Runs for 3 days.

CRESTED BUTTE REEL FEST

T 970 349 2600
F 970 349 1384
W www.crestedbuttereelfest.com

Founded in 1998, a competitive festival for films under 40 minutes in the categories of animation, experimental, live-action narrative (comedy, drama, science fiction, action or musical) and documentaries under 60 minutes.

CUCALORUS FILM FESTIVAL

T 910 343 5995
F 910 343 5227
E mail@cucalorus.org
W www.cucalorus.org

Founded in 1994, a 4-day festival in Wilminton, North Carolina, showing documentaries, feature films and shorts.

DAMAH FILM FESTIVAL

T 310 237 5436
W www.damah.com

Founded in 2001, an annual festival of short films with spiritual topics.

Submissions Policy
Films must be under 30 minutes.

DENVER INTERNATIONAL FILM FESTIVAL

Denver Film Society 2601 Blake Street Suite 301 Denver CO 80205
T 303 595 3456
F 303 595 0956
E dfs@denverfilm.org
W www.denverfilm.org

Founded in 1978, the festival screens films from around the world including new international releases, cutting-edge features, documentaries, and short subjects. Hosts panels and seminars, as well as Q&A sessions with the director, cast and crew of the films. Annually for 10 days.

DURANGO INDEPENDENT FILM FESTIVAL

PO Box 1587 Durango CO 81302
T 970 375 7779
F 970 375 1437

E info@durangofilm.org
W www.durangofilm.org

Founded in 2001, a competitive film festival for independent films. Accepts entries for shorts, documentaries and feature films on all subject matter. Runs over 5 days.

Submissions Policy
Feature length films should be over 50 minutes and shorts should be 49 minutes or under in duration.

EAST LANSING FILM FESTIVAL

T 517 980 5802
F 517 336 2750
W www.elff.com

Founded in 1997, the festival focuses on presenting a diverse selection of independent and foreign features, documentaries, shorts and student films. The festival also hosts the Lake Michigan Film Competition which showcases films from Wisconsin, Illinois, Indiana and Michigan. Held annually over a period of 5 days.

FIERY FILM FEST

T 505 693 0906
E director@fieryfilmfest.org
W www.fieryfilmfest.org

Established in 2001 in Clovis, New Mexico, showing animation, comedy, documentary, drama, action, sci-fi, horror and experimental genres.

FILM COLUMBIA

T 518 392 1162
E entries@filmcolumbia.com
W www.filmcolumbia.com

Founded in 2000. Presents work by independent filmmakers in the Hudson River region. The programme includes features, documentaries, short selections and student films.

Submissions Policy
In order to qualify, a principal of the film, (director, producer, screenwriter, actor, production company or locale) must be

connected to the Hudson River region, from New York City to Canada.

A FLICKERING IMAGE FESTIVAL

3233 Grand Avenue Suite N-110 Chino Hills CA 91709
E   shortsfest@actorsbone.com
W   www.actorsbone.com/Shorts/index.html

Contacts
N. Barry Carver *Festival Director*

Competitive festival which screens ten winners' short films in Hollywood. All genres are welcomed but films must last a maximum of thirty minutes. The event is held once a year, with screenings of winning films in January.

Submissions Policy
Unsolicited applications are welcomed. All entries, whether in the top ten or not, receive written feedback from judges.

FLORIDA FILM FESTIVAL

T   407 644 6579
F   407 629 6870
W   www.floridafilmfestival.com

Founded in 1992 and produced by the Enzian Theater, screening narrative and documentary features and shorts, animation and midnight movies. Hosts several educational forums. The Festival is a qualifying festival for the Oscars in the category of live action short films.

FORT LAUDERDALE INTERNATIONAL FILM FESTIVAL

1314 East Las Olas Boulevard #007 Fort Lauderdale FL 33301
T   954 760 9898
E   info@fliff.com
W   www.fliff.com

Founded in 1986, screening over 200 films from around the world. Held annually for over a month.

FULL FRAME DOCUMENTARY FESTIVAL

T   919 687 4100
F   919 687 4200
E   info@fullframefest.org
W   www.fullframefest.org

Founded in 1998 in Durham, North Carolina, a documentary film festival showcasing more than 100 films over 4 days. The festival also has panel discussions, seminars, and question and answer sessions.

GREAT LAKES INDEPENDENT FILM FESTIVAL

Great Lakes Film Association PO Box 346 Erie PA 16512
T   814 873 5069
E   Fest@greatlakesfilmfest.com
W   www.greatlakesfilmfest.com

Founded in 2002, dedicated to showcasing independent films in the digital medium. Accepts submissions of independently produced feature length and short length films and scripts in the genres of documentary, horror, experimental, religious/spiritual, animation, and all genres of music videos and gay/lesbian.

THE HAMPTONS INTERNATIONAL FILM FESTIVAL

141 W. 28th Street Street Ste. 300 New York NY 10001
T   212 695 4793
F   212 563 9655
W   hamptonsfilmfest.org

Established in 1992, the festival highlights narrative features, documentaries and shorts, and offers diverse programming with breakthrough films by new directors, premieres by established filmmakers, panel discussions and special events with guests from the industry. Takes place annually.

Submissions Policy
Submission of material is subject to an application fee. It is a requirement that films may not have been released theatrically or shown on television in the US prior to the festival.

LOUIS VUITTON HAWAII INTERNATIONAL FILM FESTIVAL

T   808 528 3456
F   808 528 1410
E   program@hiff.org
W   www.hiff.org

Founded in 1981, showing feature films, documentaries, short films, Hawaii-themed films, music videos and student films. Runs for 2 weeks.

HAZEL WOLF ENVIRONMENTAL FILM FESTIVAL

PO Box 22695 Seattle WA 98122
T 206 624 9725
E info@hazelfilm.org
W www.hazelfilm.org

Contacts
Grace Stahre *President*

Founded in 1998, specializing in documentaries, fiction, animation and web media with an environmental theme. Includes filmmaking and environmental workshops and panel discussions, and 'meet the filmmaker coffees'. Recent films shown include *McLibel* and *Buyer Be Fair*. The event is held annually, lasting 3–4 days in March/April.

Submissions Policy
Unsolicited applications are welcomed by email.

HEARTLAND FILM FESTIVAL

200 S. Meridian Street Suite 220 Indianapolis IN 46225-1076
T 317 464 9405
F 317 464 9409
E info@heartlandfilmfestival.org
W www.heartlandfilmfestival.org

Founded in 1991, aiming to recognize filmmakers whose work explores the human journey and the positive values of life.

HOLLYWOOD FILM FESTIVAL

8306 Wilshire Boulevard Ste. 2057
Beverly Hills CA 90211
T 310 407 3596
F 310 943 2326
E info@hbff.org
W www.hbff.org

Contacts
Tanya Kersey *Founder/Executive Director*

An annual celebration of black cinema drawing together established filmmakers and emerging

artists. Established in 1999, activities include public screenings, competitions for filmmakers and scriptwriters (with a staged reading of the winning script) and a 'Pitchathon' for those trying to sell ideas and screenplays. Held in June, lasting 6 days.

Submissions Policy
Welcomes unsolicited applications by email.

HOLLYWOOD INTERNATIONAL FILM FESTIVAL

T 310 288 1882
F 310 288 0060
E info@hollywoodawards.com
W www.hollywoodawards.com

Founded in 1997, a competitive festival with a mandate to highlight international films made by the global creative community. Runs for 5 days.

Submissions Policy
Submissions are accepted monthly. Features, documentaries, short subjects and music videos are eligible for the competition.

HOPE AND DREAMS FILM FESTIVAL

PO Box 131 Hope NJ 07844
T 908 459 5797
E hopeanddreams@earthlink.net
W www.hopeanddreams.com

Contacts
C.L. Rusin *Festival Director*

Founded in 1998, events include workshops, social functions, talks, an awards ceremony and a DVD sales market. Screenings of features, shorts, documentaries and animation. All subjects are considered, but 'themes of hope and dreams' will be given additional consideration. Held annually, the festival takes place over a weekend in October.

Submissions Policy
Applications through the website are welcomed.

HOT SPRINGS DOCUMENTARY FILM INSTITUTE

T 501 321 4747
F 501 321 0211

E hsdfi@hsdfi.org
W www.hsdfi.org

Founded in 1992, showing quality
documentaries on a variety of topics and
themes. Held annually.

Submissions Policy
Non-fiction documentaries in all forms
(features, shorts, and student films). The
duration for shorts is 20 minutes or less.

HUMBOLDT INTERNATIONAL FILM FESTIVAL

T 707 826 4113
F 707 826 4112
E filmfest@humboldt.edu
W www.humboldt.edu

Founded in 1967, among the oldest student-run
film festivals in the world. Celebrates
independent, student and international films
that test cinematic boundaries. Films must be
under 30 minutes and have been created within
the last 5 years.

KANSAS CITY FILMMAKERS JUBILEE

4741 Central #306 Kansas City MO 64112
T 913 649 0244
F 913 649 0244
E kcjub@kcjubilee.org
W www.kcjubilee.org

Founded in 1997, a juried film festival featuring
more than 100 local, regional, national and
international films. The festival also hosts
panels and workshops for filmmakers. Held
in April.

LONG ISLAND INTERNATIONAL FILM EXPO

222 Pettit Avenue Bellmore New York
NY 11566
T 516 572 0012
F 516 572 0260
E debfilm@aol.com
W www.longislandfilm.com

Contacts
Debra Markowitz *Director*

Founded in 1998, a week-long showcase of
short and feature-length independent films of
all genres. Some of the films featured in recent
years include *Strike the Tent*, *Dorian Blues*,

Push, *My Date with Drew* and *Falling Sky*.
Held annually.

Submissions Policy
Welcomes unsolicited applications which are to
be made either by email or via
www.withoutabox.com.

LOS ANGELES FILM FESTIVAL

T 310 432 1240
E LaFilmFest@filmindependent.org
W www.lafilmfest.com

Founded in 1995, showcasing upwards
of 175 narrative features, documentaries,
shorts, and music videos. A qualifying
festival in all categories for the Independent
Spirit Awards and for the Short Films
categories of the Academy Awards. Runs
for 10 days in June.

Submissions Policy
Feature films and shorts must be in English
or have English subtitles, and must not
have had any commercial theatrical or
television play in the US. Feature-length
films should be 50 minutes or more and
short films should be under 50 minutes
running time.

LOS ANGELES INTERNATIONAL SHORT FILM FESTIVAL

T 323 461 4400
E info@lashortsfest.com
W www.lashortsfest.com

Founded in 1997, showcasing short films in the
following categories: drama, comedy,
documentary, animation, and experimental.

MALIBU FILM FESTIVAL

PO Box 4166 Malibu CA 90264
T 310 452 6688
F 310 395 8895
W www.malibufilmfestival.com

Founded in 2000. Shows over 80 international
features, documentaries and short films
from around the world. Runs for 4 days
in April. Films that have not yet screened
in Los Angeles are given priority in jury
selection.

MARGARET MEAD FILM AND VIDEO FESTIVAL

American Museum of Natural History Central Park West at 79th Street NY 10024
T 212 769 5305
F 212 769 5329
E meadfest@amnh.org
W www.amnh.org/mead

Contacts
Elaine Charnor *Artistic Co-director*

An annual festival of experimental non-fiction and documentary films. Founded in 1977, events include screenings, Q&A sessions with filmmakers, panel discussions and performances. The festival lasts 5 days and is held in November each year.

Submissions Policy
Unsolicited applications are welcomed via the website.

MEDIA THAT MATTERS FILM FESTIVAL

T 646 230 6288
F 646 230 6388
E info@artsengine.net
W www.mediathatmattersfest.org

Founded in 2001, showcasing short films on topical themes. The jury selects work on a variety of topics including gay rights and global warming, made by independent filmmakers many of whom are under the age of 21. Films include documentaries, music videos, animations and experimental work. All films run for 8 minutes or less.

Submissions Policy
Submission of material is subject to an entry fee (free for students). Films must run for 8 minutes maximum. Films of all genres are accepted. Interested in films on social and environmental issues.

MIAMI INTERNATIONAL FILM FESTIVAL

c/o Miami Dade College 25 NE 2nd Street Room 5501 Miami FL 33132
T 305 237 3456
E info@miamifilmfestival.com
W www.miamifilmfestival.com

Founded in 1984, showing films from over 50 countries. Cash awards are given in four competition categories: World Features, Ibero-American Features, World & Ibero-American Documentaries, and Short Films. Grand Jury prizes of $25,000 awarded in dramatic and documentary competitions.

MINNEAPOLIS-ST PAUL INTERNATIONAL FILM FESTIVAL

309 Oak Street SE Minneapolis MN 55414
T 612 331 7563
F 612 378 7750
E info@mnfilmarts.org
W www.mnfilmarts.org

Contacts
Al Milgrom *Festival Director*

Activities include a children's festival and an emerging filmmakers award, as well as screenings, premieres and an awards ceremony. Running since 1983, the festival shows around 150 films a year, incorporating both local and international films. Held annually for 2 weeks in April.

Submissions Policy
Welcomes unsolicited applications but prefers phone call first.

NAPA SONOMA WINE COUNTRY FILM FESTIVAL

T 707 996 2536
E wcfilmfest@aol.com
W www.winecountryfilmfest.com

Founded in 1986, the festival presents features, documentaries, shorts and animation in six categories: world cinema, Latin cinema, US cinema, arts in film, cinema of conscience and eco cinema.

THE NEW FESTIVAL

T 212 571 2170
F 212 571 2179
E info@newfest.org
W www2.newfest.org

Founded in 1989, showing local, national and international pictures to foster a greater sense of awareness and community among gay, bisexual and transgender audiences. Runs for 11 days.

Submissions Policy
Submission of material is subject to an administrative fee and films/videos should be by, about or of interest to lesbians, gay men, bisexuals or transgendered people.

NEW ORLEANS FILM FESTIVAL

843 Carondelet Street New Orleans LA 70130
T   504 309 6633
F   504 309 0923
E   info@neworleansfilmfest.com
W www.neworleansfilmfest.com

Contacts
Ali Duffey *Executive Director*

Founded in 1989, the festival includes screenings, workshops, talks and an awards ceremony. An 8 day event held annually in early October.

Submissions Policy
Welcomes unsolicited applications. A call for entries is listed on the website. Films can be entered in 5 competitive categories.

THE NEW YORK CITY HORROR FILM FESTIVAL

PO Box 8582 Woodcliff Lake NJ 07677
E   NYCHorrorfest@aol.com
W www.NYCHorrorfest.com

Contacts
Michael J. Hein *Festival Director*

Focusing solely on horror, science-fiction and thrillers, the festival 'celebrates genre films and those who make them'. Founded in 2001, events include special screenings, informative panel discussions and 'frightening fun parties'. Films include short and feature narratives, documentaries, animation and music videos. Held annually in October, the festival runs for a week.

Submissions Policy
Unsolicited applications are welcomed by email.

NEW YORK FILM FESTIVAL

165 West 65th Street Fourth Floor New York NY 10023
T   212 875 5638
E   festival@filmlinc.com
W www.filmlinc.com

Founded in 1963. Shows 30 features and 12 short films each year. Runs for 17 days.

Submissions Policy
All filmmakers, regardless of experience, are invited to submit material. There is no entry fee and films of all lengths and genres are considered.

THE NEW YORK INTERNATIONAL DOCUMENTARY FESTIVAL

T   212 668 1100
F   212 943 6396
W www.docfest.org

Founded in 1998, a 5-day event focussing on new and classic international documentaries. Every screening and seminar is followed by a panel discussion with the filmmaker, film subject(s) and other guests. Selection of material to the festival is by invitation only. If interested in submitting material, send a short synopsis, technical information, press material and director's biography to the festival and they will review it and decide on whether to extend an invitation. US films considered for the festival must have been completed within twelve months prior to the festival, and films made outside the US must have been completed within 24 months prior to the festival.

NEW YORK INTERNATIONAL INDEPENDENT FILM AND VIDEO FESTIVAL

T   702 361 1430
F   702 361 6309
E   filmmfest@aol.com
W www.nyfilmvideo.com

A competitive event founded in 1993. Hosts film, music and art events in New York and Los Angeles and has attracted major figures from around the world. Hostsed four times per year.

Submissions Policy
See website for submission procedure.

NEW YORK INTERNATIONAL LATINO FILM FESTIVAL

419 Lafayette Street 3rd Floor New York
NY 10003
T   646 723 1428
E   info@nylatinofilm.com
W www.nylatinofilm.com

Founded in 1999, showing movies from North,
Central and South America and the Caribbean
made by, about and/or for the Latino
community.

Submissions Policy
Films of all genres are considered and can be of
any form including feature narrative, short
films, documentary and experimental shorts.
Films must be in English or have English
subtitles, and cannot have been broadcast or
distributed commercially in the US prior to the
festival (exceptions are made for short films
and documentaries).

NEWPORT INTERNATIONAL FILM FESTIVAL

PO Box 146 Newport RI 02840
T   401 846 9100
E   info@newportfilmfestival.com
W www.newportfilmfestival.com

Founded in 1998, with over 100 screenings of
feature length narrative films, documentaries
and shorts. Hosts international and US
premieres. Also runs daily panel discussions
with well-known industry professionals. Held
annually.

Submissions Policy
All entries must either be in English or subtitled
in English. Feature films and documentaries
should be 60 minutes or longer, and short films
should be 30 minutes or less in duration.

NIHILIST FILM FESTIVAL

Box 36422 Los Angeles CA 90036
E   nihilist01@aol.com
W www.nihilists.net/film.html

Contacts
Elisha Shapiro *Director*

Specializes in 'amusing and challenging films',
including documentaries, animation, drama and
comedy. Founded in 1999, the festival includes
'the blessing of the TVs'. Held annually in
December.

Submissions Policy
Welcomes unsolicited applications by mail.

PALM BEACH JEWISH FILM FESTIVAL

3151 N. Military Trail West Palm Beach
FL 33409
T   561 689 7700
F   561 478 3060
E   pbjhh@jcconline.com
W www.palmbeachjewishfilm.org

Contacts
Karen Davis *Director*

Founded in 1989, screening feature films,
documentaries and shorts with a Jewish focus.
Recent films featured include *More than 1000
Words* and *A Love to Hide*. 10-day event held
annually in November/December.

Submissions Policy
Unsolicited applications are welcomed by mail.

PALM SPRINGS INTERNATIONAL FILM FESTIVAL

1700 E. Tahquitz Canyon Way Suite 3
Palm Springs CA 92262
T   760 322 2930
F   760 322 4087
E   info@psfilmfest.org
W www.psfilmfest.org

Contacts
David Lee *Marketing and Publicity Manager*

Founded in 1990, the festival includes
screenings, panel discussions, international
gala screenings and an awards ceremony.
Covers a wide range of genres including
live action, animation, documentaries
and short films. Films entered in previous
years include *Black Book* and *The Tiger's Tail*.
The event is held annually for 12 days in
January.

Submissions Policy
On-line applications are welcomed.

PAN AFRICAN FILM FESTIVAL

T   323 295 1706
F   323 295 1952
E   info@PAFF.org
W   www.paff.org

Founded in 1992 in Los Angeles, run by a
non-profit corporation dedicated to the
promotion of cultural and racial tolerance and
understanding. Each year over 100 films
shown.

Submissions Policy
The festival accepts films and videos made by
and/or about people of African descent. Films
should preferably depict positive and realistic
images and can be of any genre.

PORTLAND INTERNATIONAL FILM FESTIVAL

T   503 221 1156
F   503 294 0874
E   info@nwfilm.org
W   www.nwfilm.org

Founded in 1978. Focuses mainly on foreign
films but does include American features,
documentaries and shorts. Each year the
festival screens nearly 100 films from over
30 countries. Runs for two weeks each year.

Submissions Policy
Unsolicited preview tapes with entry may be
sent. Entries must include a synopsis of the film
and a one-page bio/filmography of the
filmmaker's background and previous works.

REAL TO REEL FILM AND VIDEO FESTIVAL

111 Washington Street Shelby NC 28150
T   704 484 2787
F   704 481 1822
W   www.ccartscouncil.org

Founded in 2000, providing a platform for
independent film, video and multimedia artists
from around the world. Runs for 4 days.

Submissions Policy
Four categories: documentary, feature length
(over 61 minutes in length), shorts (under 60
minutes in length) and animation. Each entry
must include all promotional material for the
film such as credits, film stills, and synopsis.

RED BANK INTERNATIONAL FILM FESTIVAL

T   732 741 8089
F   732 741 8093
E   mleckstein@monmouth.com
W   www.rbiff.org

Founded in 2001, showing all genres made by
both industry professionals and students from
all over the world. Cash awards for all major
category winners. Runs for 3 days.

Submissions Policy
Entries must include a synopsis of 200 words
or less.

REEL AFFIRMATIONS FILM FESTIVAL

PO Box 73587 Washington, D.C. 200
T   202 986 1119
F   202 939 0981
E   Jbilancio@oninten.org
W   www.reelaffirmations.org

Contacts
Joe Bilancio *Programs Manager*

Founded in 1991, one of the largest gay and
lesbian festivals in the world. Held annually.

Submissions Policy
The festival seeks features, shorts,
documentaries and animated works in 35mm,
DVD, Beta SP and VHS formats.

RHODE ISLAND INTERNATIONAL FILM FESTIVAL

PO Box 162 96 Second Street Newport
RI 02840
T   401 861 4445
E   401 490 6735
W   www.film-festival.org

Founded in 1997, a juried competition and
showcase for independent filmmakers from all
over the world. The festival's short film winner
qualifies for Academy Award consideration.
Runs for 6 days.

Submissions Policy
No category restrictions. Films must be
presented in their original language with
English language subtitles. Feature films should
run for 46 minutes or longer, and short films
should be 45 minutes or less.

ROCHESTER INTERNATIONAL FILM FESTIVAL

T 585 234 7411
W www.rochesterfilmfest.org

Founded in 1959. The world's oldest continuously-held short film festival. Programme includes narrative films, documentaries and animations submitted by independent filmmakers from all parts of the world. Includes films by students and professionals.

Submissions Policy
Open to films and videos in all genres. Maximum length of entries is 30 minutes. No more than two entries per filmmaker.

SACRAMENTO FILM AND MUSIC FESTIVAL

T 916 600 7029
E questions@sactofilmfest.com
W www.sacfilm.com

Founded in 2000. Submission-based and highly selective. Invites films in all genres and of all lengths. Since its inception, has screened over 400 films and videos. Annual.

Submissions Policy
Entries should include a brief synopsis. All entries must either be in English or subtitled in English.

SAN DIEGO FILM FESTIVAL

7974 Mission Bonita Drive San Diego
CA 92120
T 619 582 2368
F 619 286 8324
E info@sdff.org
W www.sdff.org

Contacts
Robin Laatz *Executive Director*

Established in 2002 to support up-and-coming independent filmmakers. Incorporates screenings, panel discussions, workshops for screenwriters and filmmakers and awards. Features full-length films, documentaries, shorts and music videos. The festival is held annually in September, lasting 5 days.

Submissions Policy
Unsolicited applications are welcomed, via application form on website.

SAN FRANCISCO INTERNATIONAL FILM FESTIVAL

T 415 561 5000
F 415 561 5099
W www.sffs.org

Founded in 1957, the longest-running film festival in the Americas and the first to showcase international productions. Screens more than 200 films and hosts more than 100 filmmakers each year. Runs for 2 weeks.

SAN FRANCISCO INTERNATIONAL GAY AND LESBIAN FILM FESTIVAL

145 Ninth Street #300 San Francisco
CA 94103
T 415 703 8650
F 415 861 1404
E boxoffice@frameline.org
W www.frameline.org

Founded in 1977, the world's largest and oldest LGBT film festival, screening films from around the world. The festival awards a $10,000 First Feature Award, the $10,000 Best Documentary Award and a $7,500 Audience Award.

SANTA BARBARA INTERNATIONAL FILM FESTIVAL

W www.sbfilmfestival.org

Running since 1986. A juried festival showing over 200 feature films and 50 short films. Also panel discussions and a student screenwriting and filmmaking competition. Annual.

SANTA FE FILM FESTIVAL

T 505 988 5225
F 505 988 4998
E info@santafefilmfestival.com
W www.santafefilmfestival.com

Founded in 2000, the festival premiers local New Mexican film, new American and foreign film including revivals, retrospectives, independent productions and mini-festivals.

Also hosts panel discussions, demonstrations, talks and workshops.

SAVANNAH FILM FESTIVAL

c/o Savannah College of Art and Design PO Box 3146 Savannah GA 31402-3146
T   912 525 5051
F   912 525 5052
E   filmfest@scad.edu
W   www.scad.edu

Founded in 1998, showcasing feature-length films and shorts from both award-winning professionals and emerging student filmmakers. The festival also hosts panel discussions and presentations by visiting artists. Feature films and videos must be no less than 40 minutes in length. Short works must not exceed 40 minutes. All entries must either be in English or subtitled in English. The entry must include a brief synopsis not longer than 100 words.

SEATTLE INTERNATIONAL FILM FESTIVAL

400 9th Avenue N. Seattle WA 98109
T   206 464 5830
F   206 264 7919
E   info@seattlefilm.org
W   www.seattlefilm.org

Contacts
Carl Spence *Artistic Director*

Established in 1975, incorporating screenings, tributes, workshops and demonstrations, panel discussions and an awards ceremony. Over 400 feature films and documentaries and shorts from more than 60 countries are presented to an audience of 160,000 each year. Films featured in recent years include *The Illusionist, The Science of Sleep, Half Nelson* and *Me and You and Everyone We Know*. Held annually in May/June and lasting 25 days.

Submissions Policy
Unsolicited applications are welcomed via the website.

SEDONA INTERNATIONAL FILM FESTIVAL & WORKSHOP

T   928 282 1177
F   928 282 5912

E   info@sedonafilmfestival.com
W   www.sedonafilmfestival.com

Founded in 1997. Features more than 125 films, including features, documentaries, foreign films, shorts, animation and student films. Many of the films screened at the festival have gone on to garner Academy Award nominations including *Genghis Blues, Spellbound* and *Why Can't We Be A Family Again*. Lasts for 5 days.

SHOCKERFEST INTERNATIONAL FILM FESTIVAL

PO Box 580450 Modesto CA 95358
T   209 537 5221
F   209 531 0233
E   director@shockerfest.com
W   www.shockerfest.com

Founded in 2002, the festival showcases films in the science fiction, fantasy, and horror genres. Runs for 2 days every year.

SHRIEKFEST

PO Box 920-444 Sylmar CA 91392
T   818 367 9161
F   818 367 9861
E   shriekfest@aol.com
W   www.shriekfest.com

Contacts
Denise Gossett *Founder/Co-director*

Established in 2001, dedicated to horror, thrillers, science fiction and fantasy films and screenplays. Includes adult and junior competitions for screenplays and films, as well as panel discussions and screenings. Recent films include *Dark Remains* and *The Other Side*. Held annually in September, lasting 6 days.

Submissions Policy
Welcomes unsolicited applications by mail or email.

SILVER LAKE FILM FESTIVAL

E   info@silverlakefilmfestival.org
W   www.silverlakefilmfestival.org

Founded in 2000 to provide a showcase for independent film in Los Angeles. It screens over

200 narrative features, documentaries and short films. In addition to its annual festival, the organization presents a monthly screening of short films throughout the year. Held annually for a period of 10 days.

SLAMDANCE FILM FESTIVAL

T 323 466 1786
F 323 466 1784
E mail@slamdance.com
W www.slamdance.com

Founded in 1995, the festival takes place each year in Utah at the same time as the Sundance Film Festival. The festival was launched to showcase undistributed films by emerging filmmakers. Festival discoveries have included directors Marc Forster (*Monster's Ball*) and Jared Hess (*Napoleon Dynamite*). Held annually in January.

Submissions Policy
Films of all genres and from any country accepted.

THE SONOMA VALLEY FILM SOCIETY FESTIVAL

589 First Street West Sonoma CA 95476
T 707 933 2600
F 707 933 2612
E filmsociety@cinemaepicuria.org
W www.sonomafilmfest.org

Founded in 1998, screening about 75 independent films annually, including feature length narratives, world cinema, documentaries, shorts and student films. Most screenings are followed by a Q&A with the stars and filmmakers.

Submissions Policy
See website for submission details.

SUNDANCE FILM FESTIVAL

Sundance Institute P.O. Box 684429 Park City Utah UT 84068
T 801 328 3456
F 801 575 5175
E Institute@sundance.org
W festival.sundance.org

Founded in 1978 as the Utah/US Film Festival, it was renamed the Sundance Film Festival in 1991. It is the largest independent cinema festival in the US. The festival comprises competitive sections for American and international dramatic and documentary films, and a group of non-competitive showcase sections, including the Sundance Online Film Festival. Held annually in January.

Submissions Policy
Submission of material is subject to an application fee.

TAMPA INTERNATIONAL GAY AND LESBIAN FILM FESTIVAL

T 813 879 4220
F 813 514 6428
E amy@tiglff.com
W www.tiglff.com

Founded in 1990, focussing on films with homosexual themes as well as transgender issues and gender roles. Held annually.

Submissions Policy
Films and videos submitted should be of interest to lesbian, gay, bisexual, intersex and/or transgendered people. The festival accepts narrative, documentary, experimental and animated films and videos (both features and shorts).

TELLURIDE FILM FESTIVAL

T 510 665 9494
F 510 665 9589
E Mail@telluridefilmfestival.org
W www.telluridefilmfestival.org

Founded in 1974, a non-competitive festival for independent film. The festival screens features and student films. Films such as *Slingblade* have premiered at the festival. Annual.

Submissions Policy
Unsolicited works may be submitted for consideration from May 1st to July 15th each year. Movies of any length, in any format, and in all genres and disciplines are eligible for consideration. Features (60 minutes or longer)

which have had any public exposure in North America prior to the Labor Day event are not eligible for consideration.

TEMECULA VALLEY INTERNATIONAL FILM & MUSIC FESTIVAL

T   951 699 5514
F   951 506 4193
E   festival@tviff.com
W   www.tviff.com

Founded in 1995. Has since screened over 700 films from more than 20 countries. Annual. Open to US and foreign films in five categories: full length features, shorts, documentaries, animation and student films. Entries must include a film synopsis, complete cast/crew credits list, stills, and complete technical information (running time). Non-English language-produced films must have subtitles or be dubbed in English.

TIBURON INTERNATIONAL FILM FESTIVAL

1680 Tiburon Boulevard Tiburon CA 94920
T   415 381 4123
F   415 388 4123
E   info@TiburonFilmFestival.com
W   www.TiburonFilmFestival.com

Founded in 2002, the aim of the festival is to strengthen cultural awareness and to create a platform for independent filmmakers.

TRIBECA FILM FESTIVAL

375 Greenwich Street New York NY 10013
T   212 941 2400
F   212 941 3939
E   festival@tribecafilmfestival.org
W   www.tribecafilmfestival.org

The Tribeca Film Festival was founded in 2002 by Robert De Niro, Jane Rosenthal and Craig Hatkoff as a response to the attacks on the World Trade Centre. Conceived to foster the economic and cultural revitalization of Lower Manhattan through an annual celebration of film, music and culture, the Festival's mission is to promote New York City as a major filmmaking centre and allow its filmmakers to

reach the broadest possible audience. Held annually.

UNITED NATIONS ASSOCIATION FILM FESTIVAL

PO Box 19369 Stanford CA 94309
T   650 725 0012
E   info@unaff.org
W   www.unaff.org

Contacts
Jasmina Bojic *Festival Director*

Focusing on international short and feature-length documentaries, includes screenings, talks and an awards ceremony. Lasting 5 days, the festival is held in October.

Submissions Policy
Call for entries is released on website.

US INTERNATIONAL FILM AND VIDEO FESTIVAL

713 South Pacific Coast Highway Suite A
Redondo Beach CA 90277-4233
T   310 540 0959
F   310 316 8905
E   filmfestinfo@filmfestawards.com
W   www.filmfestawards.com

Founded in 1967, devoted exclusively to recognition of outstanding business, television, documentary, educational, entertainment, industrial and informational productions.

VERMONT INTERNATIONAL FILM FESTIVAL

T   802 660 2600
F   802 860 9555
E   info@vtiff.org
W   www.vtiff.org

Founded in 1985 by peace and social justice activists, George and Sonia Cullinen, the festival has provided a forum for films dealing with issues of war and peace, justice and human rights, and the environment. Most years, the festival accepts independent films from around the world in any length and genres that fit into one of the three categories: Justice and Human Rights, War and Peace, or the Environment.

VISTAS FILM FESTIVAL

T 214 887 9048
F 214 887 1734
W www.vistasfilmfestival.org

Founded in 1999, a 5-day international festival of movies by or about Latinos or Latino culture. Annual.

Submissions Policy

Submissions are accepted throughout the year and all entries are considered for the main festival in September, as well as for the monthly screening series that occurs throughout the year. Non-competitive. Films must fall within the festival's focus of works by or about Latinos or Latino culture. Feature length and short films are considered for presentation.

WASHINGTON, D.C. INDEPENDENT FILM FESTIVAL

2950 Van Ness Street NW Suite 728
Washington D.C.
T 202 537 9493
F 202 686 8867
E dcindiefilmfest@aol.com
W www.dciff.org

Contacts

Carol Bidault de l'Isle *Founder/Executive Director*

Established in 1999, screening over 100 independent feature films, shorts, documentaries and animated films from around the world. Other events include seminars, discussions with filmmakers and a music festival. Held in March annually, the festival lasts 11 days.

Submissions Policy

Welcomes applications from around the world. 'All films (except opening and closing night) are chosen from an open call'.

WATERFRONT FILM FESTIVAL

PO Box 387 Saugatuck MI 49453
T 269 857 8351
F 269 857 1072
E info@waterfrontfilm.org
W www.waterfrontfilm.org

Founded in 1999, this non-competitive festival is open to films of any genre including features, shorts, documentaries and animation. Non-English language produced films must have English subtitles or be dubbed in English.

WESTCHESTER FILM FESTIVAL

148 Martine Avenue Room 107 White Plains NY 10601
T 914 995 2917
F 914 995 2948
W www.westchestergov.com

Founded in 2000, this juried festival has the following categories: feature, documentary feature, narrative short, documentary short, international, animation, screenplay, student resident and student non-resident.

Submissions Policy

Applicants must be 18 years or older.

WILLIAMSTOWN FILM FESTIVAL

T 413 458 9700
F 413 458 2702
E contactus@williamstownfilmfest.com
W www.williamstownfilmfest.com

Running since 1998, aiming to celebrate the industry, past present and future. As well as classic screenings, there are panels, seminars and discussions, and explorations of new technologies.

WITHOUTABOX

W www.withoutabox.com

Online application submission service for film festivals, connecting festivals with filmmakers and screenwriters. Also helps independent filmmakers to distribute and profit from their work.

THE WOODS HOLE FILM FESTIVAL

PO Box 624 87B Water Street Woods Hole MA 02543
T 508 495 3456
F 508 495 3456
E info@woodsholefilmfestival.org
W www.woodsholefilmfestival.org

Contacts
Judy Laster   *Executive Director*

Founded in 1989, incorporating screenings, screenplay competition with staged readings of winners, workshops and social events. Programme features around 40 features and 50 shorts including comedy, drama, documentary, animation and experimental films. All films are in competition. Held annually from last Saturday in July to first Saturday in August.

Submissions Policy
Welcomes unsolicited applications online.

WOODSTOCK FILM FESTIVAL

T   845 679 4265
F   509 479 5414
E   info@woodstockfilmfestival.com
W   www.woodstockfilmfestival.com

Founded in 2000, the festival showcases films, concerts, workshops, celebrity-led panels, and an awards ceremony. Maverick Awards are presented for Best Feature, Best Documentary, Best Short Documentary, Best Short Film, Best Student Film, Best Cinematography, Best Editing and Best Animation. Annual.

WORLDFEST HOUSTON INTERNATIONAL FILM FESTIVAL

PO Box 56566   Houston   TX 77256
T   713 965 9955
F   713 965 9960
E   mail@worldfest.org
W   www.worldfest.org

Founded in 1961 by producer/director Hunter Todd. Dedicated to the independent feature and short film and does not accept films from major studios. Presents around 55 new indie feature films and 100 short films each year. Runs for 10 days in April. Attended by over 500 filmmakers each year, films can compete in more than 200 awards categories.

Submissions Policy
A 50 to 100 word synopsis is required for all entries.

UNITED KINGDOM

10 SEC FILM FEST

Mobile Media Entertainment Ltd 2 Percy Street London   W1T 1DD
W   www.tensec.com

Described as the 'shortest film festival in the world, instant entertainment for an attention deficient universe.' Best submissions are shown on the website.

Submissions Policy
Must be a member to submit films. No fee for entering. Download and fill in a film submission form from the website for each film entered.

2 DAYS LATER SHORT FILM COMPETITION

The Community Pharmacy Gallery 16 Market Place   Margate Old Town   Kent   CT9 1ES
T   01843 223 800
F   01843 223 800
E   info@2dayslater.co.uk
W   www.2dayslater.co.uk

Contacts
Mick Etherton   *Competition Director*

Founded in 2002. Runs a competition for micro budget short horror films made in 48 hours to be shown at a screening event. Also runs weekend filmmaking workshops for novice film makers.

Submissions Policy
A competition brief is available in July on website. Deadline is 10 days before the Haloween screening. Festival is free. To become involved, approach by email in first instance.

AFRICA IN MOTION

37 McDonald Road   Edinburgh   EH7 4LY
E   info@africa-in-motion.org.uk
W   www.africa-in-motion.org.uk

Edinburgh-based festival showing a broad range of African films (old and new) and complementary events. Particularly interested in attracting young, emerging African filmmakers to submit shorts and documentaries and to talk to audiences about their work. The festival then tours other parts of the UK.

THE ANGEL FILM FESTIVAL

138 Upper Street Islington London N1 1QP
E info@angelfilmfestival.org
W www.angelfilmfestival.org

Contacts
Chirs Timms *Director*

Competition with screenings, talks
and award ceremonies for new short
films. All genres welcomed. Established
in 2005. Takes place annually over four
weeks. Scheduled for 1st-30th
September 2008.

Submissions Policy
Submissions welcomed via email.

ANIMATE THE WORLD

Barbican Centre Silk Street London EC2Y 8DS
W www.barbican.org.uk/animate

The Barbican's annual children's film
festival, founded in 2001. Shows
children's animated feature films and
shorts from around the world, together
with family animation workshops and
special events.

ANIMEX INTERNATIONAL FESTIVAL OF ANIMATION AND COMPUTER GAMES

School of Computing University of Teesside
Middlesbrough Tees Valley TS1 3BA
T 01642 342631
F 01642 342691
E chris@animex.net
W animex.tees.ac.uk

Contacts
Chris Williams *Festival Director*

Annual festival since 2000 with its roots in the
creative side of animation and computer games.
Brings together animators, directors, students,
artists, designers, writers and educators for
talks, presentations, workshops, screenings and
parties.

ASPECTS LITERATURE FESTIVAL

W www.northdown.gov.uk

Annual festival attracting leading Irish writing
talent. See website for details.

AURORA (NORWICH INTERNATIONAL ANIMATION FESTIVAL)

T 01603 756280
E info@aurora.org.uk
W www.niaf.org.uk

Festival includes screenings, seminars, debates,
live performance and installation works. Firmly
committed to showing cross-disciplinary work
and aims to present animation within the
context of the wider moving image.

Submissions Policy
Submission forms are available via the website.
Not only accepts animation but also
manipulated live action, artists' films and
installation work.

BATH FILM FESTIVAL

2nd Floor Abbey Chambers Kingston Parade
Bath BA1 1LY
T 01225 401149
F 01225 401149
W www.bathfilmfestival.org

Established in 1991 by members of Bath Film
Society, screening invited previews, arthouse
films and documentaries. Also includes a
film-makers discussion and film-related
workshops. Annual.

BELFAST FESTIVAL AT QUEEN'S

Culture & Arts Division 8 Fitzwilliam Street
Belfast BT9 6AW
W www.belfastfestival.com

Ireland's biggest international arts festival,
established in 1962. Covers all art forms
including theatre, dance, classical music,
literature, jazz, comedy, visual arts, folk music
and popular music, attracting over 50,000
visitors.

BELFAST FILM FESTIVAL

3rd Floor 23 Donegall Street Belfast BT1 2FF
T 02890 325 913
F 02890 329 397
E info@belfastfilmfestival.org
W www.belfastfilmfestival.org

Contacts
Stephen Hackett *Programmer*

Established in 2000. Runs annually in late March for 11 days. Includes screenings, talks, workshops, masterclasses, special events and short film and documentary competitions. Particular interest in international and European cinema, Japanese anime, music documentaries, documentaries with an international focus and Irish shorts.

Submissions Policy
Submissions accepted via a form on the website.

BERWICK FILM & MEDIA ARTS FESTIVAL

56-58 Castlegate Berwick-upon-Tweed Northumberland TD15 1JT
T   01289 303355
E   info@berwickfilm-artsfest.com
W www.berwickfilm-artsfest.com

A contemporary film and media arts festival, first held in 2005. Shows mainstream and art house films as well as artists' videos and films in a range of venues including the Town Hall Prison Cells, The Berwick Gymnasium, The Barrel's Ale House pub, the Ice House and the Black Hole. Other events include an artists' symposium, talks by industry professionals, an educational outreach programme run by ISIS Arts and a mobile cinema.

BETTING ON SHORTS

London Consortium Institute of Contemporary Arts 12 Charlton House Terrace London SW1Y 5AH
T   020 7839 8669
E   info@bettingonshorts.com
W www.bettingonshorts.com

Contacts
Ricarda Vidal *Director*

Founded in January 2005. Run annually at the end of November. Calls for short films of all genres between two and ten minutes. Features screenings, awards and audience feedback. Audiences are invited to bet on which film will win.

Submissions Policy
Submissions encouraged via email if relevant to an announced festival theme. Past themes

include "Playtime", "Vacancy" and "Mad or Bad". See website for more details. Deadline end of August.

BEYOND TV INTERNATIONAL VIDEO FESTIVAL

Undercurrents Old Exchange Pier Street Swansea SA1 1RY
T   01792 455900
E   info@undercurrents.org
W www.undercurrents.org

Shows a broad range of short movies, documentaries, music videos and animation themed around social or environmental activism.

Submissions Policy
Check website for information on submitting films.

BFM INTERNATIONAL FILM FESTIVAL

BFM Xcel Ltd 379/381 High Street Stratford London E15 4QZ
T   0207 540 0560
F   0207 540 0550
E   festival@bfmmedia.com
W www.bfmmedia.com

Established in 1998, week-long festival screening the work of black filmmakers from the UK and the rest of the world. Other events include Q&A sessions and the BFM Short Awards which recognize new and emerging black talent. Films featured in recent years include *Four Brothers* and *Life and Lyrics*, as well as films from the African continent. The festival is held annually in September.

BIRDS EYE VIEW FILM FESTIVAL

Unit 310a Aberdeen Centre 22-24 Highbury Grove London N5 1HJ
T   020 7704 9435
E   info@birds-eye-view.co.uk
W www.birds-eye-view.co.uk

Contacts
Rachel Millward *Festival Director*

Annual festival founded in 2005 running for six days. Next held in summer/autumn 2008. Screens international features, documentaries and short films by female directors. Also features masterclasses and workshops on all aspects of filmmaking.

Submissions Policy
Unsolicited applications welcomed. Submission guidelines and forms appear on the website.

BITE THE MANGO FILM FESTIVAL

National Media Museum Bradford West Yorkshire BD1 1NQ
T 01274 203 311
F 01274 203 387
E btm@nationalmediamuseum.org.uk
W www.bitethemango.org.uk

Contacts
Addy Rutter *Director*

Annual festival established in September 1995. Features interviews, talks, workshops and an industry weekend. Particular focus on films that draw influences from Africa, South Asia, Central America and the Far East.

Submissions Policy
Unsolicited scripts invited via email.

BRADFORD ANIMATION FESTIVAL

W www.nationalmediamuseum.org.uk/baf

Founded in 1994, a major animation festival curated by the National Media Museum. Includes screenings from around the world, talks, workshops and special events with leading industry names.

Submissions Policy
Information on how to submit entries available via the website.

BRADFORD INTERNATIONAL FILM FESTIVAL

National Media Museum Pictureville Bradford West Yorkshire BD1 1NQ
T 01274 203 320
F 01274 203 387
W www.bradfordfilmfestival.org.uk

Contacts
Bill Lawrence *Head of Film*

Festival founded in 1995 for new cinema from around the world but focusing on that from Lithuania, Slovenia, the Netherlands and the Czech Republic. Features screenings, screentalk interviews, masterclasses and the yearly film and music conference, Crash Symposium. Held annually at the £60 million National Media Museum for 16 days; the 14th festival begins February 29th 2008.

BRITDOC

E festival@britdoc.org
W www.britdoc.org

One of the UK's most important festivals of documentary production, run by the Channel 4 British Documentary Film Foundation. Held annually over three days, attracting international film producers, distributors and financiers.

CAMBRIDGE FILM FESTIVAL

Arts Picturehouse 38-39 St Andrews Street Cambridge CB2 3AR
T 01223 500082
F 01223 462555
E info@cambridgefilmtrust.org.uk
W www.cambridgefilmtrust.org.uk

Major film festival held each July, established in 1977 and relaunched in 2001. Shows selection of films alongside an eclectic range of specialist interest programmes at the three-screen Arts Picturehouse and assorted other arts venues in the town. Also runs several touring events.

Submissions Policy
Those wishing to submit a film can either download a form from the website or use the submission page on the withoutabox.com service. Particularly keen to receive locally- or regionally-produced work.

CAN LEICESTER INTERNATIONAL SHORT FILM FESTIVAL

T 0116 2621265
E info@lineout.org
W www.lineout.org

Annual festival which began in 1996 to serve the East Midlands but has since gained an international profile.

Submissions Policy
Seeks films from all over the world, of any genre and by filmmakers of any age.

Submission is free and there is no limit on number of times an individual can enter. Download the submission form from website.

CARDIFF FILM FESTIVAL

Unit 1 Ty Cefn 14-16 Rectory Road Cardiff CF5 1QL
w www.cardifffilmfestival.co.uk

Contacts
Sarah Howells *Festival Director*

Founded in Aberystwyth in 1988. Includes screenings, workshops and Q&A sessions with directors. Specializes in short and feature films, documentaries, animation and live action film (international and Welsh).

Submissions Policy
Unsolicited applications welcomed via email.

CELTIC MEDIA FESTIVAL

249 West George Street Glasgow G2 4QE
T 0141 302 1737
E info@celticfilm.co.uk
w www.celticfilm.co.uk

First held in 1982. Aims to promote the languages and cultures of the Celtic countries on screen and in broadcasting during an annual three-day event.

CHELTENHAM INTERNATIONAL SCREENWRITER'S FESTIVAL

c/o Arturi Films Ltd Fern House Bath Road Stroud Gloucestershire GL5 3TL
T 01453 753 440
F 01453 753 990
E info@screenwritersfestival.com
w www.screenwritersfestival.com

Contacts
David Pearson *Festival Director*

Founded in 2006. Annual four day event exploring the art, craft, education and business of screenwriting. Advisory board members and regular contributors include Julian Fellowes (*Gosford Park*), Olivia Hetreed (*Girl With a Pearl Earring*) and Bill Nicholson (*Gladiator*). Takes place in and around Cheltenham Film Studios. Sessions include masterclasses, keynote speeches, networking events, screenings,

seminars, workshops and educational events for schools. Caters for all skill levels. Scheduled for the first week of July 2008.

Submissions Policy
Manuscripts only accepted for specific festival initiatives. Application instructions available on the website.

CHICHESTER FILM FESTIVAL

Chichester Cinema New Park Road Chichester West Sussex PO19 7XY
T 01243 786650
E info@chichestercinema.org
w www.chichestercinema.org

Running since 1992. Includes audience-selected awards for best feature and best film short.

CHILIFILM FESTIVAL

PO Box 4288 London N19 4WY

Contacts
Jane Garfield

Held yearly as part of the Brick Lane Festival. Features eight hours of animation, music, short film and documentaries from around the world.

CINEM@TIC

Technology Innovation Centre Millennium Point Curzon Street Brighton B4 7XG
T 0121 331 5400
F 0121 331 5401

Contacts
Steve Smith *Centre Manager*

Short film festival founded in 2002 featuring free screenings, talks and a prize competition. Runs annually for two days.

Submissions Policy
Unsolicited applications accepted via email.

CINEMAGIC INTERNATIONAL FILM FESTIVAL FOR YOUNG PEOPLE

49 Botanic Avenue Belfast BT7 1JL
T 028 9031 1900
F 028 9031 9709
E info@cinemagic.org.uk
w www.cinemagic.org.uk

Established in 1989 and now the largest children's film festival in Great Britain and Ireland. Runs for 17 days and includes screenings, premieres, special guests, discussions, competitions and masterclasses in all aspects of filmmaking. There are prizes for best feature and best short for a teenage audience (judged by a jury aged 15–18) and best feature and best short for a children's audience (judged by a jury aged 8–14).

Submissions Policy
Entry form and regulations available on the website.

CO-OPERATIVE YOUNG FILM MAKERS FILM FESTIVAL

PO Box 53 New Century House Manchester M60 4ES
T   0161 246 2216
E   jason.brookes@co-op.co.uk
W   www.3bears.co.uk/festival/info.html

Young Film Makers is organized and funded by The Co-operative Group. The festival is held at the National Media Museum in Bradford. Over two days there are screenings of more than 100 short films as well as 20 workshops and masterclasses.

CORNWALL FILM FESTIVAL

The Old Grammar School West Park Redruth Cornwall TR15 3AJ
T   01209 204655
E   info@cornwallfilmfestival.com
W   www.cornwall-film-festival.co.uk

Annual festival with programme of screenings, skills development and networking. Submissions to the festival are restricted to films where a member of the creative team (writer, director, producer) are resident in Cornwall. Selection is made in three different categories: competition; screening; videotheque. Submission forms available on the website.

DEAD BY DAWN

E   info@deadbydawn.co.uk
W   www.deadbydawn.co.uk

Horror film festival run in association with Filmhouse and held in Scotland. Instructions on how to submit a film available on the website (for both features and shorts).

DEAFFEST, THE DEAF FILM AND TELEVISION FESTIVAL

Light House The Chubb Buildings Fryer Street Wolverhampton WV1 1HT
T   01902 716055
E   info@light-house.co.uk
W   www.light-house.co.uk

Established in 1998, catering for deaf film-lovers. Its programme includes films, panel discussions, networking opportunities and social events, all of which are free.

DISCOVERING LATIN AMERICAN FILM FESTIVAL

E   info@discoveringlatinamerica.org
W   www.discoveringlatinamerica.com

Established in 2002, showing Latin American feature films, shorts and documentaries. Also hosts debates, talks and Q&A sections. Held annually.

DOCUMENT INTERNATIONAL HUMAN RIGHTS DOCUMENTARY FILM FESTIVAL

c/o Mona Rai 268 Albert Drive 2/1 Pollokshields Glasgow G41 2RJ
T   0141 429 0185
E   docfest@gmail.com
W   www.docfilmfest.org.uk

Established in 2003, providing a platform for both established and emerging documentary filmmakers to screen their work related to international human rights issues.

EAST END FILM FESTIVAL

T   020 7613 7676
W   east.filmlondon.org.uk

Founded in 2001, exploring the potential of cinema to cross cultural, political and artistic boundaries. Films in the programme come from around the world. Screenings take place in venues across East London. Nitin Sawhney is the festival's patron.

EDINBURGH INTERNATIONAL FILM FESTIVAL

88 Lothian Road Edinburgh EH3 9BZ
T 0131 228 4051
F 0131 229 5501
E submissions@edfilmfest.org.uk
W www.edfilmfest.org.uk

Running since 1947, one of the UK's most important film festivals. Notable films screened in the last few years include *Mrs Brown, The Full Monty, La Vie Revée des Anges, East is East, Run Lola Run, Billy Elliot, American Splendor, Motorcycle Diaries* and *Tsotsi.*

Submissions Policy
Accepts submissions including shorts, features, animation, documentary and music video that are no older than 18 months at the time of the festival. Download the relevant forms and regulations from the website or submit via the online submissions service withoutabox.com. Deadline for all features and shorts is usually in April and for animation and Mirrorball films in June.

MEDIAGUARDIAN EDINBURGH INTERNATIONAL TELEVISION FESTIVAL (MGEITF)

117 Farringdon Road London EC1R 3BX
T 020 7278 9515
F 020 7278 9495
E mgeitf@profileevents.com
W www.mgeitf.co.uk

Major annual event for the television industry, founded in 1976 and hosted at the Edinburgh International Conference Centre. Explores key industry issues and offers excellent networking opportunities.

EDINBURGH MOUNTAIN FILM FESTIVAL

E stevie@edinburghmountainff.com
W www.edinburghmountainff.com

Established in 2003 and held each October in Edinburgh. An independent festival geared towards outdoor enthusiasts. Seeks 'exciting, unusual and intriguing new films' to show.

EMERGEANDSEE

T 0781 7288 797
E nathalie@emergeandsee.org
W www.emergeandsee.org

Voluntary organization founded in 2000, showing student work at regular cinema events in London (Curzon Cinema, Soho), Berlin and Budapest. Also distributes show reels to international festivals and cinemas. Submissions can be made via the website.

ENCOUNTERS INTERNATIONAL SHORT FILM FESTIVAL

Watershed Media Centre 1 Canon's Road Harbourside Bristol BS1 5TX
T 0117 929 9188
F 0117 952 9988
E info@encounters-festival.org.uk
W www.encounters-festival.org.uk

Major short film festival.

Submissions Policy
Filmmakers submitting work are requested to complete an online submission form and to send a DVD copy of the film for consideration. Deadline for submissions is normally end of May but check on website.

END OF THE PIER INTERNATIONAL FILM FESTIVAL

PO Box 213 Bognor Regis West Sussex PO21 2ZL
T 07812 806085
E info@eotpfilmfestival.com
W www.eotpfilmfestival.com

Held each May. Showcases high quality independent film from around the globe. Aims to gain recognition for new, low budget and independent filmmakers via a competition. Runs a wide-ranging education programme plus talks, seminars and master classes. Entry guidelines available on website.

FILMSTOCK INTERNATIONAL FILM FESTIVAL

c/o 24 Guildford Street Luton LU1 2NR
T 01582 402 200
E contact@filmstock.co.uk
W www.filmstock.co.uk

Running since 2000, devoted to independent shorts, features and documentaries. Shows around 150 films, selected from an open submission scheme. Paper entries can be downloaded from the website or via withoutabox. (£15 for short film/short documentary up to 25 minutes; £20 for features/feature documentary). Runs Filmschlock, 'an evening of how film should not be done'.

FIRECRACKER SHOWCASE: LONDON'S EAST ASIAN FILM FESTIVAL

Firecracker Media Ltd 27 Old Gloucester Street London WC1N 3XX
T   020 7449 3427
E   info@firecracker-media.com
W   www.firecracker-media.com

Organizes festival-style events in London to bring exposure to the cinema of East Asia.

FLIP INTERNATIONAL ANIMATION FESTIVAL

Light House Media Centre The Chubb Buildings Fryer Street Wolverhampton WV1 1HT
T   01902 716055
E   flip@light-house.co.uk
W   www.flipfestival.co.uk

Contacts
Peter McLuskie *Festival Co-ordinator*

Founded in 2004, a festival of animated films including screening, talks, workshops and awards. Films featured have included *Toy Story, Howls Moving Castle* and *Spirited Away*. Held over three days each Oct.

Submissions Policy
For tickets call the box office. To become involved contact by email.

FRIGHTFEST

10 Wiltshire Gardens Twickenham TW2 6ND
T   020 8296 0555
E   info-frightfest@blueyonder.co.uk
W   www.frightfest.co.uk

Contacts
Ian Rattray *Co-Director*

UK's premiere horror film festival. Runs annually, featuring screenings and presentations of fantasy, thriller and horror films. Established in 2000.

Submissions Policy
Unsolicited material welcomed. Submissions process outlined on website.

GLASGOW FILM FESTIVAL

Glasgow Film Theatre 12 Rose Street Glasgow G3 6RB
T   0141 332 8128
W   www.gft.org.uk

Informal celebration of international cinema.

HULL INTERNATIONAL SHORT FILM FESTIVAL

Suite 12 The Danish Buildings 44/46 High Street Hull HU1 1PS
T   01482 381512
F   01482 381517
E   office@hullfilm.co.uk
W   www.hullfilm.co.uk

Contacts
Laurence Boyle *Festival Director*

Established in 2000, dedicated to the exhibition and creation of short films. Activities include screenings, lectures, masterclasses and educational events. Committed to promoting new work and developing critical discussion. The festival is held annually and lasts 4–5 days.

Submissions Policy
Unsolicited applications are welcomed by mail.

I-BLINK FILM FESTIVAL

ceMAP Coventry University Priory Street Coventry CV1 5FB
E   info@i-blink.org
W   www.i-blink.org

A film festival and international scriptwriting competition for cutting edge short films. Prizes for the ten winners include loan of cameras, edit suite and accessories, training at Pinewood Studios and a copy of professional scriptwriting software FinalDraft 7. The three top films will also win: 1st Prize - €5000; 2nd Prize - €2000;

3rd Prize - €1000. All entrants receive professional feedback on their scripts.

IMAGES OF BLACK WOMEN FILM FESTIVAL

PO Box 54145 London W5 9DA
T   07876 155 228
E   info@imagesofblackwomen.com
W   www.imagesofblackwomen.com

An annual celebration of women of African descent working both in front of and behind the camera.

INTERNATIONAL FESTIVAL OF FANTASTIC FILMS

E   Gil@manchesterfantasticfilms.co.uk
W   www.fantastic-films.com

Weekend-long festival of science fiction, fantasy and horror movies, held in Manchester. Includes guest interviews, discussions, panels, special events, presentations, auctions, artshow and poster exhibition, dealer room, themed dinner, parties and screenings. Also runs competitions for independent and amateur films.

INTERNATIONAL MANGA AND ANIME FESTIVAL

First Floor London County Hall Belvedere Road London SE1 7BP
W   www.imaf.co.uk

First held in 2004 to meet the demand for Manga- and Anime-related activities. Administers a drawing/animation competition, which had a prize pot of $75,000 in 2006. Also runs screenings, art exhibitions, workshops, talks and opportunities to meet the professionals.

ITALIAN FILM FESTIVAL

7 Regent Terrace Edinburgh EH7 5BN
T   0131 556 3454
F   0131 556 3454
E   richard.mowe@which.net
W   www.italianfilmfestival.org.uk

Founded in 1994, showing films (features, shorts and documentaries) by established Italian directors at venues throughout the UK. Held annually.

JUMP CUT

ICA The Mall London SW1Y 5AH
T   020 7930 0493
E   jumpcut@ica.org.uk
W   www.ica.org.uk

Festival for young people aged 11–19 to showcase their creative talent in film-making. Screens short films as well as offering workshops, such as scriptwriting for drama.

KENDAL MOUNTAIN FESTIVAL

c/o Brook House Caldbeck Cumbria CA7 8EU
T   01697 478 542
E   filmentry@mountainfilm.co.uk
W   www.mountainfilm.co.uk

Contacts
John Porter *Director*

Founded in 1979. Runs annually in the third week of November for 10 days. Includes screenings, competitions, five day film school, 48-hour filmmaking marathon, book festival, workshops, seminars and exhibitions. All film types encouraged but especially those with a link to adventure, the culture of mountain communities and the environmental/economic issues affecting them. 2003 featured the gala premiere of *Touching the Void*.

Submissions Policy
Unsolicited applications welcomed. Entry details and regulations on the website.

KINOFILM - MANCHESTER INTERNATIONAL SHORT FILM FESTIVAL

W   www.kinofilm.org.uk

Kino aims to promote the short film format through exhibition, distribution, promotion and education. For information on entering films for the festival, see the website.

LANDCRAB FILM FESTIVAL

E   information@landcrabfilmfestival.co.uk
W   www.landcrabfilmfestival.co.uk

Short film festival held annually in Dorset, featuring films from recognized filmmakers and amateurs alike.

LATIN AMERICAN FILM FESTIVAL

436A New Cross Road London SE14 6TY
T 020 8692 6925
E info@latinamericanfilmfestival.com
W www.latinamericanfilmfestival.com

Founded in 1990. Dedicated to promoting the distribution and appreciation of Latin American films in the UK, featuring a mix of film screenings and associated events.

LEEDS INTERNATIONAL FILM FESTIVAL

T   0113 247 8398
E   filmfestival@leeds.gov.uk
W www.leedsfilm.com

Reputation as one of the UK's most progressive and important film festivals and the UK's largest regional film festival. Running since the 1980s.

Submissions Policy
Looks for striking and innovative features and shorts of any genre from across the world. To download an entry form see the website or email for more information.

LIVERPOOL FILM FESTIVAL

Toxteth TV 37-45 Windsor Street Liverpool L8 1XE
T 07763 486 141
E info@liverpoolff.com
W www.liverpoolff.com

Annual festival, screening a mixture of local and international films. Aims to unite filmmakers, commercial organizations, academic institutions, enthusiasts and community groups. Has a partnership with the Future Shorts network to host the Liverpool Future Shorts monthly screenings event for short films.

LLANBERIS MOUNTAIN FILM FESTIVAL

T 01286 871534
E info@llamff.co.uk
W www.llamff.co.uk

Eclectic programme of films, talks, poetry, photography and art, from Wales and beyond. Aims to capture the spirit of adventure and celebrate mountain art, sport and culture worldwide.

THE TIMES BFI LONDON FILM FESTIVAL

W www.lff.org.uk

London showcase of the best new films from around the world. Celebrated its 50th anniversary in 2006. Shows mix of films that would not otherwise get a UK screening and those that will get a release in the autumn or spring.

LONDON AUSTRALIAN FILM FESTIVAL

E film@barbican.org.uk
W www.barbican.org.uk/australianfilm/home

Annual since 1994, showing all major Australian feature film releases. Based at the Barbican Centre in London. Also offers a shorts programme in association with Flickerfest, Australia's leading international short film festival.

LONDON CHILDREN'S FILM FESTIVAL

T 020 7382 7368
E film@barbican.org.uk
W www.londonchildrenfilm.org.uk

Launched in 2005 and held over 9 or 10 days at London's Barbican Centre. Film programme includes previews and premieres, new world cinema, documentaries, archive titles, shorts, films made by young people and sing-a-long film. Also runs an extensive education programme before and during the festival.

LONDON INTERNATIONAL ANIMATION FESTIVAL

c/o The Film and Video Workshop 319-321 Holloway Road London N7 9LF
T 020 7607 8660
F 020 7607 8660
E info@liaf.org.uk
W www.liaf.org.uk

Contacts
Nag Vladermersky *Director*

Annual festival founded in 2003. Lasts one week, usually the last week of August. Strives to screen the best and most recent animated films from Britain and abroad. Also features retrospective and themed sessions, workshops and international guests.

Submissions Policy
Submissions via email.

LONDON LESBIAN AND GAY FILM FESTIVAL

w www.llgff.org.uk

Established in 1986, the third largest film festival in the UK. Usually held in March/April and then tours from May to September around 40 towns and cities across the UK and Ireland. Presents an eclectic programme of feature films, shorts, artists' film and video and experimental work, as well as discussions and special events.

LONDON SHORT FILM FESTIVAL

Curzon Soho Cinema 99 Shaftesbury Avenue London W1D 5YD
E info@shortfilms.org.uk
w www.shortfilms.org.uk

Contacts
Philip Ilson *Co-Director*

Annual film festival lasting about 10 days and founded in 2004. Screens all types of short film: drama, animation, documentary, experimental, low-budget. Also features talks and multi-media events. Next scheduled for January 2008.

Submissions Policy
Unsolicited applications welcomed via email.

LOVEBYTES DIGITAL ARTS FESTIVAL

The Workstation 15 Paternoster Row Sheffield S1 2BX
T 0114 221 0393
E info@lovebytes.org.uk
w www.lovebytes.org.uk

Held annually during March/April, bringing together film-makers, computer programmers, graphic designers and musicians from all over the world.

MENISCUS FILM FESTIVAL

w www.meniscusfilms.com

Held annually at the Whitgift Cinema in Grimsby, screening a range of independent cinema releases and hosting several other events throughout the year.

MID ULSTER FILM FESTIVAL

T 078 4312 1064
E info@midulsterfilmfestival.com
w www.midulsterfilmfestival.com

Held in An Creagan in Omagh. Now in its 4th year. Programme includes feature films, short films and documentaries.

Submissions Policy
Entry applications available via the website.

MIDLANDS BFM INTERNATIONAL FILM FESTIVAL

T 0121 678 6039
E midlands@bfmmedia.com
w www.bfmmedia.com

Festival with stated aim of being a vehicle for black British talent. The closing night includes the Short Film Awards, a highlight for new writers, directors, actors and cinematographers. Linked with Time Out's 'London on Screen' season.

NATIONAL ASSOCIATION OF WRITERS' GROUPS (NAWG) OPEN FESTIVAL OF WRITING

The Arts Centre Biddick Lane Washington Tyne & Wear NE38 2AB

The Association launched in 1995 and encompasses 150 affiliated groups and over 100 individual members. Aims to bring cohesion and fellowship to isolated writers' groups and individuals. Has held several festivals, originally in Washington, Tyne & Wear and latterly at St Aidan's College, University of Durham.

NORTHERN LIGHTS FILM FESTIVAL

(Temporary address until 2008) Tyneside
Cinema Old Town Hall West Street Gateshead
NE8 1HE
T   0191 261 7674
E   info@nlff.co.uk
W   www.nlff.co.uk

Contacts
Stephanie Little *Festival Director*

One week festival held annually in
November. Founded in 2003. Features
screenings, talks, educational workshops
and the largest short film award in the UK.
Specializes in features, documentaries,
shorts and animation from the UK and
northern Europe.

Submissions Policy
Script submissions welcomed via the website.

ONEDOTZERO

Unit 212c Curtain House 134-146 Curtain
Road London EC2A 3AR
E   info@onedotzero.com
W   www.onedotzero.com

Founded in 1996, since when it has collated
and commissioned over 200 hours of original
programming for its annual digital film festival
and related projects. Now tours to 60 major
cities around the world.

OPTRONICA

E   mail@optronica.org
W   www.optronica.org

Festival of visual music presented by the British
Film Institute, Addictive TV and Cinefeel.
Features live audiovisual performances,
screenings, illustrated talks, workshops and
related special presentations.

OSKA BRIGHT FILM FESTIVAL

Carousel Community Base 113 Queens Road
Brighton East Sussex BN1 3XG
T   01273 234 734
F   01273 234 735
E   enquiries@carousel.org.uk
W   www.oskabright.co.uk

Contacts
Mark Richardson *Artistic Director*

First film festival anywhere in the world run by,
and for, people with a learning disability.
Established in 2004. On odd years the
Brighton-based festival lasts two days and
offers screenings, workshops, bursaries and an
awards ceremony. On even years the previous
year's festival tours the UK.

Submissions Policy
Submissions must be no longer than 10
minutes. Further details via email or phone.

OUTSIDERS: LIVERPOOL LESBIAN AND GAY FILM FESTIVAL

15 Sandon Street Liverpool L8 7NS
T   0151 703 0548
E   llgff2004@yahoo.com
W   www.outsidersfilmfestival.com

Contacts
Matthew Fox *Festival Director*

Screens current and classic shorts and feature
films with gay, lesbian, bisexual or transgender
themes. Other activities include masterclasses,
exhibitions, workshops, social events and
monthly screenings throughout the year. Past
films featured include *Shortbus*, *Unveiled* and
Pink Narcissus. The festival is held annually
over a period of two weeks.

Submissions Policy
Welcomes any film submissions with gay,
lesbian, bisexual or transgender content or
makers.

OXDOX INTERNATIONAL DOCUMENTARY FILM FESTIVAL

The Jam Factory 27 Park End Street Oxford
OX1 1HU
E   info@oxdox.com
W   www.oxdox.com

Festival with a theme of 'Documenting the Real
World'. Subjects in 2007 included China, the
Mafia, women in Islamic countries and city life.
Administers an audience award for the Best
Feature Documentary and Best Short film while
a panel selects Best Student Film and Best
Dance Film.

PURBECK FILM FESTIVAL

8 Salisbury Road Swanage BH19 2DY
T   07939 968238
E   info@purbeckfilm.com
W   www.purbeckfilm.org.uk

Long-running rural film festival. Aims to show wide range of themed films and to serve areas without easy access to public cinema. Presents over eighty films along with their associated notes, personal introductions and discussions.

QUICKFLICK WORLD LONDON

E   nick@qfworld.tv
W   www.qfworld.tv

A global digital film festival held simultaneously once a month in cities across the globe. Each festival has a theme and a set technical parameter. The finished films are then screened and critiqued.

RAI INTERNATIONAL FESTIVAL OF ETHNOGRAPHIC FILM

Royal Anthropological Institute 50 Fitzroy Street London W1T 5BT
T   020 7387 0455
F   020 7388 8817
E   film@therai.org.uk
W   www.raifilmfest.org.uk

Contacts
Susanne Hammacher *RAI Film Officer, Festival Manager*

Biennial festival specializing in international ethnographic documentary and anthropological filmmaking. Features screenings, workshops, talks and exhibitions.

Submissions Policy
Unsolicited applications welcomed via email/website.

RAINDANCE FILM FESTIVAL

81 Berwick Street London W1F 8TW
T   0207 287 3833
F   0207 439 2243
E   info@raindance.co.uk
W   www.raindance.co.uk

Contacts
Elliot Grove *Founder*

International festival screening around 90 feature films and documentaries and 150 shorts. Founded in 1993, the event has previously hosted UK premieres of *Pulp Fiction*, *Blair Witch Project* and *Memento*. Held annually for 12 days in September/October.

RUSHES SOHO SHORTS FESTIVAL

E   info@sohoshorts.com
W   www.sohoshorts.com

Annual event for both established filmmakers and newcomers. Founded in 1999 and now receives over 2,000 entries from around the globe. Films must be no longer than 12mins without credits and should be submitted on both DVD and Beta Tape. (SAE required for return). Awards festival held in Leicester Square and the main venue is the Curzon Cinema in Soho.

SAND-SWANSEA ANIMATION DAY

SAND Office Swansea Institute of Higher Education Mount Pleasant Swansea West Glamorgan SA1 6ED
T   01792 481194
E   sand@sihe.ac.uk
W   www.sand.org.uk

Founded in 2000, an international CGI (computer generated imagery) event which includes a conference, workshops, seminars and film screenings. Tailored primarily for the Creative IP Industries and individuals interested in animation and digital media. Held annually over 5 days.

SHEFFIELD DOCFEST

The Workstation Paternoster Row Sheffield S1 2BX
T   0114 272 5141
F   0114 276 1849
E   info@sidf.co.uk
W   www.sheffdocfest.com

Contacts
Heather Croall *Director*

Established in 1994, the programme includes public screenings, pitching competitions and networking events. Among the workshop activities are a 'Student DocDay Afternoon' and a Newcomers Day for aspiring filmmakers. Also hosts 'MeetMarket', an event matching documentary makers with UK and international buyers. Recent films featured include *Black Gold* and *A Crude Awakening*. Held annually, the festival lasts between 4 and 7 days.

Submissions Policy
Unsolicited applications are welcomed through an online submission process.

SHOWCOMOTION YOUNG PEOPLE'S FILM FESTIVAL

Showroom Cinema Paternoster Row Sheffield S1 2BX
T   0114 276 3534
F   0114 249 3204
E   info@showcomotion.org.uk
W www.showcomotion.org.uk

Contacts
Kathy Loizou *Festival Director*

Founded in 1998, the festival screens short and feature films for young people from across the world. Incorporates talks and discussions, workshops, premieres and award ceremonies. Past films featured include *Hoodwinked*, *Offside*, *Eat Dog Cat Mouse* and *Midsummer Dream*. The festival is also host to the Showcomotion Children's Media Conference, bringing together producers, broadcasters, filmmakers and commissioners. Held annually in July, lasting for two weeks.

Submissions Policy
A call for submissions is made in January but entries are accepted all year round.

SIGNALS INTERNATIONAL SHORT FILM FESTIVAL

Victoria Chambers St Runwald Street Colchester CO1 1HF
T   01206 560 255
F   01206 369 086
E   info@signals.org.uk
W www.signals.org.uk

Contacts
Andy Roshay *Director*

Short film festival running yearly for six days. Established in 2005. Includes screenings, talks, exhibitions, workshops and an awards ceremony. Scheduled for 7–12 October 2008.

Submissions Policy
Unsolicited material accepted via email.

SUPER SHORTS

E   admin@supershorts.org.uk
W www.supershorts.org.uk

Over 700 short films shown across London venues. Films then go on a national tour.

SUTTON FILM FESTIVAL

10 Endale Close Carshalton Surrey SM5 2HB
T   020 8669 0855
E   info@suttonfilmfestival.co.uk
W www.suttonfilmfestival.co.uk

Contacts
Marq English *Organiser*

One-day festival founded in 2002 to showcase new film talent. Includes screenings and networking events. Encourages all genres of short films alongside music promos, documentaries and trailers. Scheduled for autumn 2008.

Submissions Policy
Submissions via email/letter. No phone calls.

UK BRASILIAN FILM FESTIVAL

5 Durham Yard Unit 10 Teesdale Street London E2 6QF
T   020 7729 1332
E   info@somethingfrombrasil.org
W www.somethingfrombrasil.org

Festival celebrating the diversity of Brazilian films and paying homage to Black Brazilian cinema. Programme includes features, medium-length films and shorts covering a broad panorama of documentary, fiction and experimental formats.

UK JEWISH FILM FESTIVAL

Finsbury Business Centre 40 Bowling Green Lane London EC1R 0NE
T   020 7415 7178
E   info@ukjff.org.uk
W www.ukjewishfilmfestival.org.uk

Founded in 1997 in Brighton, home of the founder, Judy Ironside. In 2003 the festival went to eight venues including Bristol, Birmingham, Manchester and Glasgow and has subsequently become a national event. Screenings are often accompanied by visiting directors and speakers.

VIVA! SPANISH FILM FEST

w   www.vivafilmfestival.com

Founded in 1995, showcasing Spanish and Latin American features, shorts and documentaries. All films are in Spanish with English subtitles.

WATERSHED

1 Canon's Road Harbourside Bristol
BS1 5TX
T   0117 927 6444
F   0117 921 3958
E   bulletin@watershed.co.uk
w   www.watershed.co.uk

Contacts
Anja Datton *Communications Coordinator*

Founded in 1982, a dedicated media centre that hosts a variety of events such as the Encounters Short Film Festival, the Depict! Awards for Short Films and a Japan Film Season. Also home to the Bristol Screenwriters' Group.

WILDSCREEN FESTIVAL

Ground Floor The Rackhay Queen Charlotte Street Bristol BS1 4HJ
T   0117 328 5950
F   0117 328 5955
E   info@wildscreen.org.uk
w   www.wildscreenfestival.org

Founded in 1982 to encourage and applaud technical excellence in film, television and interactive productions about the natural world. Held every 2 years.

Submissions Policy
Refer to website for submission information.

WOOD GREEN INTERNATIONAL SHORT FILM FESTIVAL

Film and Video Workshop Hungerford School Hungerford Road London N7 9LF
T   020 7607 8660
E   lou@filmworkshop.com
w   www.woodgreenfilmfestival.com

Founded in 2003, showing a selection of films and specialist programmes over three days. Focuses on short films of 5–10 minutes.

WOW! WALES ONE WORLD FESTIVAL

Taliesin Arts Centre University of Wales Swansea
T   01239 615066
F   01239 615066
E   sa3657@eclipse.co.uk
w   www.wowfilmfestival.org

Founded in 2002, with over 30 different films from around the world. Held at various venues throughout Wales.

CANADA

THE 3 AMERICAS FILM FESTIVAL

E   festival@fc3a.com
w   www.fc3a.com

Five-day festival held in Quebec City, showcasing films from across the Americas with a focus particularly on independent films.

Submissions Policy
Submissions welcomed through the website.

ANTIMATTER UNDERGROUND FILM FESTIVAL

636 Yates Street Victoria British Columbia
V8W 1L3
T   250 385 3327
F   250 385 3327
E   info@antimatter.ws
w   www.antimatter.ws

Contacts
Deborah de Boer *Curator*

Founded in 1998. Dedicated to the exhibition and nurturing of film and video as art.

Showcases all genres of experimental film
(primarily shorts), through screenings,
installations, performances and media hybrids.
Strives to be completely free from commercial
and industry agendas. Runs annually for
9 days. Scheduled for 26th September–4th
October 2008.

Submissions Policy
Unsolicited applications welcomed via email.

ATLANTIC FILM FESTIVAL, HALIFAX

PO Box 36139 Halifax Nova Scotia B3J 3S9
T 902 422 3456
F 902 422 4006
E festival@atlanticfilm.com
W www.atlanticfilm.com

Founded 1980 and held annually in September.
Screenings run alongside a 'Strategic Partners'
co-production conference, the 'alfresco
filmFesto' outdoor summer film series and
several industry panel, discussion, master class
and lecture initiatives. Sister project for young
people, 'ViewFinders: International Film
Festival for Youth', takes place annually in
April.

Submissions Policy
Script submissions encouraged. Application via
website.

BANFF MOUNTAIN FILM FESTIVAL

The Banff Centre Box 1020 Banff Alberta
T1L 1H5
T 403 762 6100
F 403 762 6444
E arts_info@banffcentre.ca
W www.banffcentre.ca

One-week festival held annually, founded in
1975. Screens around 50 short films with a
focus on high-adrenaline mountain stories. Also
presents talks, shows and discussion
opportunities with top filmmakers and
adventurers. Prize-money for competitions up
to CA$4,000. Later tours 30 countries with a
total audience of more than 170,000 people.

Submissions Policy
Submissions welcomed. Details and deadlines
on the website.

BANFF WORLD TELEVISION FESTIVAL

W www.bwtvf.com

Television festival established in 1980.
Focused on the development of business
and creative opportunities for those
in television programming. Features
seminars, master classes, pitching
opportunities and the high-profile
Banff World Television Awards
(in Partnership with Alberta Film).

CALGARY INTERNATIONAL FILM FESTIVAL

Suite 210 308-11 Avenue S.E. Calgary
Alberta T2G 0Y2
T 403 283 1490
F 403 283 1498
E info@calgaryfilm.com
W www.calgaryfilm.com

Established in 1999 as a non-profit
organization. Aims to provide an
annual world-class cinema event
for the citizens of Calgary and the
surrounding area.

CANADIAN COMEDY FESTIVAL AND AWARDS

E info@canadiancomedyawards.ca
W www.canadiancomedyawards.ca

Celebration of the best Canadian
comedic talent in stand-up, television
and film. Held annually in London,
Ontario by The Comedy Network.
Features four days of stand-up shows,
workshops and awards.

CANADIAN FILM CENTRE'S WORLDWIDE SHORT FILM FESTIVAL

T 416 445 1446 ext. 81
E shortfilmfest@cdnfilmcentre.com
W www.worldwideshortfilmfest.com

Held annually in Toronto. Activities
include screenings of international short
films, a symposium on short filmmaking
and an awards ceremony. Features Screenplay
Giveaway Prize with winner receiving
prizes worth $100,000. Held in June, lasting
six days.

CANADIAN FILMMAKER'S FESTIVAL

E   info@canfilmfest.ca
W   www.canfilmfest.ca

Non-profit organization devoted to
the celebration, promotion and
advancement of Canadian filmmakers.
Exclusively features Canadian films
and provides valuable showcasing
and networking opportunities for
homegrown talent.

CINEFEST – SUDBURY INTERNATIONAL FILM FESTIVAL

47 Durham Street Sudbury Ontario P3E 3M2
T   705 688 1234
F   705 688 1351
W   www.cinefest.com

Established in 1989, screening more
than 100 films each year including
domestic and international productions,
films from Northern Ontario and aboriginal
productions.

Submissions Policy
Submissions are welcomed via the website.

DAWSON CITY INTERNATIONAL SHORT FILM FESTIVAL

T   867 993 5005
E   dawsonarts@yknet.ca
W   www.kiac.org/filmfest

Founded in 1999, screening over 60 films each
year. Other events include workshops, guest
speakers and panel discussions.

EDMONTON INTERNATIONAL FILM FESTIVAL

#201 10816A – 82 Avenue Edmonton Alberta
T6E 2B3
T   780 423 0844
F   780 447 5242
E   info@edmontonfilmfest.com
W   www.edmontonfilmfest.com

Held annually for nine days in October.
Emphasis placed on 'discovery'. Features
a mix of feature-length films, light
documentaries and short films from around
the world.

FANTASY WORLDWIDE FILM FESTIVAL

37 Langford Avenue Upper Level Toronto
Ontario M4J 3E4
T   416 406 2224
F   416 406 2224
E   info@fantasyworldwide.com
W   www.fantasyworldwide.com

Contacts
Johanna Kern *Executive Director*

Festival launched in February 2005 to promote
fantasy filmmaking in Canada and around the
world. Includes screenings, seminars and award
ceremonies. Interested in feature films, shorts,
documentaries and animation focusing on
world mythology, fantasy (no horror),
mysticism, magical realism, science fiction,
historical fiction, legend and artetype. Runs
annually in October for 3–5 days.

Submissions Policy
Welcomes submissions via email. All
filmmakers from beginner to veteran
encouraged to apply.

FREEZE FRAME INTERNATIONAL FESTIVAL OF FILMS FOR KIDS OF ALL AGES

465-70 rue Arthur Street Winnipeg Manitoba
R3B 1G7
T   204 943 5341
F   204 957 5437
E   info@freezeframeonline.org
W   www.freezeframeonline.org

Provides film screenings and video production
workshops for kids and teens. Goes on tour
and runs a family film day, showing an hour
of international animated shorts followed by
a 3-hour animation workshop.

FUTURE SHORTS CANADA

44 Charles Street West #1212 Toronto
Ontario M4Y 1R7
T   416 915 9585
E   jasper@futureshorts.ca
W   www.futureshorts.com

Aims to develop a wider audience for short
film. Currently screening in Toronto but soon
expanding to Halifax, Vancouver and
Montreal.

GIGGLESHORTS

T 416 924 7201
E giggles@giggleshorts.com
W www.giggleshorts.com

Festival of international comedy shorts, held at the Brunswick Theatre in Toronto.

HOT DOCS CANADIAN INTERNATIONAL DOCUMENTARY FESTIVAL

110 Spadina Avenue Suite 333 Toronto
Ontario M5V 2K4
T 416 203 2155
F 416 203 0446
W www.hotdocs.ca

North America's largest documentary festival, founded in 1993. Annually shows over 100 cutting-edge domestic and international documentaries. Runs industry programmes to promote professional development, and market and networking opportunities for documentary professionals. Also hosts the Toronto Documentary Forum, a limited-seating international market event for buyers and sellers.

IMAGE AND NATION: MONTRÉAL INTERNATIONAL LGBT FILM FESTIVAL

#404 4067 Boulevard St. Laurent Montréal
Québec H2W 1Y7
T 514 285 4467
F 514 285 1562
E info@image-nation.org
W www.image-nation.org

Contacts
Katharine Setzer *Director of Programming*

Lesbian, gay, bisexual and transgender festival founded in 1987. Screens feature length, short and documentary films along with filmmaker talks and special presentations. Interested in film works from all genres made by and for an LGBT audience. Does accept television productions upon occasion. Past screening examples include *20 Centimetres* by Ramon Salazar (2006) and *Reinas* by Manuel Gomez Pereira (2006). Takes place annually over 11 days. Scheduled for 13th-23rd November 2008.

Submissions Policy
Unsolicited applications welcomed via email or website.

INSIDEOUT – THE TORONTO LESBIAN AND GAY FILM AND VIDEO FESTIVAL

219–401 Richmond Street West Toronto
Ontario M5V 3A8
E inside@insideout.ca
W www.insideout.on.ca

Held over 11 days in May, promoting film and video by or about lesbian, gay, bisexual and transsexual people. Hosts screenings, artist talks, installations and discussions, featuring more than 275 films and videos from across the world.

MONTREAL INTERNATIONAL FESTIVAL OF NEW CINEMA & MEDIA (FESTIVAL DU NOUVEAU CINÉMA DE MONTRÉAL)

3805 Boulevard Saint-Laurent Montréal
Quebec H2W 1X9
T 514 282 0004
F 514 282 6664
E info@nouveaucinema.ca
W www.nouveaucinema.ca

Founded in 1971, aims to be a forum for audiences to discover original new works, particularly in cinéma d'auteur and digital creation. Features over 300 works from more than 40 countries.

MONTREAL WORLD FILM FESTIVAL

1432 de Bleury Street Montréal Québec
H3A 2J1
T 514 848 3883
F 514 848 3886
E info@ffm-montreal.org
W www.ffm-montreal.org

Aims to be a forum for quality cinema from around the world. Includes jury-chosen awards and People's Choice awards (for most popular Canadian film, best film from Latin America, best documentary and best Canadian short).

NICKEL INDEPENDENT FILM FESTIVAL

PO Box 1644 Stn. C St John's Newfoundland
A1C 5P3
T   709 576 FEST
E   inckelfestival@yahoo.ca
W   www.nickelfestival.com

Contacts
Baptiste Neis *President*

Festival for independent film founded in 2000.
Showcases film and video of all lengths and
genres once a year, usually in the last week of
June for five days. Includes screenings,
workshops, awards, Q&A, musical
entertainment, master classes and readings.
Scheduled for 26–30th June 2008.

Submissions Policy
Submissions welcomed via
www.withoutabox.com.

NSI FILMEXCHANGE CANADIAN FILM FESTIVAL

Suite 400 141 Bannatyne Avenue Winnipeg
Manitoba R3B 0R3
T   204 956 7800
F   204 956 5811
E   filmexchange@nsi-canada.ca
W   www.nsi-canada.ca/filmexchange

Annual celebration of Canadian screen
achievement, bringing together writers,
producers, directors and executives with
emerging talent. Shows features and shorts and
runs numerous events including masterclasses,
competitions, discussions and networking
events. Also operates SnowScreen, an outdoor
10 x 8 foot movie screen made of snow.

OTTAWA INTERNATIONAL ANIMATION FESTIVAL

2 Daly Avenue Suite 120 Ottawa Ontario
K1N 6E2
T   613 232 8769
F   613 232 6315
E   info@animationfestival.ca
W   www.ottawa.awn.com

Largest animation event of its kind in North
America. Events include screenings, panels,
workshops and parties.

PLANET IN FOCUS: INTERNATIONAL ENVIRONMENTAL FILM AND VIDEO FESTIVAL

455 Spadina Avenue Suite 304 Toronto
Ontario M5S 2G8
T   416 531 1769
F   416 531 8985
E   information@planetinfocus.org
W   www.planetinfocus.org

Contacts
Kim Haladay *Administative and Development
Co-ordinator*

Environmental film and video festival
founded in 1999. Features over 50 screenings
along with workshops, round table
discussions, pitch sessions, awards ceremonies
and talks. Recently screened films include
Conflict Tiger (animal rights documentary)
and *Terra* (short animation). Runs annually
for one week. Scheduled for 24–28th
October 2008.

Submissions Policy
Unsolicited applications welcomed. Details on
website.

REELWORLD FILM FESTIVAL

438 Parliament Street Suite 300 Toronto
Ontario
T   416 598 7933
F   416 585 2524
W   www.reelworld.ca

Festival celebrating diversity in
international filmmaking. Provides
screenings, seminars, workshops and
special events. Run in conjunction with
the ReelWorld Foundation.

TORONTO AFTER DARK FILM FESTIVAL

3219 Yonge Street Suite 346 Toronto Ontario
M4N 3S1
E   info@torontoafterdark.com
W   www.torontoafterdark.com

A week-long showcase of new
international horror, sci-fi, fantasy
and thrillers (features and shorts). Held
in October.

TORONTO INTERNATIONAL FILM FESTIVAL

2 Carlton Street Suite 1600 Toronto Ontario
M5B 1J3
T 416 967 7371
W www.tiffg.ca

Founded in the 1970s and now a major festival
on the world stage.

Submissions Policy
Films may be submitted via form available on
website.

TORONTO INTERNATIONAL LATIN FILM FESTIVAL

100 Seaton Street Toronto Ontario M5A 2T3
T 416 364 3131
F 416 359 9238
E info@tilff.com
W www.tilff.com

Festival presenting mostly independent films
from Latin America, Southern Europe and
Quebec. Held annually in October, lasting
eight days.

Submissions Policy
Welcomes submissions through the website.

TORONTO JEWISH FILM FESTIVAL

17 Madison Avenue Toronto Ontario
M5R 2S2
T 416 324 9121
F 416 324 8668
E tjff@tjff.ca
W www.tjff.ca

Aims to showcase Jewish culture, heritage
and the diversity of the Jewish experience in
Canada and around the world via the medium
of cinema. Includes feature films,
documentaries and shorts.

TORONTO REEL ASIAN INTERNATIONAL FILM FESTIVAL

401 Richmond Street West Suite 309 Toronto
Ontario M5V 3A8
T 416 703 9333
F 416 703 9986
E info@reelasian.com
W www.reelasian.com

Established in 1997, showcasing contemporary
Asian cinema and work from the Asian
diaspora. Annual event lasting five days,
offering screenings, forums, workshops and
galas. Festival also spotlights one Canadian
artist from the Asian filmmaking community
each year.

VANCOUVER ASIAN FILM FESTIVAL

455 Prior Street Vancouver British Columbia
V6A 2G3
W www.vaff.org

Aims to promote independent North American
Asian filmmakers and to act as a springboard
to bigger film festivals. Committed to
supporting both emerging and established
artists. Held annually in November.

VANCOUVER INTERNATIONAL FILM FESTIVAL

W www.viff.org

Founded in 1981, over 150,000 people attend
almost 600 screenings of films from more than
50 countries. Also runs a film and television
forum with many leading names in the field.

Submissions Policy
Submission forms available from website.

VANCOUVER INTERNATIONAL JEWISH FILM FESTIVAL

6184 Ash Street Vancouver British Columbia
V5Z 3G9
T 604 266 0245
F 604 266.0244
W www.vijff.com

Screens around fifty films from across the
world, including new films and classics of
Jewish interest. Also features awards ceremony,
panel discussions and gala events.

VANCOUVER QUEER FILM FESTIVAL

Out On Screen 405–207 West Hastings Street
Vancouver British Columbia V6B 1H7
T 604 844 1615
F 604 844 1698
W www.outonscreen.com

Festival promoting the production and
exhibition of independent queer media art.

Hosts free professional development workshops.

VANCOUVER STUDENT FILM FESTIVAL

w   www.vsff.com

Established in 2005, screening films by student filmmakers and graduates from Vancouver. Aims to raise awareness of young talent throughout the area.

THE VICTORIA INDEPENDENT FILM AND VIDEO FESTIVAL

808 View Street Victoria British Columbia V8W 1K2
T   250 389 0444
F   250 389 0406
E   festival@vifvf.com
w   www.vifvf.com

Contacts
Donovan Aikman *Programmer*

Founded in 1995. Runs annually for 10 days. Scheduled for 1st-10th February 2008. Screens over 140 films including 50 features. Includes an international film co-production financing conference (Trigger Points Pacific) alongside parties, gala openings and master classes. Features narrative, documentary, experimental and animation films from Canada and around the world.

Submissions Policy
Unsolicited applications welcomed with official entry form.

WORLD OF COMEDY FILM FESTIVAL

T   416 487 7574
E   info@worldcomedyfilmfest.com
w   www.worldcomedyfilmfest.com

Held in Toronto during March, celebrating the comedy film. Mixture of new movies from around the world and old classics. Also serves as an industry marketplace and networking event.

WORLDWIDE SHORT FILM FESTIVAL

E   shortfilmfest@cfccreates.com
w   www.worldwideshortfilmfest.com

Major festival of short films from Canada and around the world.

IRELAND

CORK FILM FESTIVAL

Emmet House Emmet Place Cork
T   021 427 1711
F   021 427 5945
E   info@corkfilmfest.org
w   www.corkfilmfest.org

Contacts
Eimear O'Herlihy *Festival Manager*

Founded in 1956. Includes screenings, features, documentaries, shorts, workshops and seminars, an awards ceremony and 'meet the film-maker' events. Shows films of all genres, including fiction, documentary, experimental and student. Special focus on gay and lesbian films. Held annually and lasts for 8 days.

Submissions Policy
Welcomes unsolicited applications. Entry forms are available on-line each year from January to June.

CORK YOUTH INTERNATIONAL FILM ARTS FESTIVAL

Coláiste Stiofáin Naofa Tramore Road Cork City
T   021 4273526
F   021 4306019
E   ftfranwc@eircom.net

Established in 1980, a festival of film for the young, especially those involved in youth clubs, schools and community groups.

DARK LIGHT DIGITAL FESTIVAL

69 Dame Street Dublin 2
T   01 670 9017
E   contact@darklight-filmfestival.com
w   www.darklight-filmfestival.com

Established in 1999, screening short films, feature films, animation, mobile films and documentaries. Ranges from student films to household-name directors.

DUBLIN INTERNATIONAL FILM FESTIVAL

Filmbase Curved Street Temple Bar Dublin 2
T   01 635 0290
E   info@dubliniff.com
W   www.dubliniff.com

Founded in 2002, screening films from around the world.

FRESH FILM FESTIVAL

69 O'Connell Street Limerick
T   061 319 555
F   061 319 555
E   info@freshfilmfestival.net
W   www.freshfilmfestival.net

Founded in 1997, aimed at young people up to the age of 18. Includes a competition for films made by children aged 7 to 18, and screens feature films for schools with study guides. Held for a week during spring.

Submissions Policy
Welcomes unsolicited applications and prefers to be contacted via email.

GALWAY FILM FLEADH

Cluain Mhuire Monivea Road Galway
T   091 751 655
F   091 735 831
E   gafleadh@iol.ie
W   www.galwayfilmfleadh.com

Contacts
Miriam Allen *Managing Director*

Founded in 1988, including screenings, talks, workshops, award ceremony and film fair. Screens films of all genres. A 6-day event held annually.

Submissions Policy
Does not accept unsolicited applications.

KERRY FILM FESTIVAL

Samhlaiocht The Old Presbytery Lower Castle Street Tralee County Kerry
W   www.kerryfilmfestival.com

Screens animation films, short documentaries, short narratives and student films. The main feature of the festival is a short film competition, which focuses on young filmmakers.

Submissions Policy
A synopsis of 100 words must be submitted with the application form.

MOVIES ON THE SQUARE

12 East Essex Street Temple Bar Dublin 2
T   01 677 2255
F   01 677 2525
E   info@templebar.ie
W   www.templebar.ie

Contacts
Grainne Millar *Head of Cultural Development*

Founded in 1999, a 12-week programme of free outdoor movies screened at the Temple Bar on Saturday nights. Also runs a short film award competition. Screens an eclectic mix of films ranging from musicals to black and white classics.

Submissions Policy
Welcomes unsolicited applications. Contact the Cultural Department on 01 677 2255 or via email.

PINTSIZE FILM FESTIVAL

14 St. Stephens Green Dublin 2
E   info@pintsizefilmfest.com
W   www.pintsizefilmfest.com

Dedicated to internet videos, such as those seen on YouTube, Google Video and Myspace.

Submissions Policy
Videos can be entered in the categories of Comedy, Music, Animation, People and Documentary. Should be less than 4 minutes 40 seconds in duration.

AUSTRALIA

ADELAIDE FILM FESTIVAL

12 King William Road Unley SA 5061
T   08 8271 1029
F   08 8271 9905
E   info@adelaidefilmfestival.org
W   www.adelaidefilmfestival.org

Founded in 2003, screening films from over 40 countries. Shows feature films, documentaries, shorts, music videos and animations. Introduced a juried Best Feature Film award in 2007 (cash prize of A$25,000).

THE ALLIANCE FRANÇAISE FRENCH FILM FESTIVAL

257 Clarence Street Sydney NSW 2000
T   02 9267 1755
F   02 9283 2589
W www.afsydney.com.au

Contacts
Pascale Reuter *Cultural Events Assistant*

Francophone festival with over 250 screenings including a wide range of new French films never seen before in Australia. Fosters interaction between Australian and French cultures. Lasts 1 week in March/April.

BRISBANE INTERNATIONAL FILM FESTIVAL

Level 3 The Regent 167 Queen Street Brisbane QLD 4000
E   biff@biff.com.au
W www.biff.com.au

Contacts
Anne Demy-Geroe *Executive Director*

Established in 1991, events include screenings, seminars and awards. Covers international films, films on filmmaking, experimental work and shorts. In previous years the festival has featured films such as *A Prairie Home Companion*, *The Wind that Shakes the Barley* and *U-Carmen eKhayelitsha*. Held annually, the festival lasts 3 weeks.

Submissions Policy
Welcomes unsolicited applications. Tickets are available from website or box office.

FLICKERFEST

PO Box 7416 Bondi Beach Sydney NSW 2026
T   02 9365 6877
F   02 9365 6899
E   coordinator@flickerfest.com.au
W www.flickerfest.com.au

Founded in 1992, Australia's premiere international short film festival. There is

a main competitive programme, a short documentary competition, Australian competition and a number of additional programmes and forums out of competition.

Submissions Policy
Films must be no more than 30 minutes in length. All productions must have been completed within 2 years of the closing date and must be in English or have English subtitles.

MELBOURNE INTERNATIONAL ANIMATION FESTIVAL

PO Box 1024 Collingwood VIC 3066
T   03 9375 1490
F   03 9376 9995
E   info@miaf.net
W www.miaf.net

Founded in 2005, screening about 200 animated films from over 30 countries. Highlights of the festival include many guest artists and visiting animators, both local- and foreign-based. Held annually. See website for submission information.

MELBOURNE INTERNATIONAL FILM FESTIVAL

1st Floor 207 Johnston Street Fitzroy VIC 3065
T   03 9417 2011
F   03 9417 3804
E   miff@melbournefilmfestival.com.au
W www.melbournefilmfestival.com.au

Founded in 1951, showcasing new Australian cinema alongside films from over 50 countries. Held over 19 days each winter.

Submissions Policy
Submission of material is subject to an entry fee. Films made in languages other than English must have English subtitles. No training or advertising films. Films 30 minutes or less are eligible for entry in the Best MIFF Shorts Competition with the exception of the documentary category, which accepts films of 60 minutes or less. Feature films must be Victorian premieres in order to be eligible for screening.

MELBOURNE QUEER FILM FESTIVAL

MQFF Festival Office 6 Claremont St
Sth Yarra VIC 3141
T   03 9827 2022
F   03 9827 1622
E   info@melbournequeerfilm.com.au
W   www.melbournequeerfilm.com.au

Founded in 1991, the festival includes
programmes such as the 'Queeries: Bent
On Film Youth Program'. Shows
international shorts and feature films,
documentaries, foreign language films
and experimental works. Presents the
City of Melbourne Emerging Filmmaker
Award and hosts a series of forums and
lectures. Held annually.

THE REALM OF THE SENSES

E   simon@realmofsenses.com
W   www.realmofsenses.com

Founded in 2001, an outdoor festival
with a primary focus on screening
short films from Australia and New Zealand.
Offers prizes of A$35,000 to the best
three films in competition (films have to
be made in the past 2 years). Held
annually. Email for submission
information.

REVELATION: PERTH INTERNATIONAL FILM FESTIVAL

PO Box 135 South Fremantle
WA 6162
T   08 9335 3904
E   info@revelationfilmfest.org
W   www.revelationfilmfest.org

Contacts
Megan Spencer *Director*

Established in 1997, activities include
workshops, masterclasses, screenings
and talks. Recently featured films
include *Spellbound*, *Ambulance* and
The Aura. Annual event lasting 10 days
in July.

Submissions Policy
Welcomes unsolicited applications. The festival
is ticketed, available from venues.

ST KILDA FILM FESTIVAL

Private Bag 3 Post Office St Kilda
VIC 3182
T   03 9209 6490
E   filmfest@portphillip.vic.gov.au
W   www.stkildafilmfestival.com.au

Founded in 1983, showcasing both
local and international short films. It
screens 100 Australian short films and
hosts international sessions from the
Interfilm Berlin International Short
Film Festival (Germany), Clermont
Ferrand Short Film Festival (France)
and the Sao Paulo International Short
Film Festival (Brazil). Held annually
over 6 days.

SYDNEY INTERNATIONAL FILM FESTIVAL

Suite 102 59 Marlborough Street Surry Hills
NSW 2010
T   02 9318 0999
F   02 9319 0055
E   info@sydneyfilmfestival.org
W   www.sydneyfilmfestival.org

Founded in 1954, screening a variety of films
across genres from over 50 countries. Held over
17 days in June. See website for submission
information.

TRASHARAMA A-GO-GO

PO Box 376 Goodwood SA 5034
E   jero@trasharama.com.au
W   www.trasharama.com.au

Contacts
Jero Cocksmith *Festival*

Touring short film festival established
in 1997. Films under 15 minutes in
length, including 'schlock horror,
cheesy sci-fi, bad taste comedy and
other filmic disasterpieces'. Tours across
Australia, visiting more than 15 cities and
regional areas.

Submissions Policy
Welcomes unsolicited international applications
by email. Event is ticketed and can be bought
at venues.

TROPFEST

62-64 Riley Street East Sydney NSW 2010
T   02 9368 0434
F   02 9360 1594
W   www.tropinc.com

Founded in 1993, a free, public, outdoor, short film festival held in locations across Australia. From more than 800 entries, 16 finalists are selected each year to premiere to an audience of more than 150,000 people via simultaneous satellite screenings in Sydney, Melbourne, Brisbane, Canberra, Perth, Hobart and eight regional locations around Australia. Held annually in February.

Submissions Policy
For submission films must be no longer than seven minutes, must never have been shown publicly before and must contain the Tropfest Signature Item (varies each year; in 2007 it was 'sneeze').

NEW ZEALAND

ALLSHORTS FILM FESTIVAL

PO Box 217 Takaka 7172 Golden Bay
E   allshorts@paradise.net.nz
W   www.allshorts.org.nz

Free festival held in the Village Theatre at Takaka each October. Restricted to New Zealand residents who are thirteen years and over.

Submissions Policy
Any visual content will be considered but should not exceed five minutes and should be submitted on a pal region 0 DVD (along with completed entry form). No prize money but judges choose 20 entries for the 'Festival Selection'.

AUCKLAND INTERNATIONAL FILM FESTIVAL

PO Box 9544 Marion Square Wellington 6141
T   04 385 0162
F   04 801 7304
E   festival@nzff.co.nz

Founded in 1970 as a component of the Auckland Festival. Has over time become a fund-raising event subsidizing live arts. Entry forms and regulations for submitting films are available for download on the website. Volunteer positions are available on application to assist with the festival.

BELLADONNA CANTERBURY SHORT FILM FESTIVAL

PO Box 1351 Christchurch
T   03 365 6151
W   www.belladonna.org.nz

Founded in 2002, held annually in July. Showcases works across genres including documentaries, media art, experimental works, narrative and dance films. All films must be the work of a New Zealand citizen or resident.

Submissions Policy
Drama/documentary films should be no more than 15 minutes in duration and dance/experimental films no more than 10 minutes.

BIG MOUNTAIN SHORT FILM FESTIVAL

PO Box 221 Ohakune 5461
W   www.bigmountain.co.nz

Contacts
Jeff Bollow *Director*

Founded in 2006, events include screenings of 'budget' and 'no budget' short films from around the world, seminars, Q&As and an awards ceremony. Held annually in October, lasting 3 days.

Submissions Policy
Does not welcome unsolicited applications. Festival is free to attend.

DOCNZ FILM FESTIVAL

Level 2 1 College Hill Freemans Bay
Auckland 1011
T   09 309 2613
F   09 309 4084
E   info@docnz.org.nz
W   www.docnz.org.nz

Founded in 2004, an annual international documentary film festival with a competitive element.

Submissions Policy

Accepts documentary films in three different categories: short (less than 30 minutes); medium (30–70 minutes); feature (over 70 minutes). Entries must include a short and long written description of the film (including credits) plus entrant filmography.

HUMAN RIGHTS FILM FESTIVAL

PO Box 24 423 Wellington
T 04 496 9616
E filmfestival@humanrights.net.nz
W www.humanrightsfilmfest.net.nz

Founded in 2005, featuring international and local documentaries and dramatic films with a strong human rights theme. Screenings are followed by a speakers' forum.

Submissions Policy

Accepts submissions of feature films, documentaries and shorts with a strong human rights theme. A synopsis of 80 to 100 words should be included with the entry.

LATIN AMERICAN FILM FESTIVAL

W www.rialto.co.nz

Founded in 2002, screening new and classic Latin American films. The festival is programmed by the ambassadors of relevant countries. All films are screening for the first time in New Zealand.

MAGMA SHORT FILM FESTIVAL

PO Box 6211 Whakarewarewa Rotorua
T 07 349 0029
E info@magmafilm.org.nz
W www.magmafilm.org.nz

Contacts
Kiri Jarden *Director*

Founded in 2006 as a forum for short film in digital media. Held over four days in late November and features contributions from leading NZ actors, filmmakers and production companies. An awards ceremony is held on the last night of the festival. Tickets available on-line, at selected outlets or on the door.

Submissions Policy

Film entries must be accompanied by an official entry form for selection consideration. Showcase films may be submitted by producers/directors not wishing their film to be part of the competition.

SHOW ME SHORTS FILM FESTIVAL TRUST

PO Box 6685 Wellesley Street Auckland 1141
T 02 142 7553
W www.showmeshorts.co.nz

Focus on short films with a strong New Zealand/Australia component.

Submissions Policy

Films of any genre qualify but they should be no less than 3 minutes and no more than 30 minutes long.

THE WAIROA MĀORI FILM FESTIVAL

PO Box 85 Nuhaka 4165
T 06 837 8854
F 06 837 8761
E maorimovies@gmail.com
W www.manawairoa.com

Contacts
Leo Koziol *Festival Director*

Indigenous festival founded in June 2005. Screens films featuring Māori cast and crew. Also workshops and talks with filmmakers, awards night presentations and scholarships for emerging talent. Annual event in June lasting four days.

Submissions Policy

Encourages submissions of feature films, short films and documentaries with an indigenous theme. Applications via email.

WELLINGTON FILM FESTIVAL

PO Box 9544 Marion Square Wellington 6141
T 04 385 0162
F 04 801 7304
E michael@nzff.co.nz
W www.enzedff.co.nz

Annual festival founded in 1972, with a long-standing tradition of supporting New Zealand filmmakers. Presents a non-competitive, invited season of new films, encompassing a wide variety of genres, themes and styles.

Submissions Policy
Films must not have been publicly screened in New Zealand before (requirement waived for invited, archival and retrospective programmes). The organizers prefer 35mm, original language prints (with English subtitles if foreign-language).

WELLINGTON FRINGE FILM FESTIVAL

PO Box 9207 Te Aro Wellington
T   04 938 0219
W www.fringefilmfest.co.nz

Founded in 1987, one of the leading forums for New Zealand filmmakers to show their work. The festival also hosts a special competition to promote originality and innovation within a given theme and time frame.

Submissions Policy
15-minute limit for all drama, animation and experimental films; 30-minute limit for documentaries.

The filmscripts of twenty years ago would, by and large, fail to satisfy modern audiences. Today's cinemagoers pick up hints and allusions with almost frightening speed. Indeed, they resent having a plot set out too plainly. They like to make the links, to interpret the hints, to engage with the story as they would with an interactive game.

David Puttnam

'PLAY IT AGAIN, SAM'
SCREENWRITING IN A VIRTUAL WORLD...

Andrew S. Walsh sees the future and it works

RICK
You know what I want to hear.

SAM
No, I don't.

RICK
You played it for her and you can play it for me.

SAM
Well, I don't think I can remember it.

[*AS SAM HOLDS HIS GAZE, RICK LEANS OVER THE PIANO AND SMASHES HIM IN THE FACE WITH A BOTTLE...*]

Writing for games is not like writing for the silver screen. The worst a cinemagoer can do to a story is to answer their phone, mutter into their popcorn, or walk out. They can't attempt to make Humphrey Bogart kiss Ingrid Bergman, or shoot Victor Laszlo. This is because the viewer is passive.

A game, however, requires a player not a viewer, it demands interaction. A game asks the player to experience the story by walking through it, not view it from the outside. This means the player can – to an extent – dictate how the story is told and even what that story is. In a game Rick could hit Sam for refusing to play 'As Time Goes By'.

Toto, I've a feeling we're not in Kansas anymore

Contrary to the title, this article is not about screenwriting. Screenwriting does not exist in games. Games contain games scripts and are written by gameswriters. The evolution of gameswriting and writers is a new phenomenon and it has arisen as those working in games have realized that the comfy Kansas world of the screenplay has been picked up by a twister and dropped into a world where magic is real and nothing is what it seems.

As the stunned screenwriter gets to his feet surrounded by Munchkins and bits of relocated housing, to get his bearings he must repeat the simple mantra 'viewers view, but players play'. This will lead to the next step in converting from screen to game, the realisation that while it is a general truth that the most important thing in a movie is the script...this is not the case in games. In games the most important thing is gameplay. Without gameplay a game is not a 'game'.

This means that any story and dialogue appearing in a game must serve the gameplay first and the narrative second. Whilst this might be a terrifying thought, it does not mean that story is unimportant; many of the big-selling titles of the gameworld are story driven, or story centred. Story serving gameplay does not have to be a direct conflict, rather a happy alliance. When well combined the two elements of story and game bring out the best in each other and create an incredible experience – a story you can step into.

Give me a camera and a place to stand and I can move the world

When the first films to tell stories were shot they used a static camera shooting a single set, to all intents and purposes they were stage plays with a camera placed in front of them. Then, as technology and the craft of screenwriting developed so came the cut, sound, colour, the steadicam and from a medium that was seen as novelty was born a new way of telling stories, separate from books, separate from theatre...'The Movies'.

Eighty years later along came games. Purely visual at first, games evolved to include text-based adventures, the first story-driven games. Written in the style of a novel these games were essentially books chopped into paragraphs which allowed the reader a few different ways to move through the story (turn left/turn right, shoot the girl/kiss the girl) and allowed the reader the feeling of control. Later as the power of machines increased and game graphics improved, so story and pictures could be combined.

With the introduction of animated graphics the games industry assumed that they could tell stories in the same way as they were told in movies. Games including stories took linear narratives, chopped them into small packets and presented them interspersed on either side of sections of gameplay. These linear narrative scenes are called cutscenes and are defined by the fact that the player cannot control them; in essence, they are sections of a movie. The addition of cutscenes to games had the advantage of presenting players with a story while showing off the best graphics and offering the originating company a chance to reinforce or create an IP (Intellectual Property) which it could market and protect. However, such non-interactive linear scenes have many drawbacks. Just as shooting a single set with a static camera would not provide the world with *Gone with the Wind* or *Citizen Kane*, neither would cutscenes bring out the true potential of gameswriting.

It's alive! It's alive!

By 1942, the film industry had evolved from its single shot beginnings so when *Casablanca*, a film based upon the stage play *Everybody Comes to Rick's*, was made there was no thought of simply shooting the playscript. Instead, the play was adapted and rewritten to meet the demands of the filmmakers and their audience. Similarly, gameswriting techniques have evolved beyond limiting a game's story to chopped-up sections of movie that are separate from the gameplay. While the cutscene remains an important tool for gameswriters, gameswriting is evolving subtler ways of storytelling that allow the two elements of gameplay and narrative to intermix. Just as film moved away from shooting stageplays, so games have moved away from imposing the strictures of screenwriting upon games.

Houston, we have a problem

While the screenwriter may master the short film, the novella and the feature while playing with different genres and methods to explore the narrative, the way the story is delivered is always the same. Movies are watched by an audience on a screen. Games do not have this single form.

Platforms

A 'platform' is the hardware upon which games are played. This could be an arcade machine, a mobile phone, a games console, a

PC, or a handheld device, to name but a few of the game-delivery platforms. Each of these platforms has its own intrinsic strengths and weaknesses that change the way that a game and its story may be experienced. While games consoles such as an X-Box 360 or Playstation 3 deliver the latest stunning graphics and complex AI (Artificial Intelligence) capable of allowing the game to respond to the player's every move, mobile phones offer games similar to those available on personal computers twenty years ago, with dialogue appearing as text and a limited series of choices (interactions) for the player. This means that the differences between writing for one platform and another may be as broad as those between writing a novel and a screenplay, yet both fall within the sphere of gameswriting. As gameswriters are likely to write across a wide variety of platforms during their career, they will need to learn the strengths and weaknesses of the platforms they work with if they are to write the best scripts for each.

Games Genre

Once the writer has begun to establish the technical limitations and opportunities offered by the platform for which a game is being developed, there is a second key element to take into account before starting work. Before narrative genre, the gameswriter must first examine the game genre. This will change not only the style of story, but also the way in which it can be told. When conceiving a sports game, the game designer (responsible for devising how a game works and how it interacts with the player) will create an experience as close to the real sport as possible. Time will be taken up with working out how to create a realistic, enjoyable and playable scissor kick rather than designing a complex speech engine to deliver the writer's sparkling lines. (A speech engine is that part of the game specifically tasked with delivering speech.)

Another thing worth noting is that sports games rarely have a story, though they will often contain large amounts of commentary dialogue demanding a lot of writing. Unlike the movies, games can exist with no narrative and no characters, or employ both in complex ways. A MMORPG (Massively Multiplayer Online Role-Playing Game), on the other hand, will demand a vast amount of world and character design. Players enter a free-form storyworld in which they can easily play forty hours a week for several years. The games genre therefore effects how writers can tell their story and the tools they will have to do that.

The list below will give you an idea of the major categories of game genre.

- *Role-playing games (RPGs)*. Here the player takes on a role in order to go on a quest. The narrative genre can be fantasy, sci-fi or more down to earth. These are the most dialogue-heavy type of game. *Fable*, for example, has 200,000 or more lines of dialogue. The RPGs are amongst the longest in terms of their length of gameplay and the game's narrative.
- *Action games*. These can have a tiny amount of writing (*Doom 3*, *Mortal Combat*), or they can have their own movie style storyline (*Metalgear Solid*).
- *Sims* (short for simulation) put the player in control of an element of life, be it controlling a city (*SimCity*), running a railway system (*Railway Tycoon*), or managing someone's life (*The Sims*).
- *Strategy games* are generally militarily-oriented. They pit the player against the platform, or against other players. Some are turn-based, others take place in real time (RTS – Real-Time Strategy games).
- *Platform games* range from 2D side-scrollers to newer 3D.
- *Sports*. Players engage with their favourite sports as a player, a team or a manager. These games often have commentaries even when there is no interaction between the characters.
- *Racing games*. Many racing games take an approach that is more *Fast and Furious* than Formula One sports games. These sometimes have background stories and dialogue within them (the *Driver* series).
- *Flight Sims*. Pilot a Sopwith, a 747 or a starcruiser. There is often little or no dialogue and rarely a story or characters.
- *Children's games*. Niche versions of the above, generally with lower budgets and often with text rather than spoken word.

Gameswriting, therefore, must take account of the differences that exist in a wide and varied set of platforms and games genres before considering narrative genre, character, plot and other skills central to more established media.

The greatest event in motion picture history – starring a hundred elephants!

Why does a platform and games genre affect storytelling? Surely anything and everything can be done in a game? If a game is about sports, why can't there be complex speech? Beyond matters of choice and relevance, there is a simple fact that many non-gameswriters ignore or simply don't realise…most games are very expensive to create.

The reason for this is simple. As games take place in a virtual world, *everything* in that world must be created. Before a hundred elephants can be added to a game they must be designed, drawn and animated. The ground, the trees and sky surrounding the elephants must be generated. If the elephants can touch an object then each object must have a relevant animation and sound effect so as to react as if touched. If the object falls over, the game's physics engine must be able to make the object bounce or land on the ground rather than fall through the floor, shoot into the sky or simply fail to react. The game's AI system must understand when to trigger these animations and sounds as well as what the consequences of this will be, i.e. a loud noise might be 'heard' by a guard and bring him running.

Adding an elephant to a game and making it interact with the virtual world is a complex and therefore expensive process. Expense leads to decisions about what will and will not be included in a game. This is one reason why in some games where characters can jump they cannot talk and in others they are verbose, but unable to jump or climb.

Part of a gameswriter's job is to hide games design limitations and to make them appear normal within the gameworld. Consequently, the writer has two jobs. First, he must use his skill to disguise the gameplay by making it part of the narrative. This can be achieved by making the need to inform players of what they must do within the game – the need to attack a fortification, kiss the girl, or save Victor Laszlo – blend into the story. In other cases, it means finding story reasons to make the game's design demand for a level involving, say, motorbikes, fit with the characters and the narrative. The second part of the gameswriter's job is to service the narrative. Good designers will understand the need to reorder or rework gameplay elements if it makes the story (and therefore the game) a better experience.

When design and story work together the result is a game such as *Halflife*, where the story and gameplay cannot be extricated. They are interwoven to make one uniform experience...and one that sold a lot of copies.

You talkin' to me?

The most obvious way to interweave narrative and gameplay is to place story information within the levels themselves rather than limit the story to moviestyle cutscenes. Such interweaving is most often achieved through the game's dialogue. This takes many different forms, each of which changes the way a story is told and the game experienced.

- *Cutscene dialogue*. Contained within small pre-recorded and structured sections, cutscenes remove control from the player to deliver information. These sections are the part of gamewriting that is closest to screenwriting, but can distance the player from the story as they are separate from the gameplay.
- *Timed dialogue*. This dialogue starts following a particular event, i.e. a character opening a door, and runs through from start to finish as a recorded piece. Gameplay continues, but the player's actions will not affect the dialogue, merely trigger it.
- *Interactive dialogue*. In some games the player is able to hold conversations with other characters. Such dialogue often gives the player options as to how the conversation can proceed and will respond to the player's actions and decisions.
- *Barks*. These are short lines such as orders, pain response, taunts, etc. They are triggered by the player's actions and are responsive to the player's interaction with the game.
- *Incidental dialogue*. This dialogue is placed in the world to make it feel alive. For example, as the player's character walks down a street, she might hear other people holding conversations, or reacting to the way the character looks or behaves.

The sorts of dialogue options available to the gameswriter are predetermined by the game's speech engine and the complexity of its AI.

I'm sorry, Dave, I'm afraid I can't do that

One of the crucial elements in advanced writing models is Artificial Intelligence. A game's AI system not only allows characters to react to game events but describes how the game understands the player's actions and how it must respond to them. Early AI models were full of holes. One oft-quoted problem was with games where a player could shoot one of a pair of guards without the second guard reacting or, indeed, noticing the death of his companion. More advanced and well-implemented AI models allow characters to anticipate a player's moves and to react to the player's actions. This means that game characters are imbued with intelligence and senses, i.e. guards can see characters who are in the wrong place, or hear a noise and react to it. The more complex the AI model, the greater is the range of ways the story can be told since the characters and game are more capable of responding to the gameplayers' actions and the world they are creating within the game.

Here's Johnny!

Games characters break down into two groups, one controlled by the player, the other controlled by the game's AI system:

- *PC.* The player takes the role of a Player Character (PC). There may be a single PC in a game or the player maybe able to move between different characters (sometimes the different members of the PC's team/party) or there may be a number of PCs played by different players within the same game.
- *NPC.* Characters who are not controlled by a player are termed Non-Player Characters (NPCs). These can be enemies, allies or neutrals the PC meets along their way. All of these will be controlled by the game itself and will be capable of reacting to the player within set parameters.

Characterisation, AI models, speech design and a knowledge of platforms are only the tip of the iceberg when learning how to write for games. But this introduction should give screenwriters an insight into the differences which exist between screenwriting and gameswriting. There is no reason why a screenwriter cannot make the transition from screenwriting to gameswriting, but such a shift means accepting and exploring these differences. It means playing games and learning about the ways stories are told, about how to create non-linear plots or stories told over much longer periods than in movies. Moreover, the differences don't stop merely at the writing. For instance, a gameswriter will often write more than just the game script. It is by no means unusual for the writer to be required to write everything from a concept document and story designs through to dialogue, advertising copy, the games manual and blurb for the back of the box. Just as the writing is different, so the industry within which the gameswriter operates is also different from the film industry.

Forget it, Jake – it's Chinatown

The games industry is split into two parts, developers and publishers. Primarily, games are produced by developers. Many of these are small, single-title operations prone to financial collapse and takeover. These developers provide content to publishers who then release it to the world. There are a number of big players such as Electronic Arts (EA) and Sony that both develop and publish games.

Unlike other media, it is extremely rare for computer games companies to commission original ideas from writers. It is also worth noting that with ideas and scripts, companies often work on a buyout which excludes residual deals. This may soon change as the big name writers begin to demand extended rights over their creations.

Show me the money!

With such a huge range of games projects it is impossible to set out a comprehensive pay scale. Some games are as short as 100 words, while others, such as *X-Files*, need a 250-page shooting script. This said, Writers' Guilds are setting minimum fee structures. These can be checked on the relevant websites.

The first step is to find a job and this generally means going it alone. Few agents understand the needs of the games industry or have established contacts within it. The closest the industry gets to representation is a small number of all-in-one agencies that offer developers a one-stop shop for scriptwriting through to recording.

Gameswriting jobs are often advertised on company and gaming websites via recruitment agencies and, very occasionally, in newspapers and magazines. But most contacts come by word of mouth.

I'm going to make him an offer he can't refuse

When approaching a games company, a screenwriter must have evidence of their writing ability. This does not have to be a games script. A television, film, or even a theatre script will do. What is important is matching the sample to the genre of game that is being made i.e. an action sample for an action game. On a technical level, gameswriters do not have to be either programmers or games designers. But they must understand their medium. The games industry is rife with stories of screenwriters who have been hired at Hollywood-level fees only to deliver unusable scripts. Unsurprisingly, this has made some companies wary of employing professional writers.

One reason why some writers fail when making the move into games from other media is a lack of commitment to a project. Just as a screenplay will evolve once the film starts production, so a games script will also evolve. Changes to the gameplay necessitate changes to the script. Alterations may be as simple as the change of a button to a lever but can regularly stretch to characters disappearing and whole levels being cut. If the writer is unavailable to make changes, the final script can be confusing at best and a nonsense at worst. A games script requires tender loving care from its conception through to the day the game hits the shelves.

This means that some games companies are keen to have writers based onsite and involved in the development process from the first day until the last. But they don't really need the writer there every day, just involved in the process for the duration. Many established gameswriters work as freelancers moving from contract to contract, company to company. They often work on several titles at the same time.

You're going to need a bigger boat

In the UK, US and beyond, the various international Writers' Guilds produce information to help writers break into the games industry and to find their way within it once they have made the move. The Writers' Guild of America and the Writers' Guild of Great Britain have published a set of guidelines for writers and for people working with writers in the games industry which are available on the internet or by post.

Distinct from the Guilds, the International Games Developers Association (IGDA) is an active body that connects professionals within the games industry and provides a platform for discussion of industry matters. The IGDA boasts a writers' SIG (Special Interest Group) which meets to discuss and promote games-writing.

I think this is the beginning of a beautiful friendship

Stories have had a rough start in the world of games, but then it was the same at the start of the movie industry. Encouragingly, the quality of stories is improving across the games industry. This is partly thanks to the development of improved AI, with faster machines and more sophisticated speech engines but mostly it is because gameswriting has evolved into its own distinct form of storytelling. The industry is realising that it cannot simply adopt the methods used to tell story in film. As this revolution continues, so writers are being given more tools with which to tell stories. They are also allowed more time to do the job and are employed earlier in the development process. While the opportunities for work are increasing, any screenwriter hoping to make the transition between media is expected to be familiar with games and gameswriting. This is not something to be afraid of, rather a challenge to be met head on. After all, it's all about learning to tell stories as well as possible in a brave new world, one where you can step into the action and make your own reality.

Andrew S. Walsh has written for television, radio, theatre, film animation and has worked on more than twenty-five games for companies such as EA, Sony, SEGA and Eidos.

Talking of agents, when I opened the morning paper one morning last week I saw that it had finally happened: somebody shot one. It was probably for the wrong reasons, but at least it was a step in the right direction.

Raymond Chandler, 17.12.1951 (from *The Raymond Chandler Papers, Selected Letters and Non-Fiction*, 1909–1959, edited by Tom Hiney and Frank MacShane)

AWARDS AND PRIZES

UNITED STATES OF AMERICA

ACADEMY AWARDS (THE OSCARS)

Academy of Motion Picture Arts and Sciences
Academy Foundation 8949 Wilshire Boulevard
Beverly Hills CA 90211
T 310 247 3000
W www.oscars.org

The world's most prestigious film awards,
presented annually since 1929. Ceremony held
in Los Angeles in January. Voting by Academy
members is conducted by secret ballot. Includes
awards for best original and best adapted
screenplays.

ACCLAIM FILM SCREENWRITING AWARD

300 Central Avenue Suite 501 St Petersburg
FL 33701
E acclaimfilms@go.com
W acclaimtv.netfirms.com

Contacts
Frank Drouzas *Co-ordinator*

Founded in 2001, running two awards a year
(Spring/Summer and Fall/Winter) for feature-
length scripts. $1,000 cash prize for winner; all
finalists receive consideration from established
production companies. Also offers TV
scriptwriting contests.

Entry Policy
Awards are open to all writers worldwide.
Scripts must not have been optioned or sold.

AMERICAN ACCOLADES SCREENWRITING COMPETITION

2118 Wilshire Boulevard Suite 160
Santa Monica CA 90403
F 310 576 6026
E info@AmericanAccolades.com
W www.americanaccolades.com

Founded in 2000, this screenplay contest aims
to find and usher emerging talent into the
Hollywood mainstream marketplace. Over
$5,000 in cash and prizes plus meetings with

Hollywood executives. There are 5 category
winners and 1 Grand Prize winner. Past Grand
Prize winners include Lon Harris, David Zorn
and Danny Howell.

Entry Policy
The competition is open to most writers but
screenplays must not be produced, optioned,
or purchased at the time of submission.
Submission is subject to an entry fee.

AMERICAN ACCOLADES TV/SHORT CONTEST

2118 Wilshire Boulevard Suite 160B
Santa Monica CA 90403
F 310 315 1132
E info@americanaccolades.com
W americanaccolades.com

Founded in 2000, this competition offers
$6,000 in prizes and a $1,000 grand prize. The
competition has many categories including
1/2 –hour shows (or pilots), 1-hour shows,
short films and short screenplays.

Entry Policy
Entry is open to all screenwriters and directors.
Submission is subject to an entry fee.

AMERICAN GEM SHORT SCRIPT CONTEST

PO Box 54050 Irvine CA 92619
W www.filmmakers.com

Founded in 2001, offering cash prizes
to the value of $1,000 for the first
place winner, as well as cash prizes for
4 runners-up. Previous winners of the
competition include Michael Ugulini
(*Parched*), Ronald Bramhall
(*The Veteran*) and Marc Calderwood
(*The Christmas Card*).

Entry Policy
Entry is open to anyone (except employees).
Submissions must be short film (narrative),
up to 45 pages in length in any genre,
and must be possible to produce on
a low budget. Submission is subject to
an entry fee.

AMERICAN SCREENWRITERS ASSOCIATION/GOTHAM WRITER'S WORKSHOP

Annual ASA International Screenplay Competition 1841 Broadway Suite 809 New York NY 10023
T   513 221 7004
F   513 531 0798
E   asa@goasa.com
W   www.goasa.com

Founded in 1999, this screenplay competition offers the grand prize winner a financial reward of $5,000, as well as industry recognition and writer development. The grand prize winner is awarded the Mick Caswell Award. Previous grand prize winners include Anita Skibski (*Mine*) and Mike Miller (*Ten and a Half*).

Entry Policy
Submission of material is subject to an entry fee. Scripts must be between 80 and 130 pages in length. It must be original work that is not sold or optioned at the time of entry. A 1-page synopsis must be attached to the script.

AMERICAN SCREENWRITING COMPETITION

311 N. Robertson Boulevard Suite 172 Beverly Hills CA 90211
T   310 388 1789
E   contestdirector@flatshoe.com
W   www.flatshoe.com

Founded in 2003, offering prizes to the value of $50,000 and has a grand prize of $12,000 cash. Past grand prize winners include Bill Balas (*The Pros and Cons of Breathing*) and Kieran Shea and David Osorio (*The Outcast*).

Entry Policy
All feature length English language scripts are eligible for the competition. Each screenplay submission must include the appropriate entry fee, an official entry form, a short synopsis and the complete screenplay, which should be 70 to 150 pages in length.

AMERICAN ZOETROPE SCREENPLAY CONTEST

916 Kearny Street San Francisco CA 94133
T   415 788 7500
F   415 989 7910
E   contests@zoetrope.com
W   www.zoetrope.com

Founded in 2003, this annual contest provides the grand prize winner with $5,000. The winner and finalists will also be considered for representation by leading agencies. Past winner Michael Cahill wrote and directed *King of California*, which premiered at Sundance 2007 and starred Michael Douglas and Evan Rachel Wood.

Entry Policy
Submission of material is subject to an entry fee. Entrants must be 18 years and older and not have earned over $5,000 as a screenwriter. Screenplay submissions should be in the US Motion Picture industry standard screenplay format and approximately 87 to 130 pages in length. Submissions should be written in English.

ASIAN AMERICAN INTERNATIONAL FILM FESTIVAL SCREENPLAY COMPETITION

133 West 19th Street Suite 300 New York NY 10011
T   212 989 1422
F   212 727 3584
E   info@asiancinevision.org
W   www.asiancinevision.org

Annual competition open to all writers of Asian descent of any nationality, held in July as part of the film festival. Only unproduced full-length screenplays are eligible. Staged reading of winning script, along with other prizes.

AUGUSTA PICTURES SCREENPLAY CONTEST

PO Box 5085 Glendale CA 91221
E   diana@augustapictures.com
W   www.augustapictures.com

Contacts
Diana Osberg *Producer/Script Doctor*

Founded in 2005, competition offering winner one-on-one advice and guidance on developing the winning screenplay from screenwriter/producer Diana Osberg. Past winners: Jennifer Harrison (2005), Diana Cobbold (2006).

Entry Policy
Screenplays must not be optioned, purchased or produced at time of submission. Subject to an entry fee.

BIG BEAR LAKE INTERNATIONAL SCREENWRITING COMPETITION

PO Box 1981 Big Bear Lake CA 92315
T   909 866 3433
E   karsten33@earthlink.net
W   www.bigbearlakefilmfestival.com

The festival has been hosting the award since 2000. Past winner Iris Yamashita has worked with Paul Haggis and Clint Eastwood to write the screenplay for the Academy Award-nominated film *Letters From Iwo Jima*.

Entry Policy
Submission of material is subject to an entry fee. Screenplays should be 90 to 130 pages in length and should be written in English. Screenplays should not have been produced or optioned.

BIG BREAK INTERNATIONAL SCREENWRITING CONTEST

26707 W. Agoura Road Suite 205 Calabasas CA 91302
E   bigbreak@finaldraft.com
W   www.finaldraft.com/bigbreak

Contacts
Liz Alani *Contest Director*

Annual global screenwriting competition supporting emerging creative talent. Offers over $30,000 in cash and prizes, and executive meetings. Top 10 finalists receive prizes. Past winners include Rylend Grant and Shawn Corridan.

Entry Policy
Digital entries via the website are preferred. Optioned screenplays are not eligible. Submission is subject to an entry fee.

BLUECAT SCREENPLAY COMPETITION

PO Box 2630 Hollywood CA 90028
E   info@bluecatscreenplay.com
W   www.bluecatscreenplay.com

Founded in 1998, the competition offers a $10,000 grand prize and $1,500 for each of the finalists. Every writer who enters the competition will receive written script analysis.

Entry Policy
Submission of material is subject to an entry fee. All entries must be in English and between 80 and 145 pages in length. Screenplays must not have been purchased or optioned.

BRASS BRAD SCREENWRITING MENTORSHIP AWARD

PO Box 892410 Temecula CA 92589
T   951 587 3890
F   951 587 6350
E   brassbradmentor@aol.com
W   www.brassbrad.com

Contacts
Kimberley Seilhamer *Foundation*

Founded in 2005, mentorship scheme offering advice and guidance to help the winner move forward in the industry. Winner receives one year of bi-weekly phone conferences and script analysis, as well as prizes such as screenwriting software and online subscriptions. Past winners include Donald Cager and Elizabeth Pfeiffer.

Entry Policy
Open to residents of Canada and the USA. No collaborative work is accepted. Submission is subject to an entry fee.

CENTURY CITY FILM FESTIVAL SCREENWRITING COMPETITION

c/o MIBTP PO Box 67132 Century City CA 90067
W   www.centurycityfilmfestival.com

Annual contest with winner receiving cash award and other prizes from sponsors. Awards ceremony held in October each year. Applications through the website.

CYNOSURE SCREENWRITING AWARDS

3699 Wilshire Boulevard #850 Los Angeles
CA 90010
T   310 855 8730
E   cynosure@broadmindent.com
W   www.broadmindent.com

Founded in 1999, the competition offers two
$2,500 prizes to quality character- and
concept-driven screenplays showcasing female
and minority protagonists.

Entry Policy
The competition is open to writers from
any country. Submission of material is
subject to an entry fee. Screenplays may
not have been previously optioned,
purchased or produced. Screenplays must
be in English only, and may be of any
genre. Screenplays must be in standard US
screenplay format, between 90 and 130
numbered pages.

EMMY AWARDS

Academy of Television Arts & Sciences 5220
Lankershim Boulevard North Hollywood
CA 91601 3109
T   818 754 2800
F   818 761 2827
W   www.emmys.org

The leading awards for American television,
voted for by over 12,000 members of the
Academy. The Primetime Awards are for
excellence in national prime time programming.
There are also Daytime Emmys, awarded by
the National Television Academy in New York,
and regional and international Emmys.
Categories in the Primetime division include
outstanding writing for a comedy series, for a
drama series, for a variety, music or comedy
programme and for a mini-series, movie or
dramatic special.

FADE IN AWARD

289 South Robertson Boulevard Suite 467
Beverly Hills CA 90211
T   323 653 6065
F   323 653 6098
E   inquiries@fadeinonline.com
W   www.fadeinonline.com

Contacts
Heather Millerton *Administration*

Introduced in 1996 with over $15,000 prize
money each year. Recent winner Jon
Bokenkamp has since received sole credit on
Taking Lives, starring Angelina Jolie.

A FEEDING FRENZY – SCREENPLAY COMPETITION WITH FEEDBACK

AMLC Productions 703 Pier Avenue Suite B
#687 Hermosa Beach CA 90254
E   amlcprods@afeedingfrenzy.com
W   www.afeedingfrenzy.com

Offers feedback to all entries. Top three scripts
are distributed to production companies and
industry contacts. Feedback is 'encouragingly
blunt'.

Entry Policy
Entries should be submitted by mail or email.

FILMAKA, LLC

7955 W. 3rd Street Los Angeles CA 90048
W   www.filmaka.com

An on-line network created by a group of
independent producers, industry professionals,
and film financiers including Deepak Nayar,
Thomas Augsberger, Christopher Sharp, Robert
Herman, Tim Levy, Mahesh Mathai, Kurt
Woolner and Colin Firth. Aims to give
undiscovered filmmakers an opportunity to
show custom-made short films to industry
professionals, award prizes and find 'one truly
talented director' who will win a feature film
deal with Filmaka at the end of the year.

Entry Policy
Contests are divided into three levels, Entry,
Jury and Final. Entry level contests are held
periodically and up to 20 winners get $500. At
the Jury level contest, all winners from the
Entry Level are given $1,000 to make a second
clip on the same subject. Two winners are
selected. The first winner is given a $3,000 cash
prize and a runner-up is given a $2,000 cash
prize. The winner and runner-up move into the
final level. A special Jury prize will also be
announced at the Jury level which wins no cash
but qualifies to compete in the yearly contest in

addition to the Jury Level winners and runner ups. Final level contest happens yearly. The winners, runners-up and special jury prize winners from each jury level contest compete for the grand feature film contract and the runner-up wins $5,000 cash.

FIND THE FUNNY

531-A N. Hollywood Way #260 Burbank CA 91505
T 818 679 3845
E screenplaycontest@findthefunny.com
W www.findthefunny.com

Founded in 2005, this competition is dedicated to comedy and offers a first place prize of $2,000.

Entry Policy

Competition is open to all screenwriters 18 years of age and older. Submission of material is subject to an entry fee. Only feature-length comedy screenplays will be accepted (all genres and sub genres are acceptable – romantic comedy, action comedy, dark comedy etc). All scripts must be in English and must be between 90 and 115 pages in length. Screenplays must not have been previously optioned or sold.

GIMME CREDIT SCREENPLAY COMPETITION

4470 W. Sunset Boulevard #278 Los Angeles CA 90027
T 310 734 8516
E submissions@gimmecreditcompetition.com
W www.gimmecreditcompetition.com

Contacts
Erica Engelhardt Director/Founder

Founded in 2006, triennial contest created with the aim of giving exposure to and development advice on talented writers' short scripts. The Grand Prize-winning screenplay is produced. Awards categories for short scripts (up to 30 pages) and 'Super Shorts' of 5 pages or less. Previous winners include Alan R. Baxtor, Menotti and Benjamin Harrison.

Entry Policy
All screenplays must be in English and registered with the Writers Guild or the US Copyright Office. Open to all writers over 18.

GOLDEN GLOBES

The Hollywood Foreign Press Association 646 N. Robertson Boulevard West Hollywood CA 90069
E info@hfpa.org
W www.hfpa.org

Prestigious awards for the motion picture and television industries, administered since 1944 by the Hollywood Foreign Press Association. Includes an award for best screenplay.

HOLLYWOOD NEXUS SCREENWRITING CONTEST

2554 Lincoln Boulevard Suite 401 Marina Del Rey CA 90291
T 310 663 0656
F 310 397 8844
E cynthia@hollywoodnexus.com
W www.hollywoodnexus.com

Founded in 2002, the contest offers a grand prize of $5,000. Every entry receives feedback from the judges.

Entry Policy
Submission of material is subject to an entry fee. Entrants must be at least 18 years of age. Entries are accepted from all locations, including internationally, except Colorado and Vermont. The screenplay must not have been produced or sold.

THE MANHATTEN SHORT FILM FESTIVAL'S SCREENPLAY COMPETITION

7 East 27th Street New York NY 10016
T 212 779 2901
E info@msfilmfest.com
W www.msfilmfest.com

Contacts
Nicholas Mason Executive Director

Short film competition running since 1997. Festival takes place in 200 locations across Europe, North, South and Central America during the last week of September. Finalists' films are judged by the audience at each venue, with votes tallied and emailed to Union Square Park in New York, where the winner is announced.

Entry Policy
Entry is via the website. Tickets to screenings available from participating cinemas.

MCKNIGHT SCREENWRITING FELLOWSHIP

The McKnight Foundation 710 South Second Street Suite 400 Minneapolis MN 55401
T   612 333 4220
F   612 332 3833
W   www.ifpmsp.org/mcknight.html

Fellowship worth $25,000 awarded to two screenwriters annually, judged by two panels of industry professionals. Open to mid-career Minnesota-based writers, the fellowship is intended to provide financial assistance, professional encouragement and industry recognition.

Entry Policy
Applicants should send one completed full-length screenplay.

MONTEREY SCREENPLAY COMPETITION

Monterey County Film Commission 801 Lighthouse Avenue Suite 104 Monterey CA 93940
T   831 646 0910
F   831 655 9250
E   filmmonterey@redshift.com
W   www.filmmonterey.org

Founded in 1996, the competition awards a grand prize of $2,000 for the winning feature-length screenplay and the winning screenwriters have the opportunity to have their screenplays reviewed by a Monterey County-based film investor.

Entry Policy
Submission of material is subject to an entry fee. Submissions must be completed, feature-length scripts between 90 and 120 pages. A submitted screenplay must not have been optioned or sold at the time of submission.

NEW JERSEY SHORT SCREENPLAY FESTIVAL

PO Box 595 Cape Bay NJ 08204
T   609 823 9159
F   609 884 6722
E   bsaks47@comcast.net
W   www.njstatefilmfestival.com/screenplay.htm

Contacts
William Sokolic *Chair*

Founded in 2002, offering software of varying cost as a prize for screenplays of 45 pages or less. The writer must be from New Jersey or the state should be the primary setting. Recent winners include Susan Pelligrino.

Entry Policy
Scripts must be received by 1 November and should include an application. Scripts should be in industry-standard format.

NICHOLL FELLOWSHIPS IN SCREENWRITING

1313 Vine Street Hollywood CA 90028
T   310 247 3010
E   nicholl@oscars.org
W   www.oscars.org/nicholl

Contacts
Greg Beal *Program Co-ordinator*

Founded in 1985, up to 5 fellowships worth $30,000 are awarded each year to emerging writers. During the fellowship year winners complete an original screenplay 100–130 pages long. 2006 fellows were Alfred E. Carpenter and Mark A. Matusof, Arthur M. Jolly, Stephanie Lord, Josh D. Schorr and Scott K. Simonsen.

Entry Policy
Screenplays or teleplays which have been optioned are not eligible. Applicants may not have earned more than $5,000 as a screenwriter. Applications are only accepted by mail and are subject to an entry fee.

NICKELODEON PRODUCTIONS FELLOWSHIP PROGRAM

Nickelodeon Productions Fellowship Program 2600 Colorado Avenue Suite #256 Santa Monica CA 90404
T   818 736 3663
W   www.nick.com

Founded in 2000, the writing fellowship provides a salaried position for up to one year and offers hands-on experience writing spec scripts and pitching story ideas in both live action and animation television.

Entry Policy
The fellowship is only available to US applicants who are 18 years or older. Previous writing experience is not necessary. Applicants must submit an application form, two copies of a spec script, a one-page resume, a half-page biography, plus a submission release form and schedule A (allowing material to be read).

ON THE STORM SCREENPLAY CONTEST

PO Box 899 Venice CA 90294
T   310 582 5880
E   wotscompetition@aol.com
W www.writerstorm.com

Founded in 2006, this competition encourages submissions for any and all genres. The winning scriptwriter will receive $2,500 in cash.

Entry Policy
Submission of material is subject to an entry fee. The competition is open to all writers in all countries. All submissions should be in English. Applicants must not have made $10,000 or more on feature options or sales. Scripts should be between 90 to 120 pages in length.

ONE IN TEN SCREENPLAY COMPETITION

c/o Cherub Productions PO Box 540 Boulder CO 80306
T   303 629 3072
E   Cherubfilm@aol.com
W www.OneInTenScreenplayContest.com

Contacts
Mike Dean

Founded in 1999, screenplay contest dedicated to the positive portrayal of gay, lesbian, bisexual and transgender individuals in film. Winners receive cash prizes and submission to a major film studio. Past winners include Denise P. Meyer and Jon Zelazny.

Entry Policy
Screenplays must not have been optioned. Entries are subject to a fee.

THE PAGE INTERNATIONAL SCREENWRITING AWARDS

7510 Sunset Boulevard #610 Los Angeles CA 90046
T   323 969 0993
F   323 969 0993
E   info@internationalscreenwritingawards.com
W www.internationalscreenwritingawards.com

Contacts
Jennifer Berg *Administrative Officer*

Founded in 2003, aims to discover the most exciting new screenplays by up-and-coming writers from around the world. Over $25,000 in cash and prizes, with a $10,000 Grand Prize and gold, silver and bronze prizes in each of nine categories. Previous Grand Prize winners include Laurie Weltz and Jay C. Key, Larry Postel and Scott LaCagnin.

Entry Policy
Open to all writers over the age of 18 who have not previously earned more than $25,000 writing for film and television. Entries by mail or online.

RHODE ISLAND FILM FESTIVAL SCREENPLAY COMPETITION

Rhode Island International Film Festival PO Box 162 Newport RI 02840
T   401 861 4445
F   401 490 6735
E   info@film-festival.org
W www.film-festival.org

Award open to screenplays in all genres. Winner receives prizes valued at over $15,000. Screenplays judged on 'creativity, innovation, vision, originality and the use of language'. Also contests for lesbian, gay, bisexual and transsexual writers and for short scripts.

Entry Policy
Entry forms available online.

THE SANTA BARBARA SCRIPT COMPETITION

PO Box 4068 Santa Barbara CA 93140
E   Geoff@santabarbarascript.com
W www.santabarbarascript.com

Offers a $750 first prize for the best screenplay and has a grand prize of a $4,000 option and a staged script-reading by professional actors.

Entry Policy
Submission of material is subject to an entry fee. Screenplays should be between 85–120 pages in length.

SCREENPLAY FESTIVAL

11693 San Vicente Boulevard Suite 806
Los Angeles CA 90049
T   310 801 7896
F   310 820 2303
E   info@screenplayfestival.com
W   www.screenplayfestival.com

Founded in 2002, the feature length screenplay competition has 5 categories of competition: action/adventure, comedy, drama, family and thriller/horror. In each of the five categories, a $1,000.00 Grand Prize will be awarded.

Entry Policy
Submission of material is subject to an entry fee. Screenplays must be submitted in English and must be longer than 60 pages in length. Screenplays that have been previously optioned, sold or produced are not eligible.

SCREENWRITER SHOWCASE SCREENWRITING CONTEST

897 Oak Park Boulevard #263 Pismo Beach
CA 93449
E   contact@screenwritershowcase.com
W   www.screenwritershowcase.com

Established in 2002, competition for feature length screenplays. Prizes include screenwriting software, exposure to industry professionals and promotion on dedicated website. Previous winners include *Cinders* by Kate Pellettiere and *Bloodletting* by William D. Prystauk.

Entry Policy
Submission is subject to an entry fee.

SCREENWRITER'S CHALLENGE

130 7th Avenue #358 New York NY 10011
T   212 647 9653
W   www.nycmidnight.com

Founded in 2002, an international online screenwriters' competition. The competition has 2 rounds. In the first round writers are given 1 week to create an original short screenplay (20 pages maximum) based on an assigned genre and subject. In the second round, finalists are chosen to compete for thousands of prizes by writing a short screenplay in 24 hours.

Entry Policy
Submission of material is subject to an entry fee. Entry is open to everyone.

SCRIPT MAGAZINE OPEN DOOR CONTESTS

5638 Sweet Air Road Baldwin MD 21013
T   888 245 2228
F   410 592 8062
E   brad@scriptmag.com
W   www.scriptmag.com

Founded in 2000, the competition offers a first place prize of $3,000 and consideration for representation from AEI.

Entry Policy
Submission of material is subject to an entry fee. Screenplays must be feature length (90 to 130 pages) and written in English. Applicants must not have received consideration of any kind for any screenwriting work over a $5,000 value.

SCRIPT PIMP SCREENWRITING COMPETITION

5723 Melrose Avenue Suite 100 Los Angeles
CA 90038
T   310 401 1155
F   310 564 2021
E   competition@scriptpimp.com
W   www.scriptpimp.com

Contacts
Chadwick Clough *Contest Director*

Founded in 2003, the competition offers a grand prize of $2,500 and guaranteed circulation to over 20 production companies.

Entry Policy
Submission of material is subject to an entry fee. Entrants must be at least 18 years of age. The script must not have been produced, sold or optioned.

SET IN PHILADELPHIA SCREENWRITING COMPETITION

Greater Philadelphia Film Office 100 S. Broad
Street Suite 600 Philadelphia PA 19110
T 215 686 2668
F 215 686 3659
E joanb@film.org
W www.film.org

Contacts
Joan Bressler *Director*

Contest for screenplays set in the Greater
Philadelphia region. Prizes include the Parisi
Award for writers under 25 worth $1,000, a
regional award worth $2,500 and a Grand
Prize worth $10,000. Awarded during the
Philadelphia Film Festival. Previous prize
winners include Bruce Graham, Brian Loshiavo
and David Hoag.

Entry Policy
Submission is subject to an entry fee.

SLAMDANCE SCREENWRITING COMPETITION

5634 Melrose Avenue Los Angeles CA 90038
T 323 466 1786
F 323 466 1784
E screenplay@slamdance.com
W www.slamdance.com

Founded in 1995, dedicated to new writers.
Has a grand prize of $7,000. Accepts
screenplays in every genre, on any topic and
from every country.

Entry Policy
Submission of material is subject to an entry
fee. Screenplays must not have been previously
optioned, purchased or produced. Material
must be in English and not have received
awards from other competitions over a value
of $500.

TALENTSCOUT TV WRITING CONTEST

1484 1/2 Robertson Boulevard Los Angeles
CA 90035
T 310 276 5161
F 310 276 5134
E TV@aTalentScout.com
W www.atalentscout.com

Founded in 1991, this TV writing competition
offers a $3,000 grand prize and representation.
Only 1,000 entries will be accepted. Past
winner Marcus Folmar had his script *I'm
Perfect* produced, starring Wayne Brady, Brad
Dourif, Illeana Douglas and Malcolm-Jamal
Warner.

Entry Policy
Submission of material is subject to an entry
fee. Material submitted must not have been
bought or optioned.

THE JOHN TEMPLETON FOUNDATION KAIROS PRIZE

1041 North Formosa Avenue Formosa Bldg.
STE 217 West Hollywood CA 90046
T 760 510 8012
E contact@kairosprize.com
W www.kairosprize.com

Founded in 2006, offering a $25,000 grand
prize for scripts that teach lessons in ethics and
morality, and which are primarily spiritual. The
scripts submitted must be suitable for a G or
PG rating and must be free of foul language
(and must refer specifically to the Bible).

Entry Policy
Submission of material is subject to an entry
fee. Entrants are required to submit a 500 word
synopsis or treatment in addition to the script.
The script must be in English and must be
87 to 130 pages in length. Entrants must be
18 years of age or older, and must not have
earned money as a screenwriter.

TVWRITER.COM PEOPLE'S PILOT

Cloud Creek Ranch 3767 Marion County
5026 St Joe AZ 72675
E larrybrody@tvwriter.com
W www.peoplespilot.com

Founded in 2000, the winner of this
competition receives $500 and a 1-week
writing retreat at the Cloud Creek Institute
For The Arts. This is not a screenplay
competition and requires only the title of the
series idea, the main thrust of the storyline, the
characters and the setting. The competition is
held bi-annually.

Entry Policy
Submission of material is subject to an entry fee. The competition is open to writers at all levels and from all countries. Pilot submissions must contain a summary of the basic idea behind the show, including the setting, theme and profession. It must also have a summary of the main continuing characters, their background, appearance, personalities, interaction and a statement of the kinds of situation in which the characters will be placed.

TVWRITER.COM SPEC SCRIPTACULAR

Cloud Creek Ranch 3767 Marion County 5026 St Joe AZ 72675
T   870 449 2488
E   larrybrody@tvwriter.com
W   www.tvwriter.com

This competition has four categories - sitcom, action/drama, pilot/MOW/special and new media. The grand prize is awarded to the best entry regardless of category. The winner receives $500 and a 1-week writing retreat at the Cloud Creek Institute For The Arts.

Entry Policy
Submission of material is subject to an entry fee. The competition is open to all writers in all countries.

SIR PETER USTINOV TELEVISION SCRIPTWRITING AWARD

The International Academy of Television Arts and Sciences Foundation 7th Avenue 5th Floor NY 10019
T   212 489 6969
F   212 489 6557
E   iemmys@iemmys.tv
W   www.iemmys.tv

Contacts
Tracy Oliver *Manager, Foundation and Special Projects*

Held by the International Academy of Television Arts and Sciences Foundation, a competition for young writers of English-language television drama for a family audience. Winner receives $2,500 and a trip to New York City. A reading of the winning script is staged with professional actors.

Entry Policy
Entrants must submit a complete script lasting between 30 minutes and an hour. Open to non-US citizens under the age of 30. Email for entry form.

VISIONFEST (DOMANI VISION FILM SOCIETY)

PMB 155 6402 18th Avenue Brooklyn NY 11204
T   718 837 5736
F   718 554 0030
E   contact@domanivision.org
W   www.domanivision.org

Founded in 2004, this feature-length screenplay competition awards winners with either cash or special services prizes.

Entry Policy
Submission of material is subject to an entry fee. Screenplays should be 80 to 130 pages in length and must be in English.

WALT DISNEY STUDIOS/ABC WRITERS FELLOWSHIP

500 South Buena Vista Street Burbank CA 91521-4016
T   818 560 6894
E   abc.fellowships@abc.com
W   www.abctalentdevelopment.com

Started in 1991, offering fellowships in the feature film and television sectors with The Walt Disney Studios and ABC Entertainment, respectively. No previous experience is necessary but writing samples are required. Fellows will each be provided a salary of $50,000 for a one-year period. Recent fellowship graduates include Sean Diviny, who was hired as a staff writer on *Alias*, and Sonia Steele, who was staffed on *ER*.

Entry Policy
The programme is open to all writers.

WINFEMME MONTHLIES

PO Box 69-1774 Los Angeles CA 90069
T   310 229 5365
F   310 314 9691
E   info@winfemme.com
W   www.winfemme.com

This monthly competition runs 3 distinct categories: films or videos created by men and women which feature a female protagonist; films with a lesbian story; and films which are directed or produced by a woman. Scripts may be TV specs, TV movies, feature films, theatre plays and/or novellas.

Entry Policy
Submission of material is subject to an entry fee.

WORLDFEST HOUSTON

P.O. Box 56566 Houston TX 77256
T 713 965 9955
F 713 965 9960
E worldfest@aol.com
W www.worldfest.org

Founded in 1968, this festival hosts a screenplay competition with a $2,500 first prize. First place also includes a 1-year production option.

Entry Policy
Submission of material is subject to an entry fee. Screenplays should be between 70 to 150 pages in length. Screenplays should not have been produced.

WRITEMOVIES.COM INTERNATIONAL WRITING CONTEST

11444 Washington Boulevard Suite C-227
Los Angeles CA 90066
F 206 203 1256
E author@writemovies.com
W www.writemovies.com

Founded in 1999, award for scriptwriters from around the world. Grand prize includes $3,000 cash and guaranteed representation by TalentScout Management. Winning scripts that have been produced include *Valley of Angeles* and *The List*.

Entry Policy
Entry is open to any script which has not been bought or optioned. Scripts in English, French and German are welcome. Subject to entry fees.

WRITER'S ARC SCREENWRITING FELLOWSHIP

8332 Melrose Avenue Second Floor
Los Angeles CA 90069
E info@writersarc.org
W www.writersarc.org

This is a 10-week fellowship programme with a stipend of $3,000. Fellows are required to spend a minimum of 10 hours a week in the Arc Hub to work on their script and improve on their writing skills, as well as 4 hours a week at community events to broaden their industry awareness and experience. Offer about 5–10 fellowships a year depending on the applicant pool.

Entry Policy
No applicant may have earned money or other consideration as a screenwriter for theatrical films or television, or for the sale of, or sale of an option to, any original story, treatment, screenplay, or teleplay for more than $5,000. Applicants may not have received a screenwriting fellowship or prize that includes a 'first look' clause, an option or any other quid pro quo involving the writer's work.

WRITER'S NETWORK SCREENPLAY AND FICTION COMPETITION

289 South Robertson Boulevard Suite 467
Beverly Hills CA 90211
T 323 653 6065
F 323 653 6098
E writersnet@aol.com
W www.writersnetworkcompetition.com

Contacts
Heather Millerton *Administration*

Founded in 1993. Over $10,000 of prize money available yearly. Recent winner Frank Baldwin's script is now being directed by Spike Lee.

WRITERS GUILD OF AMERICA AWARDS

E www.wga.org/awards or www.wgaeast.org/awards

Prestigious annual awards for outstanding achievements in writing for film, TV and radio. Ceremonies held simultaneously by the East Guild in New York and West Guild in

Los Angeles. Categories include best original movie screenplay, adapted movie screenplay, documentary screenplay and numerous television awards.

THE WRITERS PLACE SCREENPLAY CONTEST

208 West 30th Street Suite 8901 New York NY 10001
T   212 436 3910
F   212 655 8528
E   contact2@thewritersplace.org
W   www.thewritersplace.org

This competition accepts full-length features and MOWs, short film scripts and TV scripts (1/2 hour). The first prize consists of money or screenwriting software.

Entry Policy
Submission of material is subject to an entry fee. The competition is open to everyone. Screenplays must be in English and must be registered with the WGA or copyrighted with the Library of Congress.

WRITESAFE PRESENT-A-THON

422 Carlisle Road Westlake Village CA 91361
T   805 495 3659
F   805 495 0099
E   admin@writesafe.com
W   www.writesafe.com

Founded in 1999, this quarterly competition is for all material registered with WriteSafe for public view. The competition has no categories. The first prize is consideration for publication, production, or representation by a panel of entertainment industry experts, and 2 free WriteSafe registrations.

Entry Policy
Competition is based on registered material.

UNITED KINGDOM

BAFTAS

195 Piccadilly London W1J 9LN
T   020 7734 0022
F   020 7734 1792

E   info@bafta.org
W   www.bafta.org

Among the most prestigious film and TV awards available in the UK. Administers several ceremonies including the British Academy Film Awards, British Academy Video Games Awards (which includes a scriptwriting award); British Academy Television Awards (including the Dennis Potter Award for outstanding writing for television) and the British Academy Children's Film & Television Awards.

BRITISH INDEPENDENT FILM AWARDS

81 Berwick Street London W1F 8TW
T   020 7287 3833
F   020 7439 2243
E   info@bifa.org.uk
W   www.bifa.org.uk

Created in 1998 to reward achievement in independently-funded British filmmaking. Ceremony held annually in central London. Among the prizes on offer are Best British 15 Second Short, British Documentary, British Independent Film, British Short Film, Foreign Independent Film and Screenplay.

BRITISH SHORT SCREENPLAY COMPETITION

c/o Kaos Films
E   info@kaosfilms.co.uk
W   www.kaosfilms.co.uk

Annual competition managed by Kaos Films in association with the National Film and Television School. Three winning scripts are produced by Kaos Films and directed by new NFTS graduates. Each will be premiered at BAFTA, entered into film festivals around the world and screened in selected cinemas in UK. Runners-up receive Movie Magic screenwriting software. Past judges have included Kenneth Branagh and producer Michael Kuhn.

Entry Policy
All genres accepted. Scripts must be 5–15 minutes screen-time. Other rules and guidelines outlined on website.

TONY DOYLE BURSARY FOR NEW WRITING

BBC NI Drama Department Broadcasting House
Ormeau Avenue Belfast BT2 8HQ
T 028 9033 8845
E tvdrama.ni@bbc.co.uk
W www.bbc.co.uk/ni/drama

Founded in memory of Tony Doyle, one of
Ireland's leading television actors. Open to
writers who 'have a different story to tell and
who are passionate about starting a writing
career in television'. Award worth £2,000.
Aims to encourage Irish writing for television
and to forge creative links between
broadcasters and writers in Ireland. Four
finalists take part in a residential seminar where
they will undergo intensive, structured, script
sessions with members of BBC Northern
Ireland Drama's development team, script
writers and producers. Previous winners include
Bill Murphy, Brian Dungan, Dominque
Maloney and Danny Stack.

Entry Policy
Submission should be either a 60- or 90-minute
script for an original television drama in
English. This can be a single drama or the first
episode of a two-parter, serial or series. For
series etc, attach a synopsis (maximum 2 pages)
outlining the remainder of the story. Submit
two typed copies of the script. Only one entry
per person. For further guidelines, see website.

EUROSCRIPT SCREENWRITING COMPETITION

PO Box 3117 Gloucester GL4 0WW
T 0780 336 9414
E enquiries@euroscript.co.uk
W www.euroscript.co.uk

Offers six-months script development worth
£1,000 and other consultancy prizes. Seeking
writers with powerful story ideas and original
voices.

Entry Policy
Submit a two page prose outline of the story
you want to develop, plus ten pages of sample
script, which can either be a complete short
film or an extract from a full length screenplay
(either the one you wish to develop through
Euroscript or another screenplay you have
completed); the sample must include a mixture

of action and dialogue. Price per entry: £35
(2007). All rights in the winning screenplay and
related materials, such as the outline, remain
with the writer.

MAKE YOUR MARK IN FILM

E info@makeyourmarkinfilm.org
W www.makeyourmarkinfilm.org

Coordinated by the Make Your Mark
campaign, a business-led, government-backed
campaign to encourage people in their teens
and twenties to develop creative ideas. Works
in partnership with CobraVision, which runs a
monthly competition to give aspiring film
makers the opportunity to show their work on
national TV (see www.cobrabeer.com/
cobravision).

MY SPACE MOVIE MASH UP

W www.myspace.com/mymoviemashup

The world's first user generated feature film,
arranged in partnership with Vertigo films and
Film4. The project unfolds in 'Ten Acts':
director search; title search; interactive script;
casting; pre-production; production; trailer;
soundtrack; mass roots market; distribution.

PAWS DRAMA FUND

OMNI Communications Limited First Floor 155
Regent's Park Road London NW1 8BB
T 020 7483 4545
F 020 7483 0934
E pawsomni@btconnect.com
W www.pawsdrama.co.uk

Contacts
Andrew Millington *Managing Director*

A fund administered by PAWS (founded in
1993) to raise the profile of science and
technology in television drama. Offers research
and development grants to writers to develop
an idea based on science or engineering into a
viable treatment for television drama.
Experienced writers may receive up to £5,000
while less experienced writers (who can
demonstrate production company-backing) get
up to £2,000. For 2007–8 most grants will go
to ideas with a women scientist or engineer in a
prominent role.

THE DENNIS POTTER SCREENWRITING AWARD

BBC Broadcasting House Whiteladies Road
Bristol BS8 2LR
T   0117 974 7586

Contacts
Jeremy Howe *Executive Producer*

Annual award established in 1995 in memory
of the late television playwright to 'nurture and
encourage the work of new writers of talent
and personal vision'. 2006 winner: Russell T.
Davies.

Entry Policy
Submissions should be made through a BBC
TV drama producer or an independent
production company.

SATYAJIT RAY FOUNDATION SHORT FILM COMPETITION

24 Southwood Lawn Road London N6 5SF
T   020 8340 5715
E   contemporaryfilms@compuserve.com
W   www.rayfoundation.mistral.co.uk

Open to all film-makers, of any age, either
resident or studying in the UK. Film should be
not more than 30 minutes running time and
should be informed by the experiences of South
Asians (Afghanistan, Bangladesh, Bhutan, India,
Nepal, Pakistan, Sri Lanka) either within their
own countries or the diaspora. All submissions
must have been completed within two years
prior to the closing date. First prize of £1,500.
See website for specific entry requirements.

UK FILM COUNCIL'S DEVELOPMENT FUND

10 Little Portland Street London W1W 7JG
T   020 7861 7861
F   020 7861 7862
E   info@ukfilmcouncil.org.uk
W   www.ukfilmcouncil.org.uk

Aims to broaden the quality, range and
ambition of UK film projects and talent being
developed. The annual budget for the
Development Fund is £4 million. The '25
Words or Less' scheme offers up to 12 writers
each year a fixed sum of £10,000 to develop a
first draft script in a specific genre. The scheme

is run three times a year and at each entry
point different genres are selected. Funding
decisions are taken by the Head of the
Development Fund.

Entry Policy
See website for further details and submission
guidelines.

CANADA

CANADIAN INDEPENDENT FILM & VIDEO FUND (CIFVF)

E   info@cifvf.ca
W   www.cifvf.ca

A private sector funding body that supports
non-theatrical film, videos and new media
projects created by Canadian independent
producers to enable lifelong learning. Various
genres considered including documentary,
docu-drama, drama and animation. Has
provided CA$17.9 million since 1991.

Entry Policy
Applications for funding are normally accepted
at two specified deadlines each year.

CANADIAN SCREENWRITING AWARDS

c/o Writer's Guild of Canada 366 Adelaide Street
West Suite 401 Toronto Ontario M5V 1R9
T   416 979 7907
F   416 979 9273
E   awards@wgc.ca
W   www.wgc.ca

Contacts
Barb Farwell *Director of Communications*

Announced annually in spring in Toronto. 'Best
Script' awards in several categories including
feature film, one-hour TV drama, documentary
and radio drama. Established in 1997. All
Writer's Guild of Canada members eligible to
apply. More details available on the website.

COGECO PROGRAM DEVELOPMENT FUND

2 Carlton Street Suite 1709 Toronto Ontario
M5B 1J3
T   416 977 8966
F   416 977 0694

E info@ipf.ca
W www.ipf.ca

Encourages the development of new Canadian drama by Canadian writers to be produced by independent Canadian producers, in English or French, or (preferably) in both languages. Runs three funding programmes: Development Programme (loans for the development of dramatic television programming, including television series, MOWs, mini-series, and animated series); Production Programme (equity investments for the production of MOWs, mini-series and pilots); Theatrical Feature Film Development Programme (corporate loans for companies with a slate of theatrical feature films in development).

Entry Policy
Application deadlines are March 1st, July 1st and October 1st.

CTV WRITER ONLY DRAMA DEVELOPMENT BENEFIT

E kmeek@ctv.ca
W www.ctv.ca

Contacts
Kathleen Meek *Manager, BCE Drama Development & Production*

Administered by CTV Inc., one of Canada's leading broadcast communications companies. Runs a CA$5 million programme for professional Canadian screenwriters, which allows for the development of dramatic screenplays for TV movies, mini-series or dramatic series. In the initial phase of development, CTV acts as producer of the project to facilitate the business aspects of the project. Working with the writer, CTV will approve the development budget, contract with story consultants and researchers, and negotiate and option underlying rights. At the appropriate stage, the project will be assigned to an independent third party producer.

Entry Policy
Normally screenwriters will have a minimum credit of 60 minutes of produced drama to be eligible for consideration.

GEMINIS

172 King Street E. Toronto Ontario M5A 1J3
T 416 366 2227
F 416 366 8454
E info@academy.ca
W www.geminiawards.ca

First broadcast in 1986, the awards celebrate excellence in Canadian English-language television in 87 categories, 6 of which are for writing.

Entry Policy
Any production which qualifies as a television production under the Canadian Radio-Television and Telecommunications Commission or the Canadian Audio-Visual Certification Office, and has had its first Canadian commercial release in English within the qualifying period on an English-language or ethnic telecaster licensed by the CRTC may enter. The programme may not be a rerun and must not have been previously entered in either the Gemini or Genie Awards. Programs previously entered for the Prix Gémeaux are eligible, subject to meeting all other Gemini eligibility criteria.

GENIES

172 King Street East Toronto Ontario M5A 1J3
T 416 366 2227
F 416 366 8454
E info@academy.ca
W www.genieawards.ca

Created in 1980 to replace the Canadian Film Awards, recognizing the best of Canadian cinema. Dramatic feature-length films (including animated features), theatrical shorts and documentaries are eligible for awards. Has an award for best original screenplay and for best adapted screenplay.

Entry Policy
Films may be submitted in either English or French. Films must be Canadian productions or co-productions, and must have had its first commercial release in Canada in a theatrical venue. A detailed synopsis of the film in both official languages must accompany the official entry form. For the screenplay awards, a

complete production script must be submitted with the entry form.

GRANTS TO FILM AND VIDEO ARTISTS PROGRAM

Media Arts Section Canada Council for the Arts PO Box 1047 350 Albert Street Ottawa Ontario K1P 5V8
T   1 800 263 5588
W   www.canadacouncil.ca/grants/mediaarts

Supports Canadian professional independent artists who use cinema and video as a mode of artistic expression. Scriptwriting Grants cover the direct costs of scriptwriting (including research for artists' documentaries) for independent film and video artworks. Grants range from $3,000 to $20,000. Eligible expenses include subsistence costs for the time spent working on the project (up to $2,000 per month per applicant); rental costs for equipment, studios, and other facilities; costs for training and/or development; fees for consultants, technicians and other participants; travel costs; contingency funds.

Entry Policy
Application forms available from website.

THE HAROLD GREENBERG FUND

BCE Place 181 Bay Street PO Box 787 Toronto Ontario M5J 2T3
T   416 956 5431
F   416 956 2018
E   hgfund@tv.astral.com
W   www.astral.com/en/theharoldgreenbergfund

Founded in 1986 by Astral Media, the first Canadian broadcaster to set up a national, non-profit private fund to support the development of film and made-for-pay-TV productions. An additional French-language programme was added in 1996. Collectively invested over CA$50 million to date. The English-language programme (sponsored by The Movie Network, Family and Viewers Choice) offers feature film script development loans as well as equity investments for both feature film and television productions. The French-language programme (sponsored by

Astral Media, Super Écran, Family and Canal Indigo) offers the same for feature films, documentaries, special events, youth dramas and music programmes.

PRIX GEMEAUX

172 King Street East Toronto Ontario M5A 1J3
T   416 366 2227
F   416 366 8454
E   info@academy.ca

Founded in 1986, celebrating excellence in Canadian French-language television.

TORONTO FILM CRITICS ASSOCIATION AWARDS

W   www.torontofilmcritics.com

Established in 1997, the association is comprised of Toronto-based journalists and broadcasters who specialize in film criticism and commentary. Every year the TFCA gives out awards to Best Canadian Film, Best Picture, Best Director, Best Actor, Best Actress, Best Supporting Actor and Actress, Best Screenplay, Best First Feature and Best Documentary.

WRITER'S FIRST PROGRAM

Telefilm Canada 360 St. Jacques Street Suite 500 Montréal Quebec H2Y 1P5
T   514 283 6363
F   514 283 8212
E   info@telefilm.gc.ca
W   www.telefilm.gc.ca

Contacts
Carrie Earl (Ontario)

Administered by Telefilm Canada, a federal cultural agency dedicated to the development and promotion of the Canadian audiovisual industry. This scheme focuses resources on promising screenwriters for the creation of screenplays likely to lead to success at the box office.

Entry Policy
Guidance and application forms available via the website. Regional contacts can be emailed via a webform on the site.

IRELAND

ARTS COUNCIL BURSARY

70 Merrion Square Dublin 2
T 01 618 0200
F 01 676 1302
W www.artscouncil.ie

The council offers a bursary award to a maximum value of €15,000 to artists. Film artists and writers are eligible for the award, but the award does not go towards the funding of a short or feature film production.

CORK FILM CENTRE/RTE SHORT SCRIPT AWARDS

Civic Trust House 50 Pope's Quay Cork
T 021 421 5160
E info@corkfilmcentre.com
W www.corkfilmcentre.com

Has disbursed an annual award to emerging filmmakers since 1999.

FILMBASE/RTE SHORT FILM AWARDS

Curved Street Building Temple Bar Dublin 2
T 01 679 6716
F 01 679 6717
E info@filmbase.ie
W www.filmbase.ie

Awards funding for six short films a year. Cash awards of €10,000 (approximately) are made to the successful candidates, along with full production facilities.

Entry Policy
Awards are open to drama, animation and experimental works to be completed on film or broadcast quality video. Scripts should be 8–15 minutes in duration. Applicants for the award must be fully paid-up members of Filmbase as of the deadline. Full-time students are ineligible.

FILMBASE/TG4 LASAIR AWARDS

Curved Street Building Temple Bar Dublin 2
T 01 679 6716
F 01 679 6717
E info@filmbase.ie
W www.filmbase.ie

Funded by TG4, the awards are open to drama, animation and other fictional works in the Irish language. Cash awards averaging €10,000 are made to the successful candidates, and there is a further award of equipment and facilities.

Entry Policy
Submissions should be between 8–26 minutes duration. Awards are made to directors. Full time students are ineligible. The applicant must be a fully paid up member of Filmbase before applying.

GALWAY FILM CENTRE/RTE SHORT SCRIPT AWARDS

Cluain Mhuire Monivea Road Galway
T 091 770748
F 091 770746
E info@galwayfilmcentre.ie
W www.galwayfilmcentre.ie

Founded in 1997, the Short Script Awards are open to emerging filmmakers with original scripts that display a strong cinematic vision and a fresh Irish perspective. Four awards are allocated from a total production fund of €38,000. Use of the facilities of Galway Film Centre is a key constituent of the awards.

Entry Policy
Films should be no more than 15 minutes in duration. Applicants must be members of the Galway Film Centre. Full-time students are ineligible.

IRISH FILM AND TELEVISION AWARDS

Irish Film and Television Academy First Floor Palmerstown Centre Kennelsfort Road Palmerstown Dublin 20
T 01 620 0811
F 01 620 0810
E info@ifta.ie
W www.ifta.ie

Founded in 2003, the awards are presented annually by the Academy to honour and celebrate outstanding Irish creativity, talent and achievement. Includes an award for best script.

Entry Policy

Open to all Irish people working in the film and television industries in Ireland and internationally.

OSCAILT (TG4 AND BORD SCANNAN NA HEIREANN)

Bord Scannán na hÉireann Queensgate 23 Dock Road Galway
T   091 561398
F   091 561405
E   info@irishfilmboard.ie
W   www.irishfilmboard.ie

Awards for short fiction film-making in Irish. Has been broadened to include fictional pieces in animation, flash animation or docu-drama projects. Although priority will be given to first-time directors and writers, the scheme is also open to film-makers with more experience. A maximum fund of €300,000 is available.

Entry Policy

Films should be between 10 and 25 minutes in duration. Applicants for the fund must normally be of Irish residence. Film-makers must have had some previous experience or training.

STELLA ARTOIS PITCHING AWARDS

W   www.galwayfilmfleadh.com/stella.htm

Screenwriters are invited to submit a one-page story idea for the screen. Five finalists are chosen to appear at the Galway Film Fleadh to make their pitch to a panel of industry experts and a public audience. The best pitch wins €5,000.

AUSTRALIA

AFI AWARDS

236 Dorcas Street South Melbourne VIC 3205
T   03 9696 1844
F   03 9696 7972
E   awards@afi.org.au
W   www.afi.org.au

Contacts

Justine Beltrame *Awards Manager*

Awards ceremony run by the Australian Film Institute, held in November/December each year.

Entry Policy

Open to Australian productions or co-productions and Australian practitioners.

AWGIE AWARDS

8/50 Reservoir Street Surry Hills NSW 2010
T   02 9281 1554
F   02 9281 4321
E   admin@awg.com.au
W   www.awg.com.au

Contacts

Jacqueline Woodman *Executive Director*

Awards run by the Australian Writers' Guild, offering AUS$100,000 in prizes each year in a range of categories including writing for screen, television and interactive media. The Monte Miller award is given to a writer of an unproduced script.

Entry Policy

To be eligible in produced script categories, writer's work must have been produced between 1 January and 31 December the previous year.

FILM CRITICS CIRCLE OF AUSTRALIA AWARDS

PO Box 673 Crows Nest NSW 1585
E   fcca@optusnet.com.au
W   www.fcca.com.au

Annual awards ceremony promoting excellence in Australian film and supporting the advancement of Australian film culture. Presented at gala dinner held in October.

THE LOGIE AWARDS

c/o Kerry O'Brien Publicity
T   03 9528 5855
E   publicity@kob.com.au

Prestigious awards for the Australian television industry awards, running since 1959. Sponsored by *TV Week* magazine.

ZTUDIO WHAT IF? AWARD FOR BEST UNPRODUCED SCREENPLAY

PO Box 55 Glebe NSW 2113
w www.ifawards.com

ZTudio and InsideFilm co-sponsor this competition for the best unproduced screenplay in Australia. Seeks screenwriters who have been proactive in seeking screenplay development but who have yet to see their work produced. The winner is flown to a country of their choice to pitch to agents or producers of their own choice.

Entry Policy
Entry forms available from the website.

NEW ZEALAND

AIR NEW ZEALAND SCREEN AWARDS

C/- SDGNZ PO Box 47-294 Ponsonby Auckland
T 09 360 2193
F 09 360 2196
E awards@sdgnz.co.nz
w www.sdgnz.co.nz

Awards for television and film. In the television category there are awards for best script in comedy and in drama, and in the film category there is an award for best script for a short film.

Entry Policy
A synopsis of 100 words or less must be included with the entry. Films must be less than 20 minutes duration and shot on film or tape. To be eligible it must have been produced in New Zealand or by a producer normally resident in New Zealand and the film cannot have been entered into the awards previously.

THE RICHIES

Richmond Road Short Film Festival 113 Richmond Road Ponsonby Auckland
T 09 376 1091
E entries@therichies.co.nz
w homepages.paradise.net.nz

Founded in 2005, this short film competition is open to any New Zealand short film (drama, documentary, experimental or animated).

Entry Policy
Films should run for 20 minutes or less. Either the writer, director, or producer must be a New Zealand citizen or a New Zealand permanent resident. All shooting formats are accepted. Music videos are not eligible.

SIGNATURE FILM

PO Box 7015 Wellesley Street Auckland 1141
T 09 366 0503
F 09 307 0835
E trevor@thefilm.co.nz
w www.thefilm.co.nz

Contacts
Trevor Haysom *Executive Producer*

A joint initiative funded by the New Zealand Film Commission, New Zealand On Air and Television New Zealand. Managed and executive produced by Trevor Haysom. Aims to facilitate the development, production and broadcast of entertaining, original and innovative films, rooted in New Zealand stories that reflect the country's multi-racial culture. Aim is to create auteur films of between 65 to 85 minutes in length, for television broadcast. A scheme for filmmakers with significant experience and not for entry-level talent.

Entry Policy
For full submission details see website.

SCRIPT ADVICE FROM BEYOND THE GRAVE

Bruce Joel Rubin recalls some supernatural assistance in getting
established in Hollywood

In the spring of 1984, my wife Blanche quit her job at Northern
Illinois University, put our house on the market, and announced
we were moving to Hollywood. She knew I would die if I did
not pursue my dream of becoming a screenwriter. That June, we
arrived in Los Angeles with our two young sons and enough
money to live for two months if we were frugal. Robert M.
Sherman, a producer friend, called me soon after with a possible
screenwriting job, adapting a novel called *Friend*. It was a
bizarre story about a young boy who builds a robot. The boy's
next door neighbour is a teenage girl he is secretly in love with,
who is badly treated by her abusive father. One day, the father
throws her down a flight of stairs and she is pronounced brain-
dead at the hospital. In despair, the boy decides to do brain surgery
on the young girl using his robot's brain to bring her back to life.
To his astonishment and ours, he succeeds. Unfortunately, the girl
comes back as a crazy person and goes around killing all the
people who have done her wrong. I turned the job down, certain
that I had not come to Hollywood to write stuff like this. I'd rather
starve.

The next morning I was sitting meditating as I do every
morning. As I observed my wandering mind, I could see that I was
still feeling smug about walking away from the project and proud
that I was maintaining my integrity in Hollywood. At that very
moment I heard a voice, the voice of my meditation teacher Rudi,
who had died eleven years before. Calling through the ether he
yelled, 'Schmuck! There is more integrity in feeding your family
than in turning down jobs.' He then insisted that I get up from my
cross-legged position, go to the phone, and call the producer. It
was seven o'clock in the morning and I thought too early to call
anyone, but then again, I don't often get directives from beyond
the grave. So I hobbled to the telephone, woke the producer and
lied that I had found a way to make this a worthy film and would
like the job. He said he was delighted and I was hired.

by Robert Pollock (Adams Media Corp,

Process by Robert A. Berman (Michael
)

eenwriting: the Writer's Road Map by
ney Ford (Garth Gardner Co, 2001)

Ken Dancyger (Butterworth-Heinemann,

writing in the New Hollywood by
kley, 2003)

Screenplay: 101 Common Mistakes Most
Denny Martin Flinn (Lone Eagle, 1999)

criptwriting by Julian Friedmann (Boxtree,

nplay by Mark Evan Schwartz (Continuum
g Group, 2007)

ove It: Screenplay Development from the
dwards and Monika Skerbelis (Lone Eagle,

writing 434: The Industry's Top Teacher
f the Successful Screenplay by Lew Hunter
)

writing Tips by Alexis Niki (LifeTips.com,

ipt Great by Linda Seger (Samuel French,

A Screenwriter on Screenwriting by Millard
eat Books, 2001)

g: The 12 Stages of Story Development by
ker (Lone Eagle Publishing, US, 2002)

Lab: Write + Sell the Hot Screenplay by Elliot
2001)

by Ronald Suppa (Premier Press, 2005)

Then, extraordinary things began to happen. I worked very hard to give the script some human dimension and when I had finished, a vice president at Warner Bros. called me. She said she was amazed that the script had made her cry. I was amazed too. The movie attracted Wes Craven as the director and it was a delight to work with him. While the movie was shooting, I was able to bring my wife and boys to the Warners lot and we all luxuriated in the excitement of being in the movie business. Ari, my youngest son (he was five then), became a mascot on the set. He fell in love with Kristy Swanson, who played the girl next door, and she was sweet enough to recognize his adoration and take him on his first date, to McDonald's. He is now twenty-four and has never forgotten it.

Unfortunately, when the movie previewed for a Wes Craven audience, they hated it. They had not come for an emotional experience and the panicked studio brass decided that we needed to put in more gore, six more scenes to be exact, each bloodier than the one before. We did, and at the next preview the audience was propelled out of its seats, literally standing on top of them, screaming with unbridled excitement and bloodlust. They especially liked the old lady who had been decapitated by a basketball, running headless through her house spouting torrents of blood from her neck. Not surprisingly, the film was given an X rating for excessive horror. With each horrific frame that was cut from the movie, Wes said we were losing another million dollars at the box office. It turns out that the film only made about $9 million, so you can imagine how many frames were cut.

I was pretty ashamed of the final product and wondered why my teacher had journeyed from the netherworld to encourage me to do it. But there is a happy ending, actually a few happy endings. Because the film got made, I got a bonus and that bonus was the downpayment on our house. My son Joshua was about to have the first peanut butter and jelly Bar Mitzvah in all of Los Angeles and was spared that humiliation by my sale of the script. And finally, a year later, in the fourth month of a horrible writer's strike when my bank account had dwindled to $400 and we were fearful of losing our home, I got my first residual cheque for what was now called *Deadly Friend*. I looked at it, saw $3,500 and was wide-eyed with excitement. I kept thanking Rudi, my teacher, for making me take this job. Then my wife looked at the cheque and gasped. She told me that I had miscounted the zeros. It was actually $35,000. *Deadly Friend* had saved our lives.

There is a moral to this tale. Don't turn down jobs in Hollywood. Take whatever the universe offers gratefully and then do your best work. You might also try meditating. It cannot hurt.

Bruce Joel Rubin is the author of three motion pictures, Jacob's Ladder, My Life *and* Ghost, *for which he won an Oscar for best original screenplay. He has also co-written* Deep Impact, Stuart Little, Brainstorm *(original story credit),* Deceived *(for which he used a pseudonym) and* Deadly Friend.

From Doing It for Money – The Agony and Ecstasy of Writing and Surviving in Hollywood, *edited by Daryl G. Nickens for the Writers Guild Foundation, published by Tallfellow Press, Los Angeles, ©2006 by The Writers Guild Foundation. Available at Amazon.co.uk and www.Tallfellow.com. Reprinted with permission from Bruce Joel Rubin, the Writers Guild Foundation and Tallfellow Press. All rights reserved.*

RECOM

Advanced
Award Le

Adventure
Books, 19

Alternative
Dancyger a

An Introdu
Essentials A
2007)

Blueprint fo
Craft and C
2004)

Breakfast wit
Meeting, Nail
Murky Waters
2004)

Characters and
Mark Axelrod (

Crafty Screenw
Epstein (Owl Bo

Creating Unforg
1990)

Creative Screenw
(Crowood Press, 2

Dealmaking in the
tions Through Fin
Press, 2002)

Easy Riders, Raging
Generation Saved H
1998)

Elements of Screenw

Everything Screenwriting
2003)

Fade in: Screenwriting
Wiese Productions, 199

Gardner's Guide to Sc
Marilyn Webber & Bon

Global Scriptwriting by
2001)

Hot Property: Scree
Christopher Keane (Be

How Not to Write a
Screenwriters Make by

How to Make Money
1995)

How to Write: A Scree
International Publishin

I Liked It, Didn't L
Inside Out by Rona
2005)

Lew Hunter's Scree
Reveals the Secrets
(Berkley Books, 2004

LifeTips 101 Screen
Inc., 2007)

Making a Good Sc
1987)

Plots & Characters
Kaufman (Really G

Power Screenwriti
Michael Chase Wa

Raindance Writers
Grove (Focal Press

Real Screenwriting

Save the Cat! The Only Book on Screenwriting You'll Ever Need by Blake Snyder (Michael Wiese Productions, 2005)

Scenario: The Craft of Screenwriting by Tudor Gates (Wallflower Press, 2002)

Screenplay Story Analysis by Asher Garfinkel (Allworth Press, 2007)

Screenplay: The Foundations of Screenwriting by Syd Field (Dell, 1979)

Screenplaying: Arming Yourself for a Shot at Screenwriting by John Scott Lewinski (Xlibris Corp, 2000)

Screenwright: The Craft of Screenwriting by Charles Deemer (Xlibris Corp, 2000)

Screenwriter's Survival Guide by Max Adams (Warner Books, 2001)

Screenwriting 101: The Essential Craft of Feature Film Writing by Neill Hicks (Michael Wiese Productions, 1999)

Screenwriting by Declan McGrath (RotoVision, 2003)

Screenwriting by Felim MacDermott & Declan McGrath (Focal Press, 2003)

Screenwriting for a Global Market – Selling Your Scripts from Hollywood to Hong Kong by A. Horton (University of California Press, 2003)

Screenwriting for Dummies by L. Schellhardt (Hungry Minds Inc, 2003)

Screenwriting for Film and Television by Roger LeRoy Miller (Prentice Hall, 1997)

Screenwriting for the 21st Century by Pat Silver-Lasky (Batsford, 2004)

Screenwriting from the Heart: The Technique of the Character-driven Screenplay by James Ryan (Billboard Books, 2000)

Screenwriting from the Soul by Richard Krevolin (Renaissance Books, 1998)

Screenwriting is Storytelling: Creating an A-List Screenplay That Sells by Kate Wright (Perigee Books, 2004)

Screenwriting Life by R. Whiteside (GP Putnam, 1998)

Screenwriting Tricks of the Trade by William Froug (Silman-James Press, US, 1992)

Screenwriting Updated: New (and Conventional) Ways of Writing for the Screen by Linda Aronson (Silman-James Press, 2001)

Screenwriting: A Manual by Jonathan Dawson & Ian Stocks (OUP Australia & NZ, 2000)

Screenwriting: Step by Step by Wendy J. Henson (Allyn & Bacon, 2004)

Screenwriting: Techniques for Success by Jimmy Sangster (Reynolds & Hearn, 2003)

Screenwriting: The Art, Craft and Business of Film and Television Films by Richard Walter (Penguin Australia, 1992)

Screenwriting: The Complete Idiot's Guide to Screenwriting by Skip Press (Alpha Books, 2000)

Screenwriting: The Sequence Approach by Paul Gulino (Continuum, 2004)

Selling Rights by Lynette Owen (Routledge, 1997)

Story and Character: Interviews with British Screenwriters by Alistair Owen (Bloomsbury, 2003)

Story: Substance, Structure, Style and the Principles of Screenwriting by Robert McKee (Methuen, 1999)

Teach Yourself Screenwriting by Ray Frensham (Teach Yourself, 2003)

The 101 Habits of Highly Successful Screenwriters: Insider's Secrets from Hollywood's Top Writers by Karl Iglesias (Adams Media Corporation, 2001)

The Art and Science of Screenwriting by Philip Barker (Intellect Books, 2002)

The Art of Screenwriting by W. Packard (Thunder's Mouth Press, 1998)

The Art of Screenwriting Simplified: The Most Comprehensive Guide for Film & Television by Willie E. Mason (Bawn Publishers Inc, 1996)

The Complete Book of Scriptwriting by Michael Straczynski (Writer's Diget, 1996)

The Definitive Guide to Screenwriting by Syd Field (Ebury Press, 2003)

The Savvy Screenwriter: How to Sell Your Screenplay (and Yourself) Without Selling Out! by Susan Kouguell (St. Martin's Griffin, 2006)

The Screenwriter's Bible: A Complete Guide to Writing, Formatting and Selling Your Script by David Trottier (Silman-James Press, US, Sept. 2005)

The Screenwriter's Guide to Agents and Managers by John Scott Lewinski (Allworth Press, 2001)

The Screenwriter's Legal Guide by Stephen F. Breimer (Allworth Press, 1999)

The Screenwriter's Problem Solver by Syd Field (Dell, 1998)

The Screenwriter's Sourcebook: A Comprehensive Marketing Guide for Screen & Television Writers by Michael Haddad (Chicago Review Press, 2005)

The Screenwriter's Story Planning Guide (Or How to Begin Working on an Idea You Don't Have) by Steven R. Gottry (Priority Multimedia Group, 1999)

The Script Selling Game: A Hollywood Insider's Look at Getting Your Script Sold and Produced by Kathie Yoneda (Michael Wiese Productions, 2002)

The Secrets of Action Screenwriting by William C. Martell (First Strike Productions, 2000)

The Tools of Screenwriting by David Howard & Edward Mabley (St Martin's Press, 1995)

The Writer's Journey: Mythic Structure for Storytellers and Screenwriters by Christopher Vogler (Michael Wiese Productions, 1992)

Top Secrets: Screenwriting by Jurgen Wolff & Kerry Cox (Lone Eagle, 1999)

Vault Career Guide to Screenwriting by David Kukoff (Vault.com, Nov. 2005)

What Happens Next? An Introduction to Screenwriting by Charles Deemer (Booksurge, 2003)

Which Lie Did I Tell? More Adventures in the Screentrade by William Goldman (Pantheon Books, 2000)

Writer's Guide to Hollywood Producers, Directors and Screenwriter's Agents (Skip Press, 2001)

Writing Screenplays That Sell by Maichael Hauge (Elm Tree, 1989)

Writing Television Sitcoms by Evan S Smith (G P Putnam's Sons, 1999)

Writing Television Comedy by Jerry Rannow (Allworth Press, 2000)

WEBSITES

www.dailyscript.com – A collection of movie scripts and screenplays.

www.finaldraft.com – Industry-standard screenwriter's software

www.imdb.com – The internet movie database site.

www.imsdb.com – Internet database of movie scripts.

www.iscriptdb.com – Movie script database.

www.screenplay.com – Software resources for screenwriters.

www.screenscripts.com – Platforms for writers to pitch their stories and ideas.

www.screenwriter.com – Advice from professional screenwriters.

www.scriptfly.com – Screenplays, articles and analysis.

www.script-o-rama.com – Movie scripts and screenplays.

www.scriptpimp.com – Screenwriting and movie screenplay database.

www.scriptsecrets.net – Offers advice from script guru William C. Martell.

www.simplyscripts.com – Free movie scripts and screenplays.

www.thescreenwritersstore.com – Complete online store.

www.wordplayer.com – Writing advice from professional including Terry Rossio and Ted Elliott.

www.writingtreatments.com – Guidance on the discipline of creating a treatment.

www.zoetrope.com – Includes a Virtual Studio where artists can submit work and producers can make movies using built-in production tools.

INDEX